ARCHAEOLOGY OF THE OUSE VALLEY, SUSSEX, TO AD 1500

A tribute to Dudley Moore and Archaeology at Sussex University CCE

Edited by

Dudley Moore[†]

Michael J. Allen

David Rudling

ARCHAEOPRESS ARCHAEOLOGY

Archaeopress Publishing Ltd
Summertown Pavilion
18-24 Middle Way
Oxford OX2 7LG

www.archaeopress.com

ISBN 978 1 78491 377 9
ISBN 978 1 78491 378 6 (e-Pdf)

© Archaeopress and the individual authors 2016

Front Cover: Piddinghoe Wharf (© Andy Gammon, Art & Design, Lewes)
Back Cover: Lewes mounds and River Ouse *c.* AD 150 (© Andy Gammon, Art & Design, Lewes)

All rights reserved. No part of this book may be reproduced, in any form or
by any means, electronic, mechanical, photocopying or otherwise,
without the prior written permission of the copyright owners.

This book is available direct from Archaeopress or from our website www.archaeopress.com

Dedicated to:

Dudley Moore[†]
(22 April 1952 – 28 January 2016)
University of Sussex alumnus, co-founder and chairman of the
Sussex University Archaeological Society

and

Archaeology at the Centre for Continuing Education, University of Sussex

Contents

Contributors xi
About the Contributors xii
Acknowledgements xiv
Preface xv
Dudley John Moore; an appreciation and tribute to 'a life well lived' xvii
Sarah Green

    Studying, archaeology, and determination xvii
    Giving back to CCE xviii
    Friendship and support xviii
    Publication xix
    Beyond Classical Archaeology xix
    Teaching xix
    Dudley outside of archaeology xix
    Book Publications: xx
    The Archaeology of the River Ouse xxi

Foreword. CCE (University of Sussex) and its three Sussex River Ouse Projects: teaching, learning and research xxi
David Rudling

    References xxii

1. Introduction: studying the Ouse Valley 1
Dudley Moore[†]

    The Ouse Valley 1
    References 3

2. Holocene geoarchaeology and palaeo-environment; setting the scene 5
Michael J. Allen

    The Study Area 5
    Geography and Topography 5
    Palaeo-environmental and Geoarchaeological Studies in the Ouse valley environs 6
        Palaeo-environmental and geoarchaeological history of the Ouse valley environs 7
        The valley geoarchaeology 7
        Sedimentation of the valley and its archaeological implications 7
        Upper Ouse (Weald) 7
        Lower Ouse 8
        Archaeological Implications 9
    Land-use and vegetation history 9
        1. The Weald 10
            Wealden conclusions 10
        2. The Lower valley and chalklands 11
        A downland land-use history for the Ouse valley 11
            Woodlands of varying sorts 12
            Creation of the Downland 12
        3. The valley floor 15
    Discussion 15
        Man and Environment 15
            Human activity and the changing environments 15
            Removing woodland or living within the woods 15
            Hidden prehistoric landscapes 15
            Cultural role of the Ouse valley 16
            Conclusions 16

Acknowledgements 16
References 17

3. Palaeolithic record of the Sussex Ouse Valley 21
Matt Pope and Jenny Brown

Key Sites 23
    The Lower Ouse (Seaford to Rodmell) 24
    The Lewes Area 24
    The Upper Ouse (North of Malling to Uckfield) 24
Discussion and future work 25
References 25

4. Mesolithic 27
Diana Jones

Early floodplain development 28
Sites on the Greensand belt 29
The Upper Ouse 30
Rock shelters of the Ouse Catchment 30
Environmental evidence 32
Discussion 33
Future work 33
Acknowledgements 34
References 35

5. Neolithic 37
Steve Sutcliffe

Into the Neolithic 37
The Neolithic Environment 38
    Environmental evidence for Neolithic forest clearance 38
    Environmental evidence for construction and agricultural practices 38
Structures and the Landscape 39
    Offham Hill Causewayed Enclosure 39
    Monument location and visibility 39
Evidence for Neolithic settlement sites 41
    Neolithic flint concentrations and findspots 41
    Bishopstone 41
    Neolithic pit depositions at Peacehaven 41
    A buried Late Neolithic/Early Bronze Age settlement site at Ashcombe Bottom? 42
Territories in Neolithic Sussex 42
    Pottery evidence for mobility and trade networks 42
Into the Bronze Age 43
Future work 43
References 43
Sources 44

6. Bronze Age, a north-south divide 45
Lisa Jayne Fisher

Bronze Age chronology 45
The emergence of the Bronze Age in the Ouse valley 45
Current records of Bronze Age activity in the Ouse valley 47
Early Bronze Age activity in the Ouse valley (2200-1600 BC) 48
    Find spots 49
    Burial sites 49
Middle Bronze Age activity in the Ouse valley (1600-1000 BC) 52
    Find spots 55
    Burial sites 55
Later Bronze Age activity in the Ouse valley (early 1150-800, late 800-600 BC) 57

  Find spots 60
  Burial sites 61
 Discussion and future work 62
 Acknowledgements 63
 References 63

7. Iron Age 65
Stuart McGregor

 Iron Age Settlements 65
  Barcombe 65
  Beddingham 65
  Ranscombe Ridge, Glynde 66
  Ringmer 66
  Malling Down 66
  Itford Hill 67
  Kingston 67
  Rodmell 67
  Peacehaven 67
  Bishopstone, Rookery Hill and Norton 67
 Wealden Iron 67
 Iron Age Hill Forts 68
  Mount Caburn 68
  Castle Hill, Newhaven 69
  Seaford Head 69
 Aerial Survey for Archaeology 69
 Discussion and future work 69
 Acknowledgements 71
 References 71

8. Impact of Rome 73
David Rudling

 The Ouse valley 73
 Roads and road-side nucleated settlements 75
  The nucleated settlement at Bridge Farm, Upper Wellingham 75
  A nucleated settlement at Seaford 77
 A Roman-period (?) barrow cemetery at Lewes 77
 Roman-period Industries in the Ouse valley 77
 Villas 78
  Newhaven villa 78
  Beddingham villa 79
  A probable villa at Firle 83
  A probable villa at Mark Cross, Laughton 84
  Barcombe villa and bathhouse 84
  The Plumpton villa 87
 The non-villa Farmsteads 87
  Bishopstone (Rookery Hill) 87
  Ranscombe Hill 89
 Discussion 89
 Acknowledgements 91
 References 91

9. Anglo-Saxons 95
Simon Stevens

 The *Adventus Saxonum* 95
 The Excavated Evidence 96
 The Beginning - The Earliest Material 96
  'Squatters' 96

  Cemeteries 96
   Rookery Hill 96
   Itford Farm 97
 The Middle - Limited Evidence of Continuity 98
  Saxonbury 98
  Itford Farm 98
  Bishopstone 98
  Religious Communities 98
 The End - 'Stable' and Defended Communities 99
  Bishopstone 99
 The Burh at Lewes 100
  The Late Saxon Countryside 101
 Discussion and future work 102
 Postscript 102
 Acknowledgements 102
 References 102

10. The Upper Ouse in the Medieval period (AD 1066 to 1499) 105
David H. Millum

 Lewes – the urban centre of the Upper Ouse 105
 Archaeological investigations of major sites in Lewes 105
  The Castle 106
  St. Pancras Priory 107
  Grey Friars 107
  St. Nicholas Hospital 107
  Baxter's Printworks, Lewes House Library and Residential sites 108
  Lewes Library 108
  Baxter's Printworks 108
  Lewes House Residential site 109
 Other Archaeological investigations in Lewes 109
 The general Upper Ouse area 110
 Discussion and future work 113
  Possible future works for volunteer projects 115
 Acknowledgements 115
 References 115

11. Lower Ouse in the Medieval period (AD 1066 to 1499) 117
David J. Worsell

 Lower Ouse valley Overview 117
 Settlements of the Lower Ouse valley 117
 Portable Antiquities Scheme (PAS) 117
 Seaford 120
  Historical context 120
 Archaeological investigations in Seaford 121
  The Crypt 122
 Archaeology of the lower Ouse 122
  Newhaven 123
  Piddinghoe 124
  Southease 124
  Rodmell 125
  Iford 126
  Beddingham 126
  Tarring Neville 126
  South Heighton 128
  Denton 128
  Norton 128
  Bishopstone 128
 Industry 128

    Discussion and future work 129
    Acknowledgements 131
    References 131

12. Research priorities for the Ouse valley 133
Michael J. Allen and David Rudling

    A Research Framework 133
    Research Themes 134
    Period by Period Research Context 134
        Lower and Middle Palaeolithic 134
        Upper Palaeolithic and Mesolithic 134
        Earlier Neolithic 134
        Later Neolithic and Early Bronze Age 135
        Later Bronze Age and Early Iron Age 135
        The Later Iron Age 135
        Roman 135
        Saxon 136
        Medieval 136
        Geoarchaeology and Palaeo-environment 136
    Summary 136
    References 137

List of Figures and Tables

1. Introduction: studying the Ouse Valley
Dudley Moore†

Figure 1.1: Mount Caburn near Lewes, by Francis Grose, watercolour on paper, 6th November 1762 (by kind permission of the Sussex Archaeological Society) 2

2. Holocene geoarchaeology and palaeo-environment; setting the scene
Michael J. Allen

Figure 2.1: The topography of the Ouse valley showing the location of the key sites. This map is reproduced from Ordnance Survey material with the permission of Ordnance Survey on behalf of the Controller of Her Majesty's Stationary Office © Crown copyright 6

Figure 2.2: Profiles of the Ouse valley at Sharpsbridge and The Brooks (after Scaife and Burrin 1983, and Jones 1971) 8

Table 2.1. Radiocarbon dates from The Brooks and Caburn (from Jones 1971; Thorley 1981, and Waller and Hamilton 2000) 9

Figure 2.3: Plan and photograph of ard marks in the Beaker soil sealed beneath Bronze Age colluvium at Ashcombe Bottom 13

Figure 2.4: Schematic model of chalkland dry valley erosion regimes; lynchet formation and valley fills (from Allen 1988, fig 6.5; 1991, fig. 5.2) 14

3. Palaeolithic record of the Sussex Ouse Valley
Matt Pope and Jenny Brown

Figure 3.1: Find spots of handaxes 23

Figure 3.2: Hand Axe, butt missing, from the Barcombe Roman villa site (drawing Jane Russell) 25

4. Mesolithic
Diana Jones

Figure 4.1: A contour map of the Ouse valley of East Sussex, highlighting locations mentioned in the text and areas of superficial geology indicating river terraces and palaeochannels (OS data © Crown copyright 2015; British Geological Survey © NERC 2015. All rights reserved.) 27

Figure 4.2: A Mesolithic tranchet axehead, one of many discovered in the 1980s on the chalk downs at Iford Hill, southwest of Lewes (© Portable Antiquities Scheme) 29

Figure 4.3: Professor Sir Grahame Clark spent formative years in Sussex collecting flint tools, earning the nickname 'Stones and Bones' at school. His excavation at Selmeston was a prelude to his work at Star Carr, where, using a multidisciplined scientific approach he helped to reverse previous neglect of the Mesolithic era (photo: Walter Stoneman, commissioned 1959, © National Portrait Gallery) 30

Figure 4.4: Rapid exploratory augering and excavation were carried out at Chiddinglye Wood Rocks in the spring of 2008 beneath the outcrop of Great-Upon-Little. Environmental samples and artefacts were sought further from the rockface than had been standard practice, and were duly recovered, protected by hillwash (photo: A. Maxted) 31

Figure 4.5: In the spring of 2011 the East Sussex Archaeology and Museums Partnership (ESAMP) constructed a conjectural Mesolithic hut of reed, hazel and heather at the Ashdown Forest Centre. Macrofossil evidence for phragmites, the common reed, has been radiocarbon dated to the Mesolithic period at many sites in southern England (© Marathon, licensed for reuse under a Creative Commons Licence) 32

Figure 4.6: A recent excavation in the Rother catchment demonstrated the potential for survival of discrete peat formations containing Mesolithic evidence in the vicinity of Sussex floodplains. Beneath a layer of gyttja mud, a sloping section of artefact-yielding peat overlying Wadhurst clay resembled a former phragmites-fringed lake margin (photo: N. Haken) 34

5. Neolithic
Steve Sutcliffe

Figure 5.1: Oval barrow, 'The Warrior Grave' or 'Camels Hump' (photo: S. Sutlciffe) 40

Figure 5.2: Barrow between Cliffe Hill and Malling Hill (photo: S. Sutcliffe) 40

6. Bronze Age, a north-south divide
Lisa Jayne Fisher

Figure 6.1: Bronze Age chronology... 45

Figure 6.2: Burial at Oxteddle Bottom, Lewes (from Horsfield 1824). This burial was actually flexed not extended as represented here 46

Table 6.1: Grinsell's barrows.. 47

Figure 6.3: Map of Grinsell's barrows (after Grinsell 1934).. 48

Figure 6.4: Main map of sites 49

Table 6.2: Settlement (footprint symbols in Figure 6.4) or field systems (chevrons in Figure 6.4) in the Early Bronze Age and Middle Bronze Age. 50

Table 6.3: Early Bronze Age find spots numbered (squares on Figure 6.4) 50

Table 6.4: Early Bronze Age burial sites in the Ouse Valley (hexagons on Fig. 6.4)... 51

Figure 6.5: Early Bronze Age Beaker from Heathy Brow, Rodmell (after Curwen 1932, with addition) 52

Figure 6.6: Cremation urns from the Lewes area (after Curwen 1954, plate 15), 1. Itford Hill; 2 and 4. Winterbourne, Lewes; 3 and 5. Cuckoo Bottom, Lewes, © Methuen Ltd. 52

Figure 6.7: Objects from the Oxteddle Bottom barrow, Lewes (from Curwen, 1954, fig. 42), © Methuen Ltd. 53

Figure 6.8: Plan of Itford Hill settlement with probable associated trackways and field boundaries (scale 400m) (after Burstow and Holleyman 1957), © CUP, reproduced from Proceedings of the Prehistoric Society 23, fig. 2 54

Table 6.5: Middle Bronze Age find spots numbered (triangles on Figure 6.4).. 56

Figure 6.9: Palstave from Lodge Farm, Newhaven (from Curwen 1936b) 56

Figure 6.10: Middle Bronze Age Palstave from Sutton Farm, Iford (from Cooper 1879a) 56

Table 6.6: Probable Middle Bronze Age Recorded burial sites and mounds (circles on Figure 6.4) 58

Figure 6.11: Possible round barrow in Isfield at TQ 4420 1823 (photo by Lisa Fisher, scales 1m)..................... 59

Table 6.7: LBA hoards, pottery finds and metal find spots (stars on Figure 6.4) 60

Figure 6.12: Later bronze finds from the Ouse valley (nos 2-4 not to scale). 1. socketed spear from Lewes (after Curwen 1954, fig. 60); 2. bronze awl from Southerham (after Wallis 1993); 3. socketed spear from Lewes (after Grinsell 1931, plate 3); 4. socketed spear with rivet holes from Lewes (after Grinsell 1931, plate 3); 5. 'carpenter's hoard' from Castle Hill, Newhaven (after Curwen 1954, fig. 61); nos 1 and 5, reproduced by permission of Methuen Ltd., and nos 2, 3, and 4 by permission of the Sussex Archaeological Society.. 61

Figure 6.13: Decorated axe from Lewes (from Shiffner 1856, 286)... 62

7. Iron Age
Stuart McGregor

Figure 7.1: Mount Caburn and Ranscombe Ridge from the southeast (photo: Stuart McGregor) 66

Figure 7.2: Aerial photograph of Mount Caburn with Lewes in the foreground (photo: Stuart McGregor) 68

Figure 7.3: Aerial photograph of the mouth of the river Ouse with Castle Hill in the bottom left corner (photo: Stuart McGregor)....... 69

Figure 7.4: ESHER Map (reproduced courtesy of the East Sussex Historic Environment Record) 70

8. Impact of Rome
David Rudling

Figure 8.1: Distribution map of various Roman-period sites in or near the water catchment area of the River Ouse (drawn by Jane Russell). 74

Figure 8.2: Bridge Farm, Upper Wellingham: Roman-period roadside settlement (produced by David Staveley)........... 76

Figure 8.3: Newhaven villa, Site 1: Structure V from the south, with part of the north wall removed. Scale: 2m (photo: Brenda Westley). 79

Figure 8.4: Plan of the Beddingham villa with its two phases of enclosure ditch. The outer and later enclosure dates to the mid-2nd century (drawn by Jane Russell). 80

Figure 8.5: The Beddingham villa: the two-phased timber 'roundhouse' and the southern masonry foundations of the villa, scales: 2m (photo: David Rudling). 81

Figure 8.6: Beddingham villa viewed from the north, scale: 2m (photo: David Rudling). 81

Figure 8.7: Beddingham villa: the Roman-period shrine. The darker area within the building contained both late Roman and early Saxon pottery, scales: 2m (photo: David Rudling). 82

Figure 8.8: Barcombe villa: Interim multi-period plan (drawn by Jane Russell). 85

Figure 8.9a: Barcombe: c. AD 40-50: The ditched enclosure with roundhouses. Remains of a Bronze Age round barrow in the foreground (drawing by Andy Gammon). 86

Figure 8.9b: Barcombe: c. AD 150: The fenced enclosure with the proto-villa and a roundhouse (drawing by Andy Gammon). .. 86

Figure 8.9c: Barcombe: c. AD 250: The winged-corridor villa and aisled building (drawing by Andy Gammon). 86

Figure 8.10: Bishopstone: General plan of the Roman-period enclosure (Bell 1977, fig. 87, reproduced with the permission of the Sussex Archaeological Society). 88

9. Anglo-Saxons
Simon Stevens

Figure 9.1: Anglo-Saxon buildings at Rookery Hill, Bishopstone (reproduced by kind permission of Martin Bell)........................ 97

Figure 9.2: Anglo-Saxon grubenhaus at Itford Farm, Beddingham (reproduced by kind permission of Richard James)................ 98

Figure 9.3: Later seventh/eighth/ninth century burials at Bishopstone (reproduced by kind permission of Gabor Thomas) 99

Figure 9.4: Anglo-Saxon features at Bishopstone (reproduced by kind permission of Gabor Thomas) 100

Figure 9.5: Reconstruction of Anglo-Saxon buildings (reproduced by kind permission of Gabor Thomas) 101

Figure 9.6: Silver penny of Edward the Elder, dated to AD 899-924 from Lewes (© Archaeology South-East)............................... 101

10. The Upper Ouse in the Medieval period (AD 1066 to 1499)
David H. Millum

Figure 10.1: Map showing the main features of medieval Lewes (from Rudling 1991, fig. 3), (plan by kind permission of Sussex Archaeological Society) 106

Table 10.1: List of extant churches in Lewes with evidence of medieval origin (Nairn and Pevsner 1965; Brent 2004) 106

Figure 10.2: Plan of Lewes Castle showing the surviving defences (from Drewett 1992, fig 2) (plan by kind permission of Sussex Archaeological Society) 107

Figure 10.3: Plan of areas excavated by Drewett between 1985 and 1988 (from Drewett 1992, fig. 4) (plan by kind permission of Sussex Archaeological Society) 107

Figure 10.4 Plan of St. Pancras Priory showing the phases of development (Gammon 2011, 11) (plan by kind permission of Andy Gammon Art & Design and the Lewes Priory Trust) 108

Figure 10.5: Plan showing the location of 1985-9 Friary excavations (Gardiner *et al.* 1996) (plan by kind permission of Sussex Archaeological Society) 109

Table 10.2: List of rural churches with evidence for medieval origin in the Upper Ouse area (Nairn and Pevsner 1965) 110

Table 10.3: List of possible references to medieval deer parks from the modern 1:25000 OS map. 110

Figure 10.6: A plan showing an interpretation of the location and approximate size of the parks of Ringmer from map research together with the location of place-name evidence (Millum 2011). 111

Table 10.4: List of excavated medieval kiln sites in Ringmer (Millum 2011)... 112

Figure 10.7: A map of central Sussex showing the locations of Ringmer-type pottery as described in Table 10.5 (Millum 2011) 112

Table 10.5: List of places where Ringmer-type pottery or tile has been discovered (Millum 2011) 113

Figure 10.8: A drawing of the aquamanile spout by Jane Russell (Gregory 2014, fig. 19, no. 80) (reproduced with permssion of the Sussex Archaeological Society) 113

Figure 10.9: A penny, possibly of Edward II, AD 1307 to AD 1327 found at Ashcombe (© Portable Antiquities Scheme; record SUR-90EE31) 114

11. Lower Ouse in the Medieval period (AD 1066 to 1499)
David J. Worsell

Figure 11.1. Medieval villages (DMV, SMV and Domesday) Crown copyright/database right 2014. 118

Ordnance Survey/EDINA supplied service... 118

Table 11.1: Settlements (DMV, SMV and Domesday)... 119

Figure 11.2: Total Portable Antiquaries Scheme (PAS) finds by parish 119

Figure 11.3: Total PAS finds – Coins by parish 120

Figure 11.5: PAS finds – Other 120

Figure 11.4: PAS finds – Personal Adornment 120

Figure 11.6: River Ouse relocation (Robinson 1999) (reproduced with permission of Phillimore and Co. Ltd.) 121

Figure 11.7: Archaeological investigations in Seaford (1976–2013), based on Gardiner (1995, fig. 1) additions by the author (for post 2000 excavations) (reproduced with permission of the Sussex Archaeological Society) 121

Figure 11.8: The Crypt, Seaford – plan of excavated features (from Gardiner 1995, fig 3, reproduced with permission of the Sussex Archaeological Society).. 123

Figure 11.9: Plan of St. Michael's church, Newhaven (from Godfrey 1940, fig 2, reproduced with permission of the Sussex Archaeological Society) 124

Figure 11.10: St. Peter's Southease tower and nave views (from Allen 1985, fig. 23, reproduced with permission of the Sussex Archaeological Society) 125

Figure 11.11: Plan of St. Nicholas church, Iford (from Godfrey 1940, fig. 5, reproduced with permission of the Sussex Archaeological Society) 126

Figure 11.12: Plan of Swanborough Grange c. 1936 (from Godfrey 1936, fig 2, reproduced with permission of the Sussex Archaeological Society) 127

Figure 11.13: Beddingham and Iford: medieval coin finds by century, recorded by PAS. 130

Contributors

Michael J. Allen, BSc, PhD, MCIfA, FLS, FSA: Bournemouth University, Department of Archaeology, Anthropology and Forensic Science, Faculty of Science and Technology, Bournemouth University, Dorset BH12 5BB, and Allen Environmental Archaeology, Redroof, Green Road, Codford, Wilshire, BA12 0NW
Email: aea.escargots@gmail.com

Jenny Brown, Independent Researcher, West Sussex

Lisa Jayne Fisher, Cert.Ed, BA, MA: Principal Archaeologist at Archaeology Services Lewes, 2 St. Johns Close, Mill Lane, South Chailey, Lewes, East Sussex, BN8 4AX
Email: info@aslewes.co.uk

Sarah Green, BA, MA, MA, PCIfA, FLS: University of Southampton and Independent Researcher; May Tree Cottage, The Street, Bramber, West Sussex, BN44 3WE
Email: bramberbones@gmail.com

Diana Jones, BA, PCIfA: 1 Broomershill Cottages, Pulborough, West Sussex, RH20 2HZ
Email: archaeosys@gmail.com

Stuart A. McGregor, PgDip: Metropolitan Police Service, London (1982-2012) and Culver Archaeological Project, Bridge Farm, Barcombe Mills Road, Barcombe, East Sussex BN8 5BX
Email: stuart.mcgregor@btinternet.com

David H. Millum, BA, MA, ACIfA: Deputy Director of the Culver Archaeological Project, Grebe, Station Road, Plumpton Green, Lewes, East Sussex, BN7 3BT
Email: david@culverproject.co.uk

Matt Pope, BSc, PhD, FSA: Senior Research Fellow, UCL Institute of Archaeology, 31-34 Gower Street, London, WC1H 0PY
Email: m.pope@ucl.ac.uk

Dudley Moore[†], BA, LLM, MPhil, MA, MSt, DPhil, PCIfA, FSA, Barrister: former Visiting Research Fellow, University of Sussex; May Tree Cottage, The Street, Bramber, West Sussex, BN44 3WE

David Rudling, BSc, MA, PhD, MCIfA, FSA: Sussex School of Archaeology, Mays Farm, Selmeston, Polegate, East Sussex, BN26 6TS
Email: david.rudling@sussexarchaeology.co.uk

Simon Stevens, BA, MCIfA: Archaeology South-East, Units 1 & 2, 2 Chapel Place, Portslade, East Sussex, BN41 1DR
Email: simon.stevens@ucl.ac.uk

Steven R. Sutcliffe, MA: Science and Engineering Placements Office Room W424, University of Brighton, Watts Building, Lewes Road, Brighton, East Sussex, BN2 4GJ
Email: s.r.sutcliffe@brighton.ac.uk

David J. Worsell, BSc, MA: University of Winchester, Department of Archaeology, Faculty of Humanities and Social Sciences, Sparkford Road, Winchester SO22 4NR
Email: david.worsell@tiscali.co.uk

About the Contributors

Mike Allen was brought up in Lewes and Brighton and knew Sussex University from a very young child visiting his father's office and lab in quantum optics (Physics and MAPS 2). He followed a number of Sussex archaeologists (Martin Bell, Peter Drewett and David Rudling) and studied at the Institute of Archaeology (BSc 1983), London, and then gained and a PhD from Southampton University (1994). For nearly 20 years he ran the environmental archaeology section of Wessex Archaeology. When he left (2007), he ran his own environmental archaeology consultancy (Allen Environmental Archaeology), was an associate staff tutor in archaeology at CCE, Sussex University (2008-2012), was a senior lecturer at Bournemouth University, and currently lectures at Oxford University. In his current freelance capacity he has very strong links with Lewes and Sussex, undertaking many commercial archaeology and research projects in East Sussex. He is an established authority in environmental archaeology and geoarchaeology.

Jenny Brown started her working life as a computer programmer and systems analyst, working in London and Nairobi. She later studied for her archaeology degree at Nottingham University, where she was taught by Dr Roger Jacobi, who became a lifelong friend and adviser. She joined Trent and Peak Archaeological Trust in the early 1990s, mostly writing desktop studies and flint reports. She retired a few years ago, and now works as a volunteer for East Sussex County Council, helping to update their HBSMR database.

Lisa Jayne Fisher was a part-time student with CCE at the University of Sussex from 2007 initially studying for a Certificate and Diploma in Archaeology before transferring to the MA in Field Archaeology and graduating in 2009. She was an assistant tutor (2006-2012) until the department closed, and supervised for the CCE excavations at the Barcombe Roman bathhouse in 2012. She has worked extensively on archaeological projects in Sussex, Hereford and Shropshire. She is a qualified teacher and was instrumental in setting up and managing the Sussex School of Archaeology, and has taught in a number of archaeological excavations and events throughout southern England, as well as directing training excavations at Isfield and Brighton. Lisa now runs Archaeology Services Lewes, a small commercial archaeology unit, she is currently a Trustee of the Sussex Archaeological Society and has been a committee member of the University of Sussex Archaeological Society since 2009.

Sarah Green studied Ancient History and Archaeology at Manchester University and later returned to study (part-time) completing a Certificate in Practical Archaeology through the CCE at Sussex. Postgraduate studies (MA in Classical Civilisation with the Open University and then an MA in Osteoarchaeology at Southampton) furthered enthusiasm, particularly in animal bone studies. Currently she is engaged in doctoral research, at Southampton, with a particular focus on animal husbandry in the Roman Empire. Along with her husband, Dudley Moore, she helped establish the University of Sussex Archaeological Society and has been Secretary since 1999. Keen to give something back, she returned to Sussex in 2007 as an associate tutor at the CCE until the department closed. Initially working alongside Dudley on Aegean and maritime archaeology, she subsequently branched out into her new passion of bones. Her day job is educational administration at an independent international college.

Diana Jones gained a degree in Archaeology and Landscape as a mature student at the University of Sussex in 2012; she was named 'best archaeology student' in 2010, and won the Whistler Prize for one of her essays the subsequent year. Her study of a modest Mesolithic flint scatter site in the Sutton End valley of the Bignor Park Estate, West Sussex (a three-year project based on her dissertation fieldwork) won here the Sussex Archaeological Society's Franz Plachy Prize for archaeology.

Stuart McGregor is a non-professional archaeologist with a diploma in Forensic Archaeology from Bournemouth University and retired Metropolitan Police officer. He is chairman of the Culver Archaeological Project.

David Millum is Sussex born and bred and became a part-time student with CCE at the University of Sussex in 2003 graduating in Landscape Studies (Archaeology) in 2008 before going on to gain an MA in Field Archaeology in 2010, whilst also securing the Whistler Prize. He supervised for CCE at the Barcombe Roman bathhouse 2010-12 and was an assistant tutor until the department closed. He has worked extensively on archaeological projects in the Ouse valley. From 2007 he supervised for the Culver Archaeological Project (CAP) at Barcombe, becoming deputy director in 2011, as they began their investigations into the newly discovered, Romano-British settlement at Bridge Farm, Wellingham; an exciting project of regional importance that carries on the excellent community engagement in archaeology originally fostered by CCE.

Dudley Moore was Sussex born and bred and a lawyer (barrister) by training who came to archaeology later in life via a part-time CCE award-bearing course at Sussex. Dudley went on to do other higher level courses at the Open University, Oxford, and Sussex, culminating in a DPhil research degree with CCE. He developed particular interests in the Aegean Bronze Age and maritime archaeology, which he put to good use as a part-time CCE associate tutor. From 2008-2012 Dudley was a Visiting Research Fellow at the CCE and it was during that time that he started putting together this book. Dudley and his wife Sarah Green established the current version of the University of Sussex Archaeological Society (USAS) and Dudley was its Chairman for 17 years until his death in January 2016. Since 1995 Dudley's main work was for an independent international college teaching law and classics.

Matt Pope is a Sussex based archaeologist and prehistorian. Having grown up in the north of Brighton, the pull of the surrounding Downland and it prehistoric landscape had already made a big impression on Matt as a young child. As a teenager he joined the Sussex Archaeological Society and began to volunteer with the Institute of Archaeology's Field Archaeology Unit during the excavation of the Brighton Bypass. Like so many before, he then went on to study at the Institute of Archaeology (London) where, after time at the University of Southampton completing his PhD, he works today teaching and researching the Palaeolithic of Northern Europe. Much of Matt's early teaching of archaeology was undertaken as a part-time associate tutor at CCE.

David Rudling is a leading expert in Roman archaeology and has spent all of his working life as a field archaeologist and archaeological tutor based in Sussex. Initially he worked for the UCL Sussex Archaeological Field Unit, and was also a part-time tutor for CCE (University of Sussex). David left his post as then director of the Field Unit to become a lecturer in Continuing Education (Archaeology) at CCE, teaching at undergraduate and postgraduate level. Following the decision by the University to close CCE, he joined the Sussex School of Archaeology as academic director; and as a founding member he currently serves on the committee of USAS and is responsible for the group's winter lecture series.

Simon Stevens was born in Sussex, and lives a stone's throw from the River Ouse. He studied archaeology at the University of York, graduating in 1992, but returned to the county of his birth, and has been lucky enough to work as a Sussex-based archaeologist ever since. A spell of training and subsequent employment at Sutton Hoo in Suffolk fostered his interest in all things Anglo-Saxon. However, over twenty years of fieldwork with Archaeology South-East, and the irreplaceable experience of acting as an associate tutor at CCE between 1997 and 2012 have broadened his horizons, and have led to a firm commitment to community engagement in archaeology.

Steve Sutcliffe moved to Sussex in 2004 and became interested in the prehistoric landscape of the area. He studied the Certificate in Practical Archaeology at the University of Sussex CCE in 2006, before eventually going on to complete the Masters in Field Archaeology there, concluding with a dissertation based on a local prehistoric flint assemblage. Since then he has continued to pursue his interest in prehistoric landscape and monuments with visits to Orkney and Lewis in Scotland, and several trips to Carnac in France. He also continues to take part in community archaeology projects based in Sussex. Steve currently works as Science and Engineering placements co-ordinator at the University of Brighton.

David Worsell, after retirement took up a long established interest in archaeology by joining the University of Sussex through the CCE. He first took the Certificate in Practical Archaeology followed by an MA in Field Archaeology as well as attending short courses. For many years he led the outreach activity for Brighton and Hove Archaeological Society and was subscription secretary for CBA South East. His studies at CCE enabled him to co-found Cuckmere Archaeology, a volunteer organisation operating in the area of the Cuckmere Valley in East Sussex. He is a member of the University of Sussex Archaeological Society (USAS), Sussex Archaeological Society and local county archaeological societies. Presently he shares his time between researching early South-West American Indian cultures and pursuing a PhD in archaeology at Winchester University.

Acknowledgements

This book is a product of the close 'archaeological community' fostered within both CCE, a popular and successful but now sadly defunct department of the University of Sussex, and the University of Sussex Archaeological Society, and it is a tribute to all of the contributors' hard work and research. Much debt is owed to Dudley Moore who encouraged and cajoled contributors to write and produce their chapters, and to his initial editing. A number of people have helped and assisted within the various period researches and they are acknowledged by the individual contributors in their own chapters, but working behind the scenes, and supporting Dudley throughout this task was his wife Sarah Green, to whom due credit is due for this books' eventual production and publication.

Small grants were obtained to assist the publication and the contributors' research and expenses. These were gratefully received from the Robert Kiln Charitable Trust, and the University of Sussex Archaeological Society. We also thank Luke Barber and the Sussex Archaeological Society for allowing many of the authors to reproduce figures from the *Sussex Archaeological Collections* in this book. Andy Gammon has been generous in allowing his artwork to adorn the front cover, and has freely allowed reproduction of other illustrations throughout this book. Julie Gardiner provided academic advice about the archaeology, as well as significant editorial advice and assistance in the final preparation of the text, especially assisting with figure formats and the final editing and production phase. We were assisted by sage comments and advice on the chapters by a number of colleagues, amongst those were Martin Bell, Matt Pope, and Luke Barber. David Millum's ability to answer last minute obscure queries in a flash is also greatly appreciated, and assisted in the smooth production of this book

The final academic and copy editing and production of this book, and taking it to publication, was undertaken by Mike Allen and David Rudling on Dudley Moore's behalf.

Preface

This book was being organised and edited by Dudley Moore (see Foreword and Introduction), but following the sad and untimely death in January 2016 of this respected and well-liked member of the Sussex archaeological community, the completion of the editing and final production of this book was undertaken by ourselves on behalf of our friend. Dudley had done all of the hard work cajoling and encouraging a disparate group of very busy contributors, and extracting a contribution from everyone, which together provides archaeological coverage from the Palaeolithic to medieval periods. Much of the preliminary editing had been done. This left us with just the arduous and laborious tasks of checking, copy editing and dealing with the publishers and the production process.

Such was the affection for Dudley that we commenced the final production of this book almost immediately after his funeral, out of a wish to do this to celebrate Dudley's contribution to archaeology, and for its publication to coincide with the conference held in his memory on the 12th November 2016. That conference started with a tribute to Dudley by Sarah Green after which a copy of this book was presented in public to her with love and gratitude.

The reasons for this volumes' two dedications are hopefully self-explanatory, but see the Foreword by David Rudling, the tribute to Dudley by Sarah Green, and Dudley's own introductory chapter.

Michael J. Allen and David Rudling
March 2016

Dudley John Moore;
an appreciation and tribute to 'a life well lived'

Sarah Green

Dudley's association and involvement with archaeology started in January 1997, coincidentally the same time that he and I got together. However, his interest in things ancient really began back at Brighton College in the heady days of the late 1960s when he first studied Ancient History at A-Level. I know he wouldn't mind me saying, because he said it himself, but in those days he was 'a bit thick' and when asked in class if he knew where Athens was, he had to admit that he wasn't entirely sure where Greece was let alone Athens! He has one of those school reports that some famous people have had published to show how much they have changed since school. Dudley had his on the wall of the downstairs toilet, a room he also referred to as his study! His headmaster wrote 'He has yet to respond to the urgency of the A-Level situation – the immediate prospect seems grim and much hard work is needed during the vacation if he is to stand any chance of success.' Consequently, he came away from school with only a few formal qualifications, but many accolades on the sports field, particularly in cricket, football and rugby. He also made friendships that lasted a lifetime, an early sign of his warm, outgoing personality.

Life intervened and ancient history took a back seat to a variety of occupations which eventually saw Dudley working within the legal profession for various firms of solicitors in Sussex and then Cardigan, Wales. He was responsible for all forms of civil actions, matrimonial and criminal matters, but when encountering his own matrimonial issues at the age of 40, he decided to enrol as a full-time student at the University of Sussex and subsequently declared that for him 'life began at 40'. His first degree at Sussex was a BA in Law (1995) which he studied with the subsidiary of Classical Literature and Philosophy. In complete contrast to his school record, he was awarded a 2:1, which he said meant he had enjoyed himself as well as studying. Bitten by the academic bug he went on to study for his bar exams, being called to Middle Temple in October 1996, he then took an LLM (Master of Laws) at Wolverhampton University (1998) and completed an MPhil back at Sussex (2001) on the law of privacy.

Studying, archaeology, and determination

Sometime during the course of his LLM, Dudley and I met and I was immediately taken by the contents of his bookshelves! Alongside the many tomes on legal matters were numerous classical works, notably Homer and Virgil. Although I obtained my degree in Ancient History and Archaeology at Manchester University in the 1980s, and had taken a career path in academic administration, I still had an interest in things ancient. Meeting Dudley reignited that flame. We took many courses together; including Nautical Archaeology Society parts 1 and 2, where I discovered that Dudley had a wide variety of interests and achievements. The NAS course was, for example, a follow-on from earlier sub-aqua days when he had dived in Cardigan and the Red Sea and reached the level of dive leader.

At that time we didn't pursue nautical or maritime archaeology any further; I am a non-diver and so it wasn't something we could naturally continue with together. However, in October 1997 I happened upon an advert for the CCE Certificate in Practical Archaeology course at Sussex. I signed us both up for the course, only telling Dudley later. Dudley's interest in, and enthusiasm for, archaeology grew from there. One of the nicest things about our relationship was that we would study courses together and so discuss them endlessly during the evenings after work, often accompanied by a glass or two of red wine. We had a friendly rivalry over essays and marks obtained and took much enjoyment working together on various topics.

The CCE course took two years and at the end of it we didn't want to lose touch with all the lovely people we had met. We hatched a plan to form an archaeological society that could be joined by those studying a Sussex University course, alumni of such courses, Sussex University staff and part-time tutors, and members of the local public interested in archaeology. Thus the current University of Sussex Archaeological Society (USAS) was established in October 1999. In keeping with our slightly less than formal approach, we decided upon a logo that I know some people weren't sure about initially: an Indiana Jones style hat and whip! Helped in those early days by fellow CCE students, Lorna and Darren Hilborn, we published the first edition of our newsletter, *The Lost Scroll*, in December 1999. In the first newsletter Dudley introduced, our very own Indiana Jones 'an archaeologist of great courage, determination and fiction', called 'Artemus Smith' which some members admitted was their favourite item.

In 2001 there wasn't the option to do a Masters level archaeology degree at Sussex, so Dudley and I both took an MA in Classical Studies at the Open University. After both successfully completing this, we were looking for the next challenge archaeologically and academically and Dudley aspired to being able to study at Oxford. I half-jokingly suggested that he might contact Professor Cunliffe, who at that time was president of the Sussex Archaeological Society and I was a trustee. Dud received a reply having emailed the Professor, which said that he was sure there was a place at Oxford for him, and that he should contact John Bennett who was not only the postgraduate admissions tutor, but whose area of expertise was the Aegean Bronze Age! So in 2003, having impressed at interview (comprising more of a discussion of rugby than archaeology), he was accepted by Brasenose College to study Classical Archaeology. He took a year off work, rented a flat in the centre of Oxford, and successfully obtained his MSt (Master of Studies) in 2004.

Whilst at Oxford, and in letters we wrote to each other, ideas for his doctoral research were formulated, and advanced over a glass of red wine. He chatted about scholars who visited Crete pre 1900 and mused whether they had identified any of the archaeological sites that Arthur Evans was later to bring to light in the early twentieth century. And so it was that the next stage of Dudley's academic path was acceptance back at Sussex CCE for doctoral study into early British travellers to Crete. It was from this time onwards that we shifted our overseas trips from Greece to Crete as Dudley followed in the footsteps of those early travellers. Despite now being back working at the college full-time, Dudley's determination meant that he completed and successfully defended his DPhil in just three years (2009).

Giving back to CCE

Whilst studying for his MA at the Open University, Dudley maintained his involvement with Sussex by becoming an associate tutor with the CCE, initially teaching on the undergraduate level Past Societies course and then offering his own courses on the Aegean Bronze Age. Subsequently, not to be put off by the closure of CCE at Sussex, Dudley joined me teaching on the Lifelong Learning Programme at Southampton University and we both also became associated with the 'Sussex Lecture Circuit', giving talks to archaeological societies and anyone else who would listen! One of my favourites of his talks was on 'The Great Escape' where he was proud at the end to show a caricature of his father (himself a PoW in Stalag Luft III) drawn by Henri Picard, one of the fifty escapees executed by the Nazis following the escape.

Friendship and support

Before we started our MAs in Classical Studies Dudley expressed an interest in visiting the site of Mycenae, kingdom of the mythical Agamemnon of Homer and excavated by Henrich Schliemann at the end of the 19th century. I made the arrangements and told him we would be staying in a place called Tolo. 'Really', he said, 'so that's where Tolo is then!'. Some 25 years previously, soon after leaving school, Dudley and a group of lads had taken a holiday to the Peloponnese in Greece, on one of the first package holidays to the area. They spent a very pleasant couple of weeks in, of all places, Tolo! One day he popped out for a walk, returning triumphantly; he had found all three of the local people who had run the bars that the boys had frequented all those years ago. Not only that, but they remembered him and his friends not only because it was the first year of the package holidays there, but because they were such nice people. This just marks one of many instances showing the long-term effect of Dudley's insatiable geniality and friendship. A number of strong friendships that continue today were formed when we joined the British School of Athens, and spent several wonderful weeks staying at the 'annexe' in Knossos.

Dudley was extremely supportive of all his friends and colleagues; that was his nature. None more than my studies, particularly when I found it hard making the transition from undergraduate to postgraduate level. He encouraged me to continue when I was so despondent with my early efforts which achieved low marks. We had many productive evenings where he told me I could do it and talked me through the feedback I had received and how to improve. It was in no small way due to his encouragement that I managed to achieve a distinction for my MA dissertation. When he was in Oxford it was my turn to support him, although not academically, but by agreeing to him being away during the week. We had some fantastic weekends during that time as we took it in turns to spend the weekend either at our home in Bramber or in Oxford itself.

Even while he studied for his DPhil at Sussex he supported and encouraged me in undertaking a second MA, this time in osteoarchaeology, at Southampton and also 'persuaded' me that I should start teaching at the CCE. Initially I helped Dudley with the Aegean courses, but as my enthusiasm for bones grew, I branched out and designed and delivered my own courses. Typically, Dud supported me to the extent that he asked me to teach him enough about bones that he could be useful during the practical sessions of the courses I taught.

Publication

After his DPhil, Dudley was appointed Visiting Research Fellow at Sussex CCE, and it was during this time that the idea for this book on the Ouse Valley was formulated. Initially it was to be a review of archaeological works already undertaken and to highlight areas of potential study for students at Sussex. Sadly, the closure of CCE meant that the impetus for the book and the potential for research projects was lost. Nonetheless, Dudley still saw the potential in a book that reviewed the current state of archaeological knowledge in the Ouse Valley, and carried on seeking sponsorship and contributions.

Alongside his work on the Ouse Valley, Dudley took time to publish his DPhil, initially as a BAR title and subsequently with Cambridge Scholars. He continued an association with the latter, going on to publish a further two books looking first at early travellers to Mycenae and then an introduction to the classical world.

Beyond Classical Archaeology

Although Dudley's love was for the Aegean, he also took a healthy interest in local organisations. We moved to Bramber in 1998 and quite quickly became involved with village life and especially the Tudor House there, St. Mary's. In 2001 Dudley was appointed as Keeper of the Keys for Bramber Castle, a title that dates back to 1291. He would joke that it was pretty tricky to lock up the castle, but nonetheless he purchased a set of old keys from eBay and displayed them on our wall, complete with a label he made stating what they were for! He also wrote and produced his own leaflet giving a brief history of the castle and would often wander up there at weekends, handing out the leaflets and speaking with visitors. At St. Mary's House both he and I volunteered as stewards and gave guided tours to visiting groups of adults and school children. Since 2012 we both served as trustees and it was always Dudley's hope to become more involved with the House as retirement approached. Sadly this was not to be. Outside of Bramber, he was a Practitioner of the Chartered Institute for Archaeologists (PCIfA), a Flag Officer of the Mary Rose in Portsmouth, a Fellow of the Society of Antiquaries (FSA) and a member of the Sussex Archaeological Society, and we both worked with the Lewes Priory Trust on their open days.

Teaching

The 'day job' was obviously important for Dudley too, and for the last twenty years he worked at Bellerbys College in Brighton, where we met. He was originally employed as a law tutor and alongside his teaching he was also the Deputy Programme Manager for the Higher Education Department, until it moved to London in 2014, and the course leader for the Diploma in Business Management. Periodically students would want to study Classical Civilisation A-Level and Dudley added this string to his bow. More recently he also became a key member and joint founder of the Enrichment Programme, was a personal tutor for the Young Oxbridge students, and managed and developed the lecture series. Just over a year ago he and I introduced a Classics society as part of the Enrichment Programme and we were delighted and proud that it became one of the most popular extra-curricular courses. Although most people who saw him at archaeology events would have seen a man casually dressed, at work he always wore a bow tie and a self-tie at that. He was jovially critical of those who wore a 'stick-on' which he could spot at any distance.

Dudley outside of archaeology

Amongst all that work and academia, was there time for anything else? Oh yes, Dudley loved his cars, his sport (although for the last few years it was watching rugby rather than playing it), his opera (he would tell the tale of how he was on the waiting list for Glyndebourne membership for 20 years before his name came up) and he also served as an Honorary Steward at Wimbledon for a number of years. Just over 7 years ago we discovered the wonderful village of Mochlos in Crete. Dudley called it 'paradise' and it certainly is. We went there as many times a year as work would allow and so it was natural that we should choose it as the venue for our marriage. Now that Dud has gone, I have returned to Mochlos for a short period of time and I am writing this piece looking out over the views that he and I enjoyed so much and where we spent so many happy times.

Returning to that school report I mentioned earlier, the headmaster concluded, 'He is a cheerful, easy going and well liked prefect. He is such an uncomplicated and thoroughly pleasant young man that I hope he will knuckle down to some hard work without chastisement.' How true those words were to prove regarding Dudley's personality throughout his life (OK, so maybe he took a while to 'knuckle down'). He was always smiling and had time for anyone and everyone, no matter who they were. He was a true inspiration to his students, his colleagues, his friends and of course his son Toby. He was also my absolute soul mate. I feel privileged to have spent 19 wonderful years with Dudley, the last 4½ as his wife, and I know that all of those who knew him felt privileged to have done so. I also know that his influence will continue because his presence is still with us and will continue to be felt through the variety of projects in his name, this book being just one of them.

Mochlos, March 2016

Book Publications:

Moore, D. 2015. *In search of the Classical World: an introduction to the Ancient Aegean.* Newcastle-upon Tyne: Cambridge Scholars Publishing.

Moore, D., Rowlands, E. and Karadimas, M. 2014. *In Search of Agamemnon: early travellers to Mycenae.* Newcastle-upon Tyne: Cambridge Scholars Publishing.

Moore, D. 2013 *Dawn of Discovery: the early British Travellers to Crete.* Oxford: Newcastle-upon Tyne: Cambridge Scholars Publishing

Moore, D. 2010. *Dawn of Discovery: the early British Travellers to Crete.* Oxford: Archaeopress, British Archaeological Report S2053.

Foreword
CCE (University of Sussex) and its three Sussex River Ouse Projects: teaching, learning and research

David Rudling

For over 40 years the Centre for Continuing Education (CCE) at the University of Sussex provided the local community, both on and off campus, with a wide range of part-time Higher Education level short courses and programmes of study covering various disciplines, including archaeology, art history, creative writing, music, and local history. By the 1990s popular award-bearing programmes were available within the CCE portfolio and after the turn of the millennium such archaeology programmes comprised separate Certificates in 'Archaeology', 'Practical Archaeology', and 'Buildings Archaeology'; a Diploma in Archaeology; a BA in Landscape Studies; a BA in Archaeology and Landscape, an MA in Field Archaeology, and MPhil and DPhil Research Degrees. Whilst these programmes of study mainly attracted 'mature' part-time students, many of whom had for various reasons not gone to university immediately after leaving school, CCE also developed two joint degrees for full-time students: Art History and Archaeology and, Geography and Archaeology. Core staffing for archaeology by the end of 2004 consisted of a Professor (Peter Drewett), a Senior Lecturer (David Rudling) and a part-time convenor (Richard Carter), plus some 20 part-time tutors – a very cost efficient model given the large provision provided. Archaeology at CCE, along with related disciplines such as geology, local history and ecology, came under the general subject grouping of 'Landscape and Locality Studies' and a key aim of teaching within this grouping was that where possible it should take place within a research context.

Archaeology at Sussex (within CCE or other departments) provided a range of students (full-time and part-time, school-leavers and mature students) with the opportunity to study within a practical framework. In response to the growth of archaeology at CCE and the need to provide topics for increasing numbers of student research assignments, dissertations and artefact study reports (especially for the very 'hands-on' MA, but also undergraduate level), in 2004 the instigation of at least one large interdisciplinary research project was considered by the Landscape and Locality Studies Group. Professor Al Thompson (former Director of CCE), had already run a successful 'Ouse Valley Oral History Project' (Holmes 2011; Holmes and Pilkington 2011). This, combined with other reasons including; the proximity (the river is only some 3 miles to the east of Sussex University), previous research, and local appeal, I suggested a Sussex Ouse Research Project to include study of both the River Ouse and adjacent areas of its water catchment area. Following much consultation and two one day public symposia (one being multi-disciplinary; the other being specifically archaeological – 'The Sussex Ouse Research Project: Evolving Landscapes 500,000 BC-AD 1500'), the decision was made to run two separate research projects; one on multi-period landscape archaeology throughout the Ouse valley, and another more interdisciplinary venture involving ecology, documentary research and oral history, designed to investigate how land in the upper Ouse might be managed to achieve biodiversity aims linked to flood alleviation (see list of project reports below).

The Archaeology of the River Ouse

The Ouse valley, which is rich in archaeological remains, had already been subjected to various archaeological fieldwork projects of different types. It was ideal from an archaeological point of view, especially as very little synthesis had yet been attempted, and there were finds and fieldwork that still required analysis and publication. My own previous archaeological research in the valley had started with medieval sites, although from 1987 onwards I had concentrated upon Roman-period settlements and land-use, firstly at Beddingham and secondly at Barcombe. After 2007 this consisted of annual research and CCE student training excavations at Barcombe. Sussex University involvement in the archaeology of the Ouse valley can, however, be traced back to 1963 when members of the University's Archaeological Society dug 'on a Norman site at Lewes Naval Prison, where several interesting finds have been made' (Thomas 1963). Subsequently, the University of Sussex Archaeological Society was involved with the important fieldwork undertaken by Martin Bell at Rookery Hill, Bishopstone, and it published an interim report on the excavations (Bell 1972).

Given that the number of core archaeology staff at CCE was small, and these people were already very busy, it was necessary by 2007 to find someone to direct the still embryonic Sussex Ouse Valley Archaeology Project. Fortunately Dudley Moore, who was nearing completion of his DPhil archaeology degree with CCE, was interested in taking on a new research role and agreed to direct the first stage of the Ouse Archaeology Project. This responsibility was formalised in 2008 when Dudley was appointed as a Visiting Research Fellow within CCE. The initial stage of the project was to undertake a period by period review of the archaeology of the Ouse valley from Palaeolithic times to *circa* AD 1500 in order to establish both what is already known for each period, and what the gaps are in our knowledge. Such information could then be used to provide the foundations for future research (Chapter 12) and to identify how such new work should be prioritised, and potentially acted upon (phase 2) in student research or even structured fieldwork programs (such as in the Cuckmere valley, Garwood 1984). It had already been decided to stop the review at AD 1500 on the basis that for more modern periods there was so much more data, together with large amounts of complimentary historical evidence. The archaeology of the River Ouse since AD 1500 was considered to be a further stage in the overall project.

This publication is testament to the work undertaken by Dudley Moore in arranging for specialists to prepare the various period reviews, and after the closure of CCE continuing to edit these reviews and to oversee the resulting monograph through to publication. The CCE legacy is further represented by the fact that the various chapters have been undertaken by former CCE students (Lisa Fisher, Diana Jones, David Millum, Dudley Moore, Stuart McGregor, Steven Sutcliffe, David Worsell), tutors (Michael Allen, Matt Pope, Simon Stevens); and staff (David Rudling). Other former CCE students and tutors who have provided illustrations include: Andy Gammon, Nicholas Haken, Andrew Maxted, Jane Russell and David Staveley.

CCE was sadly closed to new business in July 2012. This closure of a whole department specialising in widening participation, mature students and part-time study, followed a gradual raiding by the University of CCE's 'FTEs' (Full-time Equivalent student numbers) in order to expand other, full-time, parts of the institution. The loss of such FTEs, and thus the ending of award-bearing programmes of study, together with increases in course fees, undermined what had by 2005/6 become an admired, progressive and fairly sustainable range of archaeology courses fulfilling both regional and community needs. Equally regrettable, at roughly the same time as at Sussex, were closures at various other Higher Education establishments of similar part-time adult education departments or provision.

Although the closure of CCE resulted in the formal aspects of the Sussex Ouse Valley Archaeology Project coming to an end, it is encouraging that archaeological fieldwork and research continue within the valley, especially the long-term Roman-period project based on Culver and Bridge Farms under the joint direction of Rob Wallace and David Millum (two former CCE MA students), the long-running Sussex Archaeological Society project at Tidemills (Bishopstone), and more recently with renewed investigations by the new Sussex School of Archaeology at Plumpton Roman villa.

References

Bell, M. G. 1972. *Excavations on Rookery Hill, Bishopstone, Sussex. An Interim Report 1968-71*, Falmer: University of Sussex Archaeological Society.

Garwood, P. 1984. The Cuckmere Valley Project fieldwalking programme 1982–83, *Bulletin of the Institute of Archaeology* 21, 49–68.

Holmes, A. 2011. The Ouse Project: A Case Study of Applied Oral History. In: S. Trower. *Place, Writing and Voice: Studies in Oral History,* New York: Palgrave Macmillan, 127-148.

Holmes, A. and Pilkington, M. 2011.Storytelling, floods, wildflowers and washlands: oral history in the River Ouse project, *Oral History* 39, no. 2 (Autumn), 83-94.

Thomas, L. 1963. 'Archaeological Society' in *The University of Sussex Student Union Handbook*, Falmer: University of Sussex Student Union 31.

The River Ouse Project Reports (these can be downloaded from the website at http://www.sussex.ac.uk/riverouse):

Report 1: Iron Gates Mead
Report 2: Spring Farm Riverside Meadows
Report 3: Broad Mead
Report 4: Vuggles and Buckham Hill
Report 5: Freshmill Cottage and Ketches Meadow
Report 6: Uck catchment

1. Introduction: studying the Ouse Valley

Dudley Moore[†]

The embryo of this book began in September 2008 and was initiated after I had been appointed to the part-time post of Visiting Research Fellow for archaeology in the Centre for Continuing Education (CCE), at the University of Sussex. The purpose of the research was to provide an outline of the existing archaeological knowledge of the River Ouse valley in Sussex and establish particular gaps in our knowledge that may need further research. The aim was then to use this information for students of archaeology at the university to help them choose suitable topics and projects for study. Between 2008 and 2011 the concept of producing a book with both tutors and students as authors was agreed and commenced, but unfortunately in January 2012 it was announced that the University was going to close CCE and make redundant most of its faculty staff, including all of those involved in archaeology. Such actions were similar to those being undertaken to Continuing Education facilities at many universities across the country. Although these measures brought to an end any future archaeology students, and with it the need to produce potential topics for study, the research and writing by nearly all the contributors on board the '*Archaeology of the River Ouse Project*' was well underway.

The value of the project was recognised as a useful and potentially significant contribution to the region as a whole, with publication in a single volume an obvious choice. Some of the contributors are well-published authorities and former CCE archaeology staff and associate tutors, and some not quite so well-known. Of the latter, all are former CCE students of archaeology at Sussex (at various levels from Certificate, Diploma, Bachelor or Masters) and, therefore, it is a unique and eclectic collection of authors. For some, therefore, this is their first and only archaeological publication to date.

The Ouse Valley

The Ouse is a very important river with much history attached to it. A review of the early archaeology and identification of future research possibilities and priorities, are essential to our understanding of the valley. This book emphasises such archaeological potential, collating for the first time a series of archaeological essays dedicated to the valley. The review was limited to AD 1500, the end of the medieval period, as there is too much data, both archaeological and historical sources, in the sixteenth century to the modern day to cope with in this volume. It may be that a future joint archaeology/local history project, 'Phase 2' as originally intended (see Foreword by Rudling above) will one day be undertaken to cover this later period.

No consistent map has been produced and used by the project as a whole, instead the authors have provided their own individual maps of the Ouse Valley or the study area as they perceived it. I would, however, refer the reader specifically to Figure 2.1, the map in the first paper by Mike Allen, as the definitive plan. It is reproduced from Ordnance Survey material with the permission of Ordnance Survey on behalf of the Controller of Her Majesty's Stationery Office © Crown copyright, as supplied by Greg Chuter of East Sussex County Council.

The River Ouse, which flows through both the modern counties of East and West Sussex, is one of four Sussex rivers that cut through the chalk of the South Downs. It rises in Horsham in West Sussex, near Lower Beeding, and terminates its course in East Sussex at its mouth in Newhaven. There are many rivers called Ouse in Britain raising much debate about the origin and meaning of the word. The origin of the name is often taken to be *usa*, the Celtic word for water, and this is generally the most accepted. An alternative would be the Saxon word *wáse*, meaning soft mud or slime, from which our word ooze derives (Laing 2011), if so this might be appropriate in view of the Saxon origins of Lewes and the name 'Lewes' itself. The West Sussex part of the river is more correctly the upper valley, whereas the East Sussex part is the lower valley. In this volume, however, the chapters on the Medieval period (i.e. 10 and 11), both deal with areas in just East Sussex, and have been designated upper and lower respectively for convenience sake. The river's meandering course is interrupted by some 29 tributaries, many of which can be found around Isfield in the Wealden District and thereafter around Barcombe near Lewes which lies on the Greenwich Meridian. It would have been a corridor of communication from the Palaeolithic period onwards through to the present day. From Newhaven/Seaford to Lewes the river would have been navigable to fully-rigged schooners in the thirteenth and fourteenth centuries (Lewes was still approachable by smaller commercial boats up until the twentieth century).

Lewes, the county town of East Sussex, is located in a strategic gap in the Downs, cut through by the River Ouse. It and its environs are probably the most altered area over time and it has four Sites of Special Scientific Interest: Lewes Downs, Lewes Brooks, Ouse Valley Flood Plains and the Southerham Works pit. Lewes's

FIGURE 1.1: MOUNT CABURN NEAR LEWES, BY FRANCIS GROSE, WATERCOLOUR ON PAPER, 6TH NOVEMBER 1762
(BY KIND PERMISSION OF THE SUSSEX ARCHAEOLOGICAL SOCIETY)

Norman castle, built by William de Warenne, is located in a Saxon fortified town, or burgh. At the Conquest in 1066 Lewes was given to Warenne by King William and it became the administrative centre of the Rape of Lewes. Later in 1264, in the Second Baron's War, the medieval town is celebrated for the Battle of Lewes when Simon de Montfort defeated Henry III (albeit only a temporary arrangement). Today the Ouse is crossed by three bridges at Lewes, the small footbridge of Willey, Phoenix Bridge and Cliffe Bridge.

After Lewes, on its southward journey, the River Ouse passes Glynde and Rodmell. There is an early Norman church at the latter which houses a possible Saxon font. Thereafter, at Southease, a twelfth century round tower can be found (Allen 1985, see Worsell this book chapter 11, Figure. 11.10). Next on the horizon is Mount Caburn (Figure 1.1) an Iron Age hillfort; originally excavated by Augustus Pitt Rivers in 1877-78, more recently by the Sussex Archaeological Society in 1996-98, and several times in between. The river then flows through Piddinghoe (with a history related to smuggling – but more famous for its bottle-shaped brick kiln, see O'Shea 1982), then past St. Johns church which is of Norman origin.

The river finally reaches the English Channel at Newhaven. Here it has become an important harbour surrounded by two long breakwater piers. It was not always the port: prior to the mid-sixteenth century, Seaford, one of the Cinque Ports, was the main outlet of the Ouse, but this was altered (below Castle Hill, Newhaven) due to silting and changes in the coastal shingle bar (see below). During the Norman period the river was probably a tidal inlet with a number of settlements around its course. Over the years, land adjacent to the river became fertile meadow land, but in the early 15th century there was much flooding. The banks of the river south of Fletching were restored following the appointment of the Commission of Sewers in 1422. However, not long after, much of Lewes and Laughton were reduced to marshland (so much so that 400 acres of the Archbishop of Canterbury's meadow at Southerham became a fishery). With the cutting of a channel below Castle Hill in c. 1539, causing Newhaven to succeed Seaford as the port of Lewes, much of the valley was usable again for pasture. However, by the mid-seventeenth century, the river was becoming totally unnavigable by large vessels due to significant changes in the rivers morphology particularly at its mouth at Seaford and Newhaven The mouth of the Ouse at Newhaven was again artificially re-opened in 1731-3, but this was not stabilised until large breakwaters were built in the late nineteenth century (Robinson 1999, 8 and map d on page 9).

In 1790 the Ouse Navigation Act was passed to allow construction of navigation. This was as a result of Thomas Jessop's survey of the river in 1787 for the purposes of navigation up to Slaugham. It was to prove too expensive and by 1812, due to canalisation of the Ouse, navigation went only as far as Balcombe (ending at Upper Ryelands Bridge after some 22 miles and 19 locks). The trade of the Ouse was mainly lime, chalk, manure and aggregates, but navigation as far as Barcombe was not to prove a great success. This was mainly due to the introduction of the railway in the 1840s, although boats did continue up to Lewes until the 1950s. Although slowly deteriorating, the remains of most of the old locks are still visible.

Today the river, managed by the Environment Agency, is still a source of drinking water. It is also a conduit for treated sewage and provides drainage for the surrounding area. It is tidal up to Barcombe Mills and its banks (levees) have been raised in an attempt to prevent flooding which is still an ongoing problem. It is for this reason that continuing archaeological research is so important within the valley, as it is only a matter of time before some of it disappears beneath the flood waters.

References

Allen, M. J. 1985. Southease church, *Sussex Archaeological Collections* 123, 261-262

Laing, O. 2011. *To the River - A Journey Beneath the Surface,* Edinburgh: Canongate Books.

O'Shea, E.W. 1982. The restoration of a tile kiln at Piddinghoe, *Sussex Industrial History* 12, 2-23

Robinson, D. 1999. The Coast and Coastal Change, pages 8-9 in K. Leslie and B. Short (eds), *An Historical Atlas of Sussex*. Chichester: Phillimore.

2. Holocene geoarchaeology and palaeo-environment; setting the scene

Michael J. Allen

The Upper Ouse valley meanders across the Wealden Series geology largely unembanked in its northern reaches and with a narrow floodplain, widening significantly to the north of Lewes where it becomes embanked with man-made levees. South of Lewes the Lower Ouse valley slices through the chalk escarpment, and currently debouches at Newhaven where it is fringed with brickearth (see Bell 1975; 1976), and further afield, at Seaford, by deep marine gravel. Its topography is characterised by a wide flat floodplain and steep chalk valley sides rising onto the undulating downland cut by dry valleys. The general view of the Ouse valley is, however, one that belongs to the last several centuries.

The rivers of south-east England flow in deeply incised, large infilled valleys (Scaife and Burrin 1992). Significant alluvial sediment has accumulated, with over 6m at Wellingham north of Lewes and in excess of 10m in the Vale of the Brooks, and 35m at Newhaven. These appreciable depths of alluvium change the whole topographical dynamics of the valley as a corridor through the landscape, and of its dynamic relationship with the Downs in the Lower Ouse, and the Weald in the Upper Ouse. The presence of metres of alluvium in the Ouse valley (Burrin and Scaife 1984; 1988; Burrin 1985; Burrin and Jones 1991) has a dramatic impact for the comprehension of this area in the past; the valley would have been significantly deeper, and journeys between, and to and from, the valley more challenging. We also know, for instance, that the channel itself allowed rigged and masted sailing ships right up to Lewes in the medieval period (see Millum, Chapter 10).

Because the Ouse valley slices through the chalk and the Weald, as well as having its own valley floor topography and ecology, it provides a transect of Sussex archaeology. In many ways studies of the environmental archaeology and geoarchaeology of the chalk Downs are well advanced, with pioneering studies and a wealth of data (though with some surprising lacunae). The Ouse valley alluvium, as we will see, offers great palaeo-environmental potential, but outline studies are now four decades old and due for re-examination. In contrast the valley floor itself is largely devoid of any archaeological, environmental or geoarchaeological study, which reflects the lack of archaeological evidence (e.g., HER). But is this a lack of human activity, or a lack of research and recovered evidence - see for instance Allen (1988; 1991)? The Weald contains a plethora of archaeological sites. Overall they are poorly studied (Gardiner 1990), but the potential for major site-based palaeo-environmental and geoarchaeological research in the upper reaches of the valley and Weald catchment (e.g. Barcombe, Gatwick and Crawley) is high and largely untapped.

The Study Area

This book discusses the archaeology of the Ouse valley, but with no specifically prescribed definition or parameters of the 'Ouse valley', and different authors even to this book have each defined different study areas all broadly centred on the Ouse. From a purely geographical or topographical perspective the Ouse valley is defined by its watershed or catchment (cf. Monkhouse 1960; Strahler 1975) which, in its southern reaches, extend from the valley floor to the top of the short steep valley sides, and excludes the downland beyond. By contrast in the Weald, although the floodplain is moderately well-defined, it narrows from almost 1km across to just 100m beyond Isfield and Sharpsbridge with very low valley sides measured in metres rather than 10s of metres. The more dendritic form of the Ouse here gives a larger catchment and encompasses a large area of the Weald.

In order to study the cultural impact of the Ouse valley as a topographical unit, a boundary, a barrier and corridor to cultural activity, it is necessary for the study to embrace the immediate environs as well as the Ouse valley itself (Figure 2.1). This is clearly relevant particularly with regard to the changing pattern of land-use history and geoarchaeology of the Ouse. As we shall see, the sedimentation within the Ouse valley is both appreciable and related to human activity beyond the floodplain. It relates directly to activity within the Ouse catchment but also, less directly, to human activity beyond that. Consequently the study area chosen is, like those of other authors, one broadly centred on the Ouse (see Figure 2.1) not as a result of loosely defined and poorly conceived boundaries as a consequence of woolly thinking, but directly as a result of consideration of topographical, geographical, social and political considerations. The development of the environment, geoarchaeology and land-use history is discussed in terms of three topographical zones: i) the valley floor, ii) the chalkland interfluves, and iii) the Weald.

Geography and Topography

Rising near Lower Beeding the upper reaches of the Ouse and its tributaries wind their way through the

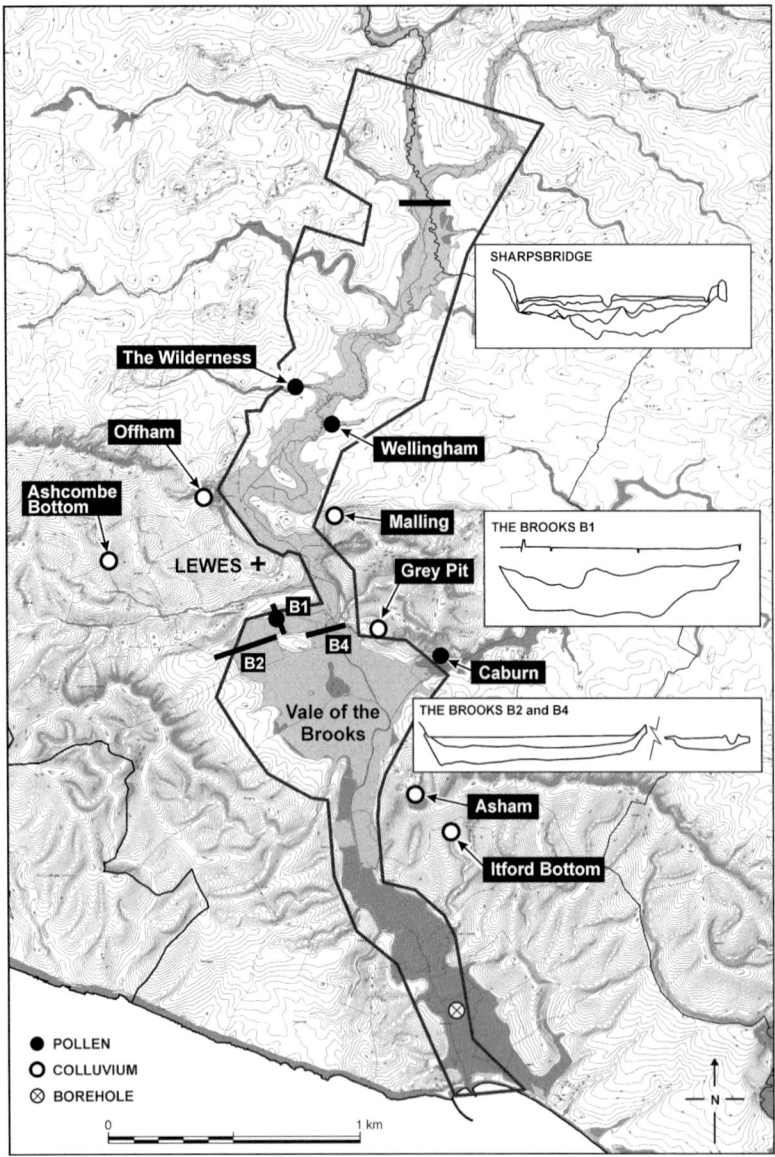

FIGURE 2.1: THE TOPOGRAPHY OF THE OUSE VALLEY SHOWING THE LOCATION OF THE KEY SITES. THIS MAP IS REPRODUCED FROM ORDNANCE SURVEY MATERIAL WITH THE PERMISSION OF ORDNANCE SURVEY ON BEHALF OF THE CONTROLLER OF HER MAJESTY'S STATIONARY OFFICE © CROWN COPYRIGHT

wide and is well-defined by clear, steep-sided, chalk slopes leading up, and on, to the Downs which rise 100 to 155 metres above the floodplain. The chalkland valley sides and valley edges of the Lower Ouse provide a clear, well-defined, interface with the chalk Downs. The Downs themselves rise to 190m at Beddingham and form the scarp slope and dip slope, the latter incised by a series of dendritic dry valleys.

Palaeo-environmental and Geoarchaeological Studies in the Ouse valley environs

This review embraces the sedimentary history and physical development of the later Holocene Ouse valley, and the vegetation and land-use history of the Ouse environs. So where does our data come from? There are a number of key sources of research. They include; geographers studying the Ouse valley (e.g. Williams 1971a; Geographical Editorial Committee 1983); palaeo-geographers and palynologists studying the Ouse sediments and vegetation history (e.g. Rob Scaife, Paul Burrin and Martyn Waller), and environmental archaeologists whose studies include research such as dry valley excavations (e.g. Martin Bell and myself), or those of soil, pollen, snail and charcoal data recovered from archaeological sites.

A number of studies of the Ouse alluvial sediments have been undertaken embracing pollen analysis. The depth and nature of the valley have been determined by the work of Jones (1981; Robinson and Williams 1983), and Bell et al. (2010), while detailed pollen analyses include those at Sharpsbridge in the Weald (Scaife and Burrin 1983), undergraduate research at Wellingham (Brooks unpubl.; Wing 1980, both quoted in Robinson and Williams 1983), that at the foot of Caburn by Waller and Hamilton (1998; 2000), and older analysis in the Vale of the Brooks by Thorley (1971; 1981). The other main source of evidence are stratified colluvial sequences (cf. French 2015) and molluscs analysed by a palaeo-geographer at Asham (Ellis 1985; 1986) and environmental archaeologists at Itford Bottom (Bell 1981; 1983) Malling, Southerham, Ashcombe Bottom and Cuckoo Bottom (Allen 1995a; 2005a; 2005b). Studies of environmental data directly from archaeological sites are limited, in part due to the lack of excavation in the Ouse corridor, but

Weald with a small, weakly defined, floodplain, but flow across deep overbank floodplain alluvium (Upper Ouse), as demonstrated by coring at Sharpsbridge (Scaife and Burrin 1983; 1992). It has many minor tributaries providing a large catchment area covering Crawley and Haywards Heath in the west, Crowborough in the north and Uckfield to the east. At Lewes, at its confluence with the Glynde Reach and the Laughton Levels, widens to a huge flat floodplain at The Brooks, only broken by Upper and Lower Rise; two knolls of Gault and Chalk (Lake et al. 1987), rising above the floodplain floor. The lower Ouse valley is a large incised valley through the chalk Downs from Lewes to Newhaven-Seaford which boasts a flat wide valley floor (up to 4km wide at the Vale of the Brooks) and deep Holocene sediments. From The Brooks southwards the Ouse valley is about 1km also to the age of some of those excavations. Where major research investigations have been undertaken recently (e.g. the Caburn), no environmental analyses were published from the Iron Age hillfort itself (Drewett and Hamilton 1999), nor indeed from recent commercial archaeological projects such as the Saxon settlement on the valley floor at Beddingham (James 2002). Other sites, such as recent Saxon features at Bishopstone were, however, fully sampled (Allen 2014), but this comprehensive acquisition of environmental data seems relatively rare. Nevertheless, land snail data is available from the Neolithic causewayed enclosure of Offham (Thomas 1977a), Neolithic to Saxon contexts at Bishopstone (O'Connor 1977; Thomas 1977b; Allen 2014), the Bronze Age round barrows at Round the Down (Allen 1995b), Itford Farm (Allen 2009) and more recent contexts at Lewes Priory (Allen 1997). No buried soils (under barrows or ramparts) have been excavated and studied (excepting a single sample from Offham). The final set of data is gleaned from charcoal from tree hollows at Itford Bottom and Ashcombe Bottom, and buried soils under colluvium at Southerham.

From this list we can see the data is sparse in some areas (Figure 2.1), and the agenda of the analysts and the projects (geographers and archaeologists) differ significantly. The former are interested in landscape and vegetation change, while the latter are also interested in those aspects, but as a product of human activity and as a basis for resource exploitation. Consequently studies undertaken within the archaeological framework are much more tightly allied to the activities and action of human populations in the past, and address changes in vegetation and land-use, and their consequences (soil erosion, colluviation, and alluviation). These studies and results help us to understand human activity, past populations, settlement and farming.

Not all palaeo-environmental and geoarchaeological work is published in archaeological journals, and even some of the key papers in collected volumes on, for instance *Archaeology under Alluvium* (Needham and Macklin 1992), do not seem to have been read by many archaeologists attempting to discuss archaeological landscapes. Consequently, I have deliberately tried to create a moderate, but far from full, bibliography to aid those future researchers. I have not, however, discussed, nor included the detailed intricacies of palaeo-environmental and palaeoecological interpretation, taphonomy and assemblage preservation bias.

Palaeo-environmental and geoarchaeological history of the Ouse valley environs

I address physical changes of the valley itself from a geoarchaeological perspective, examining the valley sediments, and pollen (vegetation history) derived from them. The areas of the chalk Downs, the Weald and the valley floor are reviewed separately.

The valley geoarchaeology

The lowering of sea-level in the Devensian (last glacial) caused the Sussex rivers to incise their channels, particularly in their lower reaches near what is now the coastline. In many cases the rivers were able to cut their floors well down below present sea-level. The Ouse valley is cut to a depth of -30 to -35m OD at Newhaven (Jones 1971; 1981, 282-88, and see below). The former floors of the valleys are now buried beneath a considerable thickness of Late-glacial and Postglacial sediments (Figure 2.2). The Ouse valley floor, like other Sussex rivers, now has very gentle gradients of about 0.1m per km between Lewes and Newhaven, as it approaches the sea. During the Devensian, however, the rivers were very much steeper and presumably much faster flowing, and the Ouse had a gradient 20 times greater (about 2m per km) between Lewes and Newhaven.

Sedimentation of the valley and its archaeological implications

The Holocene (from the Mesolithic to the medieval) geoarchaeology of the alluvium within the valley is considered here, but not the historical or earlier changes in the course of the Ouse, nor the complexities of its debouching into The Channel between Seaford and Newhaven. Historic records and sedimentary geomorphology of the changing mouth of the Ouse are summarised by Joliffe (1964), Brandon (1971), Farrant (1972), Castleden (1996, 9-18) and Bates (in Dunkin 1998) among others, and see Worsell (Chapter 11, Figure 11.6).

The Ouse is an overfit valley (i.e. a current valley too large for the river it contains) with Holocene alluvial sequences to 12m thick at Lewes (Figure 2.2), and 35m thick at Newhaven, over deep gravels and sands; the latter relate to high energy late glacial meltwater deposition. These alluvial sequences have both geoarchaeological and landscape implications (cf. Needham and Macklin 1992) and contain long stratified sequences with major palaeo-environmental (principally pollen) records (e.g., Thorley 1971; 1981; Scaife and Burrin 1983; 1992; Waller and Hamilton 1998; 2000). These pollen sequences also reference the chalklands which are generally devoid of surviving pollen. Moreover, the sediment itself can be related to larger-, and smaller-scale, activities upstream such as deforestation and tillage in both the chalklands and the Weald (Burrin 1985; Burrin and Scaife 1984; 1988; Burrin and Jones 1991), and provides indirect evidence of human activity. These sediments are fine-grained alluvial silts resulting from anastomosing channels (multi-channelled, reconnecting, braided channels) and overbank floodplain alluviation.

Upper Ouse (Weald)

Little archaeological and palaeo-environmental work has been undertaken in the higher reaches of the Ouse

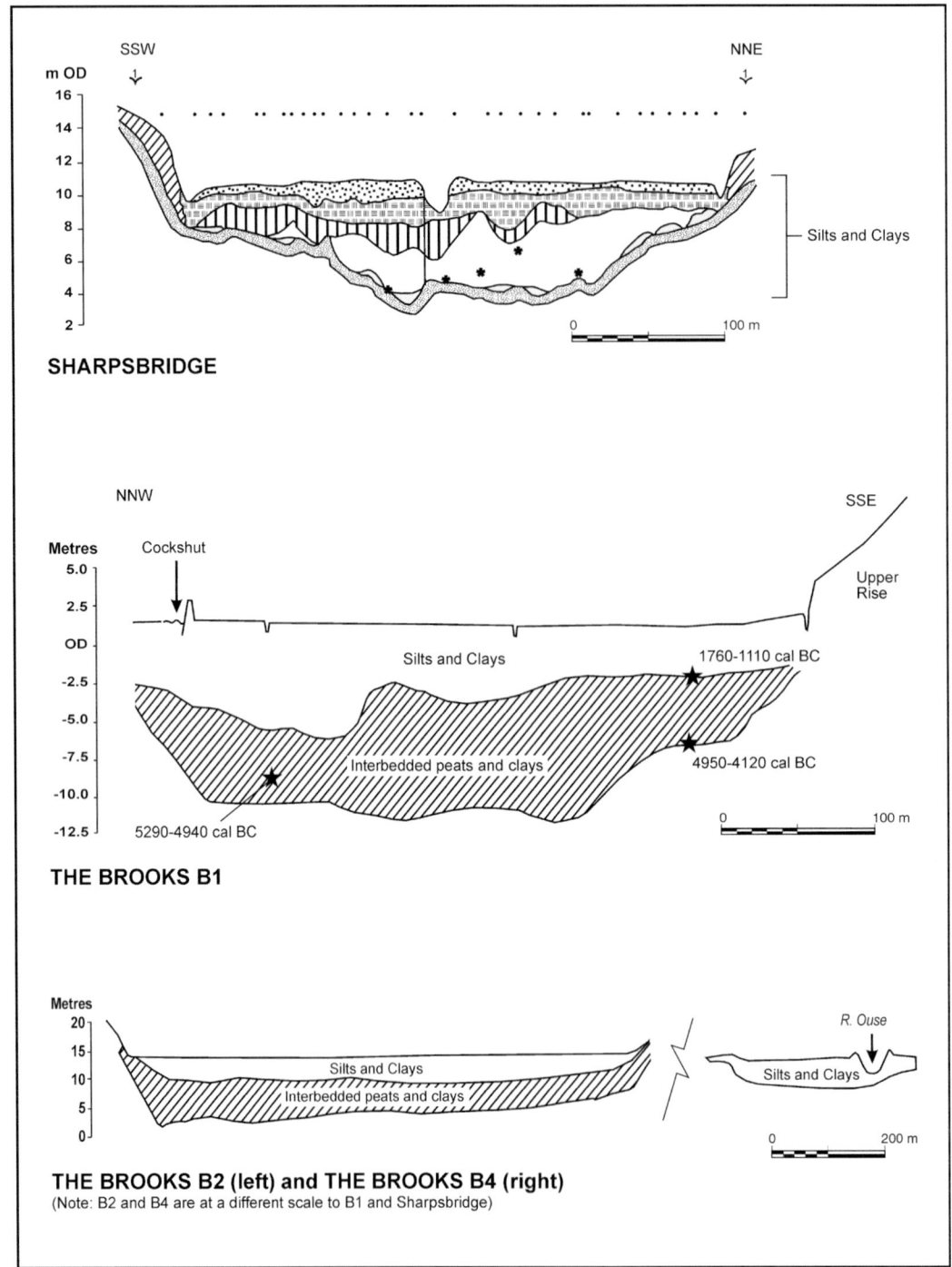

FIGURE 2.2: PROFILES OF THE OUSE VALLEY AT SHARPSBRIDGE AND THE BROOKS (AFTER SCAIFE AND BURRIN 1983, AND JONES 1971)

valley. Even in these small and minor tributaries it is likely that very deep alluvium exists. At similar locations in the Arun, at Loxwood north of Chichester for instance, where the Arun is but a small river, surprisingly deep sequences of fine-grained alluvium in excess of 5m dating from the Mesolithic to recent times were present (Wessex Archaeology 2007). In the Ouse valley, the northern most profile examined (Sharpsbridge) shows the overfit valley with nearly 6.5m of alluvium over gravels (Figure 2.2) and compares well with sequences from the Cuckmere (Scaife and Burrin 1985).

Lower Ouse

A number of boreholes taken in the Lower Ouse (from Lewes), allow us to review sequences at Wellingham Bog just north of Lewes (Robinson and Williams 1983), The Brooks (Jones 1971; Thorley 1971; 1981), the base of the Caburn (Waller and Hamilton 1998; 2000; Drewett and Hamilton 1999), as well as further south near Newhaven and at Poverty Bottom east of Rookery Hill, Bishopstone (Bell *et al.* 2010). Together these allow the characterisation of the Holocene geomorphology of the Lower Ouse.

2. HOLOCENE GEOARCHAEOLOGY AND PALAEO-ENVIRONMENT; SETTING THE SCENE

At The Brooks the alluvium was seen to increase to c. 21.3m with a gravel strewn valley base at -8 to -12m below OD. Between Lewes and Newhaven alluvium is 15-31m deep (Figure 2.2; Jones 1971, fig 5.7), and at Newhaven the valley floor is at least 25.9m below OD (Bell 1977, 2) and up to 35m below OD (Bates in Dunkin 1998, 33; Jarzembowski 2003), encompassing about 35m of stratified alluvium. Even now a dry former minor tributary and tidal inlet of the Ouse at Poverty Bottom, to the east of Rookery Hill, Bishopstone, contained 7m of fine-grained estuarine deposits to -5m OD (Bell *et al.* 2010).

Localised peat is present as bogs at Wellingham with 6m of stratified undated peat, and at the foot of Caburn with 2.8m of dated peat under floodplain edge and colluvial deposits (Table 1). The most extensive valley peat is in the Vale of the Brooks where large peat deposits up to 7.5m thick extend for about 0.5km beneath 4 to 7.5m of alluvium (Figure 2.2; Jones 1971; Thorley 1971). Peat seems to have formed from prior to 5490-4940 cal BC and continued to form in part of the Ouse valley as late as, at least, 1760-1110 cal BC (Table 1).

Overall this indicates a deep overfit valley some 35m deep at Newhaven and 7m deep at Sharpsbridge with a basal coarse gravel and sands deposited in periglacial meltwater conditions. Seawards there is a complex of interbedded silts and peaty organic beds which are deposited in low energy perimarine conditions (Thomas 2010, 9) dating from *c.* 7000 to 500 BC, and sealed by high energy shingle bar deposits.

Archaeological Implications

Clearly the environment within the valley has changed, but in simple geoarchaeological terms much of the prehistoric and early historic landscape within the early Holocene Ouse valley floor is buried by metres of fine-grained alluvium. The occurrence of woodland clearance, and potential for cereal cultivation indicated from the valley cores at Wellingham (4.5m depth) and at Sharpsbridge (4.2m depth), potentially indicate Neolithic, or later horizons, some 4-5m below the present surface. In simple terms this changes the whole topography and configuration of the prehistoric and early historic valley, and of many prehistoric viewsheds from and into the valley. More dramatically it indicates large-scale soil erosion upstream; most of the sediment to Lewes at least, is derived from the Weald and this indicates thousands or millions of tons of soil erosion, which presumably we can suggest relates to deforestation and soil erosion in the Weald.

Land-use and vegetation history

A series of key pollen sites at Sharpsbridge (Scaife and Burrin 1983), Wellingham peat bog (Brooks unpubl,; Wing 1980; Robinson and Williams 1983), the Vale of the Brooks (Thorley 1971; 1981) and the Caburn (Waller and Hamilton 1998; 2000), provide a broad vegetation history of the Ouse. What is significant about the work of Rob Scaife, Paul Burrin and Anne Thorley is that their pollen analysis is not restricted to the organic and peat deposits, but extends through the entire minerogenic silts of the floodplain alluvium. Alluvium has long been regarded as of little significance in palaeo-vegetational reconstruction because of the considerable problems of interpreting the complex taphonomy of the sub-fossil pollen and spore assemblages (Scaife and Burrin 1992, 80; Fyfe *et al.* 2013). Consequently archaeologists have believed that pollen analysis was not possible from alluvial silty sediments, and often even failed to sample well-stratified sequences where they have been related to datable archaeological horizons or events. The cores from the Ouse provide information of the valley floor vegetation and the wider landscape, although this can be difficult to interpret (see Allen 1995a, 37-8) resulting in a number of misinformed, naive and inaccurate interpretations of the wider landscape by poorly informed archaeologists. In providing a summary here, I will attempt not to fall into the same trap.

Location	Result	Calibrated date (cal BC)
Vale of the Brooks		
Lewes II; top of the peat (350-365cm), eastern floodplain edge	3190±125 BP	1760-1110
Lewes II; bottom of the peat (670-690cm), eastern floodplain edge	5674±167 BP	4950-4120
Lewes I; middle of peat (*c.* 970cm depth) main floodplain	6290±125 BP	5490-4940
Foot of The Caburn		
413cm top of peat	3610±50 BP; Beta-117544	2140-1780
527cm pollen zone 2/3 boundary	4700±50 BP; Beta 127564	3640-3370
612cm pollen zone 1/2 boundary	5570±50 BP; Beta-127565	4500-4360
690cm Base of peat	6190±50 BP; Beta-127566	5300-5010

TABLE 2.1. RADIOCARBON DATES FROM THE BROOKS AND CABURN (FROM JONES 1971; THORLEY 1981, AND WALLER AND HAMILTON 2000)

In reviewing the vegetation histories, I do not concentrate on the vegetation successions in detail, but attempt to tease out the relevant impact of human populations; in particular early disturbance of woodland, progressive woodland clearance and creation and use of open downland, the presence of disturbed soils and of pasture and cultivation. These histories can be married to sediment (alluvial and colluvial) archives, and to the archaeological record of activity, occupation and settlement.

1. The Weald

Pollen diagrams from Sharpsbridge (Scaife and Burrin 1983) provide the most relevant record of vegetation and land-use history for the Ouse within the Weald, though we can perhaps examine those at Midhurst (Scaife 2001), and Loxwood (Scaife in Wessex Archaeology 2007) to provide other valley analogies. Most of these studies suffer from poor chronological constraints, and estimates of age and date are provided by generic climatic vegetation changes, in comparison with other dated sequences in southern England (cf. Scaife 1982), or by single radiocarbon assays at strategic locations.

The earliest vegetation identified at Sharpsbridge was a pine (*Pinus*) and hazel (*Corylus*-type) dominated woodland with some birch (*Betula*), oak (*Quercus*) and ash (*Fraxinus*), with lime (*Tilia*), and notably no alder (*Alnus*), and is suggested to be earlier Mesolithic in date. Amongst the pine, birch and 'hazel' woodland was a consistent low level of grass (Gramineae) pollen and other low-growing herbs which may suggest a relatively closed canopy woodland, extending even across the 'floodplain'. However, there is significant woodland disturbance and localised clearings in this Mesolithic woodland (Sharpsbridge) which probably accompanies the archaeological evidence of dense flint scatters in the Weald (cf. Tebbut 1975; Jacobi 1978; Holgate 2003).

As the birch, pine and hazel-dominated woodland became established, increased runoff (presumably due to Mesolithic and Neolithic local woodland clearings) resulted in the erosion and removal of sediment, and deposition at Sharpsbridge. Alluvium was subsequently deposited during the Neolithic after the primary elm decline (*c.* 4400 cal BC; Scaife 1988), probably as a result of local woodland removal within the catchment. A further 6m of sediment was to accumulate at Sharpsbridge, confirming the intensity of subsequent human activity in the Wealden catchment. Further fluctuations in the woodland species at Wellingham also suggest localised clearance and disturbance of the woodland just north of Lewes. A later woodland developed, probably from the Early Bronze Age, dominated by lime in particular (on the sandy freely drained soils), with oak and elm (*Ulmus*) more dominant on heavier soils, and ash. Alder probably formed a substantial alder carr within the floodplain. What is most significant here is the evidence not of the changing composition of the woodland mosaic in the Weald, but of localised removal of local woodland and increases in grasses enabling pasture, but also tillage and cereal cultivation. These Bronze Age levels are 3-5m below the current surface at Sharpsbridge. The Middle Bronze Age levels are not represented here, but at The Wilderness, a large oak stake dating to 1680-1530 cal BC (3340±40BP, NZA-36948) was driven into peats in a minor tributary of the Ouse east of Barcombe (Allen 2011). Pollen from here indicated a floodplain dominated by alder carr woodland with a typical understory of sedges and other fen/marsh taxa. The flora of the adjacent dryland/interfluves was partially wooded with oak and hazel with some lime (Scaife pers. comm.).

The Weald saw further woodland clearance including the selective removal of the lime (possibly for building), and was associated with increased grassland, pasture and cereal cultivation, probably in the mature Bronze Age and Early Iron Age (*c.* 1750-750 cal BC). Elsewhere (at Midhurst), mass clearance of a large portion of woodland in the Weald has been dated to 950-410 cal BC (2610±100 BP, RCD-2321) in the later Bronze Age/early Iron Age (Scaife 2001). This larger scale deforestation and increase in grassland, tillage and cultivation, led to soil degradation, podsolization and the formation of some heathland communities dominated by ling/heather (*Calluna*), and was associated with the initiation of alluvium in the upper part of the valley.

Slight local expansion of the woodland and development of pine, hazel, grasses and ferns (*Dryopteris*-type) together with birch, oak and ash suggests that alluviation here resulted from Late Iron Age and Roman forest clearance and possibly charcoal production for furnaces and forges associated with Roman to Medieval Wealden Iron Industry. Lime became re-established, and alder carr became more prevalent on the floodplain as a result of increased runoff from the interfluves. Open areas were increasingly dominated with ferns suggesting continued podsolization and heathland development which had started in the Bronze Age.

Wealden conclusions

What is important about the Sharpsbridge work, combined with that at Midhurst and the Cuckmere valley, is the clear indication of anthropogenic impact (local clearance and soil destabilisation) as early as the earlier Mesolithic, as well as significant human activity and woodland clearance during the mature Bronze Age and Iron Age (Bell 1992; Allen 1995a). This represents clear activity not reflected in the current archaeological record or commonly discussed in the archaeology of the Weald. This apparent disparity, or conflict, clearly reflects a lack of archaeological investigation and engagement with the post Mesolithic, prehistoric story of the Weald, which as Bell states is a 'result of rational misconceptions of the Weald as an uncleared wild until Medieval assart (*sic.*)' (Bell 1992, 271), and clearly, despite this being recognised for nearly 25 years, more archaeological research, investigation, and engagement is still needed to redress this imbalance, but so too is the recognition of this fact by archaeologists at large. Our view of the Weald as an untouched forest throughout much of prehistory is clearly erroneous, and probably derived largely from historical sources of a wooded Weald.

The paucity of evidence in the Weald is a result of a lack of rigorous archaeological research: exacerbated by a lack of ploughing, and its associated history of fieldwalking, combined with the lack of development threats (Gardiner 1990). The consequence of prehistoric human activity such as woodland clearance and tillage is, however, clearly evidenced in the very deep alluvial sediments derived from the Weald and now choking the Ouse, and other (e.g. Cuckmere) valleys. Although little archaeological and palaeo-environmental work has been undertaken in the higher reaches of the Ouse valley, those in similar areas of the Arun at Loxwood north of Chichester, as well as Sharpsbridge suggest the presence of surprisingly deep and stratified sequences of Mesolithic to recent date even in the small minor tributaries (Wessex Archaeology 2007).

We cannot and must not continue to assume that the Weald remained a wholly impenetrable forest (Bell 1992, 271) – surely the density of Mesolithic artefacts (e.g. Jacobi 1978; etc.) indicate the presence of more open areas within the woodland. Curwen presumed this woodland density 80 years ago (and it was reinforced to an extent by Sheldon (1978)), but this was based on historic rather than archaeological or palaeo-environmental information, and as Bell states (*op. cit.*) misinformation and misconception. Thankfully we have moved from, and think more critically about, this in both archaeological and landscape/land-use terms; but not all authors have yet accepted this and many continue to pedal concepts based on assumptions made by Curwen and others over half a century ago; it is invidious to cite these, but it does not assist us in collecting new and appropriate data with which to build an informed palaeo-environmental narrative.

2. The Lower valley and chalklands

Our data for the chalklands fringing the Ouse from Lewes to the coast include pollen sequences from The Brooks and the foot of the Caburn. To this we can add the poorly dated colluvial and mollusc sequence from Asham, the better dated sequences at Southerham, Malling Hill and Itford Bottom, with a number of land snail sequences from archaeological sites including Offham, Round-the-Down, and Lewes Priory. What follows attempts to marry data from these differing and contrasting palaeo-environmental sources to give a flavour of the environments of the chalklands, which not only change temporally, but also within which we can detect spatial variation. The combination of these data is particularly important as it provides more detailed composite interpretations. Further, it is also notable that it is rare to find pollen preservation on the chalk (Dimbleby and Evans 1974) and the significance and importance of the pollen from Wellingham, the Brooks and Caburn is that they not only reference the Ouse valley, but also the adjacent chalkland from which vegetation histories (as opposed to molluscan sequences) are rare (see Scaife 1987; Allen and Scaife 2007).

The geoarchaeology of the Ouse valley is outlined above. The other main deposits of geoarchaeological interest are colluvium on the interfluves within the catchment. The Ouse valley area has seen more dry valley excavation than many others, with the pioneering work of Martin Bell in major excavations at Itford Bottom (Bell 1981; 1983), and a similar style of excavation at Ashcombe Bottom (Allen 2005a; 2005c) as well as the colluvial deposits examined from Asham (Ellis 1985; 1986), Grey Pit, Southerham and Malling Hill (Allen 1995a), and Cuckoo Bottom (Allen 2005b). These provide the opportunity of looking at long, and potentially dated, land-use sequences of the downlands, and get away from the examination of the individual site locus, which may be unrepresentative and biased, being the focus of activity thus defining it as an 'archaeological site'. The colluvial investigations have also indicated the potential for buried sites as indicated by the Neolithic pit at Malling, the Beaker site at Aschombe, the Beaker land surface at Grey Pit, Southerham as well as a Bronze Age lynchet at Malling. The analysis of the colluvium itself helps in the examination of land-use and tillage and the changing nature (depletion and degradation) of the downland soils.

Buried soils, typically under Neolithic long barrows, Bronze Age round barrows, Iron Age ramparts, and within colluvial deposits, are particularly rare in this region (see Macphail 1987). They can provide information on land-use, soil disturbance, clearance and tillage as well as the nature and vegetational potential of former downland soils, however none has been analytically studied and published. Only a single sample of land snails has been examined from a buried soil from an archaeological site – that at Offham (Thomas 1977a).

A downland land-use history for the Ouse valley

Our understanding of the nature of the prehistoric vegetation on the Downs (as the Weald) has, and is, changing. In 1937 iconic Sussex archaeologist. E. Cecil Curwen, wrote that the downs were probably 'open grassland with a variable amount of scrub' (1937, 13), but after the war and the outbreak of myxomatosis leading to proliferation of longer grass and scrub on the downs, Curwen subtly modified his view of the prehistoric downland to one 'covered with scrub with varying amount of grass' (Curwen 1954, 13). Pollen and land snail evidence has altered that, and generally provide a picture of wooded downland, open woodland, woodland clearances and ultimately the establishment of open Downs. The colluvial sequences at Asham, although poorly dated, demonstrate this well (Ellis 1985; 1986), and chronologically better data are present elsewhere.

Woodlands of varying sorts

Land snails from periglacial coombe deposits at Asham (Williams 1971b; Ellis 1985) provide confirmation of late glacial cold stage and poorly vegetated tundra conditions. The Mesolithic chalkland slopes became wooded with pine, oak, lime, elm and hazel, with probably alder carr in the Vale of the Brooks at least. Thorley suggests that the presence of bracken (*Pteridium*) hints at clearance and modification of the natural wooded environment in the Mesolithic (1971; 1981). Land snails from a tree hollow at Itford Bottom were dated to 8260-7730 cal BC (8870±85 BP, BM-1544) and indicate ancient, principally deciduous, woodland with little or no human disturbance (though the fallen tree was burnt!), and the dated charcoal from the tree hollow was pine (*Pinus*). It is possible that this fallen tree represents Mesolithic removal as the molluscan assemblage in the upper part of the tree hollow hints of a more open environment locally (Bell 1981; 1983). A later Mesolithic tree hollow at Ashcombe Bottom (Allen 1994; 2005a) also contained pine charcoal but with hazel, oak and possibly hawthorn (cf. *Crataegus*). This, with the mollusc assemblages, suggests a mature, probably deciduous, woodland at about 6000-5500 BC.

Deciduous woodland of oak and lime with an understory of hazel, cloaked the Downs in the late Mesolithic and earlier Neolithic but fluctuations in elm and lime populations suggest disturbance, and the increase of ash, which is characteristic of disturbed woodland, tends to confirm this. Species such as field maple (*Acer campestre*) and juniper (*Juniperus*) were also present at Caburn with the juniper more prevalent on the steeper slopes such as at Caburn, and the steep chalk sides of the Ouse valley corridor.

Pine had ceased to be a part of the woodland after about 5000 BC on the Caburn-Malling Down at least (Waller and Hamilton 2000, 266). Clearance for the construction of early Neolithic long barrows (such as Camels Hump on Cliffe Hill and Money Burgh above Piddinghoe) and for larger monuments such as Offham causewayed enclosure at 3950-3530 cal BC (4925±80 BP, BM-1414) are obvious. It seems, however, that at Offham the clearing was very localised (Thomas 1977a; 1982), perhaps removing the trees just far enough to see over the treeline and into the Ouse valley (which may then have been 8m deeper than today). Evidence from Neolithic pits at Bishopstone (O'Connor 1977) dated to 3350-2920 cal BC (4460±70 BP, HAR-1622) again indicates open woodland, and scrub with grassland, while the late Neolithic pit at Malling Hill (Allen 1995a) indicates open woodland and woodland disturbance. Charcoals confirm the pollen evidence with oak, hazel, ash and hawthorn predominating.

This indicates a mosaic of woodland, and of woodland clearance, some of which had already been disturbed in the Mesolithic period. The first expansion of grass on Caburn occurs at about 4400 cal. BC, and although there is no clear evidence of human causation, in view of similar suggestions in the Weald we might suggest the same anthropogenic cause here on the Chalk. There is evidence too, from colluvial deposits themselves, to suggest that the former chalkland soils were thicker brown earths (Southerham) and even argillic brown earths (brown forest soils) at Ashcombe Bottom (Allen 1995a; 1994; 2005a; Macphail in Allen 2005a). They were loess-dominated (silty) giving rise to deeper and non-calcareous soils which would enable pine growth (see Allen 1988), but were also fertile and fragile. Unfortunately no soils buried beneath archaeological monuments, long barrows or banks have been investigated except a poorly preserved buried Neolithic soil that was sampled for snails under the shallow bank at Offham; but the soil itself was not described or examined in any detail.

Creation of the Downland

The Bronze Age covers over 1½ millennia during which expanding populations, changing lifestyles and economies led to major changes of land-use on the chalkland, and transformations in the chalkland environment. In fact it was during this period that it could be argued that the downlands as we see them today, were largely created. Removal of woodland from the earlier Bronze Age for open areas for pasture and tillage (Figure 2.3) were larger than had been for the construction of individual monuments previously. The consequence was that soils were loosened, disturbed and open, thus prone to erosion. Initial clearance and opening of the landscape for herding and corralling domestic herds, and settlement activities led to soil destabilisation and erosion. From the Early Bronze Age colluvium started to accumulate in chalkland dry valley bottoms, and soils were depleted and altered on valley sides and hilltops. The clearance was not uniform with many steep slopes remained wooded, and even some foci of Iron Age activity, which we might have expect to have been cleared in preceding periods, may not have been cleared until 2000 or 1500 cal BC. Local woods also still stood probably on some hilltops and across the Downs.

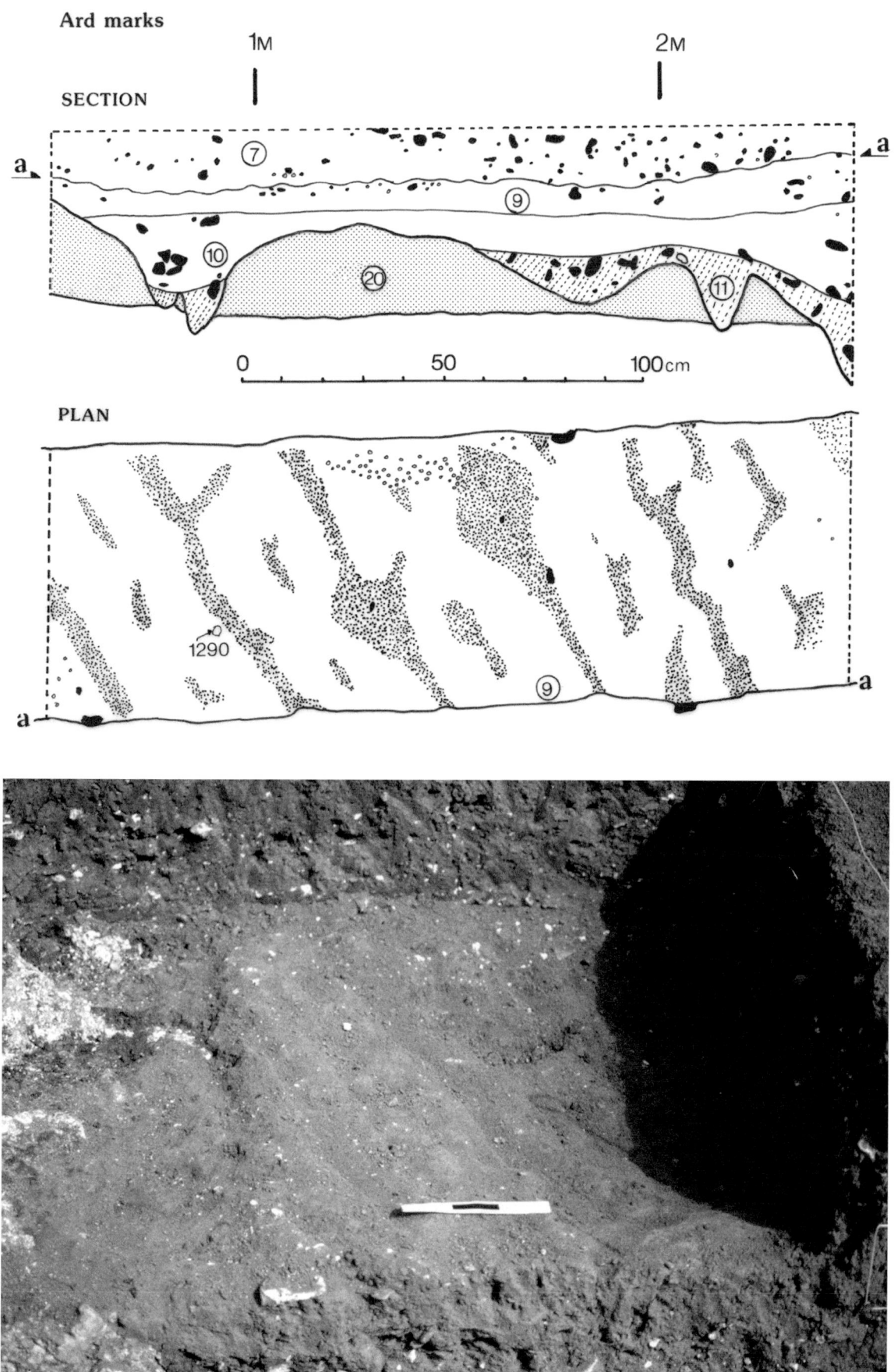

FIGURE 2.3: PLAN AND PHOTOGRAPH OF ARD MARKS IN THE BEAKER SOIL SEALED BENEATH BRONZE AGE COLLUVIUM AT ASHCOMBE BOTTOM

In the earlier Bronze Age some relatively large areas had been cleared of woodland. At Itford Bottom there are hints of a post Mesolithic tillage and possible later Neolithic woodland on less calcareous soils followed by clearance, and the development of an earthworm sorted buried soil with short grazed grassland with some disturbed ground (Bell 1981; 1983). Mixed charcoal of ash, oak, hawthorn (*Crataegus*) and pine gave a date of 2480-1770 cal BC (3720±120 BP, BM1545); but to which event this result relates is not entirely clear, if indeed all the charcoal in the buried soil even relates to a single event.

Some steep and scarp slopes such as those at the Caburn, remained wooded well into the Bronze Age and possibly later. Nevertheless on gentler slopes, hilltops and valley floors erosion of soils was exacerbated by progressive woodland clearance from the Middle, if not Early Bronze Age, which acted to accelerate local erosion and colluviation. Even the large-scale forest clearance suggested at *c*. 1000 BC, by Drewett *et al.* (1988), has been revised and can now be considered in many places to be significantly earlier (Allen 1988; 1991; etc.). The development of field systems from the mature Bronze Age, although 'embanked' by lynchets arrested some erosion (Figure 2.4), and led to lynchet build-up (see Allen 1982). Despite this, the overall trend was to increase net erosion and deposition, and to start to bury former occupation and activity areas located on the valley floors under, in some cases, several metres of colluvium (Figure 2.3). From the earlier Bronze Age the colluvium was chalkier representing the thinning of the former brown earth soils and the development of thinner and chalkier calcareous brown earths on valley sides and hilltops. Notably, settlement was no longer located in valley bottoms (such as at Ashcombe and Cuckoo Bottom) as it had been in the Early Bronze Age, but on the valley sides (such as Itford) with barrows false-crested on the ridge. This re-alignment of the settlement pattern, may in some way be related to the changing soils and their suitability for cultivation using Bronze Age technology. Even at the foot of the Down overlooking the floodplain at Itford Farm, Beddingham, very open dry conditions prevailed in the earlier Bronze Age (Allen 2009; Butler 2009).

By the mature Bronze Age and certainly the Iron Age, we can see that by comparison with other local dowlands, the soils of the Ouse valley chalklands had been denuded largely to the thin chalky rendzina soils we see today. Woodland was largely removed, but where present it survived as localised woods and forests which were managed for woodland resources for building, fuel and pannage for pigs. The downland continued to be tilled by ard, and the introduction of the plough in the Roman period, which turned and disturbed the soil rather than just scratched a shallow furrow, led to increased erosion and soil depletion, as can be seen at Southerham. *Pterdium aquilinum* (bracken) recovered by Dimbleby (1985) from Iron Age or Romano-British contexts at Ranscombe Camp, indicates the presence of acidic or loessic soils. Bracken does not exist on chalkland soils today and its occurrence suggests the survival of locally deeper soils (as at Ashcombe Bottom; Allen 2005a), into the Iron Age and Romano-British periods. Once again reinforcing the mosaic nature of the Ouse valley vegetation.

By the Saxon period this was a farmed landscape, with managed and tended woodlands. Much of the downland soils were thin and very chalky rendzinas though cultivation continued, as noted at the new Bishopstone sunken feature buildings which were largely filled with ploughwash colluvium (Allen 2014).

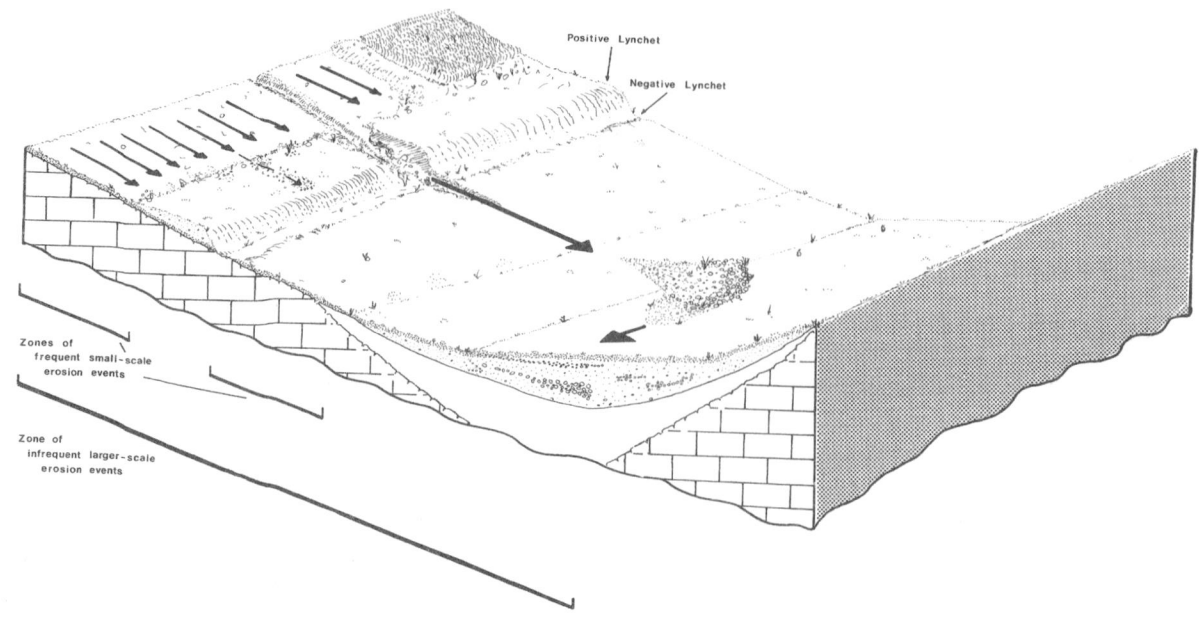

FIGURE 2.4: SCHEMATIC MODEL OF CHALKLAND DRY VALLEY EROSION REGIMES; LYNCHET FORMATION AND VALLEY FILLS (FROM ALLEN 1988, FIG 6.5; 1991, FIG. 5.2)

3. The valley floor

The valley floor is defined in part above in the pollen sequences, where as in the Weald it is seen largely as woodland with alder carr developing in the floodplain. In the lower chalkland Ouse valley, there is little evidence of prehistoric and early historic activity on the valley floor (but see discussion below).

There can be little doubt that Thorley's pollen diagrams from the Vale of the Brooks represent primarily very local catchment; that is largely just the Ouse floodplain around the Vale of the Brooks. The cores were located in the floodplain where dense alder carr exists swamping other pollen taxa (this is more relevant with regard to the interpretation of the vegetation beyond the floodplain). Her results show alder and hazel (*Corylus*-type; the latter possibly also including *Myrica gale* – bog myrtle, in this pollen type) on the valley floodplain: i.e. alder carr in the floodplain and woodland elements on its fringes. The total arboreal pollen levels in the Lewes I and Lewes II diagrams are evidently over-represented as a result of differential dispersal of pollen (Tauber 1965; 1967; Edwards 1982), especially within alluvial catchments (Burrin and Scaife 1984; 1992). Such biases can be extreme on woodland edges, and hazel, for instance, may be over-represented by as much has 500%. Care must, therefore, be exercised when using these data and previous uncritical use of Thorley's interpretations may prove unreliable. Nevertheless, alder carr dominated the vegetation in The Brooks; paludification (peatland formation) began in late Mesolithic (5490-4940 cal BC) peat continued to form as late as the Middle Bronze Age (1760-1110 cal BC). Such peat accumulation often relates to periods of environmental stability, however, woodland removal on the Downs and downland slopes would have increased surface run-off resulting in locally higher groundwater tables in valley bottoms such as The Brooks. The paludification here may not be entirely indicative of stable conditions, but in its later phases may have been maintained, prolonged and driven by anthropogenic factors. Elsewhere especially to the south of the Brooks, we have little information about the environment and land-use of the valley floor.

Discussion

Man and Environment

Human activity and the changing environments

Examination of river valley sequences has been very effective in indicating the significant presence of Mesolithic activity in the Weald; localised cycles of deforestation and regeneration, and destabilisation of the soils leading to significant alluviation. The environmental evidence suggests similar activity on the Downs with similar cyclical woodland clearances on the slopes of Caburn, on the chalk scarps around The Brooks, at Ashcombe Bottom and Itford Bottom. Thus, the environmental and geoarchaeological aspects significantly enhance the archaeological record of earlier prehistoric activity.

As Drewett suggests clearance of the Neolithic 'wildwood' of oak, elm, ash, and lime with hazel understory were often relatively small-scale and temporary (2003). Clearance for Offham did not extend much beyond the monument, and woodland regenerated after its short-lived use (see Whittle *et al.* 2011, for this revolution on the temporally ephemeral nature of these Neolithic monuments). Within these clearings local activity included farming and small-scale cultivation. We can see this on the chalk downs, and although lacking monuments, the Weald contains a number of Neolithic axes and some flint scatters (Gardiner J. 1988; Gardiner M, 1990; Holgate 2003), which allow us to postulate that some of the these activities occurred there too.

Removing woodland or living within the woods

We can be sure, that unlike the Wessex Downs where some large naturally unwooded and open areas remained in the early postglacial period, and attracted major Mesolithic activity and then Neolithic monumentalisation, the Sussex Downs and the Ouse valley contained a more-or-less continuous mosaic of woodland (Allen 2007; Allen and Gardiner 2009; Whitehouse and Smith 2004; cf. Birks 2005). We conceive the purpose of woodland removal and clearance as more than just one of moving trees to facilitate monument construction. We tend to assume a prehistoric, especially Neolithic, requirement to remove woodland. However, most of the resources for building, and the plants and animals for food, were obtained from the woods – so perhaps the creation of 'clearings' were openings *within* the wood, to enable construction, performance and special activities, such as at Offham, *within* the wood (see Allen and Gardiner 2013).

Hidden prehistoric landscapes

The Ouse valley itself is masked by metres, and millions of tons of sediment. The nature and configuration of the valley was very different in the past. The removal of the 5 to 12m of sediment may make many viewsheds, and points false-crested from the valley floor today, not possible in prehistory. Further the sediments clearly seal a whole Mesolithic to later Bronze Age alder carr landscape where the preservation of pollen and organic material may be very good. But was this area utilised for its woodland and other ecological resources during that time? Or does it harbour other ritual and community centres such as that at Shinewater in the Willingdon Levels on the edge of Eastbourne (Greatorex 2003), or a Must Farm, Cambridgeshire? The possibility of archaeological sites hidden from archaeological reconnaissance is not just restricted to the Ouse valley floor itself. The dry valleys of the downs are known to bury archaeological sites as demonstrated at Ashcombe and Cuckoo Bottom, and as suggested for much of southern England (Allen 2005c).

Cultural role of the Ouse valley

Finally in discussing the geoarchaeology and geography of the Ouse valley we can briefly consider, but not significantly address, a few other topics. The use of the floodplain has not been addressed; largely through lack of data though it must have been an important resource for farming (cultivation and pasture), wild resources, plants, reeds and of course water. Although we have seen few sets of environmental data from the Ouse valley environs, it is notable that south of Lewes, none come from the west of the valley. Is this pure accident, or does the Ouse valley mark a territorial boundary or barrier? Clearly too, the valley floor or edge of the valley floor has acted as the major communication route for the movement of herds of animals and of people, as Gardiner and Allen have argued for the Wylye valley, Wiltshire (2009). So it has acted as barrier, boundary and corridor since the Mesolithic; I hope these themes will have been addressed by other authors in their period reviews in this book.

Conclusions

Although the Ouse slices through a classic part of the Sussex Downs redolent in archaeological monuments from the Neolithic onwards, there has been surprisingly little fieldwork in the area and a general paucity of published environmental and geoarchaeological investigations. We are, therefore, in the rather surprising situation to find that except for the seminal pollen work from the Ouse valley (Thorley 1981; Scaife and Burrin 1983; 1992; Waller and Hamilton 2000), the rest of this landscape is data-poor and we know much less than is generally assumed. The area is abound with generic interpretation and assumption, based on just one or two key sites (that may not even be in this study area), and one or two long-held assumptions or conceptions deriving from the excellent, but now significantly dated work of, for instance, Curwen and Grinsell etc. Some basic assumptions of the Chalkland and Wealden divide (i.e. north (Weald) and south (chalkland)) with extensive late woodland in the latter (cf. Sheldon 1978) do not hold up to scrutiny, as Bell and others pointed out 30 years ago. The presence in prehistory of dense woodland with clearings and large clear-felled areas is clear (Scaife 2001); unfortunately the presence of extensive medieval woodland has often been taken to infer a continuum from prehistory. Retaining that assumption is dangerous and hinders continued research and advancement of interpretation. We need to prove the presence of woodland not at a regional scale (i.e. the Weald), but at the site and extra-site scale, as has been convincingly shown in Wessex. There, for instance, the assumption of an essentially uniform cloak of postglacial woodland over the Downs was proven to be wrong or inadequate for the scale of interpretation we now require (see Allen and Scaife 2007; Allen and Gardiner 2009; French *et al.* 2007; Allen 2007). We need, therefore, to prove and confirm, not assume, the existence and extent of postglacial woodland on our earlier (Mesolithic to Early Bronze Age) sites at a local and subregional scale, at every possible location, rather than assume its widespread presence. This assumption hindered research in Wessex where we now realise that large areas of downland did not become heavily wooded and they became foci of prehistoric activity from the Mesolithic and Neolithic periods. Such areas include Dorchester, Dorset (Maiden Castle, Mount Pleasant, Flagstones, Greyhound Yard, Alington Avenue, Maumbury rings etc.), Down Farm in Cranborne Chase (Wor barrow, Dorset Cursus, Firtree Feld, Wyke Down henges, etc.), Stonehenge (Amesbury 42 long barrow, Greater and Lesser Cursus, Stonehenge etc.), and possibly Avebury too (see Allen and Scaife 2007; Allen and Gardiner 2009; French *et al.* 2007; Allen 2007, and Allen forthcoming).

The prehistoric woodlands were a rich mosaic of differing woods, and the valley floor did not contain a single uniform ecology. These landscapes changed over space and time – some ephemeral while others were enduring. Just as early Mesolithic woodland clearances came and went, so did those of the Neolithic. It was not until the onset of farmers in the mature Bronze Age (established farming communities) as opposed to farming from the early Neolithic (nomadic societies involved in hunting, gathering, herding and small-scale crop growing), that the landscape started to be transformed. Even then woodland removal was not wholesale; and many now prominent and important places, may have been cloaked in woodland until late in prehistory.

The consequence of these prehistoric activities has been to transform, mould, create and re-create the Ouse valley as we see it today. Our understanding of the detail, temporal and spatial distribution of those environments still remains poor, and we should endeavour through archaeological research and commercially funded archaeology to address some of the lacuna and improve on the sketchy information provided here.

Acknowledgements

Thanks are given to Greg Chuter ESCC for allowing me to use the base map (Figure 2.1), Abby George who produced Figures 2.1 and 2.2), Dudley Moore for his patience, Rob Scaife for discussion and inspiration, and Julie Gardiner for her usual deft editorial hand, and Martin Bell for his insightful comments assisting with the clarity of the paper.

This report was supported by AEA: Allen Environmental Archaeology and limited funding from the University of Sussex Archaeological Society. While the author is wholly freelance with no other institutional funding this had to take its turn in the queue with research frameworks for South-East England, the Solent-Thames, and Avebury-Stonehenge World Heritage Site and several other research papers, authored books and edited volumes, so I apologise for any tardiness in its completion (submitted 2014).

References

Allen, L. 1982. A study of the chronological development of the Bishopstone lynchet by least-squares of the distribution of datable artefacts, *Sussex Archaeological Collections* 120, 207-8.

Allen, M. J. 1988. Archaeological and environmental aspects of colluviation in South-East England. In W. Groenmann-van Waateringe and M. Robinson (eds), *Man-Made Soils,* 69-92. Oxford: British Archaeological Reports, Int. Series 410.

Allen, M. J. 1991. Analysing the landscape: a geographical approach to archaeological problems. In A. J. Schofield (ed.), *Interpreting Artefact Scatters; contributions to ploughzone archaeology*, 39-57. Oxford: Oxbow Monograph 4.

Allen, M. J. 1994. The landuse history of the southern English chalklands with an evaluation of the Beaker period using environmental data: colluvial deposits and cultural indicators. Unpubl. PhD, thesis, University of Southampton (available at Sussex Archaeological Society library, Barbican House, Lewes).

Allen, M. J. 1995a. The prehistoric land-use and human ecology of the Malling-Caburn Downs; two late Neolithic/Early Bronze Age sites beneath colluvium. *Sussex Archaeological Collections* 133, 19-43.

Allen, M. J. 1995b. Land-use history of Round-the-Down: the molluscan evidence in Butler, C., The excavation of a Bronze Age round barrow at Round-the-Down, near Lewes, East Sussex. *Sussex Archaeological Collections* 133, 7-18.

Allen, M. J. 1997. Land Molluscs, in Lyne, M. *Lewes Priory, excavations by Richard Lewis 1969-82* pp 163-167. Lewes: Lewes Priory Trust.

Allen, M. J. 2005a. Beaker occupation and development of the downland landscape at Ashcombe Bottom, near Lewes, East Sussex. *Sussex Archaeological Collections* 143, 7-33.

Allen, M. J. 2005b. Beaker and Early Bronze Age activity, and a possible Beaker valley entrenchment, in Cuckoo Bottom, near Lewes, East Sussex. *Sussex Archaeological Collections* 143, 35-45.

Allen, M. J. 2005c. Beaker settlement and environment on the chalk downs of southern England, *Proceedings of the Prehistoric Society* 71, 219-45.

Allen, M. J. 2007. and landscape development; the molluscan evidence. In C. French, H. Lewis, M. J. Allen, M. Green, R. G. Scaife and J. Gardiner, *Prehistoric landscape development and human impact in the upper Allen valley, Cranborne Chase, Dorset*, 151-189. Cambridge: McDonald Institute Monograph.

Allen, M. J. 2009. Itford Farm (IFB 08) land snail assemblages; environment, land-use and chronology. Unpublished report for CBAS, AEA report AEA 068.20, dated 21st July August 2009.

Allen, M. J. 2011. Prehistoric Wetlands Discovery. A new Middle Bronze Age waterlogged site in Sussex. *Sussex Past and Present* 125, 6-7.

Allen, M. J. 2014. Antony Close, Bishopstone, East Sussex, (ACB 14); palaeo-environmental (charred plant, charcoal and land snail) assessment. Unpublished report for CBAS, AEA report AEA 242.01.01, dated 14th July 2014.

Allen, M. J. and Gardiner, J. 2009. If you go down to the woods today; a re-evaluation of the chalkland postglacial woodland; implications for prehistoric communities. In M. J. Allen, N. Sharples, and T, P. O'Connor (eds), *Land and People; papers in memory of John G. Evans*, 49-66. Oxford: Prehistoric Society Research Paper 2.

Allen M. J. and Gardiner, J. 2013. Not out of the woods yet: some reflections on Neolithic ecological relationships with woodland. In A. M. Jones, J. Pollard, M. J. Allen and J. Gardiner (eds.), *Image, Memory and Monumentality; archaeological engagements with the material world* 93-107. Oxford: Prehistoric Society Research Paper 5.

Allen, M. J. and Scaife, R. 2007. A new downland prehistory: long-term environmental change on the southern English chalklands, in A. Fleming and R. Hingley (eds), *Prehistoric and Roman Landscapes; landscape history after Hoskins,* 16-32. Macclesfield: Windgather Press.

Bell, M. G. 1975. Sediment analysis and periglacial landforms as evidence of the environment of southern England during the last glaciation. Unpublished BSc dissertation, University of London, Institute of Archaeology.

Bell, M. 1976. The excavation of an early Romano-British site and Pleistocene landforms at Newhaven. *Sussex Archaeological Collections* 114, 218-305.

Bell, M. 1977. Excavations at Bishopstone. *Sussex Archaeological Collections* 115.

Bell, M. G. 1981. Valley sediments as evidence of prehistoric land-use: a study based on dry valleys in south east England. Unpublished Ph.D. thesis, London University, Institute of Archaeology.

Bell, M. G. 1983. Valley sediments as evidence of prehistoric land-use on the South Downs. *Proceedings of the Prehistoric Society* 49, 119-150.

Bell, M. 1992. Archaeology under alluvium: human agency and environmental process. Some concluding thoughts. In S. Needham and M. G. Macklin (eds), *Alluvial Archaeology in Britain,* 271-76. Oxford: Oxbow Books.

Bell, M., Neal, R. and Pears, B. 2010. Bishopstone valley sediments and sea-level relationships, 12-15, in G. Thomas, *The later Anglo-Saxon settlement at Bishopstone; a downland manor in the making.* York: CBA Research Report 163.

Birks, H. J. B. 2005. Mind the gap: how open were European primeval forests? *Trends in Ecology and Evolution (TREE)* 20:4, 154-6.

Brandon, P. F. 1971. The origin of Newhaven and the drainage of the Lewes and Laughton Levels, *Sussex Archaeological Collections*, 109, 94-106.

Brooks, A. unpubl. Pollen data from Elstead, Surrey; Broxbourne and Ponders End, Hertfordshire, and Wellingham, Sussex. Unpublished student report, Dept. Plant Science, Kings College, University of London (cited in Robinson and Williams 1983).

Burrin, P. J. 1985. Holocene alluviation in south east England and some implications for palaeohydrological studies. *Earth Surface Processes and Landforms* 10, 257-271.

Burrin, P. J. and Jones, D. K. C. 1991. Environmental processes and fluvial responses in a small temperate zone catchment: a case study of the Sussex Ouse valley in southeast England. In K. J. Gregory and J. B. Thornes (eds), *Temperate Palaeohydrology*, 217-252. Chichester: Wiley.

Burrin, P. J. and Scaife, R. G. 1984. Aspects of Holocene sedimentation and floodplain development in southern England. *Proceedings of the Geologists' Association* 85, 81-96.

Burrin P. J. and Scaife, R. G. 1988. Environmental thresholds, catastrophe theory and landscape sensitivity: their relevance to the impact of man on valley alluviation. In J. L. Bintliffe, D. A. Donaldson and E. G. Grant (eds), *Conceptual Issues in Environmental Archaeology*, 211-232. Edinburgh: Edinburgh University Press.

Butler, C. 2009. An archaeological excavation at Itford Farm, Beddingham, East Sussex. Unpublished client report (CBAS: Chris Butler Archaeological Services) LW/07/0792.

Castleden, R., 1996. *Classic Landforms of the Sussex Coast.* Sheffield: Landform Guide 2, The Geographical Association.

Curwen, E. C. 1937. *The Archaeology of Sussex.* London: Methuen and Co. Ltd.

Curwen, E. C. 1954. *The Archaeology of Sussex.* London: Methuen and Co. Ltd. 2nd edn.

Dimbleby, G.W. 1985. *Palynology of Archaeological Sites.* London: Academic Press.

Dimbleby, G. W. and Evans, J. G. 1974. Pollen analysis and land snail analysis of Calcareous soils, *Journal of Archaeological Science* 1, 117-33.

Drewett, P. 2003. Taming the wild: the first farming communities in Sussex. In D. Rudling (*et al.*), *Archaeology of Sussex to AD 2000*, pp 39-46. King's Lynn: Heritage Marketing/ University of Sussex.

Drewett, P. L. and Hamilton, S. 1999. Marking time and making space: excavations and landscape studies at the Caburn Hillfort, East Sussex, 1996-98. *Sussex Archaeological Collections* 137, 7-38.

Drewett, P., Rudling, R. and Gardiner, M. 1988. *The South-east to AD2000; a regional history of England.* London: Longman.

Dunkin, D. 1998. An Archaeological Assessment (Stage 1) of the Proposed Newhaven Harbour Link Road and Associated Developments, Newhaven, East Sussex. Unpublished, Archaeology South-East Report (Project No. 776).

Edwards, K.J. 1982. Man, space and woodland edge: speculations on the detection and interpretation of human impact in pollen profiles. In M. G. Bell and S. Limbrey (eds), *Archaeological aspects of woodland ecology*, 5-22. Oxford: British Archaeological reports In. Series 146.

Ellis, C. 1985. Flandrian molluscan biostratigraphy and its application to dry valley deposits in East Sussex. In N. R. J. Fieller, D. D. Gilbertson and N. G. A. Ralph (eds), *Palaeoenvironmental Investigations: Research Design, Methods and Data Analysis*, 157-165. Oxford: British Archaeological Reports, Int. Series 226.

Ellis, C. 1986. The postglacial molluscan succession of the South Downs dry valleys. In G. de G. Sieveking and M. B. Hart (eds), *The Scientific Study of Flint and Chert*, 175-194. Cambridge: Cambridge University Press.

Farrant, J. H. 1972. The evolution of Newhaven Harbour and the lower Ouse before 1800, *Sussex Archaeological Collections* 110, 44-60.

French, C. 2015. *A handbook of geoarchaeological approaches for investigating landscapes and settlement sites.* Studying Scientific Archaeology 1. Oxford: Oxbow.

French, C., Lewis, H., Allen, M. J., Green, M. Scaife, R. G. and Gardiner, J. 2007. *Prehistoric landscape development and human impact in the upper Allen valley, Cranborne Chase, Dorset.* Cambridge: McDonald Institute Monograph.

Fyfe, R. M., Twiddle, C., Shinya, S., Gaillard, M-J., Barratt, P., Caseldine, C. J., Dodson, J., Edwards, K. J., Farrell, M., Froyd, C., Grant, M. J., Huckerby, E., Innes, J. B., Shaw, H. and Waller, M. 2013. The Holocene vegetation cover of Britain and Ireland: overcoming problems of scale and discerning patterns of openness, *Quaternary Science Reviews* 73, 132-148.

Gardiner, J. 1988. The composition and distribution of Neolithic surface flint assemblages in central southern England. Unpublished PhD thesis, University of Reading (available through ETHOS; electronic theses on line: http://ethos.bl.uk/OrderDetails.do?uin=uk.bl.ethos.278374)

Gardiner, M. 1990. The archaeology of the Weald – a survey and review. *Sussex Archaeological Collections* 128, 33-53.

Gardiner, J. and Allen, M. J. 2009. Peopling the landscape; prehistory of the Wylye valley, Wiltshire. In M. J. Allen, N. Sharples, and T. P. O'Connor (eds), *Land and People; papers in memory of John G. Evans*, 77-89. Prehistoric Society Research Paper 2.

Geographical Editorial Committee (ed.), 1983. *Sussex: Environment, Landscape and Society.* Gloucester: Alan Sutton Publishing Ltd.

Greatorex, C. 2003. Living on the margins? The late Bronze Age landscape of the Willingdon Levels. In D. Rudling (ed.), *Archaeology of Sussex to AD 2000*, pp 89-100. King's Lynn: Heritage Marketing/ University of Sussex.

Holgate, R. 2003. Late glacial and post-glacial hunter-gathers in Sussex. In D. Rudling (ed.), *Archaeology of Sussex to AD 2000*, pp 29-38. King's Lynn: Heritage Marketing/ University of Sussex.

Jacobi, R. 1978. The Mesolithic of Sussex. In P. L. Drewett (ed.), *Archaeology in Sussex to AD 1500*, p15-22. London: CBA Research Report 29.

James, R. 2002. The excavation of a Saxon *grubenhaus* at Itford Farm, Beddingham, East Sussex, *Sussex Archaeological Collections* 140, 49-56.

Jarzembowski. E. 2003. Palaeoenvironments of the Ouse Valley Project. Unpublished Manuscript.

Jones, D. K. C. 1971. The Vale of the Brooks. In R. B. G. Williams (ed.), *A Guide to Sussex Excursions*, 43-46. Sussex University: Institute of British Geographers Conference (Jan. 1971).

Jones, D. K. C. 1981. *Southeast and Southern England.* London: Methuen.

Jolliffe, I. P. 1964. The movement of shingle on the margins of Seaford Bay. Wallingford: Hydraulics Research Station, Report. INT 35.

Lake, R. D., Wood, C. J. and Mortimer, R. N. 1987. *Geology of the country around Lewes.* Memoir Geological Survey of GB, sheet 319.

Macphail, R. I. 1987. A review of soil science in archaeology in England. In H. C. M. Keeley (ed.), *Environmental Archaeology: a regional review, vol. 2*, p322-377. London: Historic Buildings and Monuments Commission for England, Occasional Paper No. 1.

Needham, S. and Macklin, M. G. (eds), 1992. *Alluvial Archaeology in Britain.* Oxford: Oxbow Books.

Monkhouse, F. J. 1960. *Principles of Physical Geography.* London: University of London Press (4th edn.).

O'Connor, T. P. 1977. Land Mollusca from the settlement. In Bell, M., Excavations at Bishopstone *Sussex Archaeological Collections 115*, 267-73.

Robinson, D. A. and Williams, R. B. G. 1983. The soils and vegetation history of Sussex, in The Geographical Editorial Committee (ed.), *Sussex: Environment, Landscape and Society*, 109-126. Gloucester: Alan Sutton Publishing Ltd.

Scaife, R. G. 1982. Late Devensian and early Flandrian vegetation changes in southern England. In M. G. Bell and S. Limbrey (eds), *Archaeological aspects of woodland ecology*, 54-74. Oxford: British Archaeological reports In. Series 146.

Scaife, R.G. 1987. A review of later quaternary plant microfossil and macrofossil research in southern England; with special reference to environmental archaeological evidence. In H. C. M. Keeley (ed.), *Environmental Archaeology: a regional review, vol. 2*. Historic Buildings and Monuments Commission for England, Occasional Paper No. 1, 125-203.

Scaife, R. G. 1988. The elm decline in the pollen record of south east England and its relationship to early agriculture. In M. Jones (ed.), *Archaeology and the Flora of the British Isles*, 21-33. Oxford: Oxford University Committee for Archaeology, Oxbow Books.

Scaife, R. 2001. The prehistoric vegetation of Midhurst: a pollen study of New Pond. In The borough ditch. Investigations at the Spread Eagle Hotel, 53-63. In J. Magilton and S. Thomas (eds), *Midhurst*. Chichester: Chichester District Archaeology, 95-102.

Scaife, R. G. and Burrin, P. J. 1983. Floodplain development in vegetational history of the Sussex High Weald and some Archaeological Implications. *Sussex Archaeological Collections* 121, 1-10.

Scaife, R. G. and Burrin, P. J. 1985. The environmental impact of prehistoric man as recorded in the upper Cuckmere valley at Stream Farm, Chiddingly. *Sussex Archaeological Collections* 123, 27-34.

Scaife, R. G. and Burrin, P. J. 1992. Archaeological inferences from alluvial sediments: some findings from southern England. In S. Needham and M. G. Macklin (eds), *Alluvial Archaeology in Britain*, 75-91. Oxford: Oxbow Books.

Sheldon, J. 1978. The environmental background. In P. L. Drewett (ed.), *Archaeology in Sussex to AD 1500*, p3-72. London: CBA Research Report 29.

Strahler, A. N. 1975. *Physical Geography.* New York and London: John Wiley and Sons, (4th edn.).

Tauber, H. 1965. Differential pollen dispersion and the interpretation of pollen diagrams. *Danmarks Geologiske Undersøgelse.* II 89, 1- 69.

Tauber, H. 1967. Investigation of the mode of pollen transfer in forested areas, *Review Palaeobotany Palynology* 3, 277-287.

Tebbutt, C. F. 1975. The prehistoric occupation of Ashdown Forest are of the Weald. *Sussex Archaeological Collections* 122, 34-43.

Thomas, G. 2010. *The later Anglo-Saxon settlement at Bishopstone; a downland manor in the making.* York: CBA Research Report 163.

Thomas, K. D. 1977a. Appendix IV: The land Mollusca from the enclosure on Offham Hill. In Drewett, P. L., The excavation of a Neolithic Causewayed Enclosure on Offham Hill, East Sussex, 1976. *Proceedings of the Prehistoric Society* 43, 201-241.

Thomas, K. D. 1977b. A preliminary report on the Mollusc from the lynchet section. In Bell, M.,

Excavations at Bishopstone *Sussex Archaeological Collections 115*, 258-64.

Thomas, K. D. 1982. Neolithic enclosures and woodland habitats on the South Downs in Sussex, England. In M. G. Bell and S. Limbrey (eds), *Archaeological Aspects of Woodland Ecology*, 147-170. Oxford: British Archaeological Reports: Int. Series 146.

Thorley, A. 1971. Vegetational history in the Vale of the Brooks. In R. B. G. Williams (ed.), *A Guide to Sussex Excursions*, 47-50. University of Sussex: Institute of British Geographers Conference (Jan. 1971).

Thorley, A. 1981. Pollen analytical evidence relating to the vegetational history of the Chalk. *Journal of Biogeography* 8, 93-106.

Waller, M. P. and Hamilton, S. D. 1998. The vegetational history of the South Downs: Mount Caburn, in J. B. Murton, C. A. Whiteman, M. R. Bates, D. R. Bridgland, A. J. Long, M. B., Roberts and M. P. Waller (eds), *The Quaternary of Kent and Sussex; Field Guide.* 115-120. London: Quaternary Research Association.

Waller, M. P. and Hamilton, S. 2000. Vegetation history of the English chalklands: a mid-Holocene pollen sequence from the Caburn, East Sussex, *Journal of Quaternary Science* 15 (3) 253–272.

Wessex Archaeology 2007. Onslow Arms, Loxwood, Chichester, West Sussex: report on the geoarchaeological field evaluation, watching brief and environmental assessment. Unpublished, Wessex Archaeology unpublished client report ref 61910.03, dated February 2007.

Whitehouse, N. J. and Smith, D. N. 2004. 'Islands' in Holocene forests: implications for forest openness, landscape clearance and 'culture-steppe' species. *Environmental Archaeology* 9, 203-12.

Whittle, A., Healy, F. and Bayliss, A. 2011. *Gathering Time: Dating the Early Neolithic Enclosures of Southern Britain and Ireland*. Oxford: Oxbow Books.

Williams, R. B. G. (ed.), 1971a. *A Guide to Sussex Excursions*. University of Sussex: Institute of British Geographers Conference (Jan. 1971).

Williams, R. G. B. 1971b. Aspects of the geomorphology of the South Downs. In R. G. B. Williimas (ed.), *A Guide to Sussex Excursions*, 35-42. University of Sussex: Institute of British Geographers Conference (Jan. 1971).

Wing, A. S. 1980. An analysis of the pollen fallout at Wellington peat bog near Lewes, East Sussex and a consideration of some of its climatic and historical implications. Unpublished B.Sc. project University of Sussex.

3. Palaeolithic record of the Sussex Ouse Valley

Matt Pope and Jenny Brown

The Sussex Ouse is one of the principal rivers of south east England, draining a significant portion of the Wealden region and with a long geological history extending back into the Tertiary period. During the first half of the twentieth century it was also considered a key locality in the archaeology of human origins, its ancient gravels having apparently produced the remains of the human ancestor *Eoanthropus dawsonii* from localities at Piltdown, Netherfield and Balcombe (Dawson and Woodward 1913). With the revelation that the Piltdown finds were fraudulent, attention rightly returned to areas of Britain which provided the genuine sequence of early human occupation. The Ouse valley and, to a wider degree, the Weald and Downs of Sussex, slipped back into the margins of the story of the British Palaeolithic. This is a situation which, apart from 14 years of focus on the archaeology at Boxgrove, has remained true to the time of writing.

In southern Britain it is the river systems of the Solent and Thames that provide the key records for long term human occupation during the Pleistocene. It is, within the region, always to these two rivers that we must look for a chronological framework which can tie into other regions and provide sites rich enough and densely concentrated enough to give us a clear understanding of Palaeolithic occupation. While significant Palaeolithic localities are found across southern Britain, from a variety of geological contexts, it is the extensive terrace sequences of these two rivers which have produced the largest concentration of finds and elicited the most concerted efforts in terms of research (Wymer 1968; 1999; Bridgland 1994; Gibbard 1994). These large systems preserve fluvial deposits at discrete altitudes as a series of terraces, the higher terraces relating to progressively earlier courses of the Thames during previous glacial-interglacial cycles. Through long histories of investigation and scientific dating programmes within these key sequences, it is now broadly possible to equate each terrace formation with a period in time and characterise each in terms of unique archaeological, climatic and ecological signatures.

Consequently, in southern Britain, we have a record spanning perhaps as much as 600k years, with terraces producing archaeology containing both the traces of handaxe-using populations of *Homo heidlebergensis*, through to later Neanderthal populations with Middle Palaeolithic technology. The deposits of the last cold stage, present at lower altitudes within the valleys, also preserve evidence for the last Neanderthal populations in northern Europe and the Upper Palaeolithic archaeology of the modern humans who replaced them.

In Sussex we have a history of research, and a plethora of both geological and archaeological localities indicating the long term history of climate change and Palaeolithic occupation in the county. The geological potential of deposits in Sussex to document both changing climate and sea level in the Pleistocene was established in the first half of the nineteenth century through published accounts of raised beaches and river terrace gravels by Mantell and Mantell (1822), Dixon (1876) and Prestwich (1859a). Early finds of extinct Pleistocene fauna were also made during this period, associated with Head and fluvial deposits of both the last and earlier glaciations; these include the Peppering elephant (Mantell and Mantell 1822), 'Asiatic elephant' from Burton Park, Duncton (Godwin Austin in Dixon 1876), 'Asiatic elephant' from Head above the Black Rock raised beach (Mantell and Mantell 1822) and, in the Ouse valley, '*Mammuthus Meridionalis*' within fluvial deposits at Barcombe church (Dixon 1876). Of these only the fossil remains from Black Rock are available for modern study, and these comprise early examples of the species *Mammuthus primigenius*. While it is likely that these other reported remains are also those of this late species, the possibility that they may be examples of *Mammuthus trogontherii* (Steppe mammoth) or *Palaeodoxon antiquus* (Straight tusked elephant) cannot be ruled out.

Systematic consideration of Pleistocene geology in the county began in the middle part of the nineteenth century with observations by the pre-eminent geologist Sir Joseph Prestwich. His focus was on mapping the raised beaches of the Sussex coastal plain, but this research directly fed into the wider academic interest in apparently ancient stone tools from deep within Pleistocene fluvial sequences. This research, carried out in partnership with the archaeologist Sir John Evans, was to culminate in the famous visit to the gravel quarries around Amiens in the Somme valley, and the pronouncement on the confirmed antiquity of humanity based on the observation of *in situ* Palaeolithic material in the pit at St. Acheul (Prestwich 1859b; Roberts and Pope 2009; Gamble and Kruyzinski 2009).

As part of the wave of both scientific and amateur interest in developing a more detailed understanding of this deeper human prehistory, active recognition and collections of Palaeolithic material became widespread during the latter half of the nineteenth century. In Sussex, it appears that the first recorded Palaeolithic handaxe was that found by Ernest Willett, son of the founding-father of Brighton Museum, Henry Willett, at Portslade,

West Sussex, in 1876. More systematic collection was undertaken by Garraway-Rice in the later nineteenth century, and Reginald Smith of the British Museum appears to have taken an interest in the county at the beginning of the twentieth century. More systematic excavation and documentation of finds was undertaken by Grinsell and the Curwens in the 1920s, and before World War II excavations by Fowler, Calkin and Curwen at Slindon, on the highest 40m (100ft) raised beach, started to focus on these deposits (now termed the Arundel-Westbourne raised beach) as a potentially productive area for collection. The valley side at Slindon Bottom was to become an extremely prolific site, to date still second only to Boxgrove in terms of volume of finds within the county. The site produced hundreds of artefacts, including both well-finished and roughed-out bifaces, and was interpreted as representing 'living-floors' associated with the raised beach (Woodcock 1981). While this interpretation has now been shown to be erroneous, the artefacts being excavated from later Head derived from *in-situ* terrestrial deposits on the valley side, it still remains a key locality in the history of Palaeolithic Sussex.

In Sussex, throughout the twentieth century, isolated finds became more routinely recognised, collected and recorded. In the mid-late twentieth century collation of existing data, as part of first Roe's gazetteer of Lower Palaeolithic sites (Roe 1968), and subsequently Andrew Woodcock's more detailed PhD thesis and subsequent publication (Woodcock 1981), demonstrated how extensive this range of available data had become, comprising by 1981 some 150 confirmed find localities. This was also the period in which Sussex was to produce two further Palaeolithic find localities which preserved primary context artefact scatters, to add to the hitherto lone site of Slindon Bottom. In 1976, excavation at a Romano-British villa in Newhaven by Martin Bell recovered mint-condition artefacts from Pleistocene involutions underlying the site. The fresh condition and extensive refitting showed that the involutions had captured a knapping scatter through periglacial processes (Bell 1976; Pope and Maxted 2008). In 1977 we also have the game-changing visit of a young PhD student, Andrew Woodcock, to Amey's Eartham Pit. His recognition of extensive fine-grained deposits overlying marine sediments of the raised beach, with *in situ*, refitting artefacts and preserved Pleistocene mammal fauna, was crucial to the discovery of the internationally important Boxgrove locality.

Through the 1980s and 1990s, Boxgrove was to dominate the discipline of Palaeolithic archaeology not only in Sussex, but across Britain and Northern Europe. The excavation seasons from 1982-1997, led by Mark Roberts, produced spectacular *in situ* archaeology associated with animal butchery and handaxe manufacture across the 1.5 km^2 of gravel extraction (Roberts and Parfitt 1999). Further discoveries of hominin remains, tooth incisors and a tibia of *Homo heidelbergensis*, were to cement Boxgrove's position as the most important Lower Palaeolithic locality in North West Europe, and to put Sussex back at the centre of the discipline for the first time since the uncovering of the Piltdown hoax. The 1990s also saw a leap forward in the understanding of Pleistocene geology in the county, most notably through the research of Martin Bates on the coastal plain of Sussex and eastern Hampshire. Bates was able to systematically test earlier observations of multiple raised beaches, preserved at discrete altitude, suggesting a model of successive high sea levels, forming beaches over 500,000 years in an area of slow but consistent tectonic uplift. The research did little to redress the paucity of finds associated with these younger raised beaches, indeed it began to raise the question as to why they appeared so poor in artefacts compared to the 40m raised beach, but it gave the county and by extension, the region, a key geochronological sequence independent of fluvial terrace sequences.

The first decade of the twenty-first century saw more detailed mapping of the Westbourne-Arundel raised beach, but a cessation of excavations at Boxgrove. Excavation by the author in 2006-2007 at the Valdoe Quarry, Boxgrove, determined the wider presence of human activity in the same MIS13 palaeolandscapes (Pope *et al.* 2009; Roberts and Pope 2009), but no further localities were either found or investigated. The author's excavations at the site of Beedings, West Sussex, (Pope *et al.* 2009) represented a shift in focus away from the raised beaches and the Lower Palaeolithic record, in an attempt to try and clarify the geological context of Upper Palaeolithic material from the Lower Greensand ridge at the site. The results of this work, showing excellent localised preservational contexts and a succession of Late Middle Palaeolithic and Early Upper Palaeolithic material, started to raise new questions for the region. How prevalent were archaeological localities on plateau and ridge contexts away from the river valleys and coastal plains? To what degree is a record of human occupation in the last glacial preserved in the region? This work, as part of wider changes in perspective on the archaeology of the English Channel region, is a developing research theme at the time of writing.

This potted history of Palaeolithic archaeology in Sussex aims to serve a very important purpose in this paper. It seeks to explain why systematic investigation of the Sussex river valleys in general, and the Ouse valley in particular, has yet to be undertaken. It is at first glance anomalous that, despite the early recognition in Sussex of the Acheulean within fluvial gravel deposits, and the development of the British sequence based on a continuity of fluvial terrace research from Smith and Dewey (1914) through to John Wymer (1968), Phil

Gibbard (1994) and Dave Bridgland (1994), that this has not yet been undertaken for Sussex. Attention was initially focused by Garraway-Rice but this did not translate into interest from the geological establishment through the twentieth century. Why should this be? The answer might be at least partially found within the Ouse valley itself and a period of a few years from 1912-1916 where an exposure of Pleistocene river gravel in Sussex had the world's attention.

Against this background of intense interest, undelivered promise, skulduggery and exceptional finds on the Sussex raised beaches, it is perhaps more understandable that the river terrace deposits of Sussex have been neglected. At the time of writing the four principle rivers which dissect the Weald and South Downs (the Arun, Adur, Ouse and Cuckmere) have yet to be subjected to systematic research, either in terms of relative geochronology, or Palaeolithic archaeology. Despite the fact that all have multiple terrace sequences, evidence for Palaeolithic human occupation, associated mammalian fauna and likely interconnection/stratification with the archaeologically important raised beach sequences of the Sussex coastal plain (Bates 2001), they have yet to attract modern archaeological or geological research. Compared to the Solent and Thames, the range and extent of terrace deposits is admittedly restricted and the contexts of existing finds are poorly understood. It is also true that no demonstrably *in situ* material has been recovered from fine grained deposits within the river gravels of the county, but the fact remains that a relatively rich and historically extensive collection of Lower and Middle Palaeolithic material has not been systematically addressed since the advent of reliable dating methodologies such as OSL and ESR.

This paper, which turns its attention to the Ouse valley, cannot begin to redress this gap in regional Pleistocene research, but it does seek to summarise the known Palaeolithic record for this single river valley, and to use this as a proxy for potential in the fluvial depositional sequences of the county and the Wealden region as a whole. Below, an attempt is made to present what is known of the Ouse valley's Lower and Middle Palaeolithic record and to try to establish what potential exists for further research and investigation.

Key Sites

Overwhelmingly the Palaeolithic record of the Ouse valley is dominated by isolated finds of handaxes, these find spots are shown in Figure 3.1. While this is also true for the Palaeolithic record of the wider region as a whole, with handaxes forming the most numerous and easily recognisable artefact class of the period, the

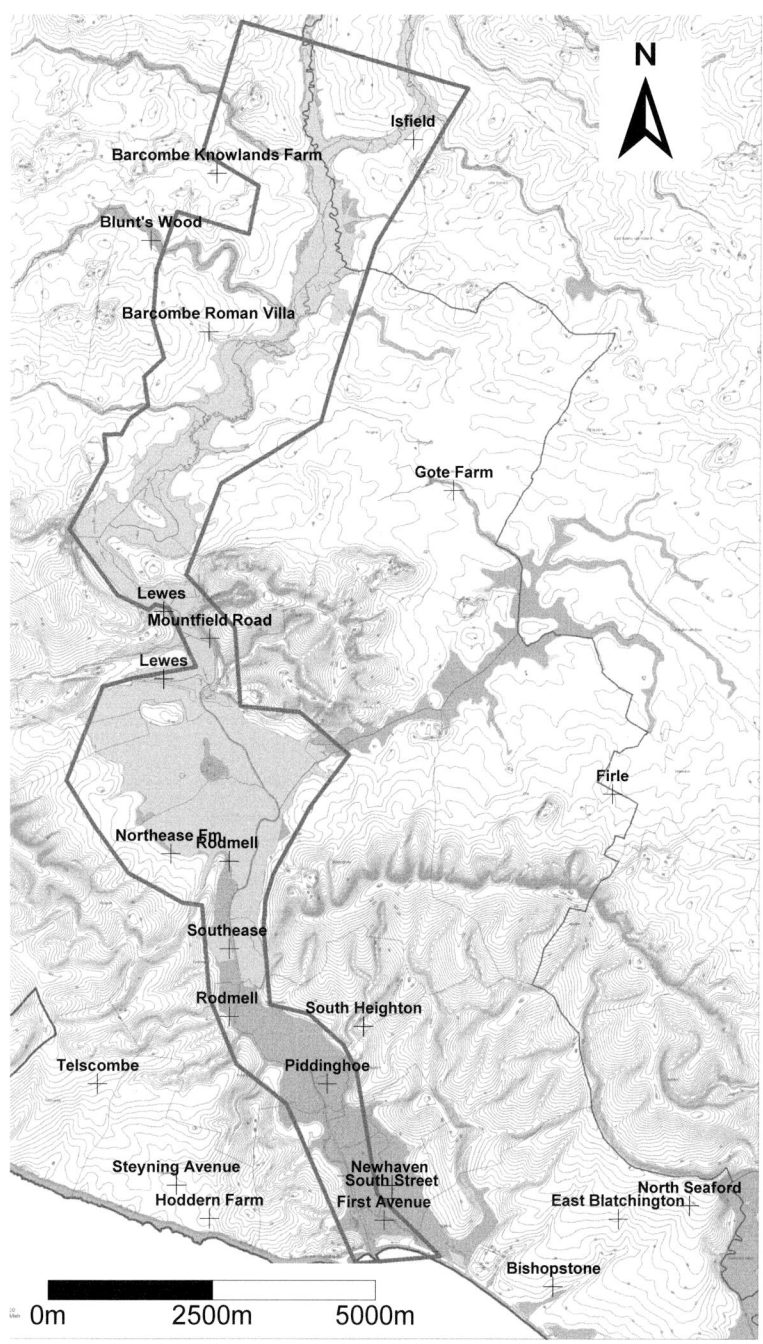

FIGURE 3.1: FIND SPOTS OF HANDAXES

situation for the Ouse valley is particularly stark. The lack of any clearly definable Middle Palaeolithic material, or large faunal accumulations, means that we have to rely on the distribution of these stone tools alone within the Ouse valley. The only exception is the recovery of preserved knapping debitage related to handaxe manufacture at Meeching Road (South Street), Newhaven (Bell 1976; Pope and Maxted 2008; see below). Beyond this occurrence, we are restricted to isolated objects, most of which were recovered as surface finds. In order to make sense of the record the find spots will be discussed in turn, grouped by three stretches of the valley, attempting to relate each find spot to likely preservation context and age.

The Lower Ouse (Seaford to Rodmell)

A single artefact is recorded by Woodcock as coming from East Blatchington, near Bishopstone. However, Woodcock introduces some uncertainty here in postulating that the artefact could have come from Bishopstone in Kent, a locality which has previously produced artefacts. To the north, recorded as being from the general vicinity of East Blatchington, an ovate handaxe and associated flint artefacts of uncertain age are in the collections of Lewes Museum (Woodcock 1981).

A number of handaxes have been found in the town of Newhaven, including the failed handaxe which forms the nucleus of the *in situ* knapping scatter from the Meeching Road/South Street site (Bell 1976; Pope and Maxted 2008). Four other handaxes have been recovered from the town, among them two fresh implements of unknown provenance and a third, iron stained and rolled implement (Woodcock 1981). Unrolled material could derive either from fine-grained fluvial deposits or from loess deposits forming components of the Head geology overlying the valley sides. Mammoth and woolly rhinoceros remains, and a further small triangular implement of 'St. Acheul' type (i.e. a handaxe), are recorded as coming from the town (Grinsell 1929); the original location and current whereabouts of these is unknown.

A further tool was found in First Avenue, Newhaven at an altitude of 30m O.D (*ibid.*). This is a lightly rolled, grey patinated piece exhibiting a Z twist on its lateral profile. It was found during building works in 1949 and is currently located in Lewes Museum.

Further up the valley, in the general vicinity of Piddinghoe (TQ4350 0300), at least two Palaeolithic artefacts have been found. Grinsell (1929, 178) mentions 'drift implements' as having come from here, though whether these were in addition to those considered by Woodcock with the hill-top palaeoliths (Woodcock 1981, 332) is not known. This general location is underlain by sands and gravels of Ouse River Terrace 2. The collections of Lewes Museum are said to contain an unfinished handaxe from Piddinghoe parish (information given on old label), but the actual implement could not be located by Woodcock.

A single handaxe was found in 2003 at South Farm, Rodmell, during metal detecting and recorded by PAS. Further handaxes are recorded from the general Rodmell area; these include two handaxes which have an ocherous patina indicating preservation within fluvial gravel, and a further white-patinated ovate which suggests derivation from the Head (Woodcock 1981). At Northease Farm, on geology also recorded as Head above the 15m contour line, two handaxes were found within 50m of each other (*ibid.*). One was found during digging at a depth of *c.* 1m, the other on the surface after ploughing. Neither was apparently water-rolled. The coincidence of proximity and position on a Head covered terrace landform does suggest the location would warrant further investigation, both through surface collection after ploughing and investigation of the sub-surface geology.

The Lewes Area

Lewes sits within the Middle Ouse, and takes in the urban area of Lewes and the widest extent of the modern Ouse floodplain between the Caburn and Beddingham. Palaeoliths were found at Mountfield (i.e. the field beneath the 'Mount') and given by Dr S. Spokes to Lewes Museum. A Palaeolithic handaxe came from Mountfield Road, TQ 418 097, and is in Lewes Museum (*ibid.*). This is of interest because it comes from just above the floodplain, potentially on accessible terrace deposits. Ambiguity exists over the number and provenance of other Palaeolithic material recorded as coming from Lewes Museum. Determining the full scope and associated documentary information to go with this material should be considered a high research priority.

Excavations at 'Lewes House' (running behind School Hill towards the foot of the hill) revealed a deep and complex fluvial and solifluction sequence existing to the south east of Lewes, with remnants of ancient river cliffs being preserved at depth. Full mapping, through borehole records, of the subsurface geology of the town would be useful in identifying areas of future development impact.

The Upper Ouse (North of Malling to Uckfield)

Moving north of the South Downs, extensive spreads of terrace gravel (Ouse 1-3) are mapped but undated. They contain an interesting, if sparse, record of Palaeolithic activity. Excavations at Barcombe Roman Villa revealed some Palaeolithic material, including a fine Acheulean handaxe from the villa itself (Figure 3.2), which might be a curated Romano-British item, and other unquantified material from field-walking at the villa site and nearby Culver Farm (Chris Butler *pers. comm.*). The Church at Barcombe apparently produced faunal material in the nineteenth century (Godwin-Austin in

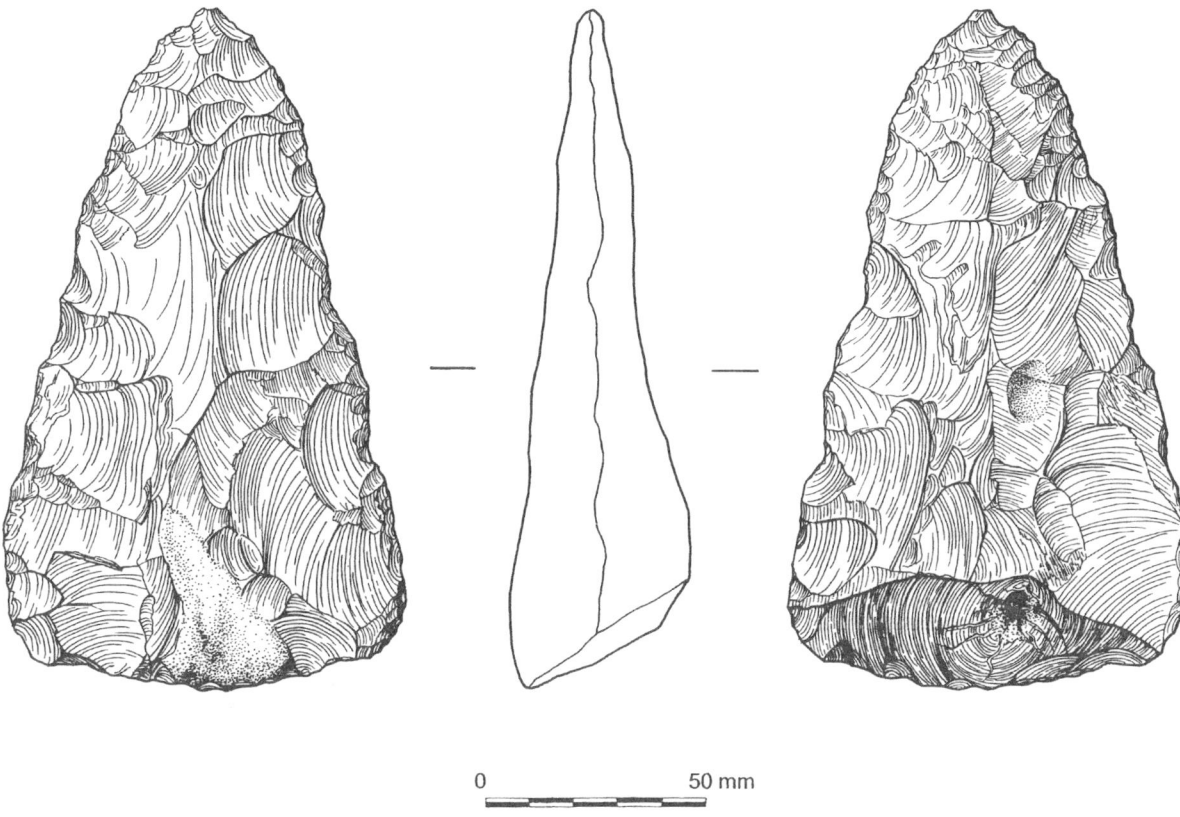

FIGURE 3.2: HAND AXE, BUTT MISSING, FROM THE BARCOMBE ROMAN VILLA SITE (DRAWING JANE RUSSELL)

Dixon 1876; Osborne-White 1924), but the whereabouts of this material is unknown. At Blunts Wood a surface find of a Palaeolithic handaxe was recently discovered, joining another surface find from Isfield, a cordate handaxe, slightly abraded, with creamy ocherous patina (Woodcock 1981), as the only other finds from the upper part of the valley.

Discussion and future work

The Ouse valley has an established, although poorly understood, record. While not all finds are uncontexualised surface ones, the lacks of firm dating frameworks for the valley, and lack of associated palaeo-environmental remains, are hampering any meaningful synthesis. Material has been recovered from clearly fluvial deposits, but also from slope and periglacial contexts, which at Meeching Road, Newhaven, were high resolution in the degree of preservation and refitting.

The Ouse valley does, however, offer enough demonstrable potential to form the basis for a complete re-evaluation of Palaeolithic archaeology in the county. Four areas offer themselves as potentially useful: river and slope deposits in Newhaven, centred on Meeching Road; the terrace sequence within the urban area of Lewes; gravel terrace sequences at Barcombe; and valley edge Clay-with-Flints and Downland slope contexts around Bishopstone. Geoarchaeological-led fieldwork, and a dating program focused on the terrace deposits, could both unlock understanding of the existing record and bring into focus new sites and new areas of potential. Until this is done, and HER and museum records updated accordingly, Piltdown will still continue to cast its shadow over early prehistory in the valley.

References

Bates, M. R. 2001. The Meeting of the Waters: raised beaches and river gravels of the Sussex Coastal Plain/Hampshire Basin. In Wenban-Smith, F. F. and Hosfield, R. (eds), *Palaeolithic archaeology of the Solent River.* Lithic Studies Society Occasional Paper 7, 27 – 45, London: Lithic Studies Society.

Coastal Plain, Southern England, U.K. *Quaternary Science Reviews 16,* 1227–1252.

Bell, M. 1976. The excavation of an early Romano-British site and Pleistocene landforms at Newhaven. *Sussex Archaeological Collections* 114, 218-305.

Bridgland, D. 1994. *The Quaternary of the Thames.* London: Chapman and Hall.

Dawson, C. and Woodward, A. S. 1913. On the discovery of a palaeolithic Human Skull and Mandible in a flint-bearing gravel overlying the Wealden (Hastings Beds) at Piltdown, Fletching (Sussex). *Quarterly journal of the geological society* 69 (1-4), 117-123.

Dixon, F. 1876. *The Geology of Sussex,* 2nd Edition. Edited by Prof. T. R. Jones.

Gamble, C., and Kruszynski, R. 2009. John Evans, Joseph Prestwich and the stone that shattered the time barrier. *Antiquity* 83 (320), 461-475.

Gibbard, P. L. 1994. *Pleistocene history of the Lower Thames Valley*, Cambridge: Cambridge University Press.

Grinsell, L. V. 1929. The Lower and Middle Palaeolithic periods in Sussex. *Sussex Archaeological Collections* 70, 172-182.

Mantell, G. A. and Mantell, M. A. 1822. *The fossils of the South Downs; or illustrations of the geology of Sussex*, Lupton Relfe.

Osbourne-White, H. J. O. 1924. *The geology of the country near Lewes* (vol. 319). H. M. Stationery Office.

Pope, M. and Maxted, A. 2008. A refitting biface reduction scatter from Newhaven, East Sussex. *Lithics* 29, 55–63.

Pope M. I., Roberts, M. B., Maxted, A. and Jones, P. 2009. Lower Palaeolithic Archaeology at the Valdoe, West Sussex. *Proceedings of the Prehistoric Society* 75, 239-263.

Prestwich, J. 1859a. On the Westward Extension of the Old Raised Beach of Brighton; and on the Extent of the Sea-bed of the same Period. *Quarterly Journal of the Geological Society*, 15(1-2), 215-221.

Prestwich, J. 1859b. On the Occurrence of Flint-Implements, Associated with the Remains of Extinct Mammalia, in Undisturbed Beds of a Late Geological Period. *Proceedings of the Royal Society of London* 10, 50-59.

Roberts, M. B. and Parfitt, S. A. 1999. *Boxgrove: A Middle Pleistocene hominid site at Eartham Quarry, Boxgrove, West Sussex*. English Heritage Monograph Series, Archaeological Report 17, London: English Heritage.

Roberts, M.B. and Pope, M. I. 2009. The Archaeological and Sedimentary Records from Boxgrove and Slindon. In R.M. Briant, M. R. Bates, R. T Hosfield and F. F. Wenban-Smith (eds), *The Quaternary of the Solent Basin and West Sussex Raised Beaches*. Cambridge: QRA Field Guide.

Roe, D. 1968. *A gazetteer of British Lower and Middle Palaeolithic sites*. London: CBA Research Report 8, 355.

Smith, R. A. and Dewey, H. 1914. The High Terrace of the Thames: Report on Excavations made on behalf of the British Museum and HM Geological Survey in 1913. *Archaeologia* (Second Series) 65, 187-212.

Woodcock, A. 1981. *The Lower and Middle Palaeolithic Periods in Sussex*. Oxford: British Archaeological Reports, British Series 94.

Wymer, J. 1968. *Lower Palaeolithic archaeology in Britain as represented by the Thames Valley*. New York: Humanities Press.

Wymer, J. 1999. *The Lower Palaeolithic Occupation of Britain*. Salisbury: Wessex Archaeology and English Heritage.

4. Mesolithic

Diana Jones

The Mesolithic period in northwestern Europe was characterised by a significant transformation of human endeavour. Marginalised by colder conditions for tens of millennia, hunter-gatherer populations manipulated increased resource opportunities stimulated by a warming climate, at a time of dramatic sea-level rise. Their selective subsistence methods and semi-sedentary settlement patterns might, in theory, have primed them to more easily adopt the agricultural and animal husbandry practices that followed, however, they hardly ran for the exit from their tenacious way of life and adapted to the inevitable only slowly in places. Current palaeogenetic research shows some indigenous hunter-gatherers lived in close proximity to immigrant farmers for many generations (Bollongino *et al.* 2013). This huge timespan of over 5000 years, half of the Holocene, is therefore of vital importance to our understanding of how and why human behaviour and belief systems began to change irretrievably, and to so comprehensively dominate the natural world.

For a period of such magnitude, however, the Mesolithic (9600-4000 BC) seems a relatively dark age for study compared to other periods of human activity in Sussex. Hundredweights of worked flint in dusty archive boxes are still the overwhelming surviving physical evidence for it. Although there were few radiocarbon dates from palaeo-environmental or organic evidence concurrent with flintworking sites when Roger Jacobi's *'The Mesolithic of Sussex'* was published in 1978, his seminal study of microlith types allowed him to propose an 'early' and 'later' chronology for the period (Jacobi 1978a). In the same year two influential landscape analyses used artefact distribution patterns to examine structural elements of the late hunter-gatherer world applicable to southeast England (Jacobi 1978b; Mellars and Reinhardt 1978). These highlighted possible geological preferences, water resources and ecological 'territories' in order to conceptualise changes in Mesolithic land use through time and provide a more explicit, humanly-shaped context for lithic artefacts. Whilst these ideas enlivened the interpretation of flintwork concentrations that continued to be found, it is perhaps the more recent studies of coastal and floodplain geomorphology, through their contribution to an understanding of local climate change sequences in the early Holocene, that have enabled a more thorough framework for what is known about the Ouse valley during the Mesolithic to now be constructed (Figure 4.1).

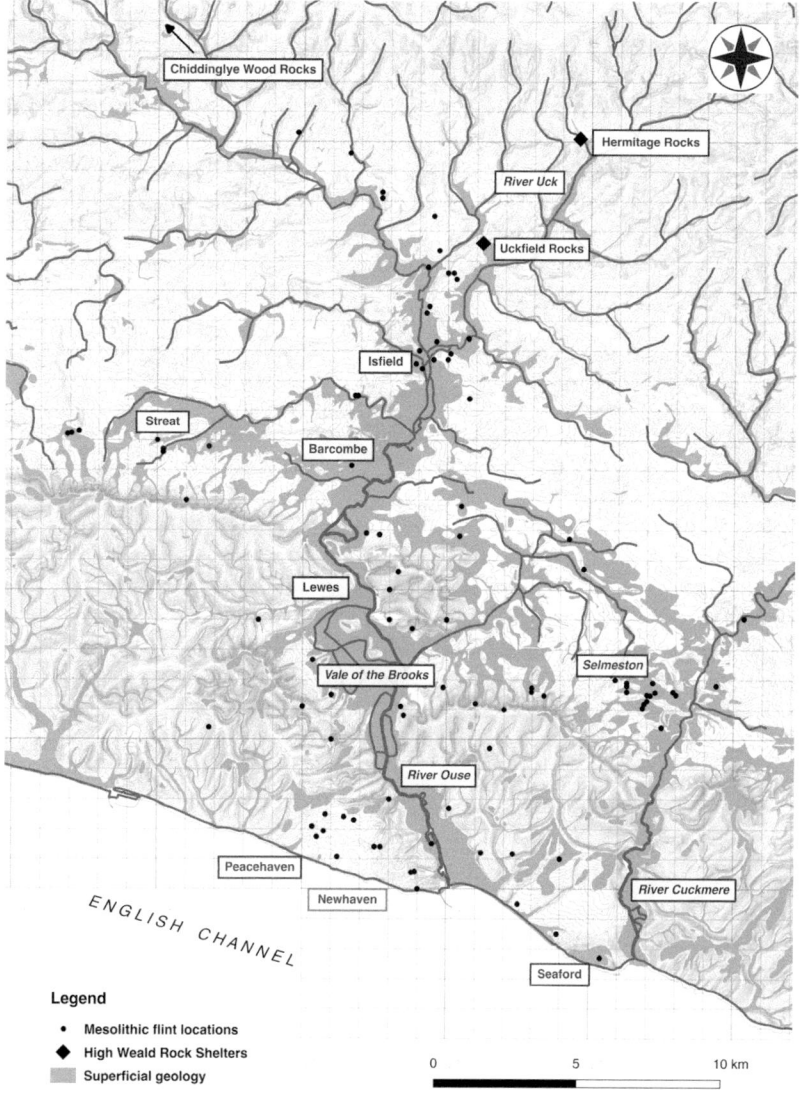

FIGURE 4.1: A CONTOUR MAP OF THE OUSE VALLEY OF EAST SUSSEX, HIGHLIGHTING LOCATIONS MENTIONED IN THE TEXT AND AREAS OF SUPERFICIAL GEOLOGY INDICATING RIVER TERRACES AND PALAEOCHANNELS (OS DATA © CROWN COPYRIGHT 2015; BRITISH GEOLOGICAL SURVEY © NERC 2015. ALL RIGHTS RESERVED.)

The Mesolithic coastline

During cold episodes of the Pleistocene the Ouse would have been one of many tributaries of a wide valley drainage system that would in time become the English Channel when a glacial lake, in what is now the North Sea area, broke through the land bridge connecting the Weald and the Artois in Northern France c. 7500 cal BC (Gibbard 2009; Waller and Long 2010). Exactly how far the mouth of the Ouse extended into this valley before the breach in the early Holocene is of some interest. Recent offshore surveys off the coast of Littlehampton have revealed Arun river palaeochannels up to 18 kilometres from the present shoreline and their drowned landforms (Wessex Archaeology 2004; Gupta et al. 2008), from which Mesolithic artefacts in peat deposits have been extracted, as at Bouldner Cliff in the Solent (Momber et al. 2011). A similar submerged channel is known to have existed for the Ouse. Vibrocore samples drawn west of Beachy Head have revealed soft sediments laminated with bands of peat, representing low energy, low tidal-range environments prior to sea level rise. Although landforms and deposits that define a more exact offshore channel at this time remain elusive (Hamblin et al. 1992; Dunkin and Bates 1998; Antoine et al. 2003), a more embayed coastline would likely have existed some 10-30 kilometres south of the present coast, allowing the development of a variety of marine habitats and resources both attractive and accessible to Mesolithic populations. However, as the glacial climate ameliorated, in the early Holocene c. 8400-6600 cal BC (9200-7800 cal BP), the Sussex coast became progressively swamped by rising sea levels at a possible average rate of 12mm per year (Waller and Long 2010), a rapid increase that would have been noticeable within lifetimes (Wessex Archaeology 2004).

The retreating cliffs at Beachy Head, when used as a measure of past erosion, suggest an early Holocene coastline of at least some five kilometres south of the present-day shore (Jennings and Smyth 1990); consequently, flintworking sites and flint scatters found near the coast would have been well inland during prehistory. Peacehaven, atop the western headland of the Ouse valley, was a particularly favoured area, where the most densely concentrated site, only two metres in diameter, yielded between 8-10,000 pieces of fine debitage and microliths that closely resembled collections from Hassocks and Horsham (Calkin 1924). Mesolithic flints were also recovered amongst the massive Bronze Age flint assemblage excavated at Peacehaven barrow in 2008, as it began to collapse into the sea (S. Birks, pers. comm.). A number of multi-period collections containing Mesolithic implements have been revealed at low elevation on southwesterly-facing dip slopes that flank the Ouse channel to the east, near its mouth, and extend along the coast. One of these was amassed through fieldwalking at Stud Farm (Bootle and Ford 1981), which overlooks the new Ouse Estuary Nature Reserve, a modest conservation tract that reflects the area's former role as a brackish and/or freshwater marsh in the early-mid Holocene, remains of which have been found tens of metres below its present level (Dunkin and Bates 1998). Findspots at Bishopstone (Bell 1977) and East Blatchington (Bell 1974) would have been within easy reach of this relatively sheltered wetland resource as well as small, now alluviated, inlets nearby. Gurney Wilson's collection of tranchet axes from the Newhaven and Seaford areas in Brighton Museum compliments the output of other local antiquarians who found tools in abundance on the chalk and in the river valleys of Sussex.

Hills and terraces surrounding The Vale of the Brooks, the wide floodplain south of Lewes, have yielded other findspots for tranchet axes, as well as pebble maceheads, as at Piddinghoe, Rodmell and South Heighton (Butler 1993). A significant flint collection gathered from the Iford and Swanborough area by the late David Cripps, an ardent fieldwalker, contained numerous flaked axeheads and picks, nine of which have been described as of the rare 'Hassocks' type (Figure 4.2). A quartzite macehead was also found in possible association with a barrow on the summit of Cliffe Hill in the nineteenth century. More recently, a small concentration of Mesolithic flintworking waste was found nearby at Lewes Golf Course and reported to the local Portable Antiquities Scheme based in Lewes. The scheme has recorded and photographed over one hundred Mesolithic artefacts from more than twenty locations within the study area over the past ten years, many of these chance finds by members of the public.

Early floodplain development

The river's prehistoric morphology is reasonably well understood. Boreholes from estuarine flats of the lower valley at Newhaven exposed a Pleistocene buried channel incised to a maximum depth of c. -26m OD (Bell 1976), containing peats, silts and clays deposited between c. 8300–500 cal BC (Dunkin and Bates 1998). Further upstream, about a quarter of the Ouse's original course was channelised to accommodate industrial traffic and alleviate flooding, which has effectively constrained natural floodplain reworking and development for the past two hundred years or more (Burrin 1985). The river course has been further stabilised by modern water extraction rates. Burrin suggested that in places the lack of an 'actively migrating Ouse' meant that parts of the river were 'relict', their depositional formation having occurred during earlier episodes of the Holocene. As much of the floodplain is now under permanent pasture, sand or gravel exposures in riverbeds that could easily reveal new evidence are rare.

An alluvial stratigraphy and vegetation history of the upper Ouse floodplain was determined through borehole and pollen analysis at Sharpsbridge, near Newick, bordering the High Weald in 1983 (Scaife and Burrin

FIGURE 4.2: A MESOLITHIC TRANCHET AXEHEAD, ONE OF MANY DISCOVERED IN THE 1980S ON THE CHALK DOWNS AT IFORD HILL, SOUTHWEST OF LEWES (© PORTABLE ANTIQUITIES SCHEME)

1983). Nearly seven metres of silts and clays were sampled. The lowest pollen zone was characterised by the usual combination of postglacial pine (*Pinus*), birch (*Betula*) and hazel (*Corylus*) present in other local study areas, particularly the Pannell valley near Romney Marsh, where their presence was thought to be dominant between *c.* 9900 and 8600 cal BC (9960±110 and 9380±100 BP, SRR-2892 and SRR-2891; Waller 1993). A comparable succession of oak (*Quercus*), lime (*Tilia*) and ash (*Fraxinus*) then followed, with evidence for a perhaps substantial alder carr community (*Alnetum*) established on floodplains throughout the remainder of the Mesolithic. The Sharpsbridge investigation was notable for the occurrence of an unexpectedly high level of alluviation in a valley consolidated by postglacial vegetation. This was thought to have been caused by transportation and deposition of substantial erosional sediments from upstream. Despite a lack of firm dating evidence, the most logical inference was that forest cover had been anthropogenically modified from the Mesolithic onwards. Later work by Waller and others on the vegetation history of the Weald, however, suggests the valley remained well wooded until at least the early Bronze Age (*c.* 2500 cal BC, Waller and Long 2010).

Although the Folkestone Formation geology of the Weald anticline (which has to date contained the most abundant collections of Mesolithic artefacts in the west of Sussex) diminishes as it reaches the Ouse, this relatively thin strip of sandstone contains some of the most sizeable flintwork collections associated with the valley, though fed by its remotest tributaries. The Ouse river cannot be considered in isolation of these minor, branching watercourses and valleys, which might have served as more well-drained, easily managed activity-settlement areas than the margins of its less predictable major floodplain (LUC 2011).

Sites on the Greensand belt

Significant Folkestone Formation finds have been recorded at Lodge Hill in Ditchling (Garrett 1976; Cohen 2008), East Chiltington, and also at Streat, where during 1996-7 a distinctive flintworking site was excavated near a spring-fed Ouse tributary, revealing four pits containing unusually high quantities of fire-cracked flint, 3000 worked pieces, including microliths, and the possible base of a temporary shelter. Charcoal in association with the flints was ^{14}C-dated to *c.* 6450-2250 cal BC (7500±40 BP, Beta-144847) and used to identify the presence of oak and hazel, as well as fruiting shrubs and trees of the *Rosaceae* family such as hawthorn (*Crataegus*), apple (*Malus*) and pear (*Pyrus*), and rarer indications of cherry (*Prunus avium*), bird cherry (*Prunus padus*) or sloe (*Prunus spinosa*). Defining the site according to the usual categories was problematic, as it possessed 'short-stay hunting camp' features but also evidence for more prolonged, specialised subsistence processes that might have had 'more to do with social interaction' (Butler 2007).

To the east of the Ouse fieldwalking activity has unearthed flint blades and flakes from cultivated land on Gault mudstone and the Lower Greensand near Ringmer and Laughton. Further east still is the prolific, late Mesolithic site at Selmeston, on a low rise between tributary sources of the Ouse, the Cuckmere river – two kilometres distant – and copious spring streams that emerge from the scarp foot of the Downs. The large flint assemblage excavated here in 1933, on the edge of a sandpit east of the church, is notable for its association with Grahame Clark, who devised a classification for microlith forms from southeast England that is still recognised today, based on the attributes of an enormous collection from the Horsham area (Jacobi 1982) (Figure 4.3). Selmeston is a site against which many others in Sussex, and beyond, have been compared for decades (Clark 1934). Surface collection predated Clark's involvement and excavations undertaken between 1963 and 1982 recovered yet more worked flints (Cartwright 1985). More recently, modest discoveries at Berwick and Chilverbridge have widened this area of known activity.

Soil micromorphology analysis at Selmeston in 1985 showed little evidence of undisturbed woodland cover during the Mesolithic, information that correlated well with Scaife and Burrin's conclusions for the upper Ouse: that people might have been subjecting the land to regular minor clearance and burning since the Boreal, c. 8300-6500 cal BC (9000–7500 BP; Macphail 1985). Clark found three 'pit-dwellings' filled with white sand, worked and burnt flints, hazel, oak and hawthorn charcoal and hazelnut shells in the orange-coloured bedrock, one of which contained traces of a hearth. Though these particular pits are now considered not to have been dwellings, the assemblages within them were certainly products of a microlithic industry, their flintwork forms closely allied to those from Peacehaven and the Horsham area. Flintwork found in later years came from more disturbed, multi-period contexts but still retained strong Mesolithic elements. In total approximately 10,000 pieces from the period were recovered (Clark 1934).

The Upper Ouse

During excavation of the Roman villa and bath house at Barcombe, situated on a sand and gravel terrace, a tranchet axe and other Mesolithic artefacts were recovered between 2000-2012. Recent surface collection undertaken within an Ouse meander at nearby Bridge Farm as part of The Culver Project yielded more than 700 worked flints of Mesolithic-Early Neolithic origin (Butler 2013).

Fields within Isfield parish have been subjected to surface collection since the nineteenth century, with a particularly avid peak during the 1920s and 30s, a time when many enthusiasts were combing Sussex for flintwork. F. P. Matthewman's collections in the Brighton museum, provenanced only to 'Isfield', include microliths (several of rare crescentic form), a tranchet axe and a petit tranchet arrowhead. The Tebbutt Collection at Barbican House, Lewes, derives from a cluster of sites in the village such as Elms Farm and Tile Barn Field, as well as Buckham Hill some two miles north, and consists of cores, blades, microliths, scrapers and various retouched flakes and debitage. Though the evidence is far from prolific overall, it does at least provide a distribution pattern for wide-ranging Mesolithic presence here, where Weald mudstone meets the rising topography of the Tunbridge Wells Sand Formation, and the River Uck, as well as the Shortbridge and Longford streams, join the Ouse. Debitage flakes have been found where several iron-rich Chalybeate springs emerge 3.5 kilometres to the northwest at Newick Park. Further north, where the Ouse forks south of Piltdown, fieldwalking on the Hundred Acre Field at Moon's Farm and in the immediate vicinity brought to light 335 pieces of Mesolithic flintwork from a larger mixed-period collection, including tranchet axes and sharpening flakes (Butler 2000).

FIGURE 4.3: PROFESSOR SIR GRAHAME CLARK SPENT FORMATIVE YEARS IN SUSSEX COLLECTING FLINT TOOLS, EARNING THE NICKNAME 'STONES AND BONES' AT SCHOOL. HIS EXCAVATION AT SELMESTON WAS A PRELUDE TO HIS WORK AT STAR CARR, WHERE, USING A MULTIDISCIPLINED SCIENTIFIC APPROACH HE HELPED TO REVERSE PREVIOUS NEGLECT OF THE MESOLITHIC ERA (PHOTO: WALTER STONEMAN, COMMISSIONED 1959, © NATIONAL PORTRAIT GALLERY)

Rock shelters of the Ouse Catchment

A cluster of High Weald Mesolithic rock shelter sites subjected to excavation, such as Hermitage Rocks, Rocks Wood and Eridge Rocks, lay to the northeast (Jacobi and Tebbutt 1981; Harding and Ostoja-Zagórski

1987; Greatorex and Seager Thomas 2000). J. H. Money, who investigated High Rocks at Tunbridge Wells, identified other sandstone outcrops of potential interest, which included Uckfield Rocks, only five kilometres away from the northernmost boundary of the study area. He believed that shelter levels had been submerged by an eighteenth-century garden landscape treatment that created an artificially dammed lake around the rocks (Money 1960, 220), but in 1979-80 an area north of the lake seemed to hold promise and was excavated. In excess of 10,000 Early Mesolithic artefacts were recovered, consisting mainly of microliths and associated debitage. Surface collection covering approximately one hectare in the same area and test pitting in a meadow to the south of the rocks revealed more early material (Hemingway 1980; 1981).

Another rock shelter site, at the remotest reach of the Ouse catchment, is Chiddinglye Wood Rocks, north of Ardingly, where augering (Allen *et al.* 2008) and two small excavations were undertaken between 2007-09. The first, on a hillslope bench overlooking the Cob stream near a distinctive stack known as Great-Upon-Little, revealed components of a microlithic toolkit (Maxted unpubl.) (Figure 4.4). The second, conducted nearer the rockface, unearthed similar microlithic elements, as well as a Neolithic leaf arrowhead fragment and flakes from a polished implement (Le Hégerat unpubl.). Sherds of Decorated or Plain Bowl and Peterborough Ware-style pottery, also ascribed to the Neolithic, were mixed amongst the flints in a disturbed context.

The same combination of flints and pottery was also found together at High Rocks and Rocks Wood. Pollen and radiocarbon dated charcoal at High Rocks suggested these might have been found in a primary context, which would have been extraordinary evidence for 'a hunting community using pottery' (Money 1962, 150). Sandy Mesolithic sites in the county, however, including rock shelters, are notorious for their lack of stratigraphic integrity. Methods of investigating fragile and complex sites like these have also changed greatly over the past fifty years. Modern doubts have therefore been expressed about the interpretation at High Rocks. It has been pointed out that 'disturbance', which could have been the more likely circumstance at High Rocks, didn't necessarily signify 'transition' (Healy 2009, 6). None of the excavators of the rock shelter sites quoted, as well

FIGURE 4.4: RAPID EXPLORATORY AUGERING AND EXCAVATION WERE CARRIED OUT AT CHIDDINGLYE WOOD ROCKS IN THE SPRING OF 2008 BENEATH THE OUTCROP OF GREAT-UPON-LITTLE. ENVIRONMENTAL SAMPLES AND ARTEFACTS WERE SOUGHT FURTHER FROM THE ROCKFACE THAN HAD BEEN STANDARD PRACTICE, AND WERE DULY RECOVERED, PROTECTED BY HILLWASH (PHOTO: A. MAXTED)

as Stone Farm Rocks near East Grinstead (Oliveira and Tebbutt 1985), expressed certainty of secure stratigraphy. Of the two sites where hearths and charcoal were found, only High Rocks possessed Neolithic pottery, but the radiocarbon dates obtained could not be accurately applied to the artefact contexts. The compelling question of why Neolithic pottery has been found in three strategic rock shelter locations, overwhelmingly the preserve of hunter-gatherers, where no other evidence predates the Iron Age, has yet to be satisfactorily answered.

Environmental evidence

Unfortunately, dire lack of faunal and floristic evidence in Sussex constricts a fuller interpretation of lives that were heavily dependent on animal and plant resources (Figure 4.5). Bone preservation is rare in soils where Mesolithic flint scatters are most commonly found in the county. Nevertheless, bone data from sites elsewhere in southern England such as Thatcham in Berkshire (Healy *et al.* 1992), can be used to theoretically populate the Ouse valley with large mammals such as wild horse (*Equus caballus*), elk (*Alces alces*), aurochs (*Bos primigenius*), wolf (*Canis lupus*), wild boar (*Sus scrofa*) and red deer (*Cervus elaphus*) during the early Mesolithic. Beaver (*Castor fiber*) was particularly well represented among the bones at Thatcham. It is interesting to speculate about the beaver's possible role in the alteration of wet woodland on the Ouse floodplain at this time, and the opportunities this might have afforded humans in their exploitation of its ready-felled timber, navigable canals and ponds that would have provided conditions in which freshwater aquatic species could thrive. The only evidence of this to date, however, is a piece of possibly beaver-gnawed Early Bronze Age wood recovered from an excavation at Friars Oak, Hassocks (Butler 2000, 63).

A few clues for plant use were also evident at Thatcham. Although charred hazelnuts predominated, as at many other Mesolithic sites (e.g. Oakhanger, Hampshire, Dimbleby 1960), use-wear analysis of flint tools implied soft fibres were being processed using microliths at this fen location – perhaps wild parsnips or carrots – emphasising a wider range of uses for tools traditionally viewed as components of hunting toolkits than had previously been supposed (Grace 1992). Blade analysis

FIGURE 4.5: IN THE SPRING OF 2011 THE EAST SUSSEX ARCHAEOLOGY AND MUSEUMS PARTNERSHIP (ESAMP) CONSTRUCTED A CONJECTURAL MESOLITHIC HUT OF REED, HAZEL AND HEATHER AT THE ASHDOWN FOREST CENTRE. MACROFOSSIL EVIDENCE FOR PHRAGMITES, THE COMMON REED, HAS BEEN RADIOCARBON DATED TO THE MESOLITHIC PERIOD AT MANY SITES IN SOUTHERN ENGLAND
(© MARATHON, LICENSED FOR REUSE UNDER A CREATIVE COMMONS LICENCE)

from North Park Farm in Surrey has shown herbaceous plant fibres were also being processed for bedding or basketry (Donahue and Evans 2013). DNA samples extracted from sediments at the submerged Mesolithic site at Bouldner have recently revealed the surprising presence of einkorn wheat in the form of flour as early as *c*. 7000 cal BC, highlighting an increasing capacity to detect plant use during this period using emergent biotechnologies (Smith *et al*. 2015).

The Mesolithic landscape of southern England had once been described as one of thick, primary forest, on soils of uniform, wind-blown periglacial loess. It now seems likely, however, that tracts of land in Sussex might have had a continuously open aspect from the Late Glacial onwards (Birks 2005; Whitehouse and Smith 2004; Bell and Brown 2008), in some part due to the profoundly transformative presence of herds of grazing animals and human intervention. Burning in particular is thought to have promoted the formation of clearings advantageous to hunting, creating heathland environments (Mellars and Reinhardt 1978, 263). Greater precipitation *c*. 8000 BP shaped highly productive fen and wet woodland, providing lush vegetation and waterfowl habitat. Coastal resources seem to have been an essential part of Mesolithic subsistence. Sites where these were harvested have largely been lost through sea level rise and isostatic adjustment; those still extant on land, such as Culverwell on Portland, contain shell midden evidence for the use of mostly gastropod molluscs such as limpets (*Patella spp.*), edible periwinkles (*Littorina littorea*) and the dog whelk (*Nucella lapillus*), gathered so intensively that their abundance may even have been threatened *c*. 6000 cal BC (Mannino and Thomas 1998).

Discussion

The people who moved through the early Holocene landscape of Sussex lived amid a period of rapid climate change, and seem to have made detectable environmental responses to it. The lithic distribution record for the Ouse valley – despite being skewed by agricultural disturbance or varying intensities of archaeological fieldwork – implies that, although Mesolithic people were ranging throughout its major floodplain area to hunt, fish, fowl and forage, using the waterways as travelling arteries, their principal homebases tended to be situated on free-draining chalk or sandy tracts, particularly along tributaries or within easy reach of springs and ecotonal resource areas.

A common and complicating feature of this record has been the discovery of Mesolithic flintwork amid tools more diagnostic of the Neolithic or Bronze Age. While multi-period flint scatters might once have been viewed as 'contaminated' evidence for any one point in time, some recent studies have used this coexistence of artefacts as an opportunity: to examine them in terms of the long-term, social construction of 'persistent places' in the landscape (Barton *et al*. 1995). In this way, reinforced by ethnographic evidence, it seems likely that certain sites in the Ouse valley were endowed with special meaning, as destinations or meeting points revisited over successive generations. This perception of remembrance and continuity considerably humanises our understanding of Mesolithic and later communities and adds valuable substance to the narratives we construct about them. It also provides an enhanced foundation, alongside economic fact, upon which to layer new research.

Future work

Today's modern, holistic outlook, which attempts to extract social inferences from data, has reduced emphasis on the purely typological scrutiny of flint artefacts that prevailed during much of the twentieth century. In 2007-8 a South East Research Framework was designed to plan future archaeological aims and objectives. It concluded that, ideally, broad landscape studies were now needed to examine palaeo-environmental evidence synchronous with Mesolithic artefacts, as well as excavations that secured high quality information from securely stratified and dated contexts (LSS 2004; Pope *et al*. 2007). From these, it was hoped that more information about ritual, belief and cultural differences could be extracted. Testing local assumptions about the Mesolithic, such as preference for the Greensand, the use of tranchet axes for forest clearance and the identification of pits as 'dwellings', was also encouraged.

Investigation of numerous small sites was thought to be particularly important for 'building up the overall mosaic of environmental information over time' (de Moulins *et al*. 2008). These could profitably be found through efforts to locate relict wetlands of the Ouse catchment in areas least subject to modern disturbance, especially those adjacent to shallow slopes or terraces. Localised peat formations in silted tributaries, oxbows or pools containing anaerobically preserved artefacts of any period have been considered rare in East Sussex, perhaps in part because their locations are patchy and elusive, today disguised as cultivated floodplains, waste ground or wooded field boundaries, as at two recently investigated sites: one near Stonegate in the Rother catchment (Haken unpubl.), the other at The Wilderness near Barcombe (Allen 2011). Hazelnuts were found in test pits at both locations; at Stonegate they were charred, found beneath a fen peat layer with over 70 flints, including an axe-sharpening flake and an obliquely-truncated microlith, charcoal, remains of pine and birch trees and macrofossil evidence (Figure 4.6). The Wilderness produced a waterlogged hazelnut and several undiagnostic flints lying atop gravels, at the base of a 40cm-thick peaty palaeosol, indicative of a possible Mesolithic woodland floor (Allen 2010, 5).

Fieldwork was also undertaken in the autumn of 2014 to record and sample a submerged forest emerging from intertidal peat along a two-kilometre span of the East Sussex coastline at Pett Level (S. Timpany, pers. comm.). Well-preserved tree trunks and stumps on the shoreline at low tide had previously obtained radiocarbon dates of c. 6200-6300 cal BC. Early indications show the forest possessed clearings, and had also experienced phases of marine inundation and recolonisation during prehistory.

This recent research illustrates untold potential for further discovery on the ground. The use of aerial or satellite photography to pinpoint landscape anomalies such as standing water, dry depressions, bands of vegetation or trees, cropmarks and sinuous boundaries, comparable to the survey of potential palaeochannels undertaken for the Trent valley basin (Baker 2007), could help lead to the identification of new sites. There is undoubtedly more scope for fieldwork at rock shelter sites within the study area, which have for the most part only been examined at a constricted scale, with limited technological means and virtually no environmental sampling. Investigations such as these may yet hold the key to understanding to what extent hunter-gatherers might have mixed with more settled communities during the liminal Late Mesolithic.

The restoration of flint artefacts in local archives to prominent, imaginative displays is also needed. Most assemblages and collections are restricted to storage for years on end, having been studied or appreciated only rarely. It is as if they are considered too remote in time to be relevant to anyone but specialists today, an attitude not in step with the recent surge of research into human origins. The Mesolithic flintwork of the Ouse valley was a refined component of a tradition shaped by human cognitive development for millions of years, a tradition and narrative that is increasingly relevant to the identity of people in modern Sussex, who should be given the opportunity to become more aware of their lithic legacy.

Acknowledgements

Special thanks to Dr Richard Carter for editorial advice, Greg Chuter (Assistant Archaeologist, East Sussex County Council) for assistance with HER (Historic Environmental Record) information and Stephanie Smith (Finds Liaison Officer, East Sussex) for access to Portable Antiquities Scheme data. Thanks also to Emma Butterfield at the National Portrait Gallery for permission to reproduce figure 4.3.

FIGURE 4.6: A RECENT EXCAVATION IN THE ROTHER CATCHMENT DEMONSTRATED THE POTENTIAL FOR SURVIVAL OF DISCRETE PEAT FORMATIONS CONTAINING MESOLITHIC EVIDENCE IN THE VICINITY OF SUSSEX FLOODPLAINS. BENEATH A LAYER OF GYTTJA MUD, A SLOPING SECTION OF ARTEFACT-YIELDING PEAT OVERLYING WADHURST CLAY RESEMBLED A FORMER PHRAGMITES-FRINGED LAKE MARGIN (PHOTO: N. HAKEN)

References

Allen, M. J. 2010. *Barcombe: The Wilderness 2010 - geoarchaeological fieldwork résumé.* Unpublished report for the Culver Project. Available from: <culverproject.co.uk>.

Allen, M. J. 2011. Prehistoric Wetlands Discovery. A new Middle Bronze Age waterlogged site in Sussex. *Sussex Past and Present* 125, 6-7.

Allen, M. J., Carter, R. and Maxted. A. 2008. Rapid Field Investigation Methods and a New Mesolithic Site Approach for the Weald, UK. *PAST (The Newsletter of the Prehistoric Society)* 59, 5-8. Available from: <www.prehistoricsociety.org/publications/publication/past_59_july_2008>.

Antoine, P., Coutard, J., Gibbard, P., Hallegouet, B., Lautridou, J.-P. and Ozouf, J. 2003. The Pleistocene rivers of the English Channel region. *Journal of Quaternary Science* 18, 227–43.

Baker, S. 2007. *The Paleochannel record in the Trent Valley UK: contributions towards cultural heritage management: The Palaeochannel survey methodology.* Available from: <intarch.ac.uk/journal/issue20/3/2.3.html>.

Barton, R. N. E., Berridge, P. J., Walker, M. J. C. and Bevins, R. E. 1995. Persistent places in the Mesolithic landscape; an example from the Black Mountain upland of South Wales, *Proceedings of the Prehistoric Society* 61, 81-116.

Bell, M. 1974. Mesolithic Finds from East Blatchington. *Sussex Archaeological Collections* 112, 155-6.

Bell, M. 1976. The Excavation of an early Romano-British Site and Pleistocene Landforms at Newhaven, Sussex. *Sussex Archaeological Collections* 114, 218-305.

Bell, M. 1977. Excavations at Bishopstone. *Sussex Archaeological Collections* 115.

Bell, M. and Brown, A. 2008. *Southern regional review of geoarchaeology: windblown deposits.* Research Department Report Series. 5-2009. English Heritage, Fort Cumberland.

Birks, H. J. B. 2005. Mind the gap: how open were European primeval forests? *Trends in Ecology and Evolution (TREE)* 20:4, 154-156.

Bollongino, R., Nehlich, O., Richards, M.P., Orschiedt, J., Thomas, M.G., Sell, C., Fajkošová, Z., Powell, A. and Burger, J. 2013. 2000 Years of Parallel Societies in Stone Age Central Europe. *Science*, 10 October 2013. Available from: <DOI: 10.1126/science.1245049>.

Bootle, D.T. and Ford, S. 1981. A flint collection from Stud Farm, Newhaven, East Sussex. *Sussex Archaeological Collections* 119, 206-8.

Butler, C. 1993. Some Flint Implements from South Heighton, East Sussex. *Sussex Archaeological Collections* 131, 198.

Butler, C. 2000. *Saxon settlement and earlier remains at Friars Oak, Hassocks, West Sussex.* BAR British Series 295. Oxford: Archaeopress.

Butler, C. 2007. A Mesolithic Site at Streat Lane, Streat, East Sussex. *Sussex Archaeological Collections* 145, 7-31.

Butler, C. 2013. *Bridge Farm, Barcombe 2013 Excavation – Prehistoric flintwork.* Unpublished report for The Culver Project. Available from: <culverproject.co.uk>.

Burrin, P. J. 1985. Holocene Alluviation in Southeast England and Some Implications for Palaeohydrological Studies. *Earth Surface Processes and Landforms* 10, 257-71.

Calkin, J. B. 1924. Pygmy and other Flint Implements found at Peachaven. *Sussex Archaeological Collections* 65, 224-41.

Cartwright, C. 1985. The Flintwork, pp. 10-13 in D. Rudling, 'Recent Archaeological Research at Selmeston, East Sussex'. *Sussex Archaeological Collections* 123, 1-25.

Clark, J. G. D. 1934. A Late Mesolithic Settlement Site at Selmeston, Sussex, *Antiquaries Journal* 14, 134-158.

Cohen, P. 2008. Lodge Hill, Ditchling, East Sussex. Unpublished report submitted in partial fulfillment of the requirements for the degree of MA in Field Archaeology, University of Sussex.

de Moulins, D., Bates, M., Branch, N., Smith, W., Symmonds, R., Stevens, C., Hamilton, J. and Bayley, J. 2008. *Notes on the South-East Research Framework public seminar on the Environment theme.* Available from: <https://shareweb.kent.gov.uk >.

Dimbleby, G.W. 1960. Fossil Pollen and Charcoal, pp. 255-262 in W.F. and W.M. Rankine, 'Further Excavations at a Mesolithic Site at Oakhanger, Selborne, Hants'. *Proceedings of the Prehistoric Society* 26, 246-262.

Donahue, R. E. and Evans, A. A. 2013. Lithic Microwear Analysis, pp. 80-84 in P. Jones, *A Mesolithic 'persistent place' at North Park Farm, Bletchingley, Surrey.* Spoilheap Publications Monograph 8, Surrey County Archaeology Unit.

Dunkin, D. and Bates, M. 1998. *An Archaeological Assessment (Stage 1) of the Proposed Newhaven Harbour Link Road and Associated Developments, Newhaven, East Sussex.* Archaeology South-East Pro. No. 776.

Garrett, S. 1976. A Mesolithic Site at Lodge Hill, Ditchling. *Sussex Archaeological Collections* 114, 326.

Gibbard, P. 2009. *Britain's island heritage: half a million years of history.* Available from: http://www.cam.ac.uk/research/news/britains-island-heritage-half-a-million-years-of-history.

Grace, R. 1992. Use Wear Analysis, pp. 53-63 in Healy *et al.*, 'Excavations of a Mesolithic site at Thatcham'. Proceedings of the Prehistoric Society 58, 41-76.

Greatorex, C. and Seager Thomas, M. 2000. Rock shelter stratigraphy: Excavations at Eridge. *Sussex Archaeological Collections* 138, 49-56.

Gupta, S., Collier, J., Palmer-Fengate, A., Dickinson, J., Bushe, K. and Humber, S. 2008. *Submerged Palaeo-Arun and Solent Rivers: Reconstruction of Prehistoric Landscape and Evaluation of Archaeological Resource Potential,* Chapter 5. Available from: <http://archaeologydataservice.ac.uk/archives/ view/ palaeoarun_eh_2007/>.

Hamblin, R. J. O., Crosby, A., Balson, P. S., Jones, S. M., Chadwick, R. A., Penn, I. E. and Arthur, M. J. 1992. *The Geology of the English Channel*. British Geological Survey United Kingdom Offshore Regional Report. London: HMSO.

Harding, A.F. and Ostoja-Zagórski, J. 1987. Excavations in Rocks Wood, Withyham, 1982. *Sussex Archaeological Collections* 125, 11-32.

Healy, F., Heaton, M., and Lobb, S.J. 1992. Excavations of a Mesolithic site at Thatcham. Proceedings of the Prehistoric Society 58, 41-76.

Healy, F. 2009. Causewayed enclosures and the Early Neolithic: the chronology and character of monument building and settlement in Kent, Surrey and Sussex in the early to mid-4th millenium cal BC. *South East Research Framework resource assessment seminar*. Available at: <https://shareweb.kent.gov.uk>.

Hemingway, M. F. 1980. Preliminary Explorations at the Rocks, Uckfield, East Sussex. *Sussex Archaeological Newsletter* 31, 109-210.

Hemingway, M. F. 1981. Further Explorations at The Rocks Early Mesolithic Site, Uckfield, East Sussex. *Sussex Archaeological Society Newsletter* 34, 243.

Jacobi, R. 1978a. The Mesolithic of Sussex. *Archaeology in Sussex to AD 1500: Essays for Eric Holden*, P.L. Drewett (ed.). CBA Research Report 29, 15-22.

Jacobi, R. 1978b. Population and landscape in Mesolithic lowland Britain. *The Effect of Man on the Landscape: the Lowland Zone*, J.G. Evans and S. Limbrey (eds). CBA Research Report 21, 75-85.

Jacobi, R. 1982. Mesolithic Findspots near Horsham. *Warnham Historical Society Contribution* 5. Available from: <http://www.warnhamsociety.org.uk/ History/MesolithicFindspotsNearHorsham.pdf>.

Jacobi, R. and Tebbutt, C. F. 1981. A Late Mesolithic Rock-Shelter Site at High Hurstwood, Sussex. *Sussex Archaeological Collections* 119, 1-36.

Jennings, S. and Smyth, C. 1990. Holocene evolution of the gravel coastline of East Sussex. *Proceedings of the Geological Association* 101 (3), 213-224.

LSS (Lithic Studies Society) 2004. Research Frameworks for Holocene Lithics in Britain. Available from: http://www.lithics.org/docs/Research Frameworks ForHoloceneLithicsInBritain.pdf.

LUC (Land Use Consultants) 2011. South Downs Integrated Landscape Character Assessment. Appendix F: Major River Floodplains, 193. Available from: <http://www.southdowns.gov.uk/planning/integrated-landscape-character-assessment>.

Macphail, R. 1985. Soil report, pp. 2-3 in D. Rudling, 'Recent Archaeological Research at Selmeston, East Sussex'. *Sussex Archaeological Collections* 123, 1-25.

Mannino, M.A. and Thomas, K.D. 1998. Mesolithic middens and molluscan ecology: a view from southern Britain. *Archaeology International* 2, 17-19.

Mellars, P. and Reinhardt, S.C. 1978. Patterns of Mesolithic Land-use in Southern England: a Geological Perspective. *The Early Postglacial Settlement of Northern Europe*, P. Mellars (ed.). London: Duckworth.

Momber. G, Satchell, J. and Gillespie, J. 2011. Bouldnor Cliff. *British Archaeology* 121, 30-35. York: Council for British Archaeology.

Money, J.H. 1960. Excavations at High Rocks, Tunbridge Wells, 1954-1956. *Sussex Archaeological Collections* 98, 172-221.

Money, J.H. 1962. Excavations at High Rocks, Tunbridge Wells, 1954-56: Supplementary Note. *Sussex Archaeological Collections* 100, 149-151.

Oliveira, D.L. and Tebbutt, C.F. 1985. A Rock Shelter at Stone Rocks, East Grinstead. *Sussex Archaeological Collections* 123, 246-250.

Pope, M., Wells, C., Maxted, A., Farr, L., Allen, M. and Carter, R. 2007. *Notes on the South East Research Framework public seminar on the Upper Palaeolithic and Mesolithic periods*. Available from: https://shareweb.kent. gov.uk.

Scaife, R.G. and Burrin, P.J. 1983. Floodplain Development in and the Vegetational History of The Sussex High Weald and Some Archaeological Implications. *Sussex Archaeological Collections* 121, 1-10.

Smith, O., Momber, G., Bates, R., Garwood, P., Fitch, S., Pallen, M., Gaffney, V. and Allaby, R.G. 2015. Sedimentary DNA from a submerged site reveals wheat in the British Isles 8000 years ago. *Science* 347, 6225, 998-1001.

Waller, M. P. 1993. Flandrian vegetational history of south-eastern England: Pollen data from Pannell Bridge, East Sussex. *New Phytologist* 124, 345-69.

Waller, M. and Long, A. 2010. The Holocene Coastal Deposits of Sussex: A Re-evaluation. *Romney Marsh: Persistence and Change in a Coastal Lowland*, M. Waller, E. Edwards and L. Barber (eds), Romney Marsh Research Trust, 1-21. Available from: <http://eprints.kingston.ac.uk/16410/1/01Waller_and_Long_offprint.pdf>.

Wessex Archaeology 2004. Seabed Prehistory: Gauging the Effects of Marine Aggregate Dredging. Available from: www.wessexarch.co.uk/projects/marine/alsf/seabed_prehistory/index.html.

Whitehouse, N.J. and Smith, D.N. 2004. 'Islands' in Holocene forests: Implications for Forest Openness, Landscape Clearance and 'Culture-Steppe' Species. *Environmental Archaeology* 9, 203-212.

5. Neolithic

Steve Sutcliffe

Following the River Ouse valley north from Seaford up to Newick there is a variety of evidence for Neolithic activity, including a causewayed enclosure and two oval long barrows. Much archaeological work has already been carried out in the area and, in particular, the work of Peter Drewett has been key to furthering our understanding of Neolithic activity in the Ouse valley. Apart from the major sites at Offham and Bishopstone, much of the evidence for the Neolithic period is artefactual, in the form of flint and pottery concentrations, or axe findspots. Communal monuments overlooking the river valley, such as the causewayed enclosure at Offham and the oval barrow on Cliffe Hill, also suggest that there was Neolithic activity in the valley. Although there is much potential for further sites to exist, it is likely that the evidence for these is buried under hillwash and river sediment (see Allen, Chapter 2). The implications of this, with regards to the Early Neolithic (c. 4000-3300 BC), later Neolithic (c. 3300-2900 BC), and Late Neolithic (c. 2900-2500 BC) are discussed below.

Into the Neolithic

In the Early Neolithic, crop cultivation and animal domestication, the defining agricultural practices of the Neolithic, are likely to have been adopted only as part of a gradual process, with hunter-gathering practices continuing beyond the Mesolithic period. Hunter-gatherers were dependent upon movement in the landscape, and the ability to exploit a wide range of resources. This would have required well established patterns of mobility and subsistence, changes to which would have developed across many generations. Although it seems likely that migration from the continent introduced agricultural practices, there is no evidence to suggest any rapid acceptance of them was brought about through colonisation or conquest.

Drewett (2003) suggests that Early Neolithic activity in the nearby Cuckmere valley may have been directly derived from the final Mesolithic activity patterns in the area. The same may be true of the Ouse valley, although the evidence for late Mesolithic activity there is more limited. Flint assemblages at High Hurstwood (Jacobi and Tebbutt 1981), Rocks Wood, Withyham (Harding and Ostoja-Zagorski 1987), and High Rocks, Tunbridge Wells (Money 1960) suggest some late Mesolithic activity at these sites, possibly for hunting or foraging expeditions along the Ouse and into the Weald, as many of these sites tend to be located inland towards the Weald. Evidence for late Mesolithic activity in the southern part of the valley is even more limited, although a fieldwalking exercise at Moon's Farm (Butler 2001) recovered a small amount of Neolithic and Early Bronze Age flintwork in amongst a predominantly Mesolithic flint assemblage. The later finds included two polished axe fragments, an ovate, a chisel arrowhead, and a barbed-and-tanged arrowhead.

The free-draining river terrace gravels at Barcombe, Rodmell and Piltdown may have been more suitable for settlement than the poorer draining clay and alluvial deposits nearby (ESCC 2007) and these valleys are likely to have been utilised in the Neolithic. The fact that all of the most significant Neolithic monuments in the Ouse valley overlook the river valley suggests that it was an area of importance.

The first evidence of Neolithic activity in the vicinity of the River Ouse valley are the long oval barrows, presumed to be 37th century BC (cf. Bayliss and Whittle 2007), of Camel's Hump, Cliffe Hill (Figure 5.1), and Money Burgh, Piddinghoe, and the causewayed enclosure at Offham 3950-3530 cal BC (4925±80; BM-1414). Radiocarbon dating suggests that the last decades of the thirty-eighth century cal BC or the first half of the thirty-seventh century cal BC saw the start of a century of enclosure building in Sussex (Healy et al. 2011), including sites such as the Trundle 3900-3370 cal BC (4845±95; I-11615) and Combe Hill 3640-3010 cal BC (4590±100; I-11613), which is located approximately 20km east of Offham. There is some uncertainty regarding the sequencing, particularly as the sampling was so limited at sites such as Offham, but it appears that Offham Hill was constructed slightly later from the end of the thirty-seventh century cal BC, perhaps soon after the large enclosure at Whitehawk 3640-3380 cal BC (4757±26 BP, OxA-14178) was constructed. There is evidence of a cultural shift taking place in Sussex during this period but this would have happened over many decades. It could also be argued that the prominence of these structures in the landscape, and their endurance in the archaeological record, can obscure our interpretation of this period, particularly when other evidence is lacking. Many elements of the nomadic hunter-gatherer lifestyle are likely to have persisted well into the Neolithic period. Despite the evidence at Bishopstone for domesticated animals and plant cultivation (Bell 1977), the presence of large quantities of marine shell, and roe deer bones, on the site suggests that, at least to some extent, Neolithic ideas were being used in conjunction with existing hunter-gatherer knowledge.

The Neolithic Environment

Environmental evidence for Neolithic forest clearance

The favourable conditions for pollen preservation in the Ouse valley near Lewes has made the area a focus for environmental research, and this has provided a good overview of its prehistoric environment. Prior to forest clearance dating from the Early Neolithic it has been assumed that most of Sussex would have been wooded (Sheldon 1978). Pollen analysis from peat deposits in the Vale of Brooks, south of Lewes, confirm that the area was well wooded with deciduous oak forest and that major deforestation did not occur until the Middle Bronze Age (Thorley 1971; 1981). The pollen sequence from Wellingham, north of Lewes, also suggests deforestation of the Ouse valley in the late second-millenium BC, but indicates an additional earlier phase of opening in the vegetation $c.$ 4500 BC in the area, possibly associated with an increase in frequency of grass and cereal pollen (Wing 1980).

The Neolithic site on Rookery Hill, at Bishopstone, included 45 irregularly shaped subsoil hollows, probably tree or shrub root holes. None of the hollows could be dated any later than the Neolithic, and one of them contained a charcoal fragment and a polished quartz diorite axe or mace-head fragment, probably Neolithic in date (Bell 1977, 7). The presence of artefacts in the hollows may be suggestive of tree or bush removal coinciding with occupation during the Neolithic period. The earliest land mollusc samples taken from the Neolithic pits at the site indicate a closed, probably woodland environment. The subsequent decline in woodland species may suggest human intervention, although the evidence for this is limited (Bell 1977).

Scaife and Burrin (1983) argue that substantial alluviation within the Ouse valley was the result of forest clearance at intervals dating back to the Mesolithic period. Recent environmental research has indicated partial forest clearance in the Early Neolithic, and has provided further information regarding the nature of the clearance that took place in the Ouse valley. At Ashcombe Bottom, soil samples from the Coombe deposit surface show a long period of stability during the Mesolithic and earlier Neolithic, probably as a result of woodland coverage. There followed a period of heavy soil erosion, most likely due to woodland clearance in the Early Neolithic and possibly linked to the hilltop clearance and activity at Offham (Allen 2005, 27). Molluscan evidence from a tree hollow suggests that there was then a regeneration of woodland before another possible clearance phase in the Late Neolithic, evidenced by a layer of lower colluvium at the centre of the valley.

The colluvial and land snail sequence at Southerham Grey Pit, Ranscombe Hill, identified mature deciduous woodland, possibly of later Mesolithic or earlier Neolithic date. A slight increase in open-country species suggests a local disturbance to the forest floor, indicating a slightly more open woodland that probably dates to the Neolithic (Allen 1995). Similarly, the mollusc assemblages from a lynchet at Malling Hill featured a Neolithic pit dominated by shade-loving species, and again with evidence of limited clearance and an opening of the woodland. The assemblage was notable for the severity of the change in species from the pit to the colluvial deposits, suggesting 'truncation of the pit and a hiatus within the sequence' (Allen 1995, 33).

The emerging picture of the Neolithic environment in the Ouse valley is still one of sporadic forest clearance within a generally well wooded environment. However, the impact of clearance activity seems to have been fairly dramatic at some sites, such as Malling Hill, whereas at other sites in the Ouse valley there appears to have been a more gradual transition.

Environmental evidence for construction and agricultural practices

The causewayed enclosure at Offham featured no significant open-country molluscan fauna component in its buried soil and ditch fills (Thomas in Drewett 1977, 237). Clearance at the site took place only for the purpose of building the enclosure, which appears to have been located in a small forest clearing, isolated from any areas of open-country. Another possibility is that it was only used for a short period before woodland regenerated in the area. Similarly, the enclosure at Combe Hill also appears to have been constructed in close woodland (Drewett 1994). This excludes the possibility of the land surrounding these sites being used for arable or pasture prior to the building of the enclosure, and contrasts with other Sussex enclosures constructed prior to 3000 BC, for example Whitehawk, that were built in an area that was extensively cleared beforehand (Thomas in Drewett 1977).

Other areas of the Ouse valley do show forest clearance alongside evidence of agricultural practices, woodland management, and possible settlement. Although the slopes of Mount Caburn remained wooded throughout the Neolithic, pollen analysis shows concentrations of browse-resistant species such as juniper and yew at its foot, which may be evidence of animal husbandry (Waller and Hamilton 1998). Pollen sequences derived from peat deposits at the bottom of Mount Caburn suggest that woodland management techniques such as coppicing, pollarding, or shredding may have been taking place from the beginning of the Neolithic (Drewett and Hamilton 1999, 19). By $c.$ 3750 cal BC the presence of cereal grains suggest limited planting in clearings at the bottom of the Caburn slope, followed by a period of woodland regeneration from $c.$ 3450 cal BC.

Structures and the Landscape

Offham Hill Causewayed Enclosure

The remains of a small causewayed enclosure on Offham Hill consist of two roughly concentric incomplete circles of discontinuous banks and ditches, the eastern side of which has been destroyed by a nineteenth century chalk pit. It is one of several causewayed enclosures in Sussex. In keeping with other Sussex causewayed enclosures, Offham dates from the Early Neolithic. It is false-crested, located on a north-facing slope directly west of the river, suggesting orientation towards the river valley.

The structure was initially thought to be D-shaped, rather than continuous, with an open side facing the scarp slope (Drewett 1977, 203). However, a recent survey (RCHME 1997) has questioned whether there was an open side, on the basis that the enclosure is almost perfectly circular rather than slightly angular.

A deliberate burial of a crouched, articulated, male in his early twenties (O'Connor in Drewett 1977) was excavated from a small pit towards the northern end of the outer ditch. Another possible deliberate burial, comprising half a mandible of an individual in his/her late thirties, was found at the western entrance of the enclosure. A pit containing sherds from a single round-based pot (deposited as sherds), flint waste flakes, a leaf-shaped arrowhead, and a seemingly purposeful selection of animal bone is also likely to have been buried deliberately as the pottery sherds were cleanly broken and unabraded. No seed or grain was present in the ditches but disarticulated human bone, pottery, and worked flint was also present. Much of this material is heavily abraded suggesting surface wear prior to its accumulation in the ditch silts. Drewett (1977, 226) suggests that evidence at Offham would be consistent with an exposure burial site, where human bone on the surface would have decomposed leaving only that which found its way into the ditches remaining. Comparisons with the assemblage at the Alfriston oval barrow (Drewett 1975) further suggests that the primary function of the enclosure was burial.

The molluscan sequences suggest that the inner ditch may have been dug first in a small clearing in the woodland, with the outer bank and ditch being added slightly later, still in close woodland (Thomas in Drewett 1977). This may be significant as the inner enclosures at Offham, Whitehawk, The Trundle, and Combe Hill appear to be broadly similar in scale and these sites may have initially been more alike (Drewett 1978a) The Offham site shows little evidence of activity in the surrounding area and was not extensively cleared until a later period, suggesting that any related domestic site would have been located elsewhere, most likely in the river valley below. The low percentage of implements in the flint assemblage, and the small pottery fragments, suggest a specialised function for the site. Like most of the Sussex enclosures, excluding Whitehawk and The Trundle, both ditches at Offham appear not to have been modified after their initial construction. This may suggest that Offham was a ritual enclosure, or at least that it had a different purpose to the further developed settlement enclosures such as Whitehawk and The Trundle. It is possible that the initial enclosures at these larger sites had a similar function to the enclosure at Offham, and that their later expansion was due to them being in a preferred location for development.

Monument location and visibility

Drewett (*et al.* 1988) suggests that the Offham causewayed enclosure would have provided extensive views over the treetops of the lower slopes and across the river valley, providing woodland clearance outside the enclosure extended to a minimum of 15m. Depending on the extent of the clearance around the enclosure, it would probably have also been easily located from the low-lying river valley, due to its position on the slope and the absence of trees. However, viewed from the valley below, the surrounding woodland may have obscured the enclosure itself. It is also worth noting that the valley floor has since gained several metres of alluvium so the view would have been different to the one we experience today. Perhaps, in this instance, it was the view offered across the valley from the monument that was of greatest importance.

The two Neolithic oval barrows in the area under consideration are both located on slopes facing the Ouse, clearly suggesting an orientation towards the river valley. The oval barrow known as Money Burgh, in Piddinghoe, is located on an east-facing slope in close proximity to the river. Unfortunately, unskilled excavation has meant much of the evidence from the barrow is irretrievable but according to the granddaughter of the original excavator, the upper portion contained a skeleton and 'other antiquities' (ESHER 2012). The wider end of the barrow faces the river and it is likely to have been specifically positioned in this way. Whatever its function, evidence suggests it was meant to be a prominent feature in the landscape when viewed from the river valley below.

The size and orientation of the oval barrow (Figure 5.1), also known as 'The Warrior's Grave' or 'The Camel's Hump', on the north-east slope of Cliffe Hill, Lewes, suggest it was meant to be seen from the river valley, and from some distance. The steep incline of The Combe just south-west of the barrow allows for a dramatic sighting between Cliffe Hill and Malling Hill. The positioning of the barrow between the two hills (Figure 5.2), particularly given the spectacular rounded 'belly' shape of The Combe in between, may also have been of significance. When viewed from the Lewes valley the

Figure 5.1: Oval barrow, 'The Warrior Grave' or 'Camels Hump' (photo: S. Sutlciffe)

Figure 5.2: Barrow between Cliffe Hill and Malling Hill (photo: S. Sutcliffe)

widest, and most impressive, end of the barrow is seen protruding above the hill horizon, despite it not actually being situated on the hilltop. Visibility of the monument from the north and south is poor, again suggesting it was meant to be seen from the Lewes valley where it is likely that there would have been an associated domestic site.

Throughout the valley, monuments occur where there is raised land in close proximity to the river. The Offham enclosure and Money Burgh oval barrow are examples of this. They perhaps suggest an orientation towards the river itself, rather than the valley. The River Ouse is likely to have been an important transport route and if a monument was of importance, a position visible from the river would ensure that it was seen by many people. Alternatively, there may have been some significant activity taking place on the river and these sites were being used to view this activity. It is possible that the locations of the above monuments held special significance long before anything was built there. The characteristics of the landscape itself may have taken on monumental significance. For example, although Mount Caburn has only produced sparse evidence for Neolithic activity, it seems likely that its impressive shape in the landscape would have made it a significant landmark for Neolithic people travelling up the Ouse valley.

Evidence for Neolithic settlement sites

Neolithic flint concentrations and findspots

The ESHER records Neolithic flint concentrations, possibly evidence of either camps for temporary foraging expeditions or more permanent settlement, in Sharpsbridge (MES3156), Houndean (MES2009), Newick (MES16627), Isfield (MES16701), and Newhaven (MES1801 and MES1794). These concentrations are often part of multi-period assemblages, showing the recurring use of particular sites over different periods.

Field survey in the Houndean-Ashcombe area has produced extensive flint scatters of Neolithic to Early Bronze Age character (Biggar 1978), particularly on the crest of the spur between Houndean and Ashcombe Farms, sloping down to the A27 Lewes-Brighton road. The flint types, which included polished and unpolished flint axes, scrapers, and knives, are characteristic of Neolithic sites both in Sussex (Drewett in Biggar 1978, 147), as well as sites further afield such as Windmill Hill and Durrington Walls, Wiltshire. The high concentration of flintwork in the area suggests that a Neolithic-Early Bronze Age settlement may have existed there, before being destroyed by the activities of later Iron Age or Romano-British settlements in the area. Likewise, concentrations of Neolithic flint and sporadic pottery finds, from Castle Hill, Newhaven (Field 1939) are possibly the remains of a series of Neolithic settlement sites on the Downs.

Fifteen findspots for Neolithic axes, axe fragments, or axe roughouts are also recorded: six were found on separate occasions in Lewes, four in Newhaven, two in Fletching, and single finds were made in Barcombe and Buxted.

Bishopstone

The hilltop site at Bishopstone (Bell 1977), overlooking the English Channel, features two large Neolithic pits containing animal bone, worked flint, pottery, marine shell, and cereal remains. The bones of cattle, sheep, and pig suggest domesticated animals were being kept, and the carbonised remains of emmer wheat, spelt wheat, and six-row barley were present, some of the earliest evidence for cereals in Sussex. The archaeological material from the site was generally Early Neolithic in character, and the pits are a typical characteristic of Neolithic domestic sites throughout the United Kingdom.

The pit with the most abundant finds (pit 357) was about 2m in diameter, roughly circular, and approximately 85cm deep with vertical sides and a flat floor. Before much weathering could occur the pit was backfilled with 50cm of chalk rubble containing 2437 mussel shells. After another short period of weathering, three small scoops were made in the sediment, the central of which showed evidence of burning. Charcoal from the pit was radiocarbon dated to 3360-2930 cal BC (4460±70 BP, HAR-1662). The two scoops either side had no obvious function. Shortly after this, the remainder of the pit was backfilled with chalk lumps and dark brown earth. The process is strikingly methodical. Bell comments that 'the Neolithic features seem to be round the periphery of the excavations...possibly therefore forming a rough circle of diameter about 115m (Bell 1977, 5). Drewett suggests that 'the digging and deposition of objects in pits closely parallels the deposition of objects in other contexts such as causewayed enclosure and long barrow ditches' (Drewett 2003, 43). He adds that such pits, and their contents, could be evidence of wider use of the landscape, rather than specific settlement sites.

A series of postholes and gullies were also found at Bishopstone which, given the evidence for clearance and possible settlement, could be interpreted as evidence of structural remains (Russell 2002), but the limited evidence and the agricultural damage to the site makes it difficult to make this interpretation with any certainty.

Neolithic pit depositions at Peacehaven

Excavations of a multi-period site at Lower Hoddern Farm, Peacehaven revealed a scatter of Neolithic pits, with occasional associated postholes. The pits, which varied considerably in size, shape, and contents, produced significant quantities of Early Neolithic pottery and struck flint, as well as cereal processing equipment such as saddle querns and rubbing stones.

A residual charred cereal grain with an Early Neolithic radiocarbon date of 3770-3630 cal BC (4890±35 BP, SUERC-22071) was recovered from an Iron Age context at the site (ASE 2010). Later Neolithic features and artefacts were less abundant but small assemblages of Grooved Ware and Peterborough ware perhaps indicate a continuity of activity from the Early Neolithic (ASE 2010). Excavations at Keymer Avenue, also in Peacehaven, revealed a 20m diameter hollow containing both Mesolithic and Neolithic worked flint. A number of pits containing Neolithic struck flint and pottery were also excavated from the nearby Seaview Avenue (ASE 2008).

A buried Late Neolithic/Early Bronze Age settlement site at Ashcombe Bottom?

Twenty one Late Neolithic pottery sherds were found in the lower colluvium at Ashcombe Bottom. The dry valley location of the site may indicate low-lying settlement (Allen 2005). The sherds were undecorated, domestic in nature, and were similar to Drewett's Neolithic Fabric 1 (Drewett 1980, 27), commonly found in Sussex and generally considered to be Early Neolithic, although not in all cases. As no Early Neolithic flint artefacts were found with the pottery, it could be that the sherds date to the later Neolithic. The pottery assemblage for the site was predominantly Beaker but no sherds from this period were found in the lower colluvium. Although the artefactual material was minimal, the pottery perhaps indicates Neolithic activity at the site pre-dating Beaker activity, for which there is more abundant evidence.

A flint assemblage totalling 980 pieces was collected from the site. All of the flint was chalk-derived and diagnostic pieces, in particular a group of convex scrapers, suggested the assemblage dated from the Late Neolithic-Early Bronze Age and Beaker period. Only a few large cores were found, discarded long before they had been fully reduced, and a high proportion of the waste flakes were secondary or tertiary, suggesting that primary manufacture took place elsewhere before being continued more locally. The assemblage exhibited high frequencies of retouch and featured scrapers, a transverse arrowhead, piercers, notched pieces, and a knife (Allen 2005, 17). The suggestion of a local source of flint, along with the high proportion of tools (and recurring specific tool types such as the convex scrapers) may be indicative of maintained domestic activity at the site.

Territories in Neolithic Sussex

Evidence of Neolithic settlement sites remains a rarity in Sussex, with only the dense and extensive flint scatters at Houndean-Ashcombe (Drewett 1978b) and Bullock Down, Eastbourne (Drewett 1982) providing evidence of settlement in the area. Theories regarding territorial organisation are therefore often based upon the location of the remaining Neolithic landmarks. The relatively large number of flint mines and causewayed enclosures in Sussex has enabled some interpretation of the interrelationships between the two. It has been suggested that Neolithic Sussex featured three distinct zones, divided by the valleys of the rivers Arun and Adur (Russell 2000, 73). The central block between the Arun and Adur appears to have consisted of several major flint-mining complexes, whereas the blocks either side were dominated by causewayed enclosures. The Ouse valley features no known flint mines. However, it is possible that it lost flint-mining sites on the southern edge of the Downs to coastal erosion.

Drewett (1978a) initially suggested the possibility of thirteen discrete territories in Neolithic Sussex, with rivers and their valleys located within, rather than functioning as territorial boundaries. Each territory consisted of a long barrow, with clans grouping together to build causewayed enclosures. Later, this model was modified to feature three larger territories based around the Neolithic sites at The Trundle, Whitehawk, and Combe Hill (Drewett 1994, 2003). However, variations in the density and combinations of monuments has raised questions regarding the validity of these interpretations (Kinnes 1992).

Pottery evidence for mobility and trade networks

There is some evidence of relatively far-reaching trade networks, even in the small assemblages found in the Ouse valley. For example, the very slight use of grog found in the pottery at Offham may indicate some Wealden connections (Drewett 1980, 26). Bishopstone produced an assemblage of 181 Neolithic pottery sherds, which shared similarities with those from the Trundle and Whitehawk. Bell (1977, 18) notes that four different fabric types in such a small assemblage might be a result of trade in Neolithic pottery, or at least evidence of the different geological zones used by the inhabitants.

Marine shell tempering is found in the pottery at Bishopstone. Drewett notes that in Sussex this kind of tempering is only found south of the Downs, near to sea-shore sources, highlighting the localised nature of manufacture and distribution of Sussex pottery (Drewett 1980, 26). One possible exception to this is a single sherd of pottery found at Bishopstone containing metamorphosed limestone, for which no local origin could be found (Bell 1977, 18).

The sherd from an Early Neolithic round-based bowl found at High Rocks (Money 1960) perhaps indicates food transportation. Evidence for Neolithic activity at the site was very limited, suggesting that it was only inhabited briefly and was most likely a temporary hunting camp. The presence of pottery at such a site suggests that some hunting or foraging expeditions may have strayed far enough from the main site to warrant the burden of mobile sustenance.

Into the Bronze Age

Clear evidence for Late Neolithic activity in Sussex is shown by extensive and dense flints scatters on the downland, (e.g. Biggar 1978; Gardiner 1988; David Cripps pers. collection) but settlement or occupation activity becomes more sparse and difficult to tease out in the Beaker period; and evidence from the Ouse valley is no different. There are numerous sites showing activity during both the Neolithic and Bronze Age periods but often there is little evidence to establish what activity occurred during the transition from one period to the other, and less still for the location of domestic sites. For example, the Neolithic to Early Bronze Age flint scatters found in the Houndean-Ashcombe area, like many of the multi-period flint scatters in the Ouse valley, do little more than confirm that flintworking activity was occurring at these sites during both periods. Unfortunately, the large diagnostic pottery groups and structured pit depositions that characterise the Early Neolithic activity at sites such as Bishopstone and Peacehaven are often missing from later/Late Neolithic contexts in Sussex. This may be the result of several factors. Russell (2002) suggests that people may have been living nomadic lifestyles with impermanent houses, or they may have been living in houses made from non-durable materials. Alternatively, settlements could have been destroyed by plough damage or, as recent work to the east and west of Lewes has suggested, they may have been buried beneath hillwash.

The Lynchets at Malling Hill, Lewes, featured the remains of a small, steep-sided pit in the vicinity of a Neolithic oval barrow and several Bronze Age barrows. The pit produced three sherds of Late Neolithic Peterborough style pottery from the same vessel, similar to that seen at Offham (Drewett 1977). Also, at the nearby site of Southerham Grey Pit, Ranscombe Hill, a small assemblage of Beaker pottery was recovered from colluvial deposits (Allen 1995). Beaker pottery was obtained from the dry valleys at Ashcombe Bottom and Cuckoo Bottom, just west of Lewes. The patterning of the Beaker comb-impressed wares found at Ashcombe Bottom (Allen 2005, 14) can be paralleled with the round-based Beaker sherds excavated from the Offham enclosure (Drewett, 1977, fig. 11, nos 21 and 22). The Offham enclosure itself featured 48 sherds of Beaker pottery, and there are two Early Bronze Age round barrows to the south-west of the site, part of a larger cemetery now destroyed by construction of a reservoir (Drewett 1977).

Allen (2005) suggests that further Beaker sites could be located in dry valleys and sealed by hillwash, rendering most standard forms of archaeological survey ineffective. If this is correct, further sampling with a focus on stratified colluvial and soil deposits may reveal more sites and give a better overview of this complex transition period.

Future work

What is require now is continuing research into the existing flint assemblages for the area, particularly in the context of site dating revaluations (Healy et al. 2011), incorporating and updating the information available in the HER record. Also further survey work in the vicinity of long barrows and in their surrounding areas, as recommended by Gardiner (1988). In particular, survey of the area surrounding the Piddinghoe long barrow would be recommended, along with further field work and survey at the sites of the Houndean-Ashcombe flint scatters.

In addition, a review of the Late Neolithic finds at Ashcombe-Houndean (Biggar 1978), and comparison with similar assemblages in the area would be useful.

Finally, based on the above research, consideration of alternatives to the territorial arguments put forward by Peter Drewett.

References

Allen, M. J. 1995. The prehistoric land-use and human ecology of the Malling-Caburn Downs; two late Neolithic/Early Bronze Age sites beneath colluvium. *Sussex Archaeological Collections* 133, 19–43.

Allen, M. J. 2005. Beaker occupation and development of the downland landscape at Ashcombe Bottom, near Lewes, East Sussex. *Sussex Archaeological Collections* 143, 7-33.

ASE (Archaeology South-East), 2008. Archaeological investigations at Keymer and Seaview Avenues, Peacehaven, East Sussex. In Post-excavation assessment and project design for publication, ASE report no. 2008029.

ASE, 2010. A post-excavation assessment and updated project design for excavations at the Brighton and Hove wastewater treatment works, Lower Hoddern Farm, Peacehaven, East Sussex (stage 3). In ASE report no. 2010098.

Bayliss, A. and Whittle, A. (eds) 2007. Histories of the dead: building chronologies for five southern British long barrows, *Cambridge Archaeological Journal*, 17(1) (Supplement).

Bell, M. 1977. Excavations at Bishopstone. *Sussex Archaeological Collections* 115, 1-299.

Biggar, J. T. M. 1978. A field survey of Houndean-Ashcombe and other Downland fields west of Lewes, 1972–1975. *Sussex Archaeological Collections* 116, 143-153.

Butler, C. 2001. Mesolithic and Later Flintwork from Moon's Farm, Piltdown, East Sussex. *Sussex Archaeological Collections* 138, 222-224.

Drewett, P. L. 1975. The excavation of an oval burial mound of the third millenium B.C. at Alfriston, East

Sussex, 1974. *Proceedings of the Prehistoric Society* 41, 119-152.

Drewett, P. L. 1977. The excavation of a Neolithic Causewayed Enclosure on Offham Hill, East Sussex, 1976. *Proceedings of the Prehistoric Society* 43, 201-241.

Drewett, P. L. (ed.), 1978a. *Archaeology in Sussex to A.D. 1500*, p23-30. London: CBA Research Report 29.

Drewett, P. L. 1978b. Some flintwork from Fields 2, 3, and 4. In Biggar, J. T. M., A field survey of Houndean-Ashcombe and other Downland fields west of Lewes, 1972–1975. *Sussex Archaeological Collections* 116, 143-153.

Drewett, P. L. 1980. Neolithic Pottery in Sussex. *Sussex Archaeological Collections* 118, 23-30.

Drewett, P. L. 1982. *The Archaeology of Bullock Down, Eastbourne, East Sussex: the Development of a Landscape*, Sussex Archaeological Society Monograph I.

Drewett, P. L. 1994. Dr. V. Seton Williams excavations at Combe Hill, 1962, and the role of Neolithic causewayed enclosures in Sussex. *Sussex Archaeological Collections* 132, 7-24.

Drewett, P. L. 2003 Taming the Wild: The First Farming Communities in Sussex. In D. Rudling (ed.), *The Archaeology of Sussex to AD 2000*, 39-46. Norfolk: Heritage.

Drewett, P. L. and Hamilton, S. 1999. Marking time and making space: excavations and landscape studies at the Caburn Hillfort, East Sussex, 1996-98. *Sussex Archaeological Collections* 137, 7-38.

Drewett, P. L., Rudling, D. and Gardiner, M. 1988. *The south-east to 1000 A.D.: a regional history of England*. London and New York: Longman.

ESCC (East Sussex County Council Archaeology Team), 2007. Historic Environment Resource Assessment, River Terrace Gravel Geology (Within the Ouse valley), East Sussex, Desk-Based Assessment.

Field, L. F. 1939. Castle Hill, Newhaven. *Sussex Archaeological Collections* 80, 263-273.

Gardiner, J. 1988. *The composition and distribution of Neolithic surface flint scatters in central southern England*, unpubl. PhD thesis, University of Reading.

Harding, A. F. and Ostoja-Zagorski, J. 1987 Excavations in Rocks Wood, Withyham, 1982. *Sussex Archaeological Collections* 125, 11–32.

Healy, F., Bayliss, A. & Whittle, A. 2011. Sussex. In A. Whittle, F. Healey & A. Bayliss, *Gathering Time: dating the early Neolithic Enclosures of the Southern Britain and Ireland*, 207–62. Oxford: Oxbow Books

Jacobi, R. M. and Tebbutt, F. C. 1981. A Late Mesolithic Rock Shelter Site at High Hurstwood, Sussex. *Sussex Archaeological Collections* 119, 1-36.

Kinnes, I, 1992 *Non-Megalithic Long Barrows and Allied Structures in the British Neolithic.* British Museum Occasional Paper 52. London: British Museum

Money, J. H. 1960. Excavations at High Rocks, Tunbridge Wells, 1954-56. *Sussex Archaeological Collections* 98, 173-221.

O'Connor, T. P. 1977. Appendix I: The Human Skeletal Remains. In Drewett, P. L., The excavation of a Neolithic Causewayed Enclosure on Offham Hill, East Sussex, 1976. *Proceedings of the Prehistoric Society* 43, 201-241.

RCHME (Royal Commission on the Historical Monuments of England), 1997. Industry and Enclosure in the Neolithic: Offham Hill Survey.

Russell, M. 2002. *Prehistoric Sussex.* Stroud: Tempus Publishing Ltd.

Russell, M. 2000. *Flint mines in Neolithic Britain.* Stroud: The History Press Ltd.

Scaife, R. G. and Burrin, P. J. 1983. Floodplain Development in Vegetational History of the Sussex High Weald and some Archaeological Implications. *Sussex Archaeological Collections* 121, 1-10.

Sheldon, J. 1978. The environmental background. In Drewett, P.L. (ed.), *Archaeology in Sussex to A.D. 1500,* p3-7. London: CBA Research Report 21.

Thomas, K. D. 1977. Appendix IV: The land Mollusca from the enclosure on Offham Hill. In Drewett, P. L., The excavation of a Neolithic Causewayed Enclosure on Offham Hill, East Sussex, 1976. *Proceedings of the Prehistoric Society* 43, 201-241.

Thorley, A. 1971. Vegetational history of the Vale of the Brooks. *Institute of British Geography Conference* 5, 47-50.

Thorley, A. 1981. Pollen analytical evidence relating to the vegetational history of the Chalk. *Journal of Biogeography* 8, 93-106.

Waller, M. P. and Hamilton, S. 1998. The Vegetational History of the South Downs: Mount Caburn. In Morton, J., Whiteman, C. and Waller, M. (eds), *Quaternary: Research Association Field Guide.* Cambridge: Quaternary Research Association.

Wing, A. S. 1980. An analysis of the pollen fallout at Wellington peat bog near Lewes, East Sussex and a consideration of some of its climatic and historical implications. Unpubl BSc project (University of Sussex).

Sources

East Sussex Sites and Monuments Record, 2012. East Sussex County Council [Online]. Available at: <http://www.heritagegateway.org.uk/gateway/> [accessed 11th May 2012].

Historic Environment Record, 2012. East Sussex County Council [Online]. Available at <http://www.heritagegateway.org.uk/gateway/> [accessed 6th May 2012].

6. Bronze Age, a north-south divide

Lisa Jayne Fisher

Bronze Age chronology

The dates relating the Bronze Age range from 2,500 to 600 BC which have been divided up into the following periods in Figure 6.1.

Such dates are difficult to define exactly; at times I may refer instead to the framework for ceramic traditions based in southern England, as defined by Barrett (1980). This roughly correlates as Early Bronze Age with Beakers and Collared Urns, Middle Bronze Age as Deverel-Rimbury (DR) ceramics and early Late Bronze Age as Post Deverel-Rimbury (PDR) and Later Bronze Age with Decorated Wares. There is some overlap in time frames and technologies but this is not necessarily discussed in full in this paper as it has already been eloquently discussed by others (see Seager Thomas 2008 for a more thorough chronology). Current dates for metalwork categories are also included, based on Needham (1996).

The emergence of the Bronze Age in the Ouse valley

The Bronze Age heralded a new way of life in Britain with an influx of people from the continent contributing to an explosion of exchange networks with points of convergence on either side of the English Channel (Marcigny 2012, 29). England played an important part in providing copper and tin as well as bronze trade objects such as axes. New chiefdoms and territories were established in the South of England with new rituals and ways of burying the dead. Before the beginning of the second millennium BC, round barrows were the norm. Usually they contained a single crouched inhumation in the early period with associated Beakers but there are few of these in the area of study. By the beginning of the second millennium BC collared urn cremation burials were common with other burials sometimes flexed (Figure 6.2) and secondary burials interred into barrows as urned cremations (Ray 1999, 29-30).

These monuments have come to define the period alongside the 'magic' of working with metal and a more sedentary way of life. Towards the end of the second millennium settlement and burial appears to be more closely related and to have concentrated within the Downs areas in Sussex, but with a surprising paucity of settlements within the area of study and a plethora of burial sites. Curwen (1936a) describes the finding of 843 flint arrowheads, with a broad date range, from the Wealden clays, Lower Greensands and forest ridges to the north of the Downs. This would suggest that The Wealden zone was almost certainly where hunting took place. More research is a priority in this area. It was in the Weald that environmental evidence suggests a 'wildwood' existed with little forest clearance until 1000 BC (Drewett *et al.* 1988, 112) and a large proportion of the Ouse valley study lies in this geographical zone. Consequently we have a picture of a 'sacred geography' in the area of study where individual territories appear to have distinct and separate zones with the majority of burials on the downland ridge tops, settlement within the lower lying slopes to the south and the hunting grounds to the north (Field 1998) during the second millennium BC. At present this view could suggest a north-south divide, until such a time that further excavation leads to a *contra* view. Grinsell mentions that there is a relationship between the woodlands and a lack of barrow sites (1934, 213), and this pattern is true for the Weald which has been little studied (Gardiner 1990), with only two excavated burial sites north of the Downs in the Ouse valley at Barcombe and potentially one more at Isfield. Definite dates do not, as yet, exist and should be a priority for future fieldwork (see below). Such a possibility, however, does lie at Barcombe where a ring ditch is thought to give evidence for a barrow once standing in this field, although when excavated no evidence for a burial could be found (Chris Butler pers. comm.). In addition, the discovery of an MBA cremation burial at Pond Field in Barcombe (Fisher unpubl.) has

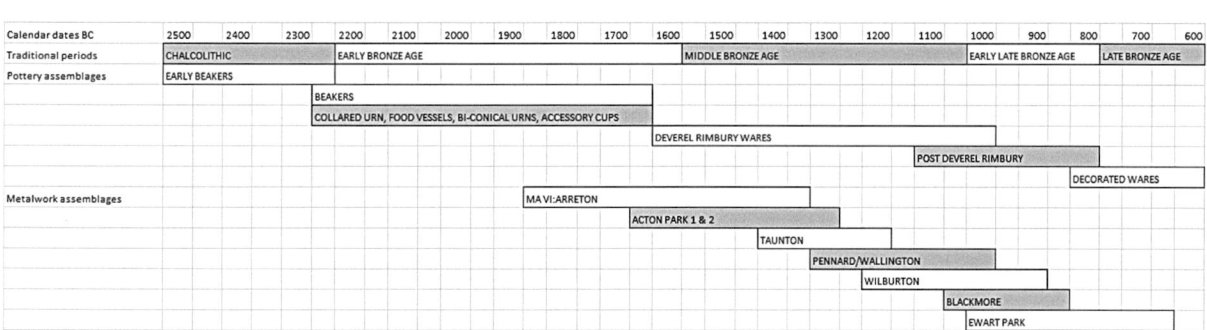

FIGURE 6.1: BRONZE AGE CHRONOLOGY

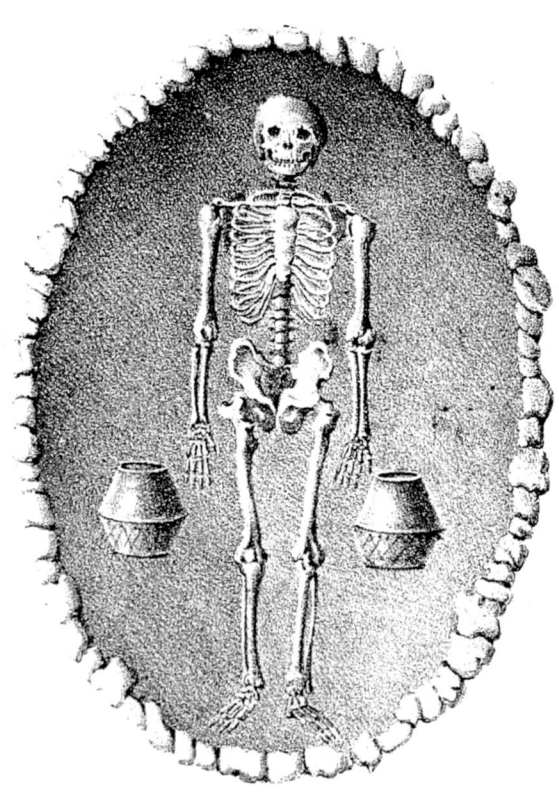

FIGURE 6.2: BURIAL AT OXTEDDLE BOTTOM, LEWES (FROM HORSFIELD 1824). THIS BURIAL WAS ACTUALLY FLEXED NOT EXTENDED AS REPRESENTED HERE

added to the database, alongside the excavation of a wooden post adjacent to the river (Allen 2011) which has been radiocarbon dated to the MBA 1680-1530 cal BC (3340±40BP, NZA-36948).

It was during the Middle Bronze Age (MBA) that farming became more widespread than the preceding Early Bronze Age (EBA), bringing new agricultural practices with associated track ways and field boundaries which were clearly linked to nearby settlements although such obvious connections cannot always be proved to be contemporary unless excavated. Such boundaries do exist within the Ouse valley but cannot necessarily be easily dated and so are difficult to place in any category, although some sites in Sussex are proving to originate in the EBA with continuity into the MBA and beyond (Judie English pers. comm.). It has been suggested that the Ouse valley was used as a transport route together with a series of droveways running from the South Downs through the Low Weald and into the High Weald (Chuter 2008). The Ouse would have been a major route way and used for direct transportation of trade items to and from the continent via the English Chanel with firm evidence for Bronze Age seafaring established in the Ouse valley with a sea wreck site at Seaford (see below).

With a suitably important navigation route such as the Ouse, it is likely that settlement and clearance took place besides the river, north of the Downs although once again, evidence is scant. We do know that by the Late Bronze Age (LBA), communities had impacted on the landscape to a high degree and as a result, the silting up of rivers caused by erosion from human activity created flooding in the Upper Ouse valley (Scaife and Burrin 1983). This would suggest that by the late period, flooding may have prevented settlement and farming in the floodplains of the Ouse.

By the beginning of the first millennium BC population pressures challenged the way of life with the smaller settlements being deserted in favour of larger, more nucleated settlements. Land was at a premium due to a deterioration of the climate and the soil quality. A wetter climate ensued and is apparent in the archaeological record alongside a paucity of burial sites, which was also reflected in other areas of England, notably that of the Upper Thames valley (Lambrick 1992). A more defended and tribal way of life followed as evidenced by the early building of enclosures on high points within the landscape such as at Castle Hill in Newhaven which likely spans the MBA and LBA (Ellison 1978, 32). This pattern lies elsewhere in Sussex, as at Hollingbury (Hamilton 1984) and Seaford Head (Hamilton 2003). Environmental evidence points to the erosion of once fertile soils on the Downs which were being tilled seasonally (Hamilton 2002, 172). This geographical shift occurred due to the low lying grounds of the river valleys suffering from high levels of flooding in the wetter months. Consequently this shift in climate forced communities into farming further upslope or on less desirable land as at Downsview and Varley Halls in Brighton (Grieg 1997; 2002). This also occurred elsewhere in Sussex, notably at Shinewater near Eastbourne (Greatorex 1997/98). Certainly in the low Wealden area of the Ouse valley, as well as the lower floodplains, we have several find spots of bronze axes and adzes which date from the LBA, giving indicators for possible forest clearance in areas not affected by flooding. This may parallel evidence from Midhurst, which points to a mass clearance of woodland dating from 1000-400 cal BC (Scaife 2001). Some may also suggest the purposeful deposit of such items, near to a water source as at Berewood, Barcombe where fifteen socketed LBA axes were found near the river in what may have been ritually placed, are similar in nature to the votive offerings at Flag Fen (Pryor and Taylor 1992, 45). Current data would suggest that there was certainly settlement activity in the Ouse valley in the Bronze Age and this has been classified as a medium potential for further sites to exist, especially within the river gravel terraces (Chuter 2008).

A list of all monuments from the Historic Environment Record (HER) database have been studied for this paper and are used throughout, referring to catalogue numbers listed as (HER) MES numbers. These, if wished, can be obtained from County Hall, in Lewes.

6. BRONZE AGE, A NORTH-SOUTH DIVIDE

Current records of Bronze Age activity in the Ouse valley

There are a lack of Bronze Age sites to the north of the extant area of study but this is not to say that settlement or burial sites do not exist; the nature of river valleys with deep sedimentation means it is highly probable that such areas of archaeological importance may be buried up to 10m deep beneath valley alluvium, Head deposits and later agricultural activity (see Allen, this volume). Widespread farming on the Downs and the river plains further downstream in the area of study may also account for a further loss of sites. In addition the bias in our understanding is further compounded by the development of hamlets, such as Barcombe, Fletching and Isfield with larger medieval towns such as Lewes and later additions such as Newhaven being developed on potential sites. To make matters worse, the classic Bronze Age monument, the round barrow, was often constructed from flint (amongst other materials) which was a desirable building resource. In antiquarian times these were often targeted for road building schemes and were quite literally wiped out with scant mumblings of 'ancient urns' being reported, as at places like Boxholt Bottom outside Lewes (Turner 1870). Finally, a lack of fieldwork in the area of study biases the evidence enormously giving us a false understanding of socio-political organisation by restricting interpretation in the Ouse valley during this period. What we can do is examine the evidence and suggest areas for potential, with regard to further research and make some sense of the spatial patterning of known sites. Such research and excavation will only reveal the true extent of such latent possibilities but when dealing with such a large area it is unlikely that the true potential of this area will ever be revealed, due to mitigating problems as highlighted above. Grinsell (1934) has already compiled a full list of barrow sites in the area which have been condensed as a separate table (Table 6.1 and Figure 6.3) limited to the areas immediately flanking the Ouse, for the purposes of this paper.

It is to be noted that a large majority of these sites have had limited excavation or little written information except in the form of a list and have been largely destroyed since his paper was written. The majority of burial sites within the area of study are round barrows. These are limited to the downland zones, with barrows in the Weald being very rare, except for some along the western Greensand ridge (Garwood 2003, 50). Grinsell also estimates that 90% of barrows are on chalk downlands (1934, 217) and has listed a minimum of 171 barrows or more in the area of study, with more barrows likely to have been in existence in the 1930s. Some of his references are vague, alluding to 'several barrows' in places. However, it should be noted that not all barrows were necessarily for burial and may have simply been ceremonial/ritual mounds devoid

Square number	Barrow numbers	Place name	Barrow type	References/comments
54 SE	20	S. Malling Without, Glynde	16 bowl barrows and 4 platform barrows. One Early Bronze Age burial	Includes rich Early Bronze Age burial at Oxteddle Bottom (*SAC* 72 and Curwen 1954) other sites commented on (*SAC* 20 and 64)
54SW	71	St. Ann without, Hamsey, St. John Without, St. Ann, South Malling	59 bowls, 7 platform barrows and 5 ring barrows Two Early Bronze Age burials	Five sites have clusters of 3-10 in size. One excavated with primary interment of woman and child and with secondary Middle Bronze Age interments (*Sussex County Mag.* 6). Possible collared urns found (*SAC* 72, also 5 and 34 and *Gent. Mag. Library, Arch.* vol 1). Also long barrow in this square
67 SW	70	Iford, Rodmell, Piddinghoe, Southease, Beddingham	All bowl barrows	1 Beaker burial (SNQ 1932), large bowl barrow at Southease (*SAC* 5) with 5 burials, nearby 1 long barrow and cluster of 24 at Rodmell
67 SE	3	South Heighton, Beddingham	All bowl barrows	'Bi-conical' cremation urn at Beddingham *SAC* 72
67 NW	15	Iford, Rodmell	All bowl barrows	Three sites have clusters of barrows 3-5 in size. One opened contained cremated remains (*SAC* vol. 3 (1931) and vol. 4 (1932))
67 NE	7	Beddingham	All bowl barrows	Some are thought to be Saxon and two maybe windmill steads. One other known as 'Gill's grave' (*SAC* 20, 23 and *Archaeologia* 46)
78 NW	5	Piddinghoe	Bowl barrows?	One site with 4 barrows now developed on (west and east of Roderick Av).

TABLE 6.1: GRINSELL'S BARROWS

of human remains but for the larger part we will never know and so without any confirmed evidence for these we must simply refer to them as barrows. These barrows have been marked by Grinsell on 6in OS maps which have been divided into quarterly squares, SW, SE, NW and NE respectively and should be numbered right to left, bottom to top within each square in relation to his map (Figure 6.3). Worthy of note is the fact that the two squares 40 and 27 to the north of the Downs do not have any barrows listed, neither does the top half of square 54.

However, we do have to exercise caution here; a list of barrows does not necessarily give us a list of Bronze Age barrows *per se*. The dating of any barrow can never be confirmed unless completely excavated with artefacts able to date the monuments. Knowing that the majority of such barrows were robbed in antiquarian times, the problem of making an assured inventory is apparent here. Note should be made that I have produced a map showing most of the Bronze Age sites which flank the Ouse in Figure 6.4 and I have mainly included those sites which look directly down upon the river valley with some lying in valley bottoms beyond the ridge tops but still within the area of research. Those further afield have not been included in this study and so important sites, such as Caburn, Ashcombe Bottom and Bishopstone have been excluded because they lie just outside the boundary of study and are not immediately adjacent to the Ouse.

Early Bronze Age activity in the Ouse valley (2200-1600 BC)

Material culture in this period consisted of a tradition of individual burial in round barrows, usually containing a single crouched inhumation with an associated Beaker but there is only one in the area of study. By the beginning of the second millennium BC Collared Urn cremation burials were common, sometimes accompanying flexed burials and secondary cremation burials. During this period, the technology for working copper, bronze and gold were introduced and kinship territories and settlements were established. Large monuments were erected although these are not as apparent in the South East as those elsewhere in the rest of England. The growth of agriculture began in the preceding Neolithic and was slowly being established.

There are no firm EBA settlements with just a couple of earthwork sites of a dubious date in the area of study, with some suggestions compiled for comparison with following MBA in Table 6.2. The field systems have been given a broad date by the HER reporters and it is unlikely that firm dates at present can be attributed to them so they are listed here as coming from a broad Bronze Age date (Figure 6.4 chevrons). This is obviously confusing and has been listed in the context of this paper as being beneficial from further exploration. However, work at Cuckoo Bottom and Ashcombe Bottom by Allen

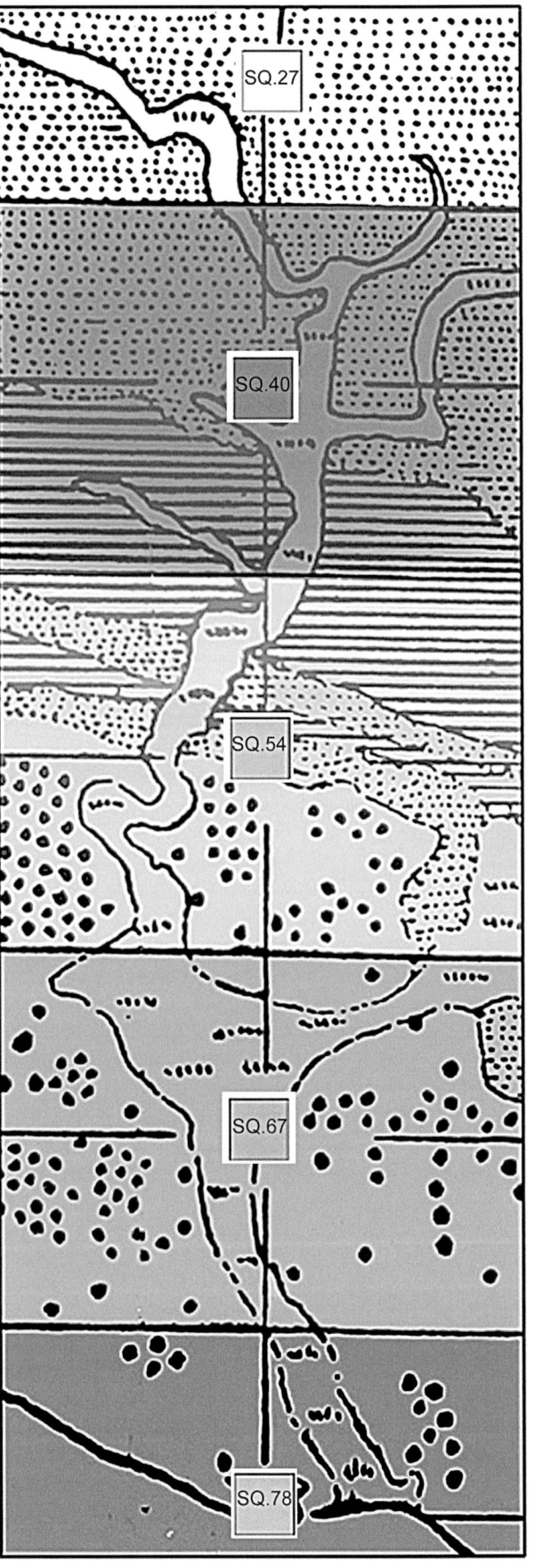

FIGURE 6.3: MAP OF GRINSELL'S BARROWS (AFTER GRINSELL 1934)

6. BRONZE AGE, A NORTH-SOUTH DIVIDE

(2005) suggests that Beaker settlements may lie in valley bottoms hidden under shallow modern colluvial deposits between 450mm–700mm deep. Several other nearby sites are also situated at Malling Hill and Southerham Grey pit (Allen 1995) with suggested EBA dates attributed by Beaker sherds found which highlights potential for further fieldwork and excavation.

Find spots

There are a few find spots with EBA dates which may suggest areas for further investigation (Table 6.3). At Itford Hill, excavations revealed ninety-five sherds of Beaker pottery but was thought by the excavator not to define the construction date of the barrow, but was suggestive of possible occupation south of the barrow (Ellison 1972; Holden 1972, 104). Although there is scant evidence for settlement and agricultural practices, we can deduce that there was certainly activity in the whole of the Ouse valley. Find spots can be interpreted in various ways, such as evidence for 'summer' camps, foraging trips, hunting trips or journeys made for trade, re-location or visiting nearby communities. However, we cannot prove any theories simply by looking at the find spots themselves other than to simply say that they are representative of activity. Within the Ouse valley are a total of nine find spots from at least the first part of the second millennium BC although two assemblages (Figure 6.4, no. 6 and no. 8) are not definite and could date from a later period. These finds appear to be spread equally to the north and south of the valley which is of interest. There are a couple of flat axes found, a nearly pure copper version from South Heighton (Grinsell 1931, 42) and a plain one 'from Lewes' exact location unknown (Grinsell 1931, 41). These are likely to give a date of between 2000-1720 BC (Drewett *et al.* 1988, 69).

Burial sites

For the EBA, burial sites (fifteen urns in total) conform to eight Collared Urn burials, one Beaker, two possible 'Food Vessel' burials, a Bi-conical urn burial and three inhumations with pottery fragments (Table 6.4). The earliest example is to the south west of Lewes at Heathy Brow, Rodmell where two bowl barrows were excavated (Curwen 1932) which were thought to be associated with a field system and a double lynchet trackway, which is yet unproved. One barrow was found to contain the remains of a skeleton with an undecorated Beaker (Figure 6.5) next to the skull. This has since been identified as an early imported Wessex/Middle Rhine beaker (Ellison 1978) likely to date to 2000 BC which is a unique as it is the only Beaker burial in the area of study. This raises interesting questions about continuity; some EBA burials follow a tradition of earlier tomb building as at Cliffe Hill, Lewes and Piddinghoe near Rodmell, where two Neolithic Long Barrows are located with no more known examples in the Ouse valley.

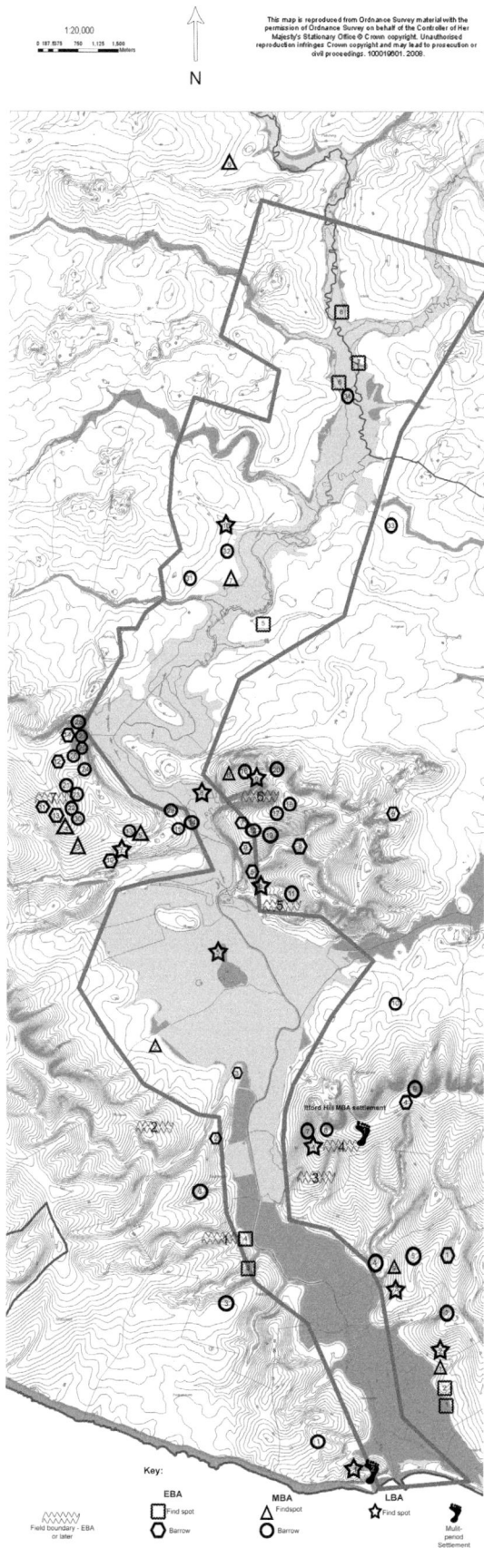

FIGURE 6.4: MAIN MAP OF SITES

Early Bronze Age	Middle Bronze Age	Source
Castle Hill (Fig. 6.4, footprint no. 2) some sherds of Beaker pottery but settlement dates mainly to Late Bronze Age		Field 1939; Hawkes 1939
Cuckoo Bottom possible Beaker valley settlement with earthworks and Beaker pottery (Fig. 6.4, chevron no. 7)		Allen 2005
Dean's Farm Piddinghoe Field system (Fig. 6.4, chevron no. 1)		MES 16401
Itford Hill settlement (Fig. 6.4, footprint no. 1) contained some earlier residual Beaker sherds but settlement features not apparent	Itford Hill settlement (Fig. 6.4, footprint no. 1) most features date to this period	Burstow and Holleyman 1957; MES 1212
	Southease Hill Field system (Fig. 6.4, chevron no. 2) broadly dated to the Bronze Age and so placed in the middle of this period	MES 1993
	Itford Down Field system (Fig. 6.4, chevron no. 3)	MES 7167
	Itford – Pooks dyke (Fig. 6.4, chevron no. 4) broadly dated to the Bronze Age and so placed in the middle of this period	MES 1211
Malling Hill, possible Beaker valley settlement with Beaker pottery and field system (Fig. 6.4, chevron no. 6)		Allen 1995
Southerham Grey Pit (Fig. 6.4, chevron no. 5) possible nearby settlement with Beaker sherds found		Allen 1995

TABLE 6.2: SETTLEMENT (FOOTPRINT SYMBOLS IN FIGURE 6.4) OR FIELD SYSTEMS (CHEVRONS IN FIGURE 6.4) IN THE EARLY BRONZE AGE AND MIDDLE BRONZE AGE.

Site or find spot	Source
Barcombe (White Bridge), a small collection of flints dating from the Palaeolithic and later (Fig. 6.4, no. 6)	MES4482
Deans Farm, Piddinghoe, Early Bronze Age pebble mace head (Fig. 6.4, no. 4)	MES 1844
Elms Farm, Isfield, Early Bronze Age flint scatter as well as earlier flints (Fig. 6.4, no. 7)	MES 4477
Isfield- small collection of crude flints found but a wide date range has been given but may include Early Bronze Age flints (Fig. 6.4, no. 8)	MES1198
Lewes – decorated flat axe although earlier, was found with a Late Bronze Age socketed axe, exact spot unknown (Fig. 6.13)	Grinsell 1931, 41; MES 1617
Newhaven, Stud Farm flint scatter of scrapers (Fig. 6.4, no. 1)	MES 1801; Bootle, D.T. and Ford, S. 1981, 206-8
Piddinghoe, Hoddern Farm, barbed and tanged arrowhead (Fig. 6.4, no. 3)	Grinsell 1931, 43
South Heighton, Copper flat axe (Fig. 6.4, no. 2)	Grinsell 1931, 42
Wellingham House Ringmer, Early Bronze Age Flint Adze (Fig. 6.4, no. 5)	MES1900

TABLE 6.3: EARLY BRONZE AGE FIND SPOTS NUMBERED (SQUARES ON FIGURE 6.4)

Site or find spot	Source
Cliffe Hill Barrow (Fig.6.4, no. 9) referred to as a Food Vessel by Ellison (1980, 33)	MES 1602; Musson 1954 no. 250
Cliffe Hill, Lewes – two secondary series Collared Urn burials (Fig. 6.4, no. 8)	Spokes 1932, 651-6; MES 1666; Musson 1954 no. 290 and 341
Cuckoo Bottom – two secondary Collared Urns (Fig. 6.4, no. 13 and Fig. 6.7, nos 3 and 5)	Allen 2005; Curwen 1954, xv, 2 and 3; Musson 1954, no. 300 and 360
Houndean, Lewes – crouched burial with flint and pottery that may have been residual (Fig. 6.4, no. 11)	Woodcock 1983
Itford Hill, Beddingham – five secondary Collared Urns including one large collared urn (Fig. 6.4, no. 4 and Fig. 6.7, no. 1)	Cooper 1879b, 238-9; Longworth 1984, pl. 187, and Musson 1954, no.3 63; MES 1210
Lewes golf course- Primary Collared Urn burial (Fig. 6.4, no. 7)	MES1602; Musson 1954, no. 342
Mount Harry, steers mill next to race-course, Lewes – secondary Collared Urn (Fig. 6.4, no. 12)	Longworth 1984, pl.142; Musson 1954, no. 346; Horsfield 1824, 45; Lower 1852, 199-200
Offham Hill – Later Collared Urn burial? (Fig. 6.4, no. 14)	Drewett 1978, 219-20; MES1509
Oxteddle Bottom, Lewes – two middle to later Collared Urn burials (Fig. 6.4, no. 6) excavated spot unclear	Horsfield 1824, 47-8; Curwen 1954, 157; Grinsell 1931, 66; Musson 1954, no.170 and 353
Round the Down Lewes Barrow (Fig. 6.4, no. 5) Collared Urn sherds found with continuity into later periods	Butler 1995; MES1665; Grinsell 1934, 262
Rodmell Beaker inhumation burial at Heathy Brow, (Fig. 6.4, no. 3) exact spot unclear	Curwen 1932,70-1; Musson 1954, no. 081
South Heighton, Biconical Urn, later Early Bronze Age exact spot unclear (Fig. 6.4, no. 1)	Drewett et al. Gardiner 1988, Musson 1954, no.380; Grinsell 1931, 66
Southease – 5 extended (?) skeletons found in a north-south orientation in a ploughed out barrow next to church. (Fig. 6.4. no. 2) Possibly earlier but unsure.	MES 1997; Lower 1852
Winterbourne, Lewes – two secondary Collared Urns (Fig. 6.7, nos 2 and 4, and Fig. 6.4, no. 10) one referred to as a Food vessel by Ellison (1978, 33)	Curwen 1954, pl. xv, 4 and 5; Musson 1954, no. 260 and 330; Grinsell 1931, 65; MES1658; Ellison 1978, 33

TABLE 6.4: EARLY BRONZE AGE BURIAL SITES IN THE OUSE VALLEY (HEXAGONS ON FIG. 6.4)

Dating of Collared Urns is another problematical area with absolute dates not always possible. The primary urns and secondary series can be attributed to the EBA, as defined by Longworth (1984, 140) and can span the earlier to later periods but usually occur before the Deverel-Rimbury phase but some lie in the transitional period in-between (Seager Thomas 2008, 20). At Lewes golf course an early Collared Urn was recovered and at Cliffe Hill, Lewes (Spokes 1932) there was a secondary series Collared Urn.

Another burial site comes from Offham hill, where the HER recorder states that several bodies were evident, with one which may possibly be an EBA burial. Another vague reference gives an account of a very large urn found at Beddingham (Cooper 1879, 238-9) near Itford. Measuring approximately 55cm high (Figure 6.6, no. 1) this urn was inverted over cremated bones in a pit cut into the solid chalk and within about two metres of this urn were four other smaller urns. These are also likely to have been EBA cremation burials although some of these really need re-dating as the Bronze Age in Sussex has been pushed back in time since a re-assessment of Bronze Age typologies (Barrett 1980).

At South Heighton a grave contained an early bi-conical urn which is likely to date from between 2000–1500 BC (Seager Thomas 2008, 27). This is a very rare form for Sussex and one of only seven known examples in the county. However, the exact find spot is not clear but Musson has drawn this complete pot (1954, no. 380). We have to also bear in mind that not all burials in this period were interred in barrows; Drewett suggests that the norm may well have been for flat graves during the period 3000-1400 BC and so we may have lost the majority of evidence or it may still be awaiting discovery (Drewett et al. 1988, 85).

Another undetermined example comes from Southease where five extended burials were uncovered in a possible

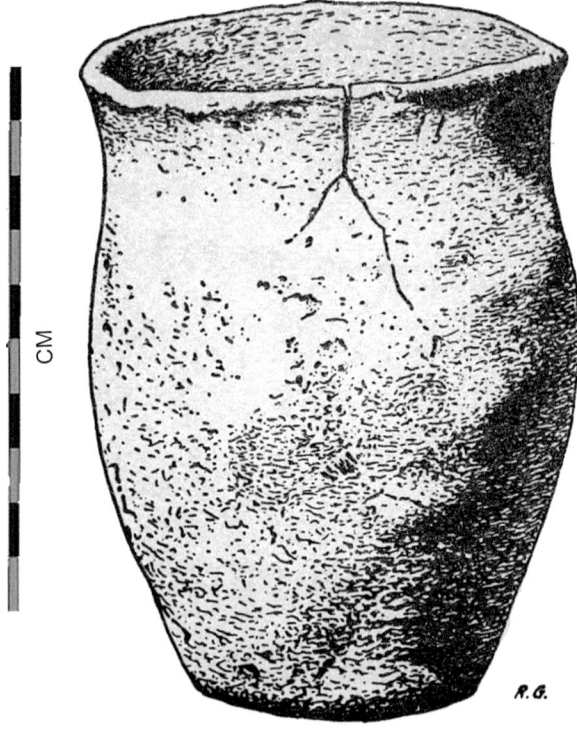

FIGURE 6.5: EARLY BRONZE AGE BEAKER FROM HEATHY BROW, RODMELL (AFTER CURWEN 1932, WITH ADDITION)

ploughed out barrow next to the church, orientated north-south. In more recent years, discoveries have been few and far between. In 1981 a crouched burial was found in Lewes (Woodcock 1983) with some nearby flint artefacts and 'flint gritted' sherds of pottery. However, these were not enough to lead the excavator to believe that they were definitely prehistoric so this should be noted, but it could possibly be an earlier grave site.

The only site excavated to modern standards is at Round-the-Down (Butler 1995). No complete pot was found but sherds were recovered using the type of ceramic technology utilised for making Collared Urns (based on decoration and form), suggesting an EBA construction date. There were subsequent DR and PDR sherds in the secondary ditch fill indicating later activity on site after construction of the barrow and so it has been listed in this paper as belonging to the earlier period.

Finally an earlier grave site worth noting was at Oxteddle Bottom (sometimes referred to as Oxsettle) in Lewes (Horsfield 1824; Curwen 1954). This contained two secondary series collared urns which was a rare occurrence in EBA Sussex as it was a rich grave, containing a necklace made from jet and amber beads and a faience brooch (Figure 6.7). Grave goods from this area are rare but it does not mean to say that they did not exist; it is highly probable that antiquarians participated in their favourite sport of tomb plundering and have possibly removed important artefacts that were associated with the burials.

Middle Bronze Age activity in the Ouse valley (1600-1000 BC)

This period saw more sedentary kinship settlements with agriculture becoming more widespread than in the previous period. Material culture included Deverel Rimbury Urns; huge bucket Urns for cremated remains

FIGURE 6.6: CREMATION URNS FROM THE LEWES AREA (AFTER CURWEN 1954, PLATE 15), 1. ITFORD HILL; 2 AND 4. WINTERBOURNE, LEWES; 3 AND 5. CUCKOO BOTTOM, LEWES, © METHUEN LTD.

6. Bronze Age, a north-south divide

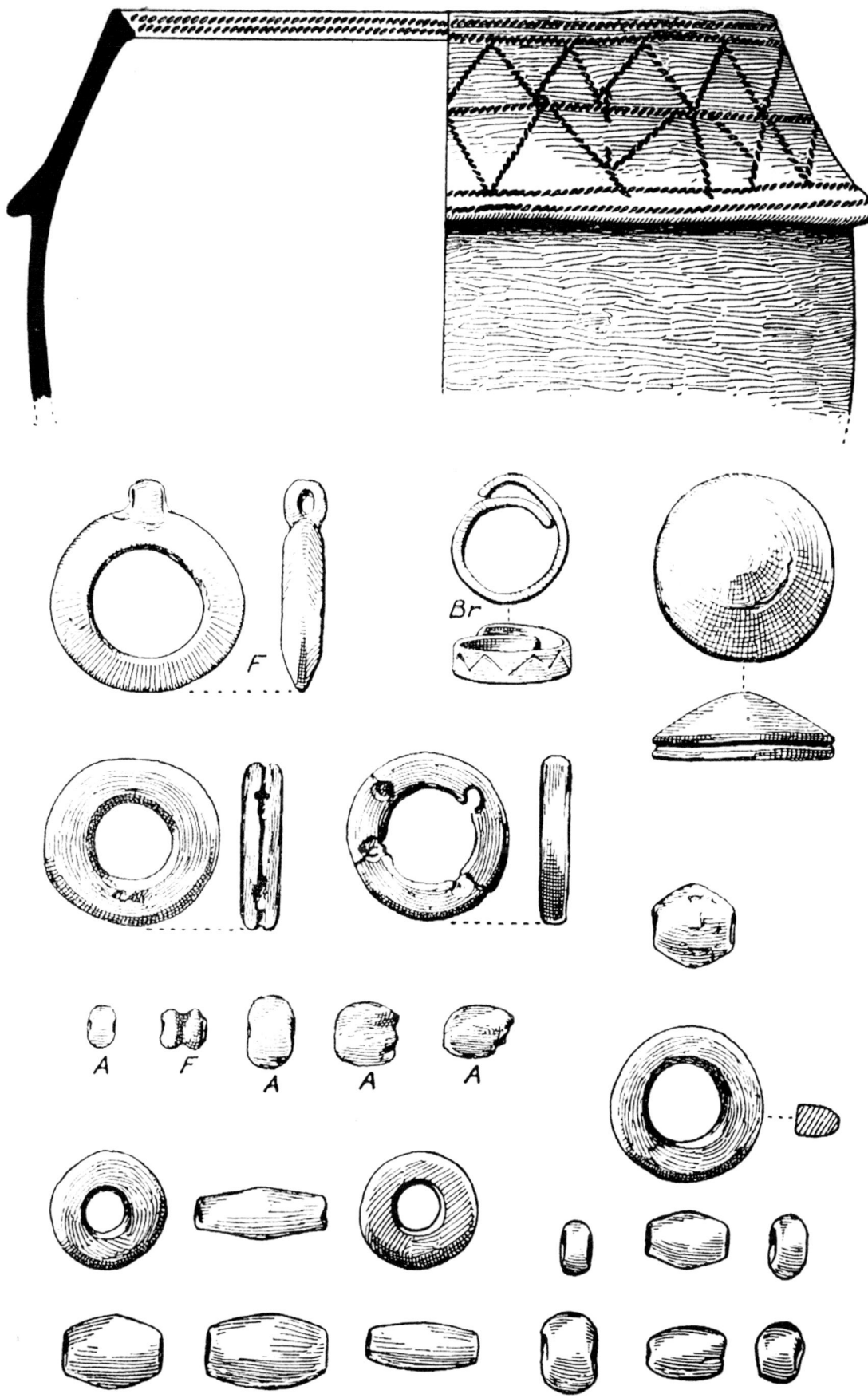

Figure 6.7: Objects from the Oxteddle Bottom barrow, Lewes (from Curwen, 1954, fig. 42), © Methuen Ltd.

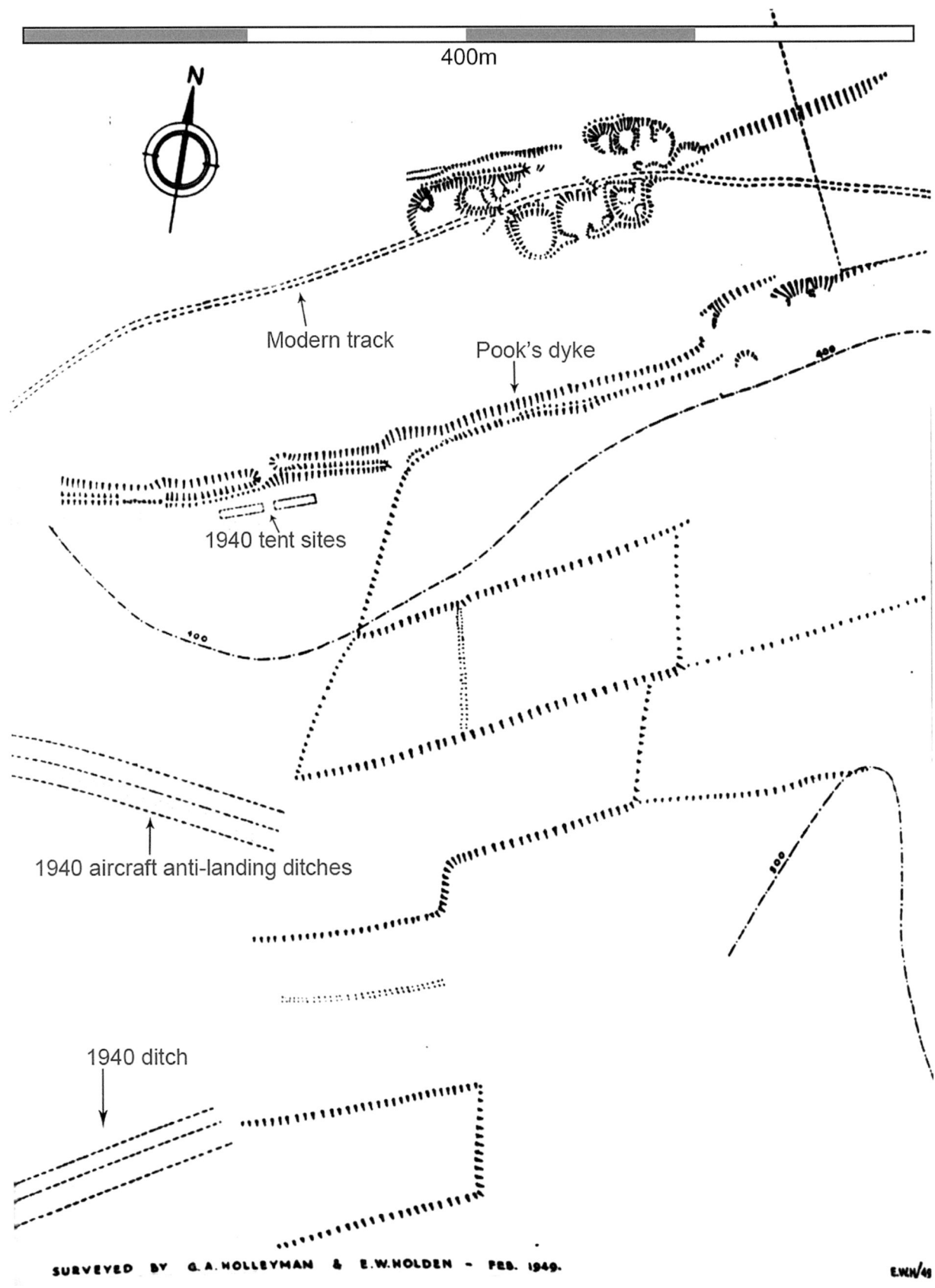

FIGURE 6.8: PLAN OF ITFORD HILL SETTLEMENT WITH PROBABLE ASSOCIATED TRACKWAYS AND FIELD BOUNDARIES (SCALE 400M) (AFTER BURSTOW AND HOLLEYMAN 1957), © CUP, REPRODUCED FROM PROCEEDINGS OF THE PREHISTORIC SOCIETY 23, FIG. 2

sometimes placed in round barrows but increasingly in flat cemeteries. There was a rise in the range of metal goods being produced which were also more skilfully crafted. Hoarding of metalwork became more prevalent during this time. Settlement appeared to lie on the southern facing slopes with Downland burial sites with the weald potentially used for hunting. A more complex social organisation emerged with track way construction and the increased use of field boundaries which led to a more divided landscape.

There are currently less than fifty known settlements for the MBA in Sussex, usually located on south facing slopes of the downs rather than on ridge tops but interestingly with only one firm example at Itford, in the area of study. Evidence that may point to settlement may also lie at Southease (Table 6.2), with a vague reference to a possible Bronze Age field system and another possible site at Castle Hill, Newhaven. Here a rescue excavation produced pottery which was dated (amongst others) to the LBA but also needs re-appraisal as it is fairly evident that some of this assemblage comprises MBA Deverel-Rimbury vessels with some continuity into the LBA and Iron Age (Hawkes 1939). This site is certainly worthy of further investigation but unfortunately the remains of an earthwork which surrounded the hill have all but gone and the rushed excavations produced pottery from the Neolithic to the Roman periods.

It would appear that the only firm evidence for an MBA settlement (Figure 6.4 star and Figure 6.8) comes almost entirely from Itford, to the east of the river between Newhaven and Lewes. The excavations are fairly well known (Burstow and Holleyman 1957). As well as an MBA settlement (previously thought to date to the LBA) there was a cemetery which, after excavation (Holden 1972), was closely associated with the nearby settlement by burial ceramics which closely match those used for domestic purposes within the settlement. It is an important site with few definite Deverel-Rimbury barrow sites found to the east of the Ouse. Radio carbon dates the settlement (from burnt grain) to the end of the MBA to 1300-1010 cal BC (2950±35BP, GrN-6167) and shows sequential development which is associated with earlier Beaker pottery, at least three barrows, a single cremation and a cremation cemetery. This cemetery may only have served one kin unit (Ellison 1978, 36) rather than the settlement as a whole, with the barrows on site providing space for the other kin units. Interestingly, Miles Russell has a theory that the enclosure at Itford is actually a henge (1997, 74-6). However, it is unlikely given the lack of evidence and is not a theory that is held by everyone. Garwood states that it is unlikely and this does highlight an unusual phenomenon in Sussex; the lack of high status henge monuments (2003, 57).

Find spots

Stray finds from the MBA have been located in nine different spots (Table 6.5), with twelve Palstaves, one copper alloy ring plus the recent excavation of a hoard of great significance near Lewes within the Ouse valley. Eight of the Palstaves have been found in or near Lewes with the exception of two at Newick church and two in the southern floodplains near Newhaven (Figure 6.9) and Iford (Figure 6.10). The presence of Palstaves in the Low Weald and lower floodplains may suggest further woodland clearance perhaps for temporary woodland camps. However, more likely is that these could be viewed as ritual deposits; Yates and Bradley (2010, 42) point out that buried metalwork may not have been meant for retrieval at a later date but were possibly an offering from the smith. Furthermore, the finds of metalwork in the Ouse valley have a 'wet' association and are concentrated on small areas of high ground above water sources (*ibid.*, 65) with none found on promontories, dry river valleys or burnt mounds. However, their study did include metalwork from both MBA and LBA and does not differentiate between the two. At present there is not a huge amount of metal recovered from the MBA in the Ouse valley but there is a large amount of MBA metalwork in Sussex as a whole. Is this indicative that metal was simply 'passing through' rather than being produced in the area? There are certainly several continental forms that would partially support such an idea but there are local objects as well.

The recent excavation of the 'near Lewes' hoard is such an example; seventy eight objects were placed in a plain urn dated between 1400-1250 BC (Stephanie Smith, pers. comm.) which adds considerably to our database of trade items with the continent during the MBA. Both local and continental forms were found with French gold discs alongside local objects, such as Sussex Loops and a lozenge shaped pin almost identical to one found in a barrow between Brighton and Lewes (Curwen 1954, 201-2). The Sussex Loops are tightly distributed local artefacts of which thirty examples have been recovered. The majority of these come from Sussex and may be the work of a single craftsman. They are generally found in pairs or groups of three but this new hoard produced five fresh examples. The importance of this hoard cannot be stressed enough and we await full publication with keen anticipation.

Burial sites

For the MBA we have some existing burial sites to the south of the Ouse valley, with scores more barrows on the Downs which were once upstanding that have now sadly disappeared. As discussed above, Leslie Grinsell made records of all existing barrows in Sussex and Figure 6.3 shows an interesting pattern with some clustering around long barrows which has already been discussed

Site of find spot	Source
Barcombe, The Wilderness. Middle Bronze Age fencepost (Fig. 6.4, no. 7)	Allen 2011
Downs near Lewes, Palstaves without loops number not defined (Fig. 6.4, no. 3)	MES 1621
Downs near Lewes, Palstave (Fig.6.4, no. 4)	MES 1629
Lewes, Wallands 3 Palstaves with loops (Fig. 4, no. 5)	Grinsell 1931, 56
Malling Hill, Lewes, Copper alloy spiral ring (Fig. 6.4, no. 6)	MES 6988
Near Lewes, important and recent hoard comprising approx. 50 objects including 4 gold discs, 5 Sussex Loops, 4 torcs, bronze rings and a quoit headed pin in a large ceramic vessel (Fig. 6.4, no. 9)	PAS no. 2011 T192
Newick Church, 2 Palstaves (Fig. 64, no.8)	MES 6904
Newhaven, copper alloy arm ring and quoit headed pin exact spot not clear	Manley and White 1996, 233-5
Newhaven, Lodge Farm Palstave no loop (Fig. 6.4, no. 1)	Grinsell 1931, 48; Curwen 1936b
Sutton Farm Iford, Palstave (Fig. 6.4, no. 2)	MES1524; Grinsell 1931, 56; Cooper 1879a

TABLE 6.5: MIDDLE BRONZE AGE FIND SPOTS NUMBERED (TRIANGLES ON FIGURE 6.4)

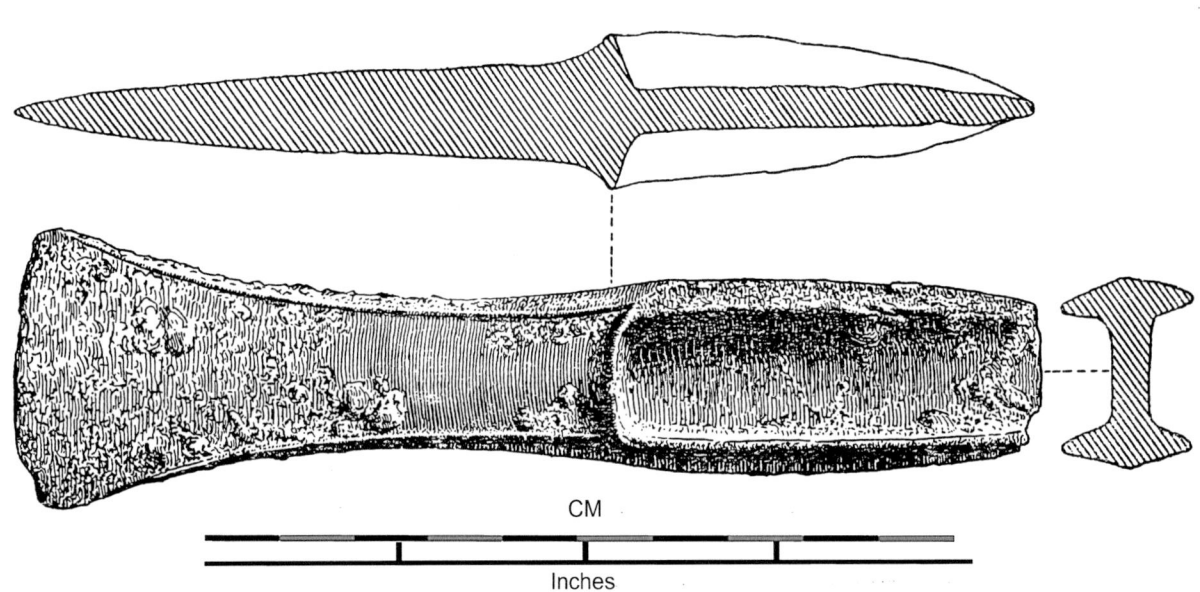

FIGURE 6.9: PALSTAVE FROM LODGE FARM, NEWHAVEN (FROM CURWEN 1936B)

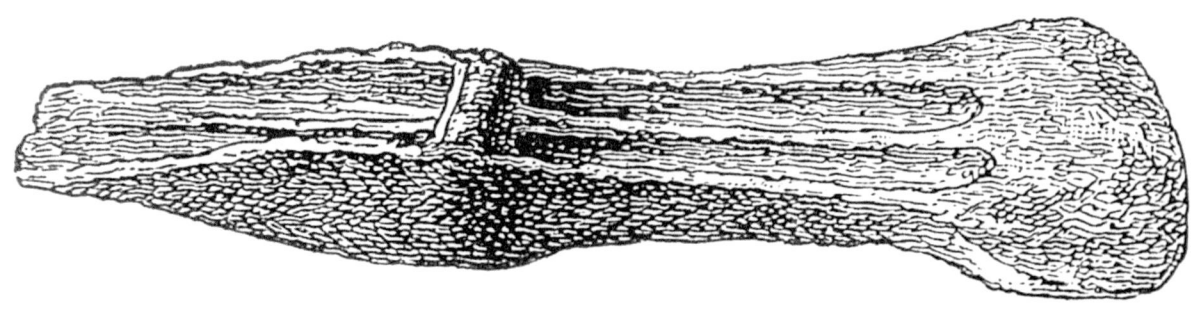

FIGURE 6.10: MIDDLE BRONZE AGE PALSTAVE FROM SUTTON FARM, IFORD (FROM COOPER 1879A)

above. MBA burials often have a concentration of cremation burials centred around one barrow, often radiating out as a flat cemetery within a liminal zone surrounding the main barrow (Drewett 1982). Some records are scant and all examples are condensed in Table 6.6, with some vague references to workmen finding archaeology when 'digging for flints' such as the urns found at Cuckoo Bottom (Anon 1888). This records four urns 'of Celtic make' (Figure 6.6, nos 3 and 5 show earlier vessels) which held cremated remains with one (not illustrated) having a 'row of small projections resembling *mammæ* or teats'. This was originally thought to be LBA in date, but the description and form brings it into the DR tradition in the MBA, with the other three recorded above as being Collared Urns.

Note should be made at this point that although the HER was consulted, several entries were made which are quite probably the same monument which has caused some confusion. Bearing this in mind, I have attempted to condense and separate where likely entries have been doubled up, to the best of my ability.

Curwen writes that there were several other barrows in the vicinity, one at Summersdene, 300m to the south-east of the Heathy Brow barrow (1932, 71). This contained no finds whatsoever and it is not likely that this was robbed previously as a thin layer of charcoal lay over the complete barrow underneath the topsoil, which was not disturbed. On Front Hill, Iford, a bowl barrow (one of a group) was excavated which also contained no diagnostic finds except a layer of charcoal and bone deposited 85cm below the surface. This barrow has no other records and should perhaps be considered as an MBA barrow by typology alone.

In 1986, another possible burial site was discovered in Lewes at Gundreda Road (Allen 1986), although no bones were found and only Iron Age pottery, two ditch profiles were revealed which may well form a ring ditch for a barrow for which a Bronze Age date is postulated, due to a lack of ditched Iron Age barrows in the county. However, Iron Age pottery found therein is cited as being residual from manuring in the area but the size and form of the ditch is similar to that elsewhere and has been compared to the ditch profiles in a barrow from Rottingdean.

North of the Downs in the Ouse valley there are only two excavated MBA burial sites both in Barcombe with two more possible sites at Isfield. At Barcombe, a ring ditch was excavated alongside Iron Age roundhouses which preceded the construction of a Roman villa. Investigations by Chris Butler and the author did not reveal a central burial. This may be due, in part, to the acidic content of the soil possibly destroying the bone; it may also denote a non burial function for the feature as no central pit was present either. MBA pottery was recovered from the site but not *in-situ*. Less than 1km to the north of the Barcombe ring ditch is the site of Pond Field, part of the Culver Farm project. During excavations in 2008 an MBA cremation pit was discovered with burnt bones contained in a fragmented urn which has been dated to the later MBA (Fisher unpubl.). This lies directly next to two parallel ditches running in a north-south direction (Rob Wallace, pers. comm.) which may be contemporary with the cremated remains. However, excavation revealed no other features or finds from the Bronze Age but there is room for interpretation here; cremated remains on the low Weald are an exciting discovery. Add to this the close position of the ring ditch in a nearby field then we could be looking for likely evidence of settlement nearby, perhaps attracted by the river terrace gravels which would give good drainage to crops in this area. Preliminary excavation of an MBA post at Barcombe gives a teasing hint of settlement activity but the full extent of this evidence remains to be seen; it could be a stock control fence or a posthole from a house (Allen 2011).

A barrow is recorded at Isfield (Figure 6.4, circle no. 34) which is logged on the HER database but is of a very dubious nature. Certainly when I set out to investigate the mound (MES4486) it was existing to a height of no more than 50cm (Figure 6.11) and did not look very barrow shaped, lying next to a system of drainage ditches in a wetland area. It is possible that it is a barrow which has suffered from alluvial flooding and consequent erosion or it is possible that it is simply a product of soil dump from ditch clearance. It would be beneficial if further fieldwork at this site would be conducted to determine the nature, age and preservation of this mound.

A second record at Isfield in the HER database marks another likely barrow which cannot be seen from the ground (Figure 6.4, circle no. 33). Having consulted several aerial photographs I would postulate that a ring ditch is visible from the air, alongside some linear marks which appear to be associated field boundaries, trackways and possible round houses and this certainly merits further investigation. In 2007 some evaluation trenches were put in by commercial archaeologists in the vicinity (Dawkes 2007) but unfortunately they did not look at this particular field and it is not possible to date this site at present.

Later Bronze Age activity in the Ouse valley (early 1150-800, late 800-600 BC)

This phase saw an increase in population, the climate grew wetter and cooler and some farmland was eroded, leading to a geographical shift in farming and territorial areas. The Downland soils were newly cultivated and

Barrow	Source
Beddingham Hill barrow (Fig. 64, no.10)	MES 1226; Grinsell 1934, 266
Cliffe Hill 2 bowl barrows (Fig. 6.4, no.18)	MES 1598
Cliffe Hill Lewes 3 barrows (Fig. 6.4, no.17)	MES 1597; Grinsell 1934, 262
Cuckoo Bottom, Lewes (Fig. 6.4, no. 30)	Anon 1888; Musson No.404
Denton, near Newhaven Multiple ring-ditch, date not definite could be earlier. Scheduled Monument 12800 (Fig. 6.4, no. 2)	MES 1797
Offham 2 bowl barrows and site of another (Fig. 6.4, no. 28)	MES 1508; Horsfield 1824, 45.
Hamsey/Offham 2 barrows ploughed out (Fig. 6.4, no. 27)	MES 1507; Grinsell 1934, 261
Hamsey Platform barrow now ploughed out (Fig. 6.4, no. 25)	MES 1487; Grinsell 1934, 261
Offham Platform barrow and two bowl barrows (Fig. 6.4, no. 24)	MES 1603; Grinsell 1934, 261
Itford Hill Bowl barrow (Fig. 6.4, no. 9) cremation cemetery representing at least 16 individuals	MES 1223; Holden 1972
Itford Down Barrow (Fig. 6.4, no. 7) two barrows nearly ploughed out	MES 1224
Itford Hill barrow (Fig. 6.4, no. 8)	MES 7172
Lewes golf course Barrow? (Fig. 6.4, no. 19)	MES 1759
Lewes Saucer barrow and 2 bowl barrows (Fig. 6.4, no. 22)	MES 1679
Lewes by County hall Inhumation, cremations in urns and barrow (Fig. 6.4, no. 13)	MES 1623; Grinsell 1934, 262
Lewes Site of ring two barrows (Fig. 64, no. 23)	MES 1680; Grinsell 1934, 261
Lewes between golf course and bible bottom skull found C14 dates to 1690-1510 BC (Fig. 6.4, no. 12)	MES 7003
Lewes site of six barrows (Fig. 6.4, no.21)	MES 1608
Lodge Hill, Piddinghoe Barrow(s), possibly barrow turned into windmill stead? (Fig. 6.4, no. 3)	MES 1843; Grinsell 1934, 268
Malling Down 2 barrows (Fig. 6.4, no. 16)	MES1601; Grinsell 1934, 262
Malling Hill 2 possible bowl barrows (Fig. 6.4, no. 20)	MES 1600; Grinsell 1934, 262
Offham Hill 2 poss.platform barrows (Fig. 6.4, no. 26)	MES 1510
Plashett Park nr.Isfield, ring ditch (Fig. 6.4, no. 33)	MES 4514
Round the Down, Ranscombe Farm 2 ring ditches situated next to 6 barrows (Fig. 6.4, no. 11)	MES 15425
Southease Hill Barrow (Fig. 6.4, no. 6)	MES 1993
St.John sub Castro, Lewes 2 barrows may have been Bronze Age but not definite? (Fig. 6.4, no. 14)	MES 7175; Bleach 1997
South Heighton Barrow? (Fig. 6.4, no. 5) circular crop mark recorded in 1990	MES 16384
South Heighton Barrow (Fig. 6.4, no. 4) former barrow destroyed by chalk quarrying by caravan park	MES 1952; Grinsell 1934
Tideway School, Newhaven Cremation (Fig. 6.4, no. 1) urned cremation	MES 1807; Bell 1974
Whitehill, Elephant and Castle, Lewes- Barrow possibly re-used as gallows mound? (Fig. 6.4, no. 15)	MES 7177; Bleach 1997
Wallands Park, Lewes. No bones but possible barrow ditch (Fig. 6.4, no. 29)	Allen 1986
Barcombe TQ 418 143 Ring ditch (Fig. 6.4, no. 31)	MES1194
Pond field, Culver cremation pit (Fig. 6.4, no. 32)	Fisher forthcoming
Isfield mound undated (Fig. 6.4, no. 34)	MES4486

TABLE 6.6: PROBABLE MIDDLE BRONZE AGE RECORDED BURIAL SITES AND MOUNDS (CIRCLES ON FIGURE 6.4)

the clearance of the Wealden areas opened up more agriculturally diverse areas above the flood plains. Early pre-hillfort enclosures were constructed on north facing spurs on the downs as defensive positions which gave rise to larger, more territorial 'warrior' kingdoms. Material culture saw further refinements in the range of metal being worked, especially concerning weapons. The larger ceremonial landscapes of the dead were no longer being constructed, in favour of smaller cremation areas.

FIGURE 6.11: POSSIBLE ROUND BARROW IN ISFIELD AT TQ 4420 1823 (PHOTO BY LISA FISHER, SCALES 1M)

The number of LBA downland settlement sites east of the river Adur is lower than those to the west and in the Ouse valley area are virtually non-existent, save one possible site at Itford (see below). This may suggest that the population may have been moving off the Downs and settling in other areas, with prime agricultural land being at a premium (Yates 2007). Evidence also suggests mass woodland clearance by the LBA certainly at Midhurst on the greensands (Scaife 2001, 101) which may have been reflected in other areas of Sussex. This is not clear; a suggestion might be a move to the Wealden area or more to the east in the marshlands, as evidenced at Shinewater (Greatorex 1997/98). However, the close proximity of some LBA hillforts on the northern edge of the Downs, close to the Weald may suggest that an important link was being nurtured (Hamilton and Manley 1997) and future fieldwork needs to make this a priority. Evidence in the ceramic records for the PDR phase show a greater use of Wealden clays, with pisolithic iron oxides in abundance, which are sourced directly from the eastern Weald and do not lie near to the Downs. This may also suggest evidence for the trading of pots for agricultural supplies although further work is needed to prove this. There was an element of continuity of settlement on the coastal plains which was established near to the rich Brickearth in the preceding MBA (Ellison 1978, 36). Drewett (Drewett *et al.* 1988, 117) suggests that after 1400 BC, ceremony and ritual decline and that social cohesion is now linked more to economics and trade development. This is certainly borne out in some excavations, especially at Shinewater, where the material culture shows that such communities took part in a much wider alliance network than in preceding periods (Yates 2007, 57), although this site could be singled out as being special. Certainly the evidence for Wealden forest clearance and the wider use of Wealden clays may support the theory for a wider network of trade and transhumance.

At a recent excavation in Itford (Figure 6.4. triangle no. 4) a horseshoe-shaped gully was found within a shallow hollow which was associated with post and stakeholes but dating was not very secure and is thought to lie somewhere within the Bronze Age (Butler 2009). At a later date an oval, flint feature was formed (consisting of natural flints placed on top of the horseshoe-shaped gully) which had at least four broken Post Deverel-Rimbury pots deposited on top of it. Next to this was an in-situ flint knapping area with some evidence for LBA knapping with a few residual earlier pieces. Fire-cracked flint was also found on this site and it is suggested that there may be a burnt flint mound nearby, close to the river. The pottery did not contain cremations and the feature is not large enough to be a house but could have been a small building of some kind so this site is a bit of a puzzle.

Find spots

All LBA find spots have been condensed in Table 6.7. There is an emergence of hoard deposits in the LBA across the whole country, especially in coastal or river estuaries where water takes on a significant ritual importance (Hamilton 2003, 73). The Ouse valley is not without its own hoards: Newhaven contains a significant hoard, the 'Carpenter's hoard' (Figure 6.12, no. 5) which may suggest a high status coastal settlement with statements being made about disposable wealth. However, the majority of the known settlement area has been eroded from the cliff-top so few features were uncovered although a small rescue excavation was made by Field (1939) during a three year period when workmen were removing flints for building materials. He recovered a large amount of pottery, some of which dated to the LBA and was assessed by Hawkes (1939) which proved to show continuity from the Neolithic through to the Romano-British although there is a lack of MBA ceramics which needs re-appraisal.

The LBA assemblage would certainly benefit from re-investigating and re-dating as a good quantity of sherds were recovered but only six types were illustrated and discussed in detail. This is the only LBA enclosure in Sussex which continues in use into the Middle Iron Age (Hamilton and Manley 1997, 98). What is important is that Hawkes identifies some continental types of pottery similar to those found at Plumpton Plain B, suggesting a West Alpine connection. Also worth noting is that a Palstave dating from the end of the MBA was found at Newhaven (Lodge Farm) as reported (Curwen 1936b, 117; Crawford 1936, 181) as coming from a likely Northern French location which may prove stronger Continental links during this period. Of interest is the lack of evidence for bronze working in the area, save one vague reference by Grinsell (1931, 57) of a founders hoard in Lewes containing socketed axes, Palstaves and thirteen lumps of copper. Some of the metal or metal objects have clearly been brought into the county by boat; a possible sea wreck site at Seaford (Drewett *et al.* 1988, 116) may give tantalising clues for such an

Hoard or find	Source
Berewood Barcombe Mills axe hoard 15 socketed and looped axes (Fig. 6.4, no. 10)	MES1189; Grinsell 1931, p59
The Brooks, Iford Spearhead (Fig. 6.4, no. 5)	MES1521
The Brooks Lewes Spearhead (Fig. 6.4, no. 8) (Fig. 6.12, no. 1)	MES1609; Anon 1856, 286; Curwen 1954; Grinsell 1931, 62
Itford, near river. Late Bronze Age features and PDR ceramics excavated by Chris Butler (Fig. 6.4, no. 4)	Butler 2009
Lewes, socketed spearhead. Exact spot unknown. (Fig. 6.12, no. 3)	Curwen 1954; Grinsell 1931, 62, *SAC*; MES 1633
Lewes, St. Anns bronze ring??Date not clear (Fig. 6.4, no.7)	Grinsell 1931, 63
Lewes, 1 socketed axe found in association with a very early ornamented flanged flat axe. Exact spot unknown	Grinsell 1931, 46,
Lewes, bronze dagger with handle, exact spot unknown	Grinsell 1931, 50; MES 1618
Lewes 'Founders hoard', 7 socketed axes, 5 looped palstaves, 13 lumps of copper exact spot not known	Grinsell 1931, 57
Lewes socketed axe with markings. Exact spot not known.	Grinsell 1931, 60; MES 1572
Lewes (barrow near??), socketed spearhead with rivet holes. Exact spot unknown.(Fig. 6.12, no. 4)	Grinsell 1931, 61; MES 1612
Malling Hill, Late Bronze Age socketed spearhead (Fig. 6.4, no. 9)	MES 6987
Newhaven, south of Foxholes farm pit containing burnt flint, charcoal and Late Bronze Age pottery with associated ditches and bank excavated by MOLAS in 2009 (Fig. 6.4, no. 2)	MES15546
Newhaven, Castle Hill carpenters hoard 2 socketed gouges, socketed axe, tanged chisel, sword-blade parts of socketed knife and awl and Late Bronze Age sherds (Fig. 6.4, no. 1 and Fig. 6.12, no. 5)	Grinsell 1931, 60; Curwen 1954; MES 1794; Musson No. 460b, 470b, 510b
Round-the-Down, Lewes some later flintwork and pottery sherds in secondary ditch fill of Early Bronze Age barrow (Fig. 6.4, hexagon no. 5)	Butler 1995
South Heighton, socketed axe, exact spot unclear (Fig. 6.4, no. 3)	Grinsell 1931, 60
Southerham, bronze awl (Fig. 6.4, no. 6 and Fig. 12, no. 2)	Wallis 1993

TABLE 6.7: LBA HOARDS, POTTERY FINDS AND METAL FIND SPOTS (STARS ON FIGURE 6.4)

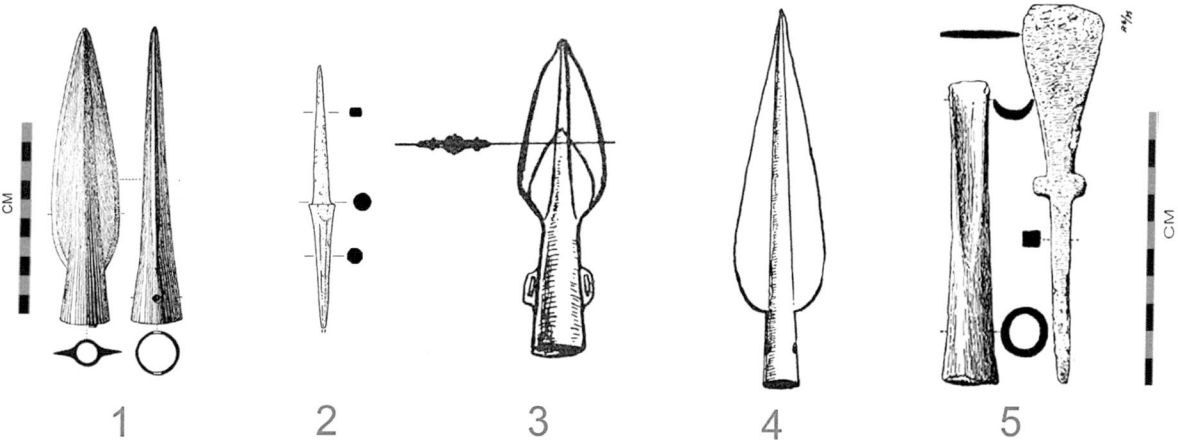

Figure 6.12: Later bronze finds from the Ouse valley (nos 2-4 not to scale). 1. socketed spear from Lewes (after Curwen 1954, fig. 60); 2. bronze awl from Southerham (after Wallis 1993); 3. socketed spear from Lewes (after Grinsell 1931, plate 3); 4. socketed spear with rivet holes from Lewes (after Grinsell 1931, plate 3); 5. 'carpenter's hoard' from Castle Hill, Newhaven (after Curwen 1954, fig. 61); nos 1 and 5, © Methuen Ltd., and nos 2, 3, and 4 by permission of the Sussex Archaeological Society

activity; although a boat was never found bronze objects were dredged up from the seabed. The Shinewater pottery assemblages also included some continental forms derived from the low countries which helps support the theory of greater continental links within Sussex. In addition, exotic metal finds have been found in the same site, notably a North Dutch/German axe (Greatorex 1997/98). So we have a real opening up of the County in the LBA, with some very real evidence of the wide distribution of continental goods and evidence of socio-economic change. New forms and technologies within ceramic traditions give rise to the idea that feasting and communal sharing becomes more prevalent (Barrett 1980) with society going through a radical change. So just where are the settlement sites? This has to be a priority for any future fieldwork.

Other metal finds spots dating from this period are illustrated in Figure 6.12 and include a bronze awl (no. 2) which was found during a metal detector survey in Southerham Farm, Lewes (Wallis 1993). This is an unusual find as only three others are known across Britain. It is thought to be LBA dating from the Ewart Park Phase 2. Probably hafted, it would have been used for piercing leather and may be evidence for domestic activity on the site, or it may simply have been lost in transition.

In Lewes (exact spot not clear) two axes were found, one being an LBA socketed axe but the other a very early and most interesting variant of a transition from a flat axe to a Palstave (Figure 6.13). This flanged axe has very unusual markings incised into the surface but it is not clear whether the two axes were found in the same context or not. This may possibly be evidence of a highly ritualised object which had been kept, apparently unused, for several hundred years before being deposited with a later axe.

At Berewood, Barcombe, a hoard of fifteen axes was recovered (Grinsell 1931, 59). These were socketed axes, placed within ½ km of the river and most likely a ritual deposit. Finally we have a recent discovery of an LBA pit containing pottery amongst other artefacts recovered by commercial archaeologists in Newhaven. This has been reported to the HER database (no. 15546) but would benefit from publication as this only exists as grey literature at present.

Burial sites

One issue that we do have to meet is also the lack of LBA burial sites. This is not just an occurrence in the Ouse valley and not even a county-wide issue but moreover a Country-wide issue. It is a well-known fact that later burial sites are effectively 'missing' from the archaeological record or at their best, rare (Brück 1995, 245). As already mentioned above, it is clear that cultural practices and lifestyles changed in the later period and obviously burial was to take a part in that cultural divergence. It is not that clearly understood but is likely to be due to various factors. During the MBA there was a norm of burial; more often than not a cremated burial placed either as a primary or secondary burial into a pre-existing round barrow with an urn inverted over the top or with the cremated bones placed inside the urn which appears to die out by the beginning of the LBA (Brück 1995, 245).

What we have to realise is that the Bronze Age monument tradition changed over more than a millennia. That is of key importance as not only did the style of barrows change over the centuries but they changed from group to group at various rates and in different ways. It is not simply a case of a ritual disappearing but slowly metamorphosing and perhaps

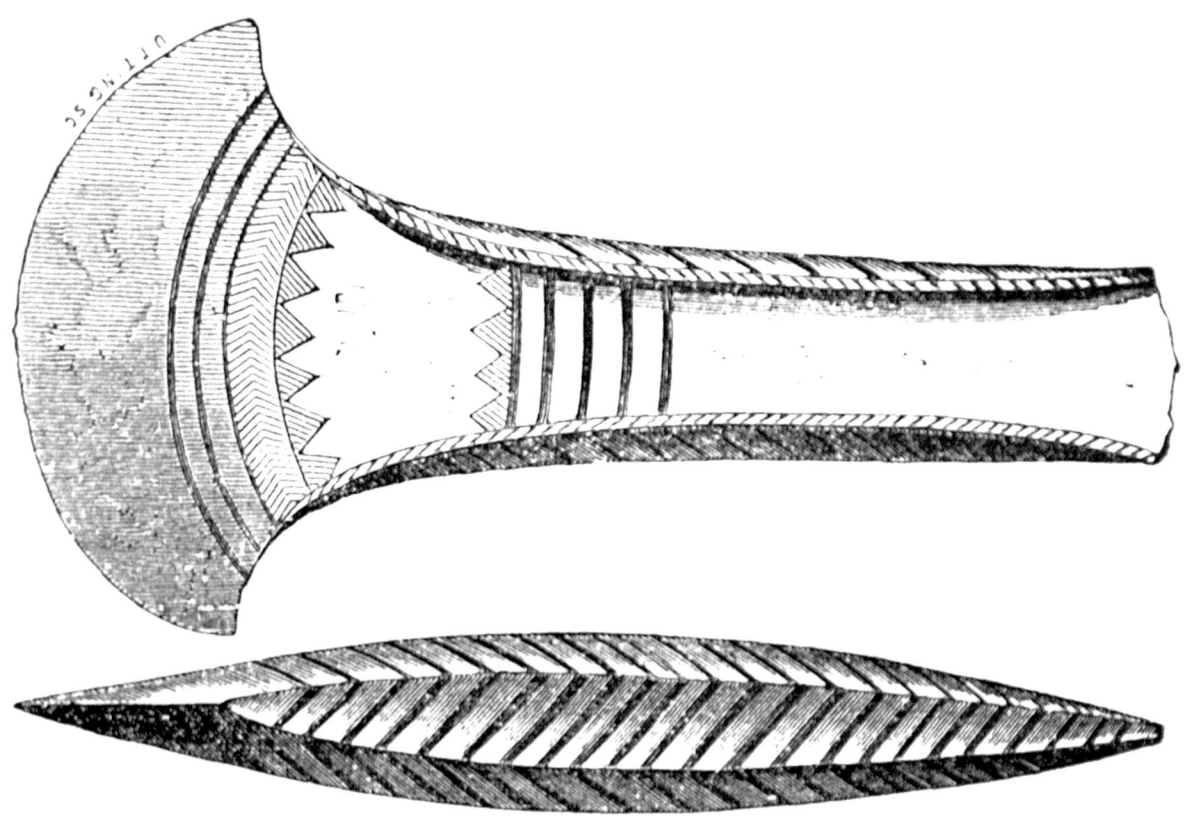

FIGURE 6.13: DECORATED AXE FROM LEWES (FROM SHIFFNER 1856, 286)

not leaving traces in the archaeological record; potentially lying un-discovered. It is possible that bodies were simply placed in the water to decompose; the river must have been of great significance and as the later period gave way to the Iron Age, a tremendous amount of ritual activity was centred around the water. Elsewhere in Sussex, Shinewater gives evidence for votive deposits in the water underneath the trackways (Greatorex 1997/98). This may go some way to support the theory that bodies were placed in the water for burial as at Flag Fen (Pryor and Taylor 1992) and at other Sussex sites there is some evidence that bodies were being buried within the settlement site itself as at Varley halls (Grieg 1997; 2002) and Mile Oak (Russell 2002). At other sites in England some evidence suggests the placement of bones within liminal zones, such as entrances and field boundaries (Ray 1999).

What we do know is that no one model fits all and that in the later period ritual and spatial geographies were changing from community to community and region to region embodying new meanings alongside new ways of disposing of the dead. So we must think, once again, that the lack of sites does not mean that activity was not taking place within the LBA of the Ouse valley.

Discussion and future work

The lack of solid, excavation data from the Ouse valley gives us a very incomplete record. We have several EBA burials but no settlement evidence; we have plenty of MBA barrows but very little firm dating and one settlement; finally we have one or two possible LBA settlements and no burials. Dating the burials that are apparent is a difficult call and has been done on the basis of chronology in the area of study. Only three known radiocarbon dates for the Bronze Age exist in the area of study (Bible Bottom, Lewes; Itford Hill and Barcombe) and only one is for the burial context of a random finding of a skull and so any further attempt at chronology of burials must derive purely from future excavation or typology of both barrows, artefacts and ceramics. Given that there are so few examples to work from and that most of the evidence from early excavations in the Victorian period have been lost, it is difficult to deduce any kind of chronological relationship between the burials in the Ouse valley. Two Bronze Age barrow sites are adjacent to Neolithic long barrows (Piddinghoe and Cliffe Hill) and could be considered as having a tenuous chronology. This is followed by eight MBA barrow sites which cluster in the vicinity of earlier EBA barrows at Southease (?), South Heighton, Itford Hill, Southerham, Cliffe Hill, Houndean, Cuckoo Bottom, and Offham Hill. However, Field (1998, 315) does maintain that is possible to establish some kind of construction order and that barrows were used to define the edges of territories thus forming boundaries between separate communities.

Future fieldwork really needs to address the imbalance of the north-south divide; further excavations need to occur at Barcombe to further understand Bronze Age activity in this area with MBA burials, a post and a later axe hoard. Initial analysis of the pottery by the author shows evidence for transitional manufacturing from Deverel Rimbury to Post Deverel Rimbury traditions and with so few DR as well as PDR assemblages in the area, I must stress again the importance of this site and Isfield, across the river, may also prove to be an area of interest. I also suggest that South Heighton is an area to watch out for; a pure copper axe find and EBA/MBA burial sites, mixed with an intriguing multi-ditched feature and later socketed axes show almost poetical continuity in this area and certainly worthy of further investigation. There is only one MBA settlement discovered in the Ouse valley and one thing is for sure: where there are burials there will be domestic activity and it is only a matter of time before other associated settlements are found. I look forward to the day when I can report the new discovery of a Bronze Age settlement in the Low Weald or near South Heighton.

Acknowledgements

I wish to thank the following people for their help with firming facts and figures and general checking: Chris Butler, Greg Chuter, Peter Drewett, Judie English, Stephanie Smith, Emma O'Connor, Mike Seager Thomas.

References

Allen, M. J. 1986. A possible barrow at Lewes, TQ 40791047. *Sussex Archaeological Collections* 124, 252-3.

Allen, M. J. 1995. The prehistoric land-use and human ecology of the Malling-Caburn Downs; two late Neolithic/Early Bronze Age sites beneath colluvial sequences. *Sussex Archaeological Collections* 133, 19-44.

Allen. M. J. 2005. Beaker and Early Bronze Age activity and a possible Beaker valley entrenchment, in Cuckoo Bottom, near Lewes. *Sussex Archaeological Collections* 143, 35-747.

Allen, M. J. 2011. Prehistoric Wetlands Discovery. A new Middle Bronze Age waterlogged site in Sussex. *Sussex Past and Present* 125, 6-7.

Anon, 1888. Archaeological discovery at Cuckoo Bottom. *Sussex Archaeological Collections* 36, 243.

Barrett, J. 1980. The pottery of the Later Bronze Age in lowland England. *Proceedings of the Prehistoric Society* 46, 297-320.

Bell, M. 1974. Tideway school, Newhaven. *Sussex Archaeological Collections* 112, 158-59.

Bleach, J. 1997. A Romano-British (?) barrow cemetery and the origins of Lewes. *Sussex Archaeological Collections* 135, 131-142.

Bootle, D. T. and Ford, S. 1981. A flint collection from Stud Farm, Newhaven, East Sussex. TQ 462 012. *Sussex Archaeological Collections* 119, 206-8.

Brück, J. 1995. A place for the dead: the role of human remains in Late Bronze Age Britain. *Proceedings of the Prehistoric Society* 61, 245-277.

Burstow, G. P. and Holleyman, G. A. 1957. Late Bronze Age settlement on Itford Hill, Sussex. *Proceedings of the Prehistoric Society* 23, 167-211.

Butler, C. 1995. The excavation of a Bronze Age round barrow at Round-the-Down, near Lewes, East Sussex. *Sussex Archaeological Collections* 133, 7-18.

Butler, C. 2009. An Archaeological Excavation at Itford Farm, Beddingham, East Sussex. Unpubl report, LW/07/0792.

Chuter, G. 2008. River Terrace Gravel Geology (within the Ouse Valley) East Sussex. *Historic Resource Assessment*. East Sussex County Archaeology team.

Cooper, J. 1879a. The Hundred of Swanborough. *Sussex Archaeological Collections* 29, 134.

Cooper, J. 1879b. On some recently discovered Ancient British Urns. *Sussex Archaeological Collections* 29, 238-9.

Crawford, O. G. S. 1936. Palstave found at Newhaven' *Sussex Notes and Queries* 6, 181.

Curwen, E. 1932. On three barrows, in the parishes of Iford and Rodmell. *Sussex Notes and Queries* 4, 70-2.

Curwen, E. 1936a. On Sussex flint arrowheads. *Sussex Archaeological Collections* 77, 15-25.

Curwen, E. 1936b. Recent presentations to the Society Museum, Lewes. Sussex. *Sussex Notes and Queries* 6, 117.

Curwen, E. C. 1954. *The Archaeology of Sussex*. London: Methuen, 2nd edn.

Dawkes, G. 2007. Archaeological trial trenching at Clay Hill, Ringmer, East Sussex. Unpubl report, Archaeology South East, report 2007140.

Drewett, P. (ed.), 1978. *Archaeology in Sussex to AD 1500*. London: CBA Research Report 29.

Drewett, P. 1982. Later Bronze Age downland economy and excavations at Black Patch, East Sussex. *Proceedings of the Prehistoric Society* 48, 321-400.

Drewett, P., Rudling, D. and Gardiner, M. 1988. *The South-East to AD 1000*. London: Longworth.

Ellison, A. 1972. The Bronze Age pottery. In E.W. Holden, Bronze Age cemetery barrow on Itford Hill, Beddingham, Sussex. *Sussex Archaeological Collections* 110, 104-113.

Ellison, A. 1978. The Bronze Age in Sussex, 30-37. In P. Drewett (ed.), *Archaeology in Sussex to AD 1500*. London: CBA Research Report 29.

Field, L. 1939. Castle Hill, Newhaven. *Sussex Archaeological Collections* 80, 263-7.

Field, D. 1998. Round barrows and the harmonious landscape: placing Early Bronze Age burial monuments in south east England. *Oxford Journal of Archaeology* 17, 309-326.

Field, L. F. 1939. Castle Hill, Newhaven. *Sussex Archaeological Collections* 80, 263-273.

Gardiner, M. 1990. The archaeology of the Weald – a survey and review. *Sussex Archaeological Collections* 128, 33-53.

Garwood, P. 2003. Round barrows and funerary traditions in the Late Neolithic and Bronze Age in Sussex. In D. Rudling (ed.), *The Archaeology of Sussex to AD 2000,* 47-68 King's Lynn: Heritage Marketing and Publications.

Greatorex, C. 1997/98. Late Bronze Age waterlogged remains at Willingdon Levels, Sussex. *Archaeology International* 1997/98, 14-15.

Grieg, C. 1997. Excavations at Varley Halls. *Sussex Archaeological Collections* 135, 7-58.

Grieg, I. 2002. Excavations at Varley Hall: a summary. In D. Rudling, *The Archaeology of the Brighton By-pass*, 267-270. London: Archetype Publications.

Grinsell, L. V. 1931. Sussex in the Bronze Age. *Sussex Archaeological Collections* 72, 30-68.

Grinsell, L. 1934. Sussex barrows' *Sussex Archaeological Collections* 75, 216-275.

Hamilton, S. 1984. Earlier first millennium pottery from the excavations at Hollingbury Camp, Sussex, 1967-9. *Sussex Archaeological Collections* 122, 55-61.

Hamilton, S. 2002. The Downsview pottery with specific reference to the Bronze Age assemblage: its forms, dating and regional implications. In Rudling, D. (ed.), *The Archaeology of the Brighton By-pass*, 170-182. London: Archetype Publications.

Hamilton, S. 2003. Sussex not Wessex: a regional perspective on southern Britain c. 1200-200 BC. In Rudling, D., *The Archaeology of Sussex to AD 2000*, 69-88. King's Lynn: Heritage Marketing and Publications, 69-88.

Hamilton, S. and Manley, J. 1997. Points of View: prominent enclosures in 1st millennium BC Sussex. *Sussex Archaeological Collections* 135, 93-112.

Hawkes, C. F. C. 1939. The pottery from Castle Hill, Newhaven. *Sussex Archaeological Collections* 80, 269-273.

Holden, E. W. 1972. A Bronze Age cemetery barrow on Itford Hill, Beddingham, Sussex. *Sussex Archaeological Collections* 110, 70-117.

Horsfield, T. W. 1824. *The History and Antiquities of Lewes and its vicinities*. Lewes: Baxter Press.

Lambrick, G. 1992. Alluvial archaeology of the Holocene in the Upper Thames Basin 1971-1991: a review. In Needham, S.P. and Macklin, M.G. (eds), *Alluvial Archaeology*, 209-226 Oxford: Oxbow monograph 27.

Longworth, I. 1984. *Collared Urns of the Bronze Age in Great Britain and Ireland,* Cambridge: Cambridge University Press.

Lower, M. A. 1852. On Miscellaneous Antiquities, discovered in, and relating to, the County of Sussex. *Sussex Archaeological Collections 5*, 198-206.

Manley, J. and White, S. 1996. A very long quoit-headed pin and a decorated annular arm ring from the Newhaven area, East Sussex. *Sussex Archaeological Collections* 134, 233-5.

Marcigny, C. 2012. History of Transmanche Relations from the Neolthic to the Iron Age. In Lehoërff, A. (ed.), *Beyond the Horizon, Societies of the Channel and North Sea 3500 years ago*, 29-32. Paris: Somogy Art publishers.

Musson, R. C. 1954. An illustrated catalogue of Sussex Beaker and Bronze Age pottery. *Sussex Archaeological Collections* 92, 106-124.

Needham, S, 1996. Chronology and periodisation in the British Bronze Age, in K. Randsborg (ed.), Absolute chronology: archaeological Europe 2500-500 BC, 121-140. *Acta Archaeologica* 67 (supp.1).

Pryor, F. and Taylor, M. 1992. Flag Fen, Fengate, Peterborough II: further definition, techniques and assessment. In B. Coles (ed.), *The Wetland Revolution in Prehistory*, 37-46. Exeter: The Prehistoric Society and Wetland Archaeology Research Project.

Ray, K. 1999. From remote times to the Bronze Age: *c.* 500,000 BC to *c.* 600 BC, p 11-39. In P. Jupp and C. Gittings (eds) *Death in England, an illustrated History*, Manchester University Press.

Russell, M. 1997. The Neolithic chalkland database of Sussex. In Topping, P. (ed.), Neolithic landscapes. *Oxbow monograph* 86, 74-6, Oxford.

Russell, M. 2002. Excavations at Mile Oak farm. In D. Rudling (ed.) *The Archaeology of the Brighton By-pass*, 5-82. London: Archetype Publications.

Scaife, R. 2001. The prehistoric vegetation of Midhurst: a pollen study of New Pond. In J. Magilton and S. Thomas (eds), *Chichester District Archaeology*, 95-102.

Scaife, R. and Burrin, P. 1983. Floodplain development in, and the vegetational history of the Sussex High Weald, and some archaeological implications. *Sussex Archaeological Collections*, 121, 1-10.

Seager Thomas, M. 2008. From potsherds to People: Sussex prehistoric pottery Collared Urns to Post Deverel-Rimbury, *c.* 2000-500 BC. *Sussex Archaeological Collections* 131, 19-51.

Shiffner, H. 1856. Two bronze celts, *Sussex Archaeological Collections* 8, 286

Spokes, S. 1932. A Bronze Age barrow. *Sussex County Magazine* 6, 651-6.

Turner, Rev. E. 1870. Miscellanies. *Sussex Archaeological Collections* 22, 192-4.

Wallis, J. 1993. A Bronze Age Awl from Southerham Farm, Lewes in the Ashmoleum Museum, Oxford. *Sussex Archaeological Collections* 131, 198-9.

Woodcock, A. 1983. A possible prehistoric burial from Houndean, Lewes. *Sussex Archaeological Collections* 121, 202.

Yates, D. 2007. *Land, Power and Prestige: Bronze Age field systems in southern England*. Oxford: Oxbow Books.

Yates, D. and Bradley, R. 2010. The Siting of Metalwork Hoards in the Bronze Age of South-East England. *The Antiquaries Journal*, 90, 41-72.

7. Iron Age

Stuart McGregor

Early in the first millennium BC the landscape of Britain was undergoing intensive agricultural change, with many farmsteads springing up, surrounded by 'Celtic' field systems. Very large, substantially built roundhouses, up to 15m in diameter were being constructed. In southern Britain they usually stood within their enclosed farmyards amid raised granaries, hayracks and underground silos used for storing seed-corn. The Ouse Valley lies within what was once the tribal lands of the 'Atrebates'. The width of the river would have averaged about 500m, much wider than at present (*c.* 5-10m). The change has been brought about by a number of environmental factors, including sea-level variations, coastal erosion and silting (Cunliffe 1973, 5; 1991, 149; 2012, 300). What is becoming clear is that most of the agricultural activity at this time, earlier in the Bronze Age and through to the Medieval period, was confined mainly to the chalk downland areas. This fact is supported by the location of surviving ancient field systems in this part of Sussex.

The area surrounding, and including, the Ouse Valley is often considered to be lacking in evidence for human activity during the period we refer to as the Iron Age (Early, Middle and Late *c.* 800 BC–AD 43), but which some modern scholars prefer to call the late prehistoric period or in this case, Sussex in the first millennium BC (Hamilton and Gregory 2000). The area selected for study stretches from Newhaven on the south coast of England and northwards towards Newick and for a few kilometres east and west. Within this area very few settlements of Iron Age date have been identified illustrating, as in other parts of the country, the fact that archaeological evidence supporting the presence of buildings made of wood and other perishable material during this period can be difficult to locate.

The East Sussex Historic Environment Record (ESHER) on-line database (www.thekeep.info) contains valuable and up-to-date information relating to all known settlement sites and find-spots in East Sussex from all historical periods and provides details of Iron Age sites and artefact finds from within the study area. Another valuable source of information is the *Sussex Archaeological Collections* published annually by the Sussex Archaeological Society. Barbican House, home to Lewes Museum and headquarters of the Sussex Archaeological Society, maintains a useful library of books and journals relating to the history and archaeology of Sussex.

From these diverse sources the known Iron Age settlement sites in the Ouse valley are located at Barcombe, Malling Down, Beddingham, Itford Hill, Rookery Hill, Bishopstone, Norton, Ranscombe Ridge, Glynde, Ringmer, Kingston, and Rodmell. Most of these sites have been discovered using traditional archaeological methods and techniques – desktop study, field walking, remote prospecting (geophysical surveying techniques), aerial reconnaissance and excavation. Some have been discovered during the course of building work or pipe laying operations. Three hill forts have also been identified, Mount Caburn, near Glynde, Castle Hill at Newhaven and Seaford Head (McCarthy and McCarthy 1975). Many modern-day scholars prefer to use the term 'hilltop enclosure' because, in most cases, archaeological investigations seem to suggest that most, including Mount Caburn, contained no buildings and therefore were not defended settlement sites. The Caburn and Castle Hill, Newhaven are of particular interest because of their significant ceramic assemblages, which are both large and span much of the period in question (Hamilton and Gregory 2000). If not hillforts, what were they used for?, animal enclosures?, places for burying structured deposits (as at Caburn), etc.?

Iron Age Settlements

Barcombe

Barcombe Roman Villa at Dunstalls Field was excavated between 2001 and 2007 (Rudling *et al.* 2010). The remains (postholes and gullies) of Late Iron Age/early Romano-British roundhouses have been identified and dated to between AD 40 and AD 150, suggesting that this type of building tradition survived long after the Roman conquest of AD 43.

Beddingham

As at Barcombe, the Romano-British villa site at Beddingham has also revealed traces of possible Late Iron Age activity/occupation. Thus the earliest feature associated with the Romano-British settlement comprises a two-phase timber ring-post structure which has been interpreted as the remains of a round 'house' or possibly a shrine (Rudling 1998, 52). Whilst dating evidence for the first-phase circular structure is lacking, the small fragments of pottery recovered from the second-phase postholes suggest a pre-Flavian but post-conquest date. Of definite Late Iron Age manufacture, however, are two coin finds; one being a bronze issue of Cunobeline and the other a silver issue of Epatticus (i.e. both are early first century AD). In addition, Dr Malcolm Lyne has also identified from the Beddingham site a very abraded sherd from an Augustan Pascual amphora (*ibid.*).

The discoveries of very late Iron Age artefacts and structures at both the Barcombe and Beddingham villa sites indicates that other early Romano-British villas may also have been located on or near pre-Conquest native farmsteads. Near the Beddingham villa site, at The Furlongs (TQ 4533 0704), a large spread of flint-tempered Iron Age pottery sherds was discovered in 2005, together with Roman pottery fragments, brooches and coins, thus indicating the presence of another multi-period settlement site (ESHER MES7264)

Ranscombe Ridge, Glynde

Ranscombe Ridge forms a narrow saddle of land between Mount Caburn and downland to the west (Figure 7.1). The ridge is separated from Caburn hill by a linear bank (which was probably revetted) and a parallel ditch. This earthwork contains a single entrance. Pottery from the lower fills of the ditch suggests that the feature was constructed during the early part of the first millennium BC. Excavations also produced worked flint, fire-cracked flint and pottery sherds dating to the Middle Iron Age. These earthworks were originally described as the bank and ditch of an unfinished settlement enclosure or hill fort (Burstow and Holleyman 1964, 55). However, it is more likely that the monument belongs to a category of land boundaries known as cross-ridge dykes (Drewett and Hamilton 1999, 15). In 1989 a gold Iron Age coin (a Gallo-Belgic 'E' stater dating to *c.* 50 BC) was found in a field to the north of Ranscombe Farm (Rudling 1992).

Ringmer

In 2007 field walking, a geophysical survey and evaluation excavation carried out on the proposed site of a reservoir at Plashets Park Farm identified a large concentration of gullies, pits and other features, which may suggest that a settlement existed at this location in the Late Iron Age. At Mill Plain, archaeological works associated with the installation of the wind turbine uncovered three pits containing Late Bronze Age and Early Iron Age pottery fragments (ESHER MES8481).

Malling Down

On the southern slopes of Malling Hill is a series of lynchets surviving to a height of about two metres indicating the remains of a 'Celtic' field system. Many artefacts have been recovered from this area suggesting continuous use from the Prehistoric to Medieval periods and the possibility of lost settlement sites in the near vicinity. Aerial photography has provided evidence for earthwork enclosures located within the field system.

FIGURE 7.1: MOUNT CABURN AND RANSCOMBE RIDGE FROM THE SOUTHEAST (PHOTO: STUART MCGREGOR)

Itford Hill

Pook's Dyke (TQ 4438 0509) on Itford Hill is another cross-ridge dyke. It consists of a large earthwork at the edge of steep slopes above a dry coombe. The bank is 7m wide and 1m high and the accompanying ditch is 6m wide and 1m deep where best preserved. The monument appears to relate to a large field system to the south and a Bronze Age settlement to the north (ESHER MES1211).

Kingston

An enclosure earthwork situated on Castle Hill near Kingston, is thought to be of Iron Age date.

Rodmell

The remains of a Late Iron Age and Romano-British settlement consisting of a trackway and roundhouses, indicated by circular depressions, can be found at Rodmell. The site, which is located on Highdole Hill and surrounded by an Iron Age field system, was partially excavated by Holleyman and Wilson in 1934 (Holleyman 1936). Four complete 'La Tene' cinerary urns containing burnt human bones were discovered at a chalk quarry at Asheham (or Asham), near Rodmell (Curwen and Curwen 1930). The urns had been buried in a row beneath a large positive lynchet, with their bases 'standing on the surface of the undisturbed chalk' (*ibid*. 255). The discovery of two finely carved bone hairpins of Roman type in one of the urns suggests that these burials may date to after the Conquest in AD 43. The importance of this discovery is that it indicates one type of location, a field bank, where we might find Late Iron Age/early Romano-British cremation burials, such discoveries being fairly rare in Sussex.

Peacehaven

To the east of Peacehaven is a large concentration of Iron Age sites and features, which may be contemporary with the settlement site at Castle Hill, Newhaven.

Bishopstone, Rookery Hill and Norton

There have been very few large scale excavations of Iron Age sites within the study area during recent years, the main one taking place at Rookery Hill, Bishopstone, just to the east of the port of Newhaven and north-west of Seaford. The results of the excavation indicated that an economy based on mixed farming was in existence. The arable influence is indicated by the presence of fields contemporary with the settlement, and by the discovery of grain, often charred, in pits and other features. The dominant cereal remains were those of spelt, followed by barley (Arthur, J. R. B., in Bell 1977, 273-5). Artefacts such as iron ploughshares, sickles for reaping, and quern stones for grinding grain have also been found. Additionally, cross-plough marks cut into the chalk subsoil were found sealed by a Late Iron Age context (Bell 1977, 252-7). The pastoral element in the economy is well attested to by the presence of animal bones, those of cattle and sheep occurring most frequently. Sheep may also have been kept for wool, and perhaps milk; certainly, spindle whorls and loom weights of baked clay or chalk are among the most common of finds on Iron Age sites, indicating the importance of spinning and weaving. Bone weaving combs are also known. There is evidence that Rookery Hill was occupied over a very long period of time. Several round barrows dating from the Bronze Age can still be seen on top of the hill. A ditch 2.4m wide and 1.2m deep, which enclosed the Iron Age settlements on the hill, was probably constructed before 500 BC. There was also an interior bank, which was levelled in the Late Iron Age and early Romano-British periods.

Another site that has recently been investigated deserves mention. This was an excavation that took place at Norton in the Bishopstone Valley, and which produced much material of Iron Age date, including, pottery sherds, metalwork, coins and a rare inhumation burial of a woman aged between 30 and 40 years. There was also evidence for a hearth and a stove at the site indicating some kind of a structure, or structures. Animal bone and marine molluscs were also present. It has long been known that the Bishopstone valley was occupied during the Iron Age with significant finds being made on Rookery Hill (see above) and at Bishopstone village (Thomas 2005). Sea levels at this time are thought to have been considerably higher than they are today. This would have resulted in this area being close to the banks of the River Ouse estuary where seafood and salt could have been obtained. Excavations in 1975 produced evidence of pottery making, weaving, farming and salt production (McCarthy and McCarthy 1975).

Wealden Iron

Iron extraction and working was taking place in the Weald as well as some farming at this time. The excess produce from these industries would no doubt have been transported to other areas by sea or northwards along the River Ouse. Perhaps trackways were used to a certain extent, but the river systems must have played a significant part in the transportation of humans and goods. The Culver Archaeological Project near Barcombe has recently identified a Roman road leading to a major settlement on the banks of the Ouse (see Rudling, Chapter 8). Many coins of Roman Imperial date and earlier have already been discovered at the site and excavations in future years will, no doubt, establish a chronology for the settlement. As with many sites throughout Britain, this one may prove to have enjoyed a long existence spanning hundreds of years.

Iron Age Hill Forts

Mount Caburn

The word Caburn may derive from the Welsh *caer bryn*, meaning 'the stronghold hill' (Glover 1997). It is more likely though, that the name derives from the old English *calde burgh*, which means cold fort. Mount Caburn is situated on the peak of an isolated hill and ridge (Ranscombe Ridge) to the south east of the town of Lewes and to the west of Glynde (Figure 7.2).

It overlooks the Ouse Valley and has been of interest to antiquarians since at least 1877, when Major General Augustus Lane Fox (later Pitt-Rivers) conducted excavations within the ramparts (Lane Fox 1881). Further excavations followed in the 1920s (Curwen and Curwen 1927) and 1930s (Wilson 1938; Hawkes 1939), the first being in 1922-6 and 1937-8 by Eliot Curwen and his son Eliot Cecil Curwen, with George Burstow and by Dr A. E. Wilson who continued in 1938 (Wilson 1937; 1938). These excavations are also discussed by Eliot Cecil Curwen in his book *The Archaeology of Sussex* (Curwen, Eliot C. 1937).

The earliest settlement was probably enclosed by a palisade enclosure. Pottery found at Mount Caburn provides the main evidence for dating the site's use from the Late Bronze Age through to the Iron Age (Drewett and Hamilton 1999). The enclosure's interior contains about 170 slight depressions, about 6m across. Excavations in the early part of the twentieth century, and more recently, have shown that most are pits of Iron Age date. The domed nature of the hilltop, which is encircled by a series of banks and ditches, constructed in phases, raises the question of functionality. The traditional interpretation of the earliest hill fort, built in about 400 BC, is of a defended settlement engaged in farming practises, based on finds which include plough shares, bill hooks, spindle whorls and loom weights (Drewett and Hamilton 1999). However, when you view the hilltop from a distance, it is immediately obvious that the area enclosed by the banks and ditches is very exposed. It is also obvious that from a distance it would have been possible to view what went on inside the earthworks. Hamilton (1998, 38) concluded that the pits within the enclosure were used for the intensive structured deposition of a wide range of Late Iron Age material culture and other finds. The enclosure on Mount Caburn, therefore, appears not to have been made as a 'defensive hill fort', but perhaps for some other reason or reasons, including possible ritual practices.

Other possibilities exist, however, and geophysical surveys conducted at a number of hilltop enclosures in Britain reveal that the interiors of many are largely devoid of major features. This might suggest, together

FIGURE 7.2: AERIAL PHOTOGRAPH OF MOUNT CABURN WITH LEWES IN THE FOREGROUND (PHOTO: STUART MCGREGOR)

with other evidence, that they may have been designed to contain animals at certain times throughout the year (Hamilton 2003, 76). However, the fact remains, that a structure like this crowning a steep hill would offer, at least, some protection to those seeking safety during periods of aggression. The recovery of 12 Type 1 potin coins of c. 100-50 BC from within the prehistoric enclosure may indicate that at the time the site was associated with social groups in north Kent and the Thames estuary (Rudling 1999, 29). Another Iron Age period coin, a bronze issue, was found in 1926 in a mole hill about 50 metres north of the Caburn. It was identified by the British Museum as being Carthaginian (c. 200 BC) and is a rare example of such coinage found in Britain (Spokes 1927). The only other recorded Carthaginian coin discovered in Sussex is an unstratified example found in 1983 near Fishbourne Roman Palace (Rudling 2003, 101).

Castle Hill, Newhaven

Castle Hill, which is situated only a few hundred metres to the west of the Roman-period and modern mouths of the River Ouse and overlooks the English channel, is the site of an Iron Age 'hill fort' which has been almost entirely destroyed by coastal erosion during the last two thousand years (Figure 7.3). Finds recovered from the site during the last 10 years include numerous Iron Age pottery sherds and coins (ESHER MES1794).

Seaford Head

The site at Seaford Head consists of a now triangular shaped enclosure surrounded by a raised dump bank and adjacent ditch. Minimal dating evidence exists, but the hill fort was constructed during the first millennium BC (Bedwin 1986).

Aerial Survey for Archaeology

Late prehistoric sites and structures are notoriously difficult to locate with the techniques currently available to archaeologists. The Light Detection and Ranging (LiDAR) System, however, is a relatively new airborne technique for detecting and locating ground features hidden within the landscape. It uses pulsed laser beams that are capable of penetrating dense tree and plant cover and will also detect slight changes in land surface heights that can reveal otherwise invisible earthworks. English Heritage is responsible for the National Mapping Programme, which provides standard procedures for mapping and recording archaeological sites and landscapes from aerial photography and LiDAR (English Heritage 2010).

Discussion and future work

So, where are we? Temporally, we are in the Iron Age (traditionally 800 BC–AD 43 in Britain). Britain is now

FIGURE 7.3. AERIAL PHOTOGRAPH OF THE MOUTH OF THE RIVER OUSE WITH CASTLE HILL IN THE BOTTOM LEFT CORNER (PHOTO: STUART MCGREGOR)

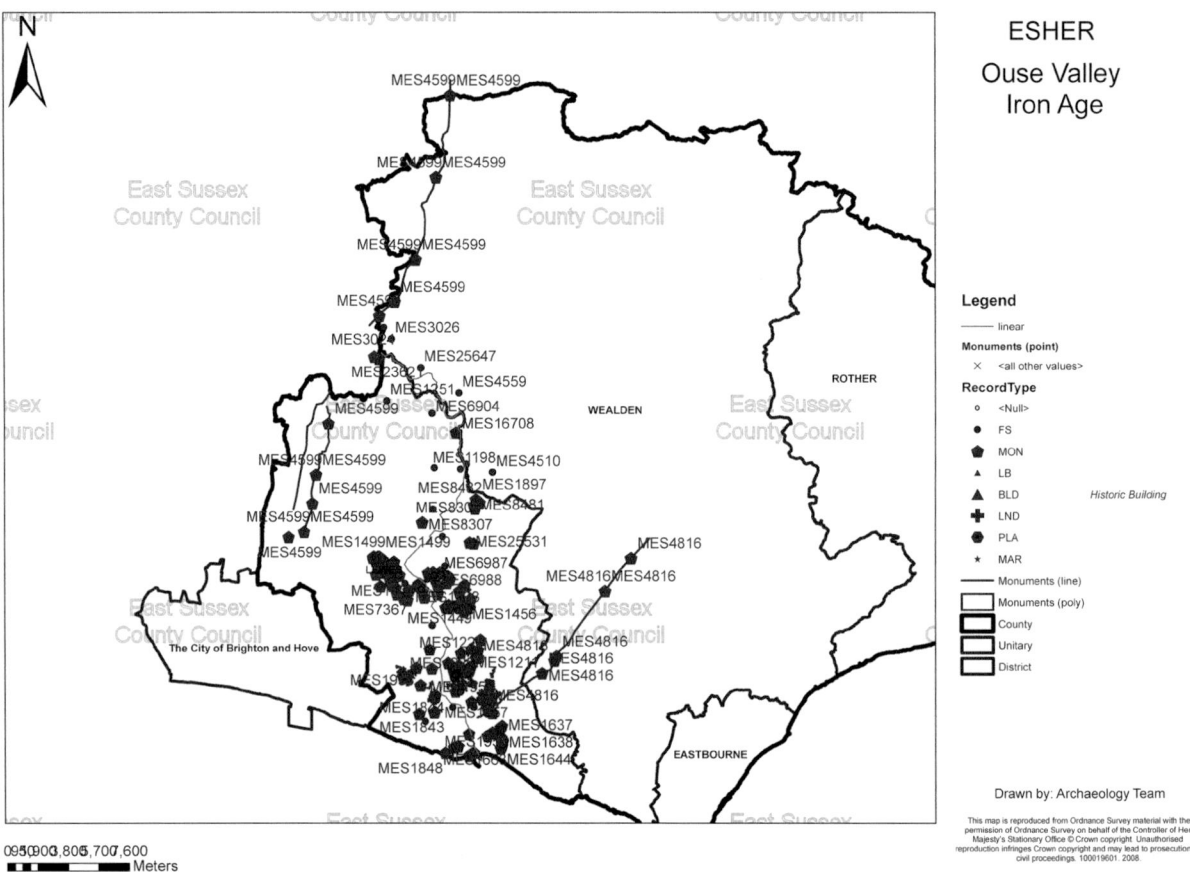

FIGURE 7.4: ESHER MAP (REPRODUCED COURTESY OF THE EAST SUSSEX HISTORIC ENVIRONMENT RECORD)

an island after the release of a titanic flood of water from a lake in North America, thousands of years previously at the end of the last Ice Age, which, in time, submerged the area we call Doggerland. The city-state of Rome has been founded (753 BC) and by about 200 BC its empire is expanding rapidly throughout the Mediterranean area and later northwards towards Gaul and Germania. In 55 and 54 BC Julius Caesar crossed the sea channel that now separates Britain from the rest of Europe, but was never to return. There is plenty of evidence for trade and contact between the peoples of the Mediterranean and coastal Britain prior to the Claudian invasion of AD 43 (Davenport 2003, 103).

Geographically, we are in the lower reaches of the Ouse valley (in East Sussex) visiting the land of Late Iron Age people probably associated with the Atrebates tribe. The Ouse itself was much larger than the relatively modest river we see today. It has been estimated that the average width was about 500m at this time and that the sea level was 4m higher than it is today. If you look at the Ordnance Survey Explorer map 122, and trace the 5m contour line from Seaford Head and Newhaven, and then north towards Newick, you will get some idea of the scale of the river two thousand years or more ago. It is almost impossible to say exactly where the coastline or rivers edge were at any stage in the ancient past, because coastal erosion, silting and the activities of humans have drastically modified the landscape, but we can attempt to visualise the scene with the evidence we have to hand.

Imagine sailing towards the mouth of the Ouse from the south during the Iron Age. You would see a wide river mouth with a defended settlement on the cliff top at Newhaven and another prehistoric enclosure at Seaford Head. The settlements at Norton Hill and Bishopstone would be accessible by sea. Having entered the river estuary, sail north along the valley between the great hills of the South Downs, rising to over 100m on either side and topped by ancient burial mounds, farmsteads and field systems, before entering a large natural water basin containing two islands, and overlooked by the impressive but fairly small Caburn hill-top enclosure. The basin is fed by two much narrower rivers, one from the east and the other from the north. It is tempting to imagine that the landscape was full of wooden structures, and that the riverside was a hive of activity with small fishing settlements, now long disappeared. Further north the small-scale production of iron, which in the Roman period became a major industry.

Identifying the places where these structures once were is proving difficult because wooden structures leave little, or no trace, in the ground. Most are discovered by accident when new roads, housing estates, car parks and other developments require the removal of topsoil. The traditional methods used by archaeologists, geophysical and aerial survey, fieldwalking, research and excavation to detect archaeological sites continue, however, to provide positive results. The development of the Portable Antiquities Scheme has also proved very useful, especially with regards to Late Iron Age coinage. Continued use of LiDAR to detect ground disturbance is also an exciting development and should prove fruitful in helping to expand our knowledge of Iron Age settlement and land-use within the Ouse valley.

Acknowledgements

My thanks go to Sophie Unger for providing all the material from the ESHER database, and David Rudling who read and commented on a draft of this chapter. David also provided additional information which has been incorporated into the current text, and Mike Allen assisted in its final production.

References

Bedwin, O. R. 1986. Excavations at Seaford Head, East Sussex 1983, *Sussex Archaeological Collections* 124, 25-33.

Bell, M. 1977. Excavations at Bishopstone. *Sussex Archaeological Collections* 115, 1–229.

Burstow, G. P. and Holleyman, G. A. 1964. Excavations at Ranscombe Camp 1959-1960, *Sussex Archaeological Collections* 102, 55-67.

Cunliffe, B. 1973. *The Regni: Peoples of Roman Britain.* London: Duckworth.

Cunliffe, B. 1991. *Iron Age Communities in Britain.* London: Routledge.

Cunliffe, B. 2012. *Britain Begins.* Oxford: Oxford University Press.

Curwen, E. and Curwen, E. C. 1927. Excavations in the Caburn, near Lewes, *Sussex Archaeological Collections* 68, 1-56.

Curwen, E. and Curwen, E.C. 1930. Lynchet burials near Lewes, *Sussex Archaeological Collections* 71, 254-57.

Curwen, E.C. 1937. *The Archaeology of Sussex.* 1st edn. London: Methuen.

Davenport, C. 2003. The late Pre-Roman Iron Age of the West Sussex Coastal Plain: continuity or change? In D. Rudling (ed.), *The Archaeology of Sussex to AD 2000*, Great Dunham: Heritage Marketing and Publications, 89-110.

Drewett, P. and Hamilton, S. 1999. Marking Time and Making Space: excavations and landscape studies at the Caburn hillfort, East Sussex 1996 – 98, *Sussex Archaeological Collections* 137, 7-37.

English Heritage 2010. The Light Fantastic – Using airborne LiDAR in archaeological survey. East Sussex Historical Environment Report, June 2015.

Glover, J. 1997. *Sussex Place Names.* Newbury: Countryside Books.

Hamilton, S. 1998. Using elderly data bases: Iron Age pit deposits at the Caburn, East Sussex and related sites, *Sussex Archaeological Collections* 136, 23-39.

Hamilton, S. 2003. Sussex not Wessex: a regional perspective on Southern Britain *c.* 1200-200BC. In D. Rudling (ed.), *The Archaeology of Sussex to AD 2000*, Great Dunham: Heritage Marketing and Publications, 69-88.

Hamilton, S. and Gregory, K. 2000. Updating the Sussex Iron Age, *Sussex Archaeological Collections* 138, 57-74.

Hawkes, C. F. C. 1939. The Caburn pottery and its implications, *Sussex Archaeological Collections* 80, 217-62.

Holleyman, G.A. 1936. An early British agricultural village site on Highdole Hill, near Telscombe, *Sussex Archaeological Collections* 77, 202-221.

Lane-Fox, A. H. 1881. Excavations at Mount Caburn Camp near Lewes, *Archaeologia* 46, 423-95.

McCarthy, E. and McCarthy, M. 1975. *Sussex River – journeys along the banks of the River Ouse (Seaford to Newhaven).* Seaford: Lindle Organisation Ltd.

Rudling, D. 1992. An Iron Age gold coin from South Malling, *Sussex Archaeological Collections* 130, 238.

Rudling, D. 1998. The development of Roman villas in Sussex, *Sussex Archaeological Collections* 136, 41-65.

Rudling, D. 1999. Pits and potin coins: a report on a new potin coin find from the Caburn, in P. Drewett and S. Hamilton 1999, 28-29.

Rudling, D. 2003. The Coin Finds from Fishbourne, 1961-1999, in J. Manley and D. Rudkin, Facing the Palace, excavations in front of the roman Palace at Fishbourne (Sussex, UK) 1995-99, Sussex Archaeological Collections 141, 99-103.

Rudling, D., Butler, C. and Wallace, R. 2010. Barcombe Roman Villa, *British Archaeology* 111, 23-27.

Spokes, S. 1927. Discovery of a Carthaginian coin near the Caburn, *Sussex Archaeological Collections* 68, 57-59.

Thomas, M. S. 2005. Understanding Iron Age Norton, *Sussex Archaeological Collections* 143, 85-115.

Wilson, A. E. 1938. Excavations in the ramparts and gateway of the Caburn, August-October, 1937, *Sussex Archaeological Collections* 79, 169-94.

Wilson, A. E. 1939. Excavations in Caburn, 1938, *Sussex Archaeological Collections* 80, 193-213.

8. Impact of Rome

David Rudling

This review of the main Romano-British remains that have been discovered in the Sussex Ouse valley provides a micro-study of settlement types, land-use, and changes over time at the eastern end of the territory of the *Regni*, a tribal grouping with its *civitas* capital at Chichester. Some settlements on the adjacent Downs show considerable elements of continuity, with the probability at Bishopstone of continuous occupation from the Late Iron Age and the possibility of unbroken continuity into the Early Saxon period. Elsewhere several of the villa settlements, such as those at Barcombe and at Beddingham, developed from more humble origins on sites established just before or soon after the Roman Conquest. None of the villas, however, were still flourishing by the end of the 4th century, by which time occupation, if it continued at all, was fairly minimal. Occupation at more nucleated settlements, such as those at Bridge Farm or Seaford, may also have ended or declined by the end of the 4th century. The presence and ultimate loss of the iron-working establishments at the northern end of the valley may have had a major impact on many of the settlements to the south, which had probably previously relied upon the iron-works as markets for their agricultural produce and other goods and services. Indeed, some of the villa-owners may have been directly involved in the iron industry (Best 2015). The apparent ending of villas and various other types of site in the valley before the end of the 4th century is considered alongside the evidence for Early Saxon occupation and burials.

The arrival of the Romans in South-East Britain in AD 43 resulted in dramatic changes to the social and economic environments, and these changes together with major developments in technology make the Roman occupation of Britain one of the most distinctive and dynamic periods in our history. For most of the last century archaeologists used Haverfield's (1912) concept of 'Romanisation', coming from a background of nationalism and imperialism, to explain the introduction to, and local adoption of, various elements of 'Roman culture' in this island. In more recent years, however, there has been a widespread questioning of the usefulness of the concept of 'Romanisation' and the development of various new theoretical approaches (Gardner 2013). Significantly, there has been a shift by many scholars in terms of viewing the archaeological record from the perspective of the indigenous Britons, rather than that of the 'invaders'/colonisers, and an asking of 'How Roman was Roman Britain?'. Thus many archaeologists today are interested in assessing the impact of Rome, rather than simply regarding Britain as a colony of Rome (Rudling 2015). In addition, researchers are increasingly looking for local variability of cultural practices and of social identities, both within the province of *Britannia* generally, but also with respect to tribal sub-divisions such as the individual *civitates*. At a more local level micro-studies of smaller areas, such as the Sussex Ouse river valley, enable comparisons to be made between sites of various types in a defined area and for the results of such studies to then be compared with either those derived from other micro-studies or significantly larger but less intense projects.

During the last 40 years the Sussex Ouse valley has been the location of a large number of archaeological investigations of Roman-period rural settlements: farmsteads, villas, more nucleated communities, as well as field-systems, iron-works, and other features of Romano-British landscapes, such as roads. The published results of such work will be reviewed in order to consider the impact of Rome after AD 43, as well as to investigate aspects of continuity or discontinuity of settlement in the valley during the Roman and sub-Roman periods.

The Ouse valley

The Ouse valley as defined here consists of the water catchment areas adjacent to the Ouse and its tributaries (Figure 8.1). Although most of the Ouse valley follows a roughly north-south route in East Sussex, cutting through the South Downs at Lewes, it originates to the north-west, at Slaugham in West Sussex. At Isfield a major tributary, the Uck, branches off to the north-east. Other significant tributaries include Glynde Reach which flows from the north-east through a gap in the Downs between Mount Caburn and Beddingham Hill to the south, and the Bevern Stream, a branch to the west of the Ouse which is fed by streams which flow near a villa at Plumpton (some 7km to the west of the Ouse) and also a pottery production site at Chiltington. The main north-south stretch of the Ouse provides a transect across the main geological zones of East Sussex, starting in the south with the chalk Downs and progressing northwards across the Gault Clay, the Lower Greensand, the Weald Clay and the Tunbridge Wells Sand. During the medieval period the river joined the sea at Seaford, but today joins it at Newhaven via a humanly created channel (Figure 11.6; Robinson 1999, 9; map d).

For further information about contacts between the inhabitants of Sussex (i.e. including the Ouse valley) with

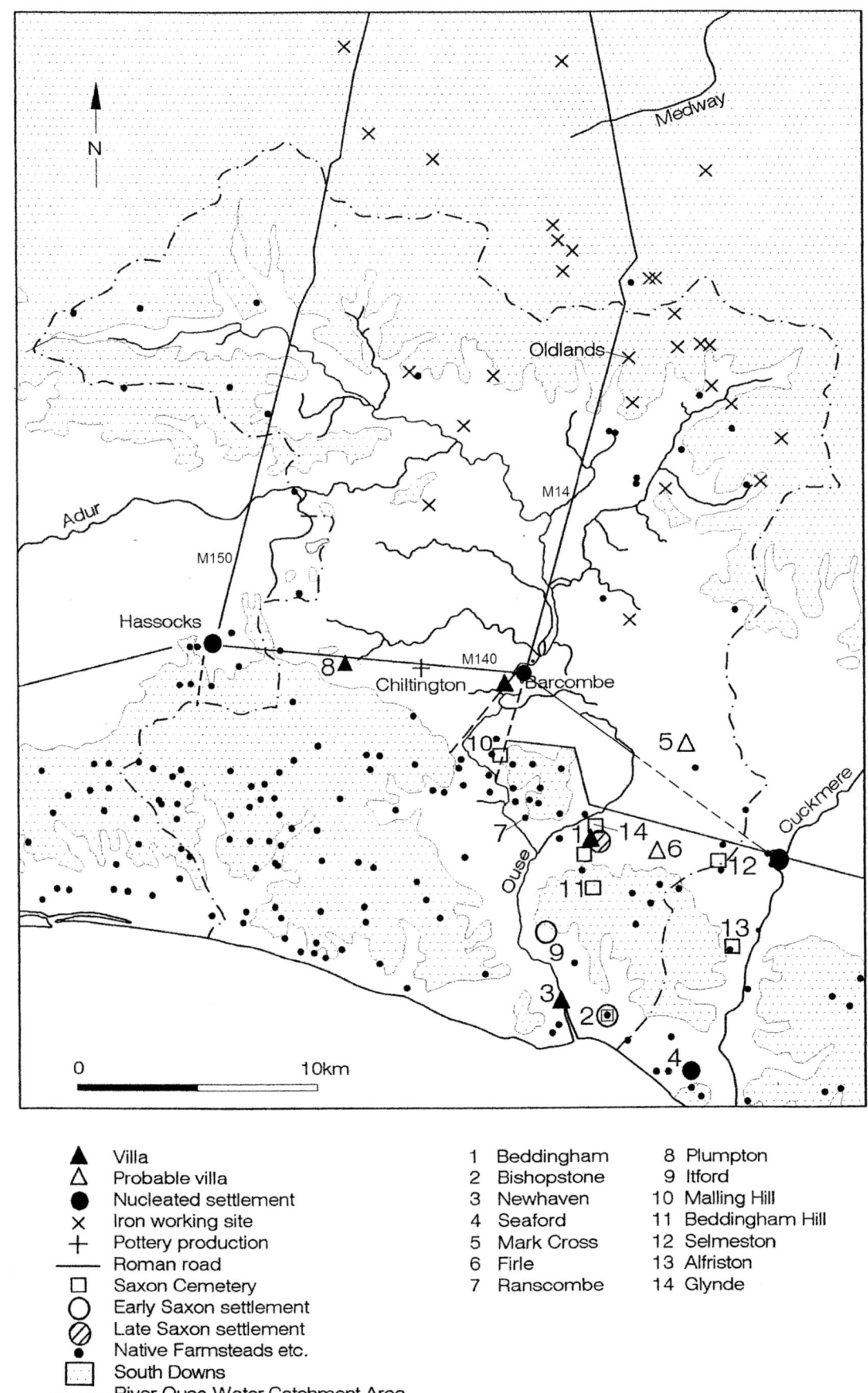

Figure 8.1: Distribution map of various Roman-period sites in or near the water catchment area of the River Ouse (drawn by Jane Russell).

the Roman world before AD 43, the Roman Conquest, the client-kingdom of Togidubnus, the establishment of the Roman *civitas* of the *Regni* after the ending of the kingdom due to the death or retirement of Togidubnus (no successor king is recorded), and the later background history of Roman-period Sussex, the reader is referred to: Cunliffe (1973), Drewett *et al*. (1988, Chapter 6); Rudling (2003a; 2008); Russell (2006) and Rudling and Russell (2015).

Roads and road-side nucleated settlements

Very important features of the Roman landscape in the Ouse valley were parts of two major roads. One of these, the 'London-Lewes Way' (Margary Road 14: M14) (Margary 1965, 124-164; 1967, 59-62) heads north-north east from Barcombe Mills towards London. Its southernmost destination has until very recently been uncertain. However, as a result of extensive geophysical survey work by the Culver Archaeological Project and David Staveley, it is now thought that the road ends at a newly discovered nucleated settlement at Bridge Farm, Upper Wellingham (Figure 8.2 and see below), where it meets the east-west orientated Greensand Way - itself another major Roman road (M 140) (Margary 1965, 165-184; 1967, 68-70) which connects the Barcombe area in the east with Hardham in West Sussex. As its name implies, this road follows for much of its route an outcrop of the Lower Greensand. Ongoing work by Staveley and others has recently confirmed that the Greensand Way continues eastwards beyond Bridge Farm and via Laughton Place joins up with the Arlington to Pevensey road (M142) (Margary 1965, 186-193; 1967, 71; Staveley forthcoming). It is not surprising that a nucleated settlement developed at the intersection of these two major Roman roads, especially as the adjacent river Ouse is both tidal and navigable at this point and thus provided the settlement with another important transport route. The combination of the now London-Barcombe road and then the possibility of onwards transportation southwards to the sea and beyond by boat would have been very important for the iron industry, but also perhaps for other industries such as timber and charcoal. Similarly, the availability of water transport at this point along the now extended Greensand Way would also have been of benefit for the movement of produce from the farmsteads and villas to both the east and west of Bridge Farm. It remains uncertain as to whether any road on the east side of the Ouse led southwards from Bridge Farm towards South Malling and Cliffe where Margary postulated there might have been a river crossing.

The settlement at Bridge Farm was probably one of a number of such nucleated sites spaced at fairly regular intervals along the east-west Greensand Way. Thus some 13km to the west was a large cemetery (and therefore presumably also a large settlement) at Hassocks, this site also being located where the Greensand Way formed a junction with an important north-south road, in this case the so called 'London-Brighton [actually Hassocks] road' (M150) (Lyne 1994). Further west is a postulated settlement at Small Dole, and beyond this the fortified camp at Hardham. Similarly, to the east of Bridge Farm at Arlington near the river Cuckmere the remains of extensive roadside settlement, including a masonry building, are suggestive of another nucleated centre (Staveley forthcoming). Yet further to the east the road terminated at the fort at Pevensey.

An example of a local access road linked to the Greensand Way was discovered in 2005 as a result of fieldwalking and trial trenching by Rob Wallace as part of the Barcombe/Culver archaeology project (Rudling *et al*. 2010, 26-7). This road, which was well constructed and had flint metalling, provided access to and from both the Barcombe villa and the nearby bathhouse. At various points along the route of this branch road are traces of roadside settlement and industrial activity. Such settlements and activity may be associated with the Barcombe villa estate. Another discovery along this road is a silver *siliqua* of Honorius minted at Milan *c*. AD 395-402. This coin, and also another of Honorius found at Bridge Farm in 2015 (Millum 2015, 7), are currently the latest dateable Roman finds from the Barcombe area. Beyond the villa and bathhouse to the south-west, the road may have continued to Offham, thus providing access to the Downs (Millum 2014a). It is likely that other such north-south access roads also provided routes to/from the Greensand Way.

The nucleated settlement at Bridge Farm, Upper Wellingham

As noted above, geophysical survey (magnetometery) at Bridge Farm, Upper Wellingham, revealed a previously unrecorded Roman-period settlement at the intersection of two major Roman roads (M14 and M140) and adjacent to the river Ouse (Millum 2013, fig. 1; Staveley forthcoming; Fig. 8.2). An extensive open settlement pattern is interrupted by a double-ditched enclosure, thus demonstrating that this site was of more than one phase. Initial excavation work in 2013 by the Culver Archaeological Project investigated some of the large enclosure ditches which were found to cut the smaller roadside ditches of the open settlement. The excavations also examined an area containing traces of industrial activity (Wallace 2014). An unexpected find was a human cremation in an urn 'within an upper context' inside the enclosure (Millum and Wallace 2013, 5). In 2014 excavations at Bridge Farm exposed another area of the site and focussed on a large (20m long) structure comprising 13 one metre wide postholes. The postholes, which averaged a metre in depth, proved to be of great importance as they contained the *in situ* remains of waterlogged posts and in one case a waterlogged moulded timber architectural fragment which had apparently been

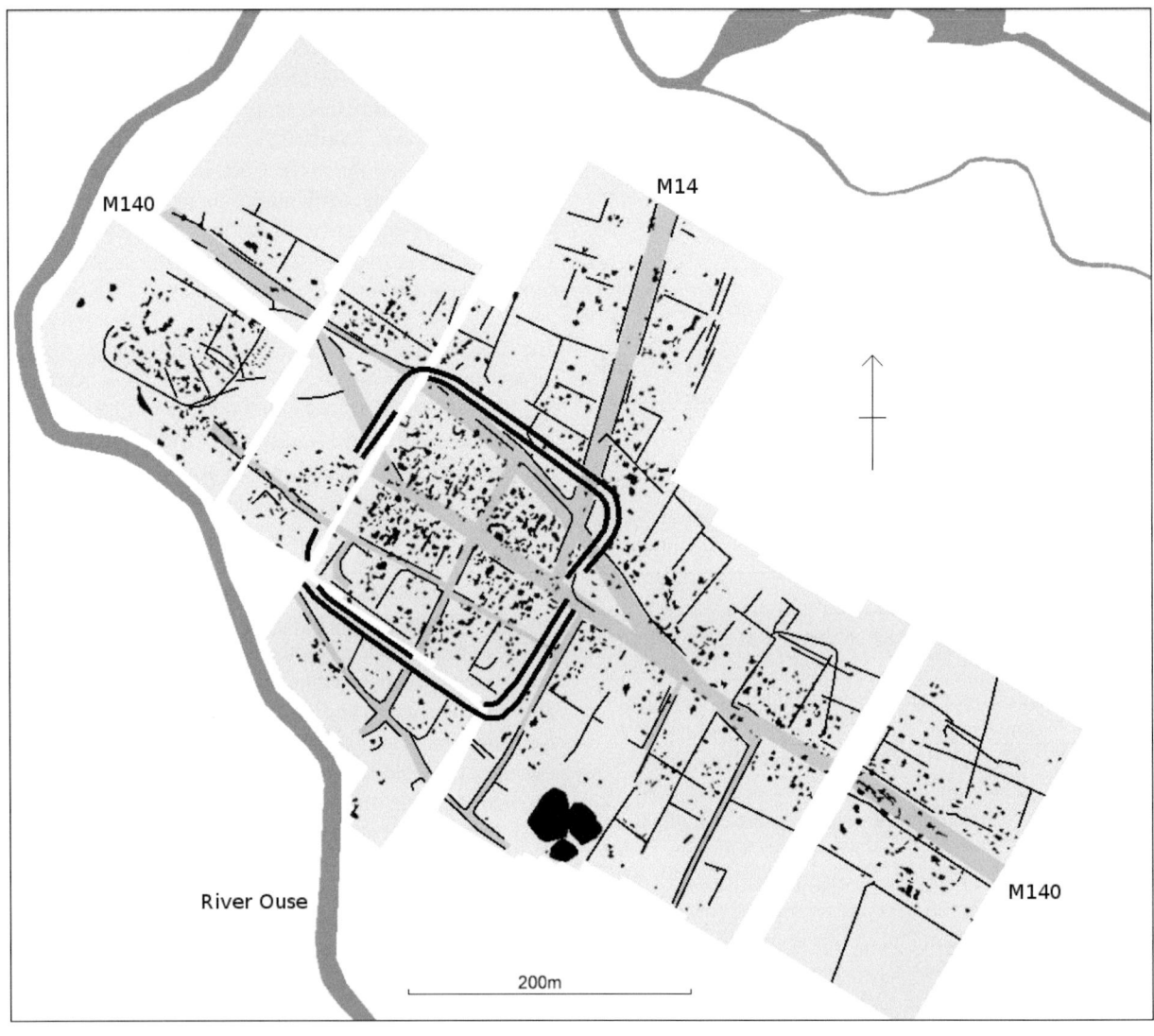

Figure 8.2: Bridge Farm, Upper Wellingham: Roman-period roadside settlement (produced by David Staveley).

used as a post-pad. Other discoveries in 2014 included: ditches, pits, hearths, postholes and two shallow wells, one of which yielded further examples of waterlogged wood (Millum 2014b).

Further excavations in 2015 concentrated upon the intersection of the double enclosure ditches with the pair of roadside ditches which continue northwards from the north-east corner of the enclosed settlement (Millum 2015). Traces of flint metalling were discovered and interpreted as further remains of the London bound road. Of great interest is the fact that this road surface appears to date to after the two late 2nd-century enclosure ditches were refilled. If so, Millum suggests that this stretch of road surface might be associated with access to the eastern road to Pevensey. Sections across the enclosure ditches again revealed 'their military-like' V-shape precision' (Millum 2015, 7), this suggesting an official purpose, perhaps associated with storing official supplies and/ or tax collecting. Mid-late 3rd-century dating evidence from above the road metalling found in 2015 suggests that the underlying double-ditched enclosure was only in use for a short period.

Prior to the discovery of the site by archaeologists, a local metal detectorist, David Cunningham, had for many years been searching various fields on Bridge Farm (including those containing the settlement site) and had found a large number of coins and other artefacts. The range of coins found start with some Roman Republican (i.e. pre-Conquest) silver *denarii* and also some Late Iron Age coins. It ends with a silver *silqua* of Gratian minted at Thessalonica in AD 375-8 (Millum 2013, fig 3). Other detector finds included a number of biconical-shaped lead weights for use with steelyard weighing scales. Such finds may indicate commercial and/or administrative activity (Booth *et al*. 2008, 154, 392). Other finds, especially coins and pottery, recovered during a surface artefact collecting survey and the initial excavations, plus the detector finds, suggest that occupation at Bridge Farm spans the period early post-Conquest to late 4th century.

Millum (2013, 58) has suggested that the settlement at Bridge Farm may have been similar to that at Westhawk Farm, near Ashford in Kent, which was also established on an important road junction (Booth *et al.* 2008). At Westhawk, which has been extensively excavated, the economic functions have been interpreted as being mainly based on farming and local market services, with perhaps an administrative role in the trade of iron. A major difference between the two sites, however, is the erection of defences at Bridge Farm. Probably dating to the late 2nd century, the double-ditched enclosure may have been thought necessary due to the site's proximity to a navigable river and the threat, real or perceived, of coastal raiding. Alternatively the defences at Bridge Farm, and those of similar date at various towns in south-eastern Britain, may have been related to more wide-ranging problems, such as a period of civil unrest or disease (Rudling and Russell 2015, 158).

A nucleated settlement at Seaford

At Seaford an early cemetery (Price 1882; Winbolt 1935, 65) may have been associated with a nucleated settlement of some importance, perhaps a port, and in 1934 an area of at least three acres of settlement activity was discovered some 500m to the west of the cemetery (Smith 1939). Pottery finds from a watching brief undertaken in 1935 during house and road construction work span the second half of the 1st century to the late 3rd or early 4th century. From elsewhere in Seaford, however, the discovery of two coins hints at later activity within the area. One of the coins, a gold solidus of Constantius II (AD 337-361), was found during trenching in *c.* 1892 (Griffith 1892). The other coin, a gold solidus of Valentinian I (AD 364-375), was found at the 'water's edge' in *c.* 1847 (*Journal of the British Archaeological Association* 2, 1847, 344). Smith (1939, 304) notes that other finds from the development site in 1935 included a 'fair quantity' of medieval pottery sherds. In medieval times, when Seaford was at the mouth of the Ouse, it functioned as the port which served the region's administrative centre at Lewes.

A Roman-period (?) barrow cemetery at Lewes

At Lewes, which in late Saxon and Norman times became a strategically important 'gap town' where the Ouse breaches the Downs (Rudling 1983, 45), the discovery of various Roman finds and burials (including a possible barrow cemetery) does not necessarily indicate that this location was the site of a nucleated settlement. Although several excavations within the town have yielded small quantities of residual Roman finds (examples being two pieces of *tegula* tile and one fragment of box-flue tile from Friars Walk (Russell 1990, 154), most of our evidence for Roman Lewes has been assembled by John Bleach (1997; Rudling 2008, 121) following a study of historical sources (e.g. old newspapers) concerning earlier discoveries. Bleach's work has revealed a number of 'forgotten' finds of Roman date including coins, burials, 'urns' and animal bones. Bleach (1997, 132-133) concludes that these and other Roman finds from Lewes indicate 'Roman and possibly earlier activity on the promontory and its western approaches'. However, Bleach suggests that much of this activity 'appears to have been of a ritual nature, and… that there were a number of mounds, at least two of which were barrows, ranged along the north-west edge of the promontory'. Although most of the finds noted by Bleach probably date to the early Roman period, four of five Roman coins found in a garden on the south side of Rotten Row have been dated by the Sussex Archaeological Society to the early 4th century (*c.* AD 317-337). Roman-period ritual activity other than burials in the Ouse valley includes the small shrine at Beddingham (see below), the finding of examples of 'special' or 'structured' deposits of animal bones and artefacts at both the Beddingham and Barcombe villas, and a possible continuation of the practice of making 'structured deposits' in pits on Mount Caburn (Rudling 2008, 118 and 124-127; Hamilton 1998, 33).

Roman-period Industries in the Ouse valley

The main industries that we have archaeological evidence for in the Ouse valley are farming and iron working. Of these farming is likely to have been the most important occupation within our study area. Thus areas of lower lying land would have been suitable for agriculture, whilst the water-meadows adjacent to the Ouse and its tributaries would have been ideal for the raising of cattle. In contrast, the waterless Downs would have been suitable for both sheep rearing and some agriculture. The evidence for farming comprises animal bones and plant remains at various settlement sites, and traces of field systems and environmental evidence as at Bishopstone (Bell 1977, 251-275) where the main agricultural crop was spelt wheat (*Triticum spelta* L.), with six-row barley (*Hordeum vulgare* L.) as a secondary crop. The large scale and intensity of agriculture undertaken in the valley may be indicated by the discovery of corn-drying ovens at both Bishopstone (Rookery Hill) and at Ranscombe Hill (see below). A possible related industry might have been water powered milling, this being an activity which is well attested in the valley during medieval and post-medieval times and survives today in the place names 'Barcombe Mills' and 'Tidemills'.

The four iron working sites closest to the Ouse, at Freshfield Brickworks, Coleham, Grange Corner and North Chailey appear to be south-western outliers of a major concentration of High Weald ironworking sites, such as Oldlands and Crabtree Farm, which would have been served by the London-Barcombe road (Cleere and Crossley 1995, 57-88 and fig. 19).

At least some of these sites had been established by the 1st century AD, with others starting in the 2nd or early 3rd centuries. At North Chailey, for instance, investigations at a site associated with ironworking, and in the vicinity of other iron workings, have yielded pottery that indicates occupation/activity during the 2nd to mid-3rd centuries (Chris Butler and Malcolm Lyne pers. comm.).

By the mid-3rd century operations at many of the Sussex iron working sites had ceased, an exception being the extensive site at Oldlands (close to the London-Barcombe road) which is thought to have still been in use at the end of the 3rd century. By the end of the 4th century it seems that all (or most) of the ironworks had closed and the labour force moved out leaving perhaps much of the Wealden forests deserted. Subsequently, during the Early Anglo-Saxon period the potential of Wealden iron-ore resources 'appears to have been unrecognised, or perhaps ignored' (Cleere and Crossley 1995, 85).

The remains of another local industry, pottery manufacture, have been found about 100m to the south of the Greensand Way at Wickham Barn, Chiltington. Two pottery kilns were excavated and their products were found to indicate a strong New Forest influence; and perhaps a migrant New Forest potter (Butler and Lyne 2001). Although archaeo-magnetic dating of the kilns proved unsuccessful, Lyne was able by seriation of the pottery assemblage and comparisons with dateable products from the New Forest kilns of Hampshire, to provide a date range for the site of *c.* AD 250-270 to *c.* AD 300-350+. With regard to the end of pottery production at the site, Lyne states that this is likely to have occurred during the mid-4th century, as post AD 370 pottery assemblages recovered from occupation sites in the vicinity include either none or very few Wickham Barn sherds.

Other important Roman-period industries in the Ouse valley probably included timber/woodland management and charcoal making in the Weald, stone quarrying/procurement on the Downs and in the Weald (note the use of flint, chalk, Sussex marble and ironstone as building materials at the Beddingham, Barcombe and Plumpton villas and at the Barcombe 'isolated' bathhouse); fishing (both freshwater and marine as evidenced by the bones of: perch, Atlantic salmon or sea trout, shad or twaite shad, herring, conger eel, cod, mackerel, sea bream, mullet, brill or turbot, plaice/flounder and other small flatfish at Beddingham villa (W. Van Neer *et al*: unpubl. specialists' report, 'The fresh and salted fish remains') and by a fish-hook and the bones of a meagre and a ? mackerel found at Bishopstone: Bell 1977, 131: 27 and fig. 63: 27, 284-5); marine mollusc procurement (including perhaps oyster farming), and probably salt making.

Villas

Six known or probable villa sites have been investigated in the Ouse valley water catchment area. Each of these sites will be considered with regard to what is known about their dating and developmental histories. For discussions about Sussex villas in general (see Rudling 1998 and 2003a).

Newhaven villa

Rescue excavations undertaken during the early 1970s in the town centre of Newhaven about 1.3km upstream from the Roman and modern mouths of the Ouse (Robinson 1999, 9 plan d), revealed traces of a Romano-British settlement bounded by a ditch (Bell 1976). Parts of five wooden and stone buildings were discovered; dating evidence indicating a start in the second half of the 1st century and ending in the Late Antonine period when the whole site was systematically levelled prior to its abandonment. Since the demolition horizons contained painted wall plaster, *opus signinum*, box-flue tiles, window glass and abundant building stone, the excavator concluded that the buildings were probably the outbuildings, including a possible granary, of a small early villa (Figure 8.3). Bell further suggested that the three excavated sites were located on a clay-with-flints deposit overlying a chalk terrace beside open water of the former Ouse estuary. Support for a potentially very early date for this villa comes from Black (1987, 155) who has identified a minimum of ten pieces of 'thin-walled' box-flue tiles among the unpublished excavation finds in Brighton Museum. Black suggests that these tiles may have been used with 'half-box' tiles (which he dates to before *c.* AD 75-80) or with *parietales* and ceramic spacers. On the basis of the presence at Newhaven of another type of flue-tile (this time roller-stamped) which dates to the late first or early 2nd century, Black also suggests that the baths at the villa 'had been modified after their original construction'. Such a postulated phase of modifications thus potentially fits with the excavator's own dating (first half of the 2nd century) for a second phase of occupation and building activity generally at the site (Bell 1976, 250).

Bell notes that part of this Roman-period settlement may have been first found in 1852, perhaps further uphill. The 19th century discoveries (now unlocated), however, which comprised traces of Roman masonry and tiles (including box-flue tiles which may have been a variety of 'half-box' type: Black 1987, 155), were in an 'upland meadow' and perhaps represent a second Roman-period stone building in the parish (Spurrell 1852; Bell 1976, 234).

Although Bell's excavations yielded a few sherds of 3rd-century pottery, nothing was found to indicate continuity of site use into the 4th century. The reasons for this villa's relatively early demise by *c.* AD 200 are unknown, but could include the threat or perceived threat

FIGURE 8.3: NEWHAVEN VILLA, SITE 1: STRUCTURE V FROM THE SOUTH, WITH PART OF THE NORTH WALL REMOVED. SCALE: 2M (PHOTO: BRENDA WESTLEY).

of coastal raiding (Rudling 2003a, 121, 124). It is also possible that occupation had moved to a new location, perhaps the now lost site recorded by Spurrell (1852), where finds included two radiate coins, one of Gallienus (AD 259-68), the other of Claudius II (AD 268-70), but even here nothing was found that can be attributed to the 4th century. It is worth noting, however, that a lack of late Romano-British pottery has also been observed for the Newhaven Castle Hill site (Bell 1976, 286). Although Bell's villa excavations yielded 'a few rather doubtful small sherds' of pottery of possible Saxon date, the stratigraphy and medieval finds indicate that the investigated sites 'were within one of the intensely cultivated fields [of the medieval settlement and its possible Saxon predecessor] of Meeching', the parish church of which (St. Michael's) is located *c*. 500m to the west on a hillside (Bell 1976, 299).

The discovery of an early and possibly elaborate villa at Newhaven is very interesting as the other 'Early' Sussex villas are generally relatively large and luxurious and sometimes, as at Fishbourne, Pulborough and Southwick, of Mediterranean- rather than north Gallic-type (Rudling 2003a, 118; Rudling and Leigh 2013, 37-39). The buildings at some of these sites share similarities in elements of design, construction and decoration, and some probably involved the same architects and craftsmen. Ownership of such a villa might have included the native aristocracy, which was left in peace to develop in the strongly philo-Roman atmosphere generated by the client kingdom of Togidubnus (Cunliffe 1973, 79). The building of such rural houses in Sussex so soon after AD 43 may have been due to a competitive desire by the local elite to display their status in a new, 'Romanised' way (Millett 1990, 94). The wide distribution of the large early villas in Sussex may be significant, each being located on a distinct block of land which might 'represent the territory over which the [indigenous] land-owning aristocracy held control (Cunliffe 1973, 79 and fig. 132). The importance after the Conquest of access to maritime and/or riverine transportation may be significant, with early villas located at Eastbourne, Newhaven, perhaps Brighton (Springfield Road), Southwick, Angmering, Arundel and Fishbourne.

Beddingham villa

During 1986 aerial reconnaissance revealed a previously unrecorded Roman-period villa near the foot of the north scarp of the Downs at Beddingham. Subsequent survey and excavation investigated the main residential building and sampled adjacent buildings and areas within the villa's two-phase ditched enclosure (Rudling 1997; 1998, 52-59; 2003b; Figure 8.4). Evidence was revealed for multi-period usage of the site from the Mesolithic to the post-medieval period, with the oldest settlement evidence dating to the Late Bronze Age/Early Iron Age. Settlement at the site may then have been abandoned until the end of the Late Iron Age or the beginning of the Roman period, when a two-phase timber round 'house' was constructed (Rudling 1997; Figure 8.5). In the Flavian period a rectangular range of five rooms with mortared flint foundations was constructed adjacent to the round 'house', and this formed the core of subsequent phases of construction/modification to this main domestic structure. Such modifications included the adding and abandonment of a suite of baths, which in *c.* AD 270 was overlain by a new range of rooms (Figure 8.6). The final development of the building, which is not securely dated, was the adding of a curiously shaped veranda with chalk foundations which involves an irregular curved section. This curved section of wall overlies the northern part of the 1st-century timber round 'house' and it is suggested that the shape of the irregular section of foundations was designed to respect the location (real or tradition) of the former ring-post structure (Figure 8.5). If this theory is correct, these chalk footings are an extremely important indication of continuity of ownership throughout a long period of the Roman occupation of Britain.

The dating of the final phase of occupation of the winged corridor villa is based mainly on pottery evidence (Lyne: unpubl. Roman and Saxon pottery report). Deposits within the new north range (i.e. the rooms above the infilled baths) yielded pottery dating to the period c. AD 270-350 and with an absence of late 4th-century forms. Similarly, the fill of an oven in the front corridor also dates to c. AD 270-350, whilst a large oven or kiln in one of the main rooms is of similar or 3rd-century date. In addition, the upper two fills of a well which is located near the winged building also date to the late 3rd/early 4th centuries. This well, the only one to be found at Beddingham, was probably carefully located some five metres behind the winged house in order to provide water for both domestic and bathing requirements. Its infilling/abandonment may thus have coincided with when the adjacent building went out of use for domestic purposes.

The demise of both the winged building and nearby well at Beddingham was not, however, the end of occupation/activity at this site. Thus just to the south of the south-west corner of the winged building (and to the west of the site of the original timber round 'house') an area of rubble with much rubbish may have been hard-standing for a small building (Figure 8.4). Whilst most of the pottery associated with the rubble spread is 3rd-century in date, there are some late 4th-century sherds, including a Hadham kilns red-ware bowl, a hook rim from the Harrold kilns in Bedfordshire, an East Sussex Ware copy of a Mayen Ware dish of Gose's form 474 (i.e. c. AD 350-420) and an Oxfordshire white ware *mortarium* of type M23 (i.e. c. AD 350-400+). In addition, Lyne's study of the pottery from the plough soil above the villa, which is nearly a quarter of all the recovered pottery from the site, shows that definite post-AD 330 sherds amount (by weight) to only 1.1% of this assemblage. This suggests that there was either very limited occupation of the villa during the late 4th century (perhaps continuing no later than the end of the third quarter), or limited use of pottery by the inhabitants.

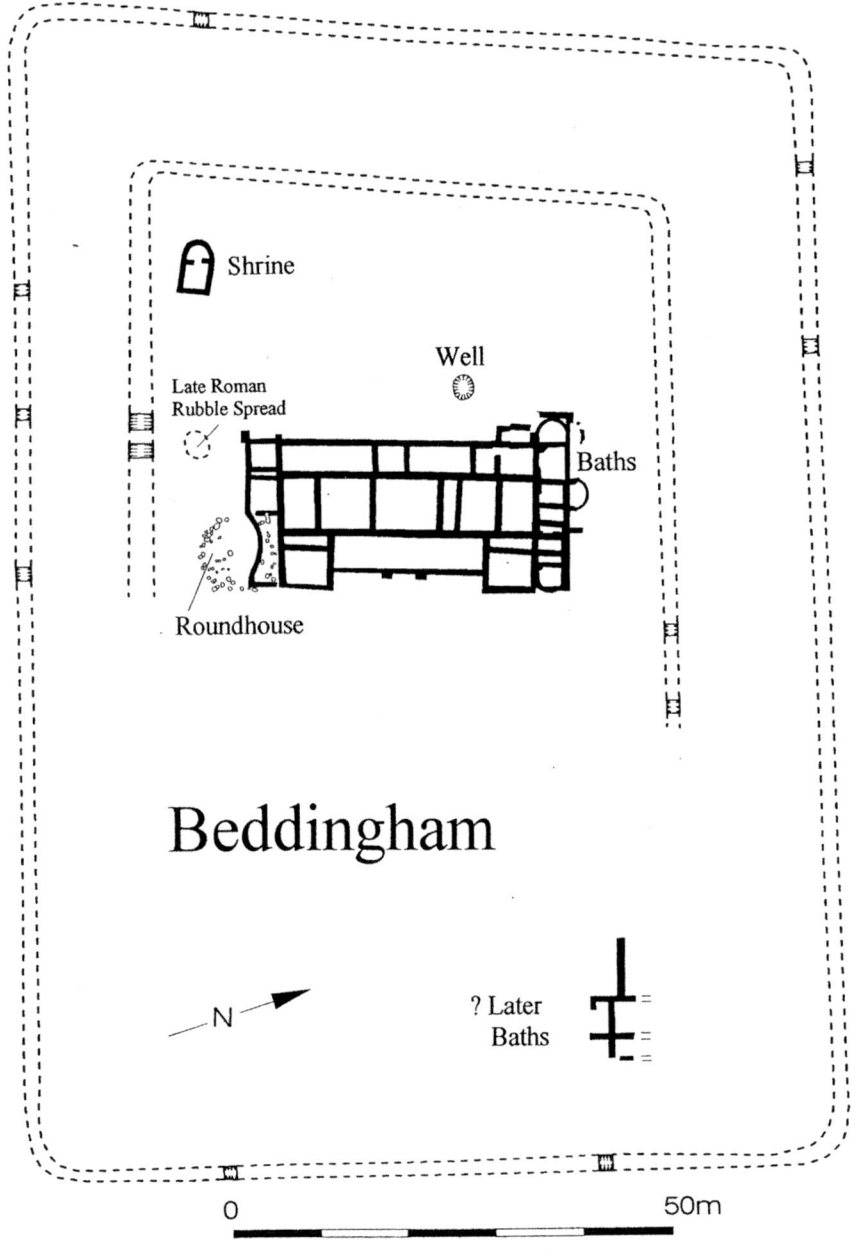

FIGURE 8.4: PLAN OF THE BEDDINGHAM VILLA WITH ITS TWO PHASES OF ENCLOSURE DITCH. THE OUTER AND LATER ENCLOSURE DATES TO THE MID-2ND CENTURY (DRAWN BY JANE RUSSELL).

FIGURE 8.5: THE BEDDINGHAM VILLA: THE TWO-PHASED TIMBER 'ROUNDHOUSE' AND THE SOUTHERN MASONRY FOUNDATIONS OF THE VILLA, SCALES: 2M (PHOTO: DAVID RUDLING).

FIGURE 8.6: BEDDINGHAM VILLA VIEWED FROM THE NORTH, SCALE: 2M (PHOTO: DAVID RUDLING).

Sixteen metres to the north-west of the rubble spread referred to above was a small, three-phase masonry Romano-British shrine (Rudling 1997; Figure 8.7). The final phase of activity within the shrine consisted of the filling of a circular cut feature at the western/apsidal end (Figures 8.4 and 8.7). The dark fill (648) of this feature yielded sherds of Saxon pottery dated to the late 4th or early 5th century. The Saxon vessels are in two fabrics: a course black sandy ware and a fine-sanded polished black ware. They include the base of a pedestal bowl; a body sherd from a rusticated vessel with random stabbing; an everted rim; the base from a jar with twin vertical grooves flanked by vertical rows of dimples; three body sherds decorated by pairs of vertical grooves separated by rows of dimples and a pedestal-based necked bowl with a carinated girth decorated with vertically slashed faceting (Rudling 1998, fig. 9; 2-7). Context 648 also yielded a number of Roman sherds, including a large and unabraded piece from a Pevensey Ware bowl dated to *c.* AD 350/370-400+. There is thus the possibility that at least some of the late 4th-century Roman pottery, which is later than the main villa building occupation, could be contemporary with some of the Saxon pottery. In addition, the two Saxon bowls with pedestal feet (*standfussgefassen*) are types which disappeared from the Saxon pottery repertoire during the mid-5th century.

Additional sherds of late Roman and early Saxon pottery were found in several features and deposits near the Roman shrine and to the west of the main villa building. These various pottery finds represent late Romano-British or early Saxon activity, perhaps 'squatter' occupation, in at least part of the former villa enclosure, but not in the main building itself.

Other as yet unexcavated parts of the villa complex may also contain evidence for late Romano-British or Saxon activity. The people involved in such activity may have been associated with the nearby 'Drayton Field' Saxon inhumation cemetery (Welch 1983, 396). This burial ground was probably first discovered in *c.*1800 when six skeletons (of which five were male) were found in a ploughed field in Beddingham parish. The associated finds included: two (?iron) swords, an (?iron) knife, beads, a buckle and fragments of a stone bracelet (*Archaeologia* 14 (1803), 273). An unpublished manuscript of *c.* 1800 may also refer to these or subsequent excavations and states that skeletons and an (?iron) spearhead were found. This document provides better locational information than the other primary account (see above) and states that the finds were made in 'Drayton Field'. Whilst such a name is not listed in the Tithe Apportionment, 'Great Drayton' field lies

FIGURE 8.7: BEDDINGHAM VILLA: THE ROMAN-PERIOD SHRINE. THE DARKER AREA WITHIN THE BUILDING CONTAINED BOTH LATE ROMAN AND EARLY SAXON POTTERY, SCALES: 2M (PHOTO: DAVID RUDLING).

only some 200m west of the villa. Although two metal detecting surveys have failed to locate any further traces of Saxon burials in what was Great Drayton field, the late Mr. John Monnington, the farmer at Preston Court Farm during the excavation project, had in his possession an iron spearhead which had been recovered from this field some years earlier. This find is of Swanton's type H2 and dates to the 5th or 6th century (Swanton 1974, 18-20). Its discovery probably confirms the general location of the Saxon cemetery, which unfortunately remains poorly understood in terms of its extent, nature and date range.

Other Early Saxon burials in the vicinity of Beddingham villa include an inhumation cemetery of primary or secondary burials in barrows on Beddingham Hill (i.e. on the Downs to the south of the villa), an inhumation cemetery at Balcombe Pit, Glynde, to the north (Welch 1983, 395-401), and a mixed inhumation and cremation cemetery on a prominent rise overlooking Glynde Reach to the north-west. The finds associated with the burials on Beddingham Hill include a copper-alloy buckle of late Roman type and dated to the late 4th or early 5th century, and a disc brooch which Welch assigned to the late 5th or early 6th century. Overall Welch suggested that these burials date to *c.* AD 500. At the Balcombe Pit site various skeletons which had been orientated west-east with the head at the west end, were discovered during 19th century quarrying for chalk. Associated finds included iron knives, pottery, glass vessels and a (?) calf skull. Three of the skeletons were in coffins. A 20th century discovery at this site had a wooden box containing grain placed under the skull. This burial was thought by Welch to be probably of Roman rather than Saxon date. If this theory is correct, the cemetery may have begun in the Roman period and continued in use into the Saxon period. The third cemetery, which was found in 2008, has only been partially investigated by archaeologists. The excavated remains comprised three inhumation burials, two possible cremations and grave goods which indicate a date range of mid-5th to mid-6th century (Beesley 2009). It can be seen from the examples discussed above that the locating of early Saxon cemeteries might help in the identification of late Romano-British inhumation cemeteries which are otherwise unknown in the Ouse valley.

Given the proximity of Preston Court farmhouse, with just one small field separating it from the Beddingham villa to its south, and in contrast to the situation at the Barcombe villa site (see below), it is surprising that the villa wall foundations at Beddingham do not show more signs of stone robbing. The fate of the above ground fabrics of the winged house, shrine and other buildings at Beddingham is unknown. Were they systematically levelled and materials salvaged for reuse elsewhere? Or were they abandoned and left to fall down, perhaps with salvaging of selected materials such as roofing tiles and lead fittings? Whilst uncertainty remains, historical sources (i.e. some of the field names of the area) indicate that the villa (-site) was perceptible during the Saxon period. Richard Coates (1990) has studied the field names and notes that on a map of 1785 the field in which the villa was subsequently discovered was called Stone Burgh. He suggests that the burgh element could date back to Saxon times and refer to a substantial masonry building. Other relevant local place names considered by Coates include various names (e.g. Comps Farm; Great Comps and Comps Wish) which contain the Old English word comps, a borrowing from the Latin campus, which Gelling (1988, 74-8) believes to denote 'land on the edge of a villa estate' – perhaps neglected arable land where the villa itself had been abandoned by the Saxon period. As the word comp went out of use at an early stage in the history of English, its usage for various place names at Beddingham indicates that the villa was perceptible 'to the Saxons in some form, physical or administrative' (Coates 1990, 6-9).

Field survey in the vicinity of the Beddingham villa has mainly consisted of metal detecting, including an extensive metal detector rally in 2005 monitored by the archaeology section of East Sussex County Council (Greg Chuter pers. comm.). These activities have revealed a large concentration of Iron Age and Roman material in a field to the south-west of the villa site. In contrast to the villa, this site (the 'Furlongs') would appear to have been occupied in the Late Iron Age as attested by finds of both Mid- and Late Iron Age pottery, a Class 1 potin coin and, perhaps, a Roman Republican denarius of Paulus Lepidus (*c.* 60 BC) which is in excellent condition. The Romano-British period is represented by pottery, metalwork and some 200 coins, most of which date to the late 3rd or early 4th centuries, but also include three bronze issues of Valens (AD 364-378). The lack of significant quantities of Roman tile may indicate the absence at this site of 'Romanised' buildings. The relationship of this site to the nearby villa is unknown, but given the small amount of Late Iron Age material found at the villa it is possible that it was the ancestral farmstead for both sites and then continued in use as a satellite farmstead after the initial stages of villa development at the other site. It was perhaps abandoned in the mid- to late 4th century, probably after the main building at the villa had already gone out of use. Possibly future excavations at this site, as at the villa, might reveal evidence for some late 4th/early 5th century activity/occupation, and thus provide a second possible settlement for some of the people who may have been buried at the nearby 'Drayton Field' cemetery.

A probable villa at Firle

Three kilometres to the east of the Beddingham villa, at Firle, metal detecting, 'rapid fieldwalking', a geophysical survey and evaluation trenches located a previously unrecorded Iron Age and Romano-British settlement within a large rectilinear enclosure (Chuter 2005). The resistivity survey and trial trenching revealed evidence for a substantial timber-framed building which the excavator suggests is 'stylistically similar to a proto-villa'. As with the Beddingham villa, this site lies at the base of the scarp foot of the Downs on a thick deposit of colluvial hill wash. The Firle site lies adjacent to Compton Wood, with here the place name word Compton being derived from the Old English cumb tūn or valley (combe) farmstead (Glover 1975, 39).

Pottery sherds from the various surveys and excavations include examples representing the Late Bronze Age/Iron Age, Roman, Early Saxon and medieval periods. Of particular interest are ten sherds of early Saxon pottery which Chuter (2005, 15) says are 'identical to Bishopstone Anglo-Saxon fabric 1 (Bell 1977, 227) and therefore of a 5th-7th century date'. Although nine of these sherds were surface finds, the tenth piece was recovered from Trench 1 in the vicinity of the postulated Roman building.

Other finds included large quantities of Roman 'brick/tile', metalwork and eight Roman coins, most of which date to the late 3rd and 4th centuries, with the most recent dateable examples being two coins attributable to the House of Constantine (i.e. early 4th century). The finds of metalwork include one definite and one possible copper-alloy Anglo-Saxon brooch. The first object is a 6th century gilded button brooch with stylised Woden decoration. The other is a probable Anglo-Saxon plate brooch. The significance of the early Saxon brooches and pottery at this site is, however, uncertain and Chuter (pers. comm.) is of the opinion that with regard to the brooches 'they are casual losses as there is a general scatter of this type of artefact around Firle'. Alternatively the brooches and pottery may provide evidence for a continuation of occupation/activity at the site into the Early Saxon period.

A probable villa at Mark Cross, Laughton

Fieldwalking 4.3km north north-east of the Firle villa, at Mark Cross, Laughton on the boundary of the Greensand and the Gault Clay, revealed a large spread of Roman material. This location is also a place noted by the farmer for the presence of a 'solid flint area', which might indicate the presence of structural remains (Masefield and Machling 1993, 1). A soil resistivity survey of part of the field located two main areas of high resistance, one of which is considered to be rectangular in shape 'with square wings protruding [to the east] from both the north and south ends' (Masefield and Machling 1993, 4). The southern end of this anomaly coincides with the area of the field with the highest concentrations of surface Roman material, including much tile (*imbrex*; *tegulae*; flat and box-flue types) and *tesserae*, and the anomaly is thus likely to be a Roman building with flint foundations – probably an east-facing winged villa.

All the pottery from this site was assessed by Malcolm Lyne. He concluded that the Roman-period sherds 'indicate occupation of the site from at least the end of the 2nd to the end of the 4th century' (Masefield and Machling 1993, Appendix 1). Lyne was also able to identify four sherds of early-mid Saxon pottery, two pieces being assigned to the 5th-6th centuries, whilst two other examples, which may be slightly later in date, were recovered from the site of the Roman building and may thus indicate possible 'squatter' occupation.

Barcombe villa and bathhouse

A programme of research and training investigations began at Barcombe in 1999. This parish lies to the north of the Downs and to the west of the Ouse (Figure 8.1). The two investigated sites are located to the south-west of the intersection at Bridge Farm of the Greensand Way and the London-Barcombe Way, close to the newly discovered Barcombe-Offham Roman road (see above), and near, and adjacent to, (respectively), St. Mary's Church.

The villa site has a very prominent setting and provides views across the Ouse valley to the Downs. Fieldwalking, geophysical survey and excavations have revealed evidence for multi-period activity on the site (Figure 8.8), including: a Bronze Age ring ditch, traces of a Bronze Age field system; four Late Iron Age and Romano-British timber roundhouses within a ditched enclosure (Figure 8.9a); a 'proto-villa' with masonry foundations (Building 1) (Figure 8.9b) which was replaced by a winged corridor building (2) (Figure 8.9c); a small bath house; a large aisled building (3) (Figure 8.9c); a well; enclosure walls; a large hall building (4) with small flanking rooms at its southern end which lies outside the main courtyard complex, and various pits, ditches and postholes (all Romano-British); later Saxon pits, postholes and a sunken-featured building; and medieval robber trenches and ditches (Rudling 2003a, 119-121; 2003b, 12-15; Rudling and Butler 2002; 2004; Rudling *et al.* 2010, 22-26). The name of the field in which the villa is located is Dunstalls Field, Dunstalls being derived from the Old English tūn-stall meaning the site (or place) of a farm (Smith 1956, 198) (see also Coates 2002).

Romano-British occupation at the site, which includes all or some of the four roundhouses, spans the first to fourth centuries. By the end of the 3rd century the principal elements of the villa as revealed by excavation comprised the winged corridor house, the aisled building and the hall building outside the courtyard complex. The first two of these buildings formed much of the northern and eastern sides respectively of the courtyard and were joined by a boundary wall. Such walling also occurs along the southern side of the courtyard but is separated from the aisled building by a large entrance into the villa complex. Dating evidence associated with the aisled building, which is thought to have been built

8. Impact of Rome

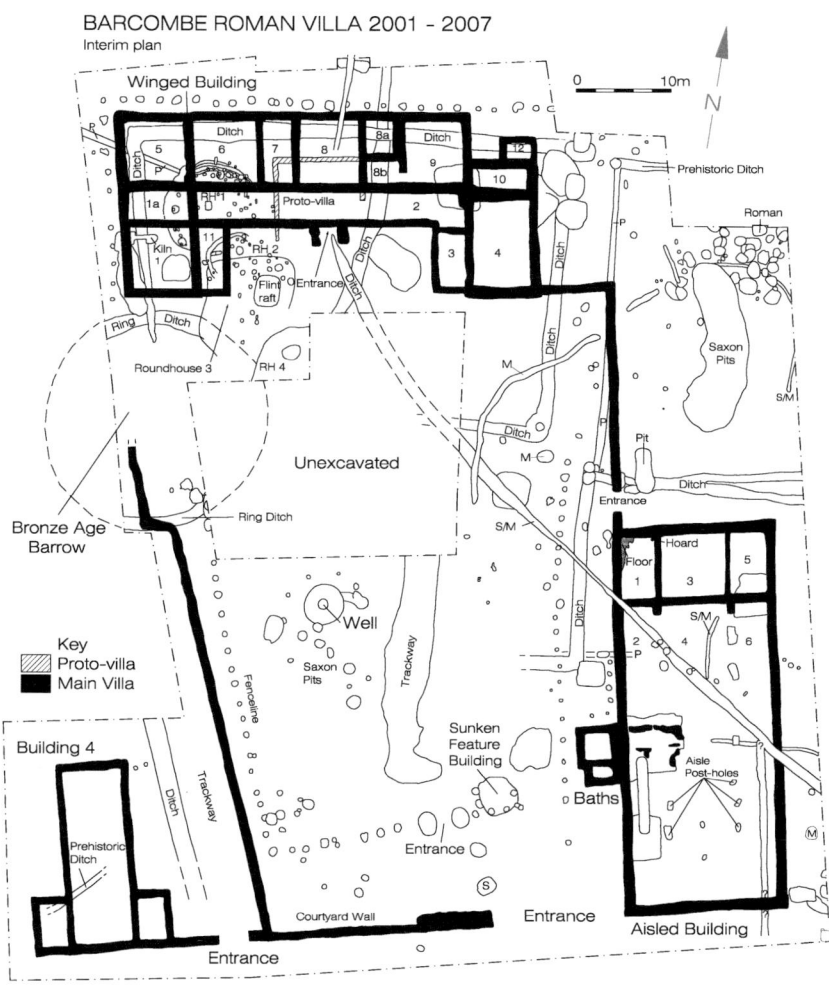

FIGURE 8.8: BARCOMBE VILLA: INTERIM MULTI-PERIOD PLAN (DRAWN BY JANE RUSSELL).

The nature and precise dating of the end of Romano-British occupation at the Barcombe villa site are unknown but, in contrast to the villa at Beddingham, that at Barcombe has not yielded any early Saxon finds. Excavations at this site have, however, revealed a number of features, mainly pits but also some postholes, which are provisionally dated to the mid–late Saxon period. A large concentration of such pits was found in the north-east corner of the trench, to the north of the aisled building and to the east of the winged building. Finds associated with these pits include pottery, animal bones, a bun-shaped ceramic loom weight and iron slag. Of possibly earlier date is a line of three postholes and a pit in the area between the small western wing room and the main entrance to the house. These four features, and the as yet undated sunken-featured building to the south, may be evidence for limited middle Saxon 'squatter' occupation amongst the ruins of the villa complex, whilst the other pits and finds indicate larger areas of later Saxon settlement and industrial activity further away from the remains of the two main Roman-period masonry buildings.

after the construction of the winged building, includes a small dispersed hoard of late 3rd century radiate coins, ending with an issue of Tacitus (AD 275-6). These coins may have been either a 'rite of commencement' (i.e. a foundation deposit) or a money hoard buried below the floor of one of the three rooms at the northern end of the building. The other coin finds from the villa site in general show an absence of coins dating to the mid- to late 4th century. Such evidence may indicate that the main phase of Romano-British occupation at the site ended c. AD 300–330. Analysis by Malcolm Lyne (pers. comm.) of the pottery finds suggests the presence of large quantities of 3rd century pottery and considerably smaller quantities of 4th century material, examples of which include a product of the Overwey kilns in Surrey which is likely to be post AD 330 and possibly as late as AD 370+. Lyne concludes that the winged house may have gone out of use by the early 4th century, whilst occupation may have continued for longer in the aisled building. It is thus possible that after the higher status winged-corridor house went out of use, perhaps as a result of the villa now having a non-resident owner, farm workers continued to live and work in other parts of the villa complex, such as the aisled building.

The second Roman-period site that has been investigated at Barcombe is a large three-phased bathhouse complex in Church Field, adjacent to St. Mary's Church (Rudling et al. 2010, 27; Millum et al. 2013). This 'isolated' bathing complex is surrounded on three sides by ditches which were used for draining both ground and waste water away from the baths and towards a large palaeo-channel which is located at the south-west corner of the field. This former channel, which may have provided a link by water with the Ouse, is today marked by a small stream running along the western boundary of the field. Dating evidence from the baths site mainly spans the 3rd-4th centuries and includes a piece of roller-stamped (die 9) box-flue tile, pottery and coins. It is possible that by the end of the 3rd century the baths and its southern ditch had gone out of use and some of its rooms used for new purposes. Activity at this site, however, continued into the late 4th century. Although the relationship between this 'isolated' bathhouse and the nearby villa is uncertain, the baths may have served the needs of the inhabitants at

Figure 8.9a: Barcombe: c. AD 40-50: The ditched enclosure with roundhouses. Remains of a Bronze Age round barrow in the foreground (drawing by Andy Gammon).

Figure 8.9b: Barcombe: c. AD 150: The fenced enclosure with the proto-villa and a roundhouse (drawing by Andy Gammon).

Figure 8.9c: Barcombe: c. AD 250: The winged-corridor villa and aisled building (drawing by Andy Gammon).

the villa and perhaps also others from elsewhere on the villa estate. Alternatively, or in addition, they may have served the inhabitants of, and visitors to, the nucleated settlement at Bridge Farm, the site being accessible by road and probably also by water.

Malcolm Lyne, who has examined all the Roman-period pottery from the Barcombe bathhouse site, has also identified two sherds of early Saxon pottery; one, from the surface of the demolition debris within the bathhouse, is a piece from a *buckelurne* with rosette stamps and vertical rouletted bands and dates to *c.* AD 450-550. Lyne (pers. comm.) suggests that this sherd hints at the possibility that an early Saxon cremation had been interred in or near the ruins of the bathhouse and had subsequently been disturbed by ploughing or stone-robbing activities.

A third possible Roman-period site at Barcombe is the location of St. Mary's Church. It is interesting to note that the fabric of the existing church, which dates from Norman times but was extensively renovated and altered in 1879, bears no obvious evidence, such as fragments of Roman tile or carved stone, for the reuse of building materials (other than probably flints) from either of the nearby Romano-British sites. However, an archaeological evaluation undertaken in advance of an application for planning permission for the construction of an extension on the south side of the church, revealed a small quantity of Roman tile, including fragments of examples of floor tiles, *imbrex, tegulae*, box-flue tiles and *tesserae* (Meaton 2004). Unfortunately all of these finds were 'residual in much later contexts' and generally the assessment excavations did not go below post-medieval deposits to the natural subsoil where earlier features may have been revealed. It is therefore possible that some, or all, of the recovered Roman tile from St. Mary's churchyard may relate to Roman-period remains that existed on the church/churchyard site. It is thought that this place was also the site of a Saxon church. It is perhaps possible that this area was also the site of a Roman-period building/s, perhaps given its more elevated location, a mausoleum or temple/shrine. Such a building/s may have been the reason for the siting of the Saxon and Norman churches.

The Plumpton villa

At Plumpton, to the north of the Downs and the Gault Clay, and some 700m to the south of the Greensand Way, is the site of a small villa (Allen 1984; Allen and Seager-Smith 1987; Rudling 2014a). The site has been investigated by three separate phases of systematic fieldwalking, two programmes of geophysical survey and excavations in 2014 and 2015. Surface indications and the results of the geophysical surveys and excavations have revealed a south facing winged corridor building orientated slightly north-west/south-east. As revealed in 2015, the eastern wing room had an apsidal southern wall, and the room to its north contained either a corn-drying oven or a form of channelled hypocaust (Rudling 2016). The discovery of box-flue tiles also indicates that the villa possessed at least one hypocaust heating system and perhaps a bath-suite. Finds of red tile *tesserae*, some smaller mosaic cubes, and painted wall plaster provide some information about internal decorations.

The most recent geophysical surveys revealed that the villa house was located within a large ditched enclosure, and probably comprised at least two phases of construction (Butler and Staveley 2014). Outside the enclosure was evidence for a number of trackways and a field system, all probably associated with the villa complex. Although dating evidence (principally pottery sherds) from the first surface artefact collecting survey indicated occupation of the villa in the 2nd and 3rd centuries but not the 4th century, a second survey undertaken by David Dunkin of University College London in 1996 recovered three coins, including a commemorative issue of Helena (mother of Constantine the Great) which is dated to *c.* AD 337-340. Subsequent coin finds during the excavations of 2014 and 2015 have included further examples of 4th century date, the youngest being a bronze issue of Magnentius minted at Trier *c.* AD 350-353. The writer plans to undertake a detailed study of all the retained finds from this villa and such work may reveal other evidence for 4th century or later activity at this site. The recent fieldwork at Plumpton is associated with a Higher Level Stewardship Agreement which is aimed to protect the full extent of the villa complex.

The non-villa Farmsteads

The majority of the Roman-period settlements in the southern part of the Ouse valley are downland farmsteads (Figure 8.1). Two have been partly excavated using modern methods.

Bishopstone (Rookery Hill)

The multi-period site at Rookery Hill, Bishopstone has yielded evidence for settlement throughout the Roman period and on into early Saxon times. The site, which is located on a hilltop which overlooks both the English Channel and the mouth of the Ouse, was also used during the Neolithic, Bronze Age and Iron Age periods (Bell 1977). A Late Iron Age unenclosed phase of occupation was followed early in the Roman period by the creation of a rectangular ditched and banked enclosure (Figure 8.10). By the late-2nd century the enclosure ditch had silted up, and during the following century activity at the site seems to have occurred at a significantly reduced level compared with the early Roman period. During the 4th century, however, and especially in its second half, there was once again more extensive activity as represented by pits, postholes and a corn-drying oven

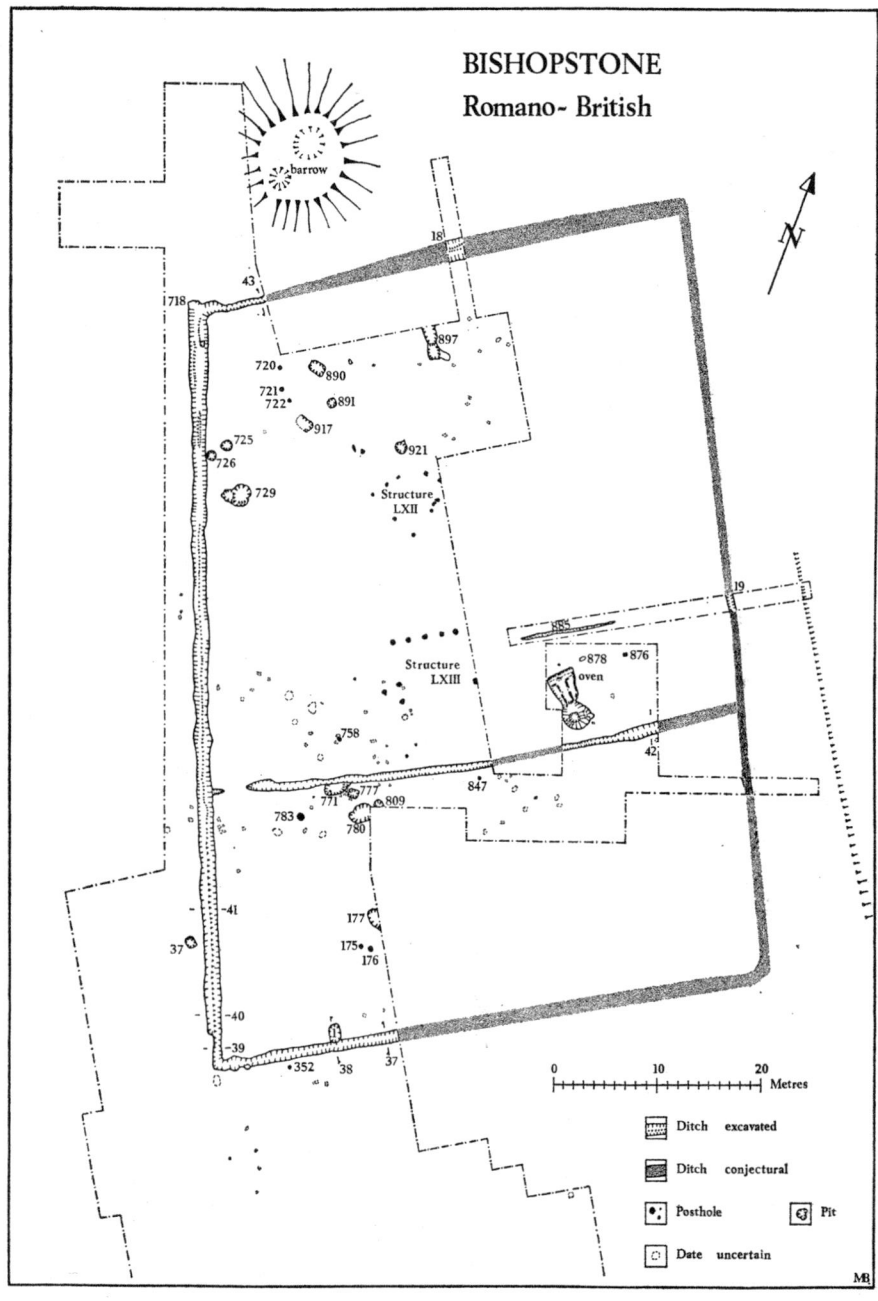

FIGURE 8.10: BISHOPSTONE: GENERAL PLAN OF THE ROMAN-PERIOD ENCLOSURE (BELL 1977, FIG. 87, REPRODUCED WITH THE PERMISSION OF THE SUSSEX ARCHAEOLOGICAL SOCIETY).

matter (only some 50% of the enclosure was excavated), it may also be due to the methods of construction used for such buildings, perhaps the use of cob or timber-framing, which may not leave any trace in the archaeological record. The author has recently discussed this issue with regard to another East Sussex downland farmstead on Bullock Down, Beachy Head (Rudling 2014b, 67). At Bullock Down the choice not to build even a modest Romanised house, such as the rectangular buildings found on the Downs at Park Brow in West Sussex (Wolseley and Smith 1927, 8), was apparently not due to poverty, the site having yielded unexpected indications of portable wealth. It is also worth noting that at least one of the earlier investigated Roman-period farmstead sites in the Ouse valley, at Highdole Hill, near Telscombe, provided evidence in the form of 'shallow circular depressions varying from 20ft. to 50ft. in diameter' which indicated the former presence of dwellings (Holleyman 1936, 202-3), although with the exception of two slightly deeper depressions, one of which 'may have served as a socket for a central post', no postholes or other features were discovered.

(Bell 1977, 139). Whilst the latest coin from the site is a possible issue of Gratian (AD 367-378), the large pottery assemblage includes the latest recognisable Roman products from this area, including Pevensey Ware which may have continued to be produced into the 5th century (Fulford 1973, 44). Bell (1977, 188) suggests that Romano-British activity at Bishopstone appears to have continued after the large corn-drying oven had gone out of use and been dismantled in order to remove the potentially useful flooring stones.

Although the absence of any recognisable domestic buildings dating to the Roman period may be a sampling

It is not known whether there was continuity or a hiatus in occupation/activity at Bishopstone between the phase of late Romano-British and early Saxon settlement (Bell 1977, 238). The area of Saxon occupation, however, is much larger than the late Roman settlement and it covered both the Roman enclosure and some of the adjacent fields, with little respect being shown for the previous features on the site. The Saxon settlement, which Bell (1977, 193) estimates to have covered some three hectares, consisted of rectangular post-built hall structures, sunken featured buildings (SFBs), fence lines and an adjacent and contemporary cemetery. Unfortunately that part of the settlement and all of the cemetery which were excavated by David Thompson remain unpublished, but Martin Bell was able from the results of his own fieldwork and what is known about Thompson's finds to suggest that the Saxon settlement at Rookery Hill dates to the 5th and 6th centuries, with the cemetery perhaps starting as early as *c.* AD 400 (Bell 1977, 238). At some time in the 6th century or perhaps later, the Saxon settlement on Rookery Hill was deserted – probably in order to establish a settlement in the valley to the east. This new valley-slope settlement, which is the site of the parish church of St. Andrew and a modern village, has been the subject of a research project (Thomas 2010).

Ranscombe Hill

The only other 'modern' excavation of a Romano-British non-villa farmstead in the Ouse valley is that which was partially investigated on Ranscombe Hill, South Malling, in advance of road construction (Bedwin 1978). The site was situated on a small south-facing spur of Lower Chalk, with a view across the Ouse floodplain and only some 620m from the course of the modern river. The features found included two ditches, a circular hearth and a corn-drying oven. Dating evidence indicates that occupation at the site started in the 1st century and continued until the late 4th/early 5th century when, as at Bishopstone, the corn-drier was deliberately infilled. Chris Green (1978, 252) who reported on the Roman pottery finds from both sites makes the interesting suggestion that the infilling of the corn-drying ovens at both Ranscombe and Bishopstone might be part of a more extensive occurrence of 'deliberate site levelling, rather than gradual abandonment and decay'. In addition, Green notes an absence at Ranscombe Hill of any early Saxon pottery.

Thus at two non-villa farmsteads in the Ouse valley late 20th-century fieldwork has revealed evidence for late 4th/early 5th century occupation and the possible deliberate in-filling of corn-driers at this time. At Bishopstone for certain, there is evidence for early Saxon occupation/activity on the site of the former Romano-British settlement.

Discussion

This review of Romano-British settlements and land-use in the Ouse valley has involved a variety of settlement types (native farmsteads, villas, and nucleated settlements) and land-uses (stone quarrying, mineral extraction, iron-works, forestry/coppicing, pottery production, arable cultivation and crop processing, animal husbandry, fishing, transportation by roads and waterways, and burial grounds/ritual locations).

With the possible exception of the early villa at Newhaven, which may have been built on a 'new' site for strategic transportation/communications reasons, the other villas (with the possible exception of that at Plumpton) in our study area may all have developed out of native farms, a pattern which is normal for many areas of Sussex and elsewhere in Britain (Applebaum 1966, 99; Rudling 1998, 50). This was certainly the case at both Beddingham and Barcombe where evidence has been found at each site for 'Iron Age type' timber roundhouses preceding the construction of the first buildings with masonry foundations. Whilst the Newhaven villa had gone out of use (or been moved to a new location) by the mid- to late 3rd century, this was the time of intense activity at both Barcombe and Beddingham. Subsequently at the end of the 3rd century/early 4th century, the principal buildings (i.e. winged corridor houses) at both of these villas went out of use, with just a few traces of later activity (perhaps 'squatter' occupation or demolition/salvage works) being recovered from in, or adjacent to, these structures. At both villas, however, there is also some limited evidence for 4th century activity elsewhere within the villa complex, but unfortunately the extent and nature of such activity is not clear. At Beddingham this later activity includes the late 4th/early 5th century 'squatter' occupation in the former shrine building by people (Romano-British or Saxon) with access to both late Romano-British and early Saxon types of pottery. Yet at neither site can continuity of occupation be demonstrated from the demise of the main house to the end of the 4th/early 5th century. At Barcombe the bathhouse site in Church Field yielded better evidence than that obtained from the nearby villa for continuity of occupation throughout the 4th century. At Plumpton, where there seems to be little if any evidence for occupation during the 1st century, the villa may have been started on a 'new' site during the 2nd century. Occupation of the site continued until the mid- 4th century. In the absence of large-scale excavations at the Firle and Mark Cross villas, the final stages of occupation at these sites are even more uncertain. If continuity of occupation did occur at some or all of the Ouse valley villas, however, possibly the owners ceased to reside at these sites which were perhaps now run by bailiffs or tenants, or maybe there were now new resident owners who could not afford, or did not want, the elaborate and expensive standards of living accommodation as in the past. Hence the abandonment of certain former domestic buildings; a fate that was not necessarily also shared at this time by all the other buildings.

We should perhaps note that elsewhere in Sussex, as in the Chilgrove valley and at Bignor in the Arun valley, some villa settlements continued to develop and expand during the early- and mid-4th century (Down 1979; Rudling 1998, 59-63; Rudling 2003a, 121-22; Rudling and Russell 2015). Thus any conclusions made here based upon Ouse valley Romano-British settlement histories are likely to be very localised. Similar studies based upon other valleys or areas (e.g. the West Sussex coastal plain) are therefore needed in order to investigate the variability of changes over time within a *civitas* or tribal region.

Despite the apparent evidence for considerably reduced domestic activity at all the Ouse valley villa settlements, there is no evidence to indicate whether there was any corresponding decline in the size or nature of the associated villa estates. Might not such estates, perhaps with absentee owners, have continued to function into the late 4th or 5th century? If not, why and how did things change? Perhaps at this time this area was, as Welch (1971, 232) hypothesised, free of a villa system and thus suitable for ceding by treaty to Saxon settlers/mercenaries? The very limited evidence for early Saxon activity at the various Ouse valley villa settlements, of which that from Beddingham is the most substantial, fits the general pattern for Saxon use of Roman sites in Sussex and Surrey, but not that for Kent where reoccupation of ruinous Roman sites may reflect a 'conscious attitude' (Drewett *et al*. 1988, 272).

Turning to the other types of Roman period settlement within the Ouse valley, I have noted the abandonment by the end of the 3rd century of most of the iron works, including the important site of Oldlands. The reasons for the end of the Wealden iron industry may have included: attacks from channel pirates; the silting up of river estuaries; and changes to both the economy and society during the 4th century (Cleere and Crossley 1995, 85). Somewhat surprisingly, during the Saxon period (and then only the later part), the Weald's still rich iron ore deposits were apparently only exploited on a small scale (Hodgkinson 2008, fig. 14; 35-6). The demise of the Roman iron working sites in the Ouse valley may in turn have had an adverse effect upon the area's agricultural villas, especially so if the iron works had previously provided markets for villa products or perhaps in some cases important revenues if they had formed parts of villa estates (Best 2015).

Elsewhere, activity at Seaford, probably one of the two largest settlements in the Ouse valley, seems to have continued into the 4th century, but perhaps at a much reduced level. At the other large nucleated site, that recently discovered at Bridge Farm, dating evidence for the final phases of occupation/activity is also uncertain, but use of this site could have continued into the mid- to late- 4th century (N.B. coins recovered during excavations in 2015 include one issued by Honorius: Millum 2015, 7). In comparison, some of the non-villa agricultural settlements within the valley, as at Bishopstone and Ranscombe Hill, and elsewhere in the region (e.g. at Bullock Down and at Burgess Hill: Rudling 1982; Sawyer 1999), show signs of increased activity in the second half of the 4th century. Could it be that some of these sites, many of which have yielded evidence for Late Iron Age/early Romano-British occupation, had periods of reduced activity during the 2nd and 3rd centuries when the villa settlements were developing and thriving? (I will return to such matters below). And later, upon the decline in the fortunes of the villas, did some of these old sites gain a renewed importance? In addition, in the late Roman period some of these non-villa sites may now have become more ideally located for settlement/agriculture (e.g. by being on higher ground or further inland) with regard to such problems (real or feared) as coastal/riverine raiding, the requisitioning (as opposed to contract purchase) of supplies by the military (e.g. the fort at Pevensey) and possibly flooding/sea level rises and alluviation (Dark and Dark 1997, 21-26) which may have occurred at sites such as Seaford, Newhaven and Bridge Farm, and at various water meadows in the valley. It is at one of the non-villa farmsteads, Bishopstone, that we have our best evidence from the valley for possible (but not certain) continuity of occupation during the transition to the Saxon period.

The relationship between villas and non-villa farmsteads in any micro-study of Romano-British rural settlements is of importance, and with regard to the Ouse valley Ernest Black (pers. comm.) has suggested to me that the presence of at least one early villa, that at Newhaven, may provide clues to what was happening later. Such a villa may have had a locally large but compact estate. If a number of farmsteads were dependencies of this (and perhaps other) large estates, the break-up of these estates, as may have happened at Newhaven by *c*. AD 200 (see above), could have resulted in a mixed pattern of different sized units, some perhaps paying rent to absentee landlords whilst others may have become owned and worked by former tenants. The growing prosperity of some of these units may have resulted in the emergence of villas such as Barcombe and Plumpton. In contrast, Beddingham villa which dates to the Flavian period, could conceivably have been a larger tenant-farm or perhaps part of a large estate gifted to a junior branch of the family or to a favoured dependent.

Ernest Black has also suggested to me that the occurrence of aisled buildings (as at Baracombe and at Bignor) may represent some sort of concentration of agricultural dependents at villas. If so this may have had an impact on the surrounding settlement pattern. Thus if such workers had families, where and how were these accommodated? Possibly some such families lived on nearby sites (see above the non-villa settlement (the 'Furlongs') which was located to the south-west of the Beddingham villa), whilst others may have been further away, such as on the Downs. Although the accommodation of some of the postulated agricultural workers in aisled buildings may have only been a seasonal thing, any such practices may help to explain the lower density of occupation/activity noted above at some non-villa sites, as at Bishopstone, during the floruit of the villas.

Generally there is a dearth of Roman-period burials in the Ouse valley, the main exceptions being the cremation cemetery at Seaford, the possible barrow cemetery and other burials at Lewes, and the remains of seven infants at Beddingham villa. However, one other discovery, at Asham, near Rodmell, may be important and perhaps provides a clue regarding the types of locations chosen in the countryside for human burials. The find at Asham comprised four Late Iron Age/early Romano-British cremation urns buried in a lynchet (Curwen and Curwen 1936). These graves may thus indicate that one type of favoured place for burial were the boundaries of fields. As elsewhere in the countryside of Roman-period Sussex, the lack of late inhumation cemeteries or individual graves in the Ouse valley is noticeable, and thus the common procedures followed at this location and at this time for the disposal of the dead are uncertain. As noted above, some late Roman-period burials may have been found on early Saxon cemetery sites in the valley. If so, these inhumation graves provide evidence for some continuity of burial ground locations.

Prior to the fieldwork of the last four decades discussed above, a major research issue affecting the Ouse valley and the area between it and the River Cuckmere to the east had been the observation made by the late Martin Welch in the early 1970s that, with the exceptions of the early cemetery at Seaford and a large number of unexcavated native settlements, the area between the rivers Ouse and Cuckmere 'is blank on the [Ordnance Survey] Romano-British map' (Welch 1971, 232). In contrast Welch noted that this 'zone' contains a concentration of 5th century Saxon settlement as represented by cemeteries at Malling Hill, Beddingham Hill, Selmeston and Alfriston, and the cemetery and settlement at Rookery Hill, Bishopstone. He went on to suggest that the area between the two rivers, 'lacking...any villa buildings and lying distant from the main villa estates', may have been ceded by treaty by the land-owning Romano-British aristocracy to Saxon settlers/mercenaries. Although Welch's settlement by treaty theory received initial enthusiasm (Cunliffe 1973, 132-135), subsequent discoveries in the Ouse valley of evidence for villas at Newhaven, Beddingham, Barcombe and Plumpton (and also probable but unexcavated villas at Mark Cross and Firle) challenged an important assumption of the theory, i.e. the absence of villas. However, the reasoning behind the treaty/enclave theory for the Ouse/Cuckmere zone could still be valid if the villa and nucleated settlement sites prove to have been abandoned or significantly in decline before, or during, the late 4th century.

Acknowledgements

I wish to thank Jane Russell for drawing Figures 8.1, 8.4 and 8.8, and Andy Gammon for producing Figure 8.9. Thanks are also due to Martin Bell for his permission to use Figures 8.3 and 8.10, to the Sussex Archaeological Society for permission to reproduce Figure 8.10 and David Staveley for permission to use Figure 8.2. David Millum helped with the digital preparation of the various illustrations, and Sophie Unger of East Sussex County Council provided Historic Environment Record details. Ernest Black kindly read and commented upon a draft of this chapter.

References

Allen, M. 1984. Plumpton Roman Villa (TQ360147), a Cursory Note, *Sussex Archaeological Collections* 122, 219-220.

Allen M.J. and Seager-Smith, R. H. 1987. Plumpton Roman Villa and its Romano-British context, pages 19-24 in M.J. Allen, R. H. Seager-Smith, E. M. Somerville, L. and P. Stevens, and P. Norman (eds), *Aspects of Archaeology in the Lewes Area.* Lewes: Lewes Archaeological Group.

Applebaum, S. 1966. Peasant economy and types of agriculture, pages 99-107 in C. Thomas (ed.), *Rural Settlement in Roman Britain.* London: Council for British Archaeology.

Bedwin, O. 1978. The excavation of a Romano-British site at Ranscombe Hill, South Malling, East Sussex, 1976, *Sussex Archaeological Collections* 116, 241-255.

Beesley, E. 2009. Beddingham, East Sussex: Investigative Conservation of Material from Three Anglo-Saxon Graves. Unpubl. Portsmouth: English Heritage Research Department Report Series 56-2009.

Bell, M. 1976. The excavation of an early Romano-British site and Pleistocene landforms at Newhaven, Sussex, *Sussex Archaeological Collections* 114, 218-305.

Bell, M. 1977. Excavations at Bishopstone, *Sussex Archaeological Collections* 115.

Best, A. 2015. Barcombe and Beddingham: Roman villas from Wealden iron?, *Sussex Archaeological Collections* 153, 63-71.

Black, E. W. 1987. *The Roman Villas of South-East England.* Oxford: British Archaeological Reports, British Series 171.

Bleach, J. 1997. A Romano-British (?) barrow cemetery and the origins of Lewes, *Sussex Archaeological Collections* 135, 131-142.

Booth, P., Bingham, A-M. and Lawrence, S. 2008. *The Roman Roadside Settlement at Westhawk Farm, Ashford, Kent: Excavations 1998-9.* Oxford: Oxford Archaeology Ltd.

Butler, C. and Lyne, M. 2001. *The Roman Pottery Production Site at Wickham Barn, Chiltington, East Sussex.* Oxford: British Archaeological Reports, British Series 323.

Butler, C. and Staveley, D. 2014. A Geophysical Survey at Plumpton Roman Villa, Plumpton, East Sussex, Unpubl. report, Project no. CBAS0450. Chris Butler Archaeological Services Report.

Chuter, G. 2005. An interim report on a Romano-British site near Compton Wood, Firle, East Sussex, Unpubl. report, Project no. 2005/07. East Sussex County Council Report

Cleere, H. and Crossley, D. 1995. *The Iron Industry of the Weald*. Second Edition. (ed. J. Hodgkinson). Cardiff: Merton Priory Press.

Coates, R. 1990. The Roman villa site at Beddingham, 5-11, in R. Coates, *Some place-names of the Downland Fringe: seven Sussex essays of 1990*. Brighton: Younsmere Press.

Coates, R. 2002. N6.1.1 A widespread and perennial problem: Dunstall(s), *Locus focus* 6 (1).

Cunliffe, B. 1973. *The Regni*. London: Duckworth.

Curwen, E. and Curwen, E.C. 1930. Lynchet Burials near Lewes, *Sussex Archaeological Collections* 71, 254-57.

Dark, K. and Dark, P. 1997. *The Landscape of Roman Britain*. Stroud: Sutton Publishing Ltd.

Down, A. 1979. *Chichester Excavations 4, The Roman Villas at Chilgrove and Upmarden*. Chichester: Phillimore.

Drewett, P., Rudling, D. and Gardiner, M. 1988. *The South-East to AD 1000*. Harlow: Longman.

Fulford, M. 1973. A fourth-century colour-coated fabric and its types in South-East England, *Sussex Archaeological Collections* 111, 41-44.

Gardner, A. 2013. Thinking about Roman Imperialism: Postcolonialism, Globalisation and Beyond?, *Britannia* 44, 1-25.

Gelling, M. 1988. *Signposts to the past*. Second edition. Chichester: Phillimore.

Glover, J. 1975. *The Place Names of Sussex*. London: Batsford.

Green, C.M. 1978. The Pottery, 245-253, in Bedwin, O., The excavation of a Romano-British site at Ranscombe Hill, South Malling, East Sussex, 1976, *Sussex Archaeological Collections* 116, 241-255

Griffith, H. 1892. Gold Roman coin found at Seaford, *Sussex Archaeological Collections* 38, 202.

Hamilton, S. 1998. Using elderly data bases: Iron Age pit deposits at the Caburn, East Sussex and related sites, *Sussex Archaeological Collections* 136, 23-39.

Haverfield, F.J. 1912. *The Romanization of Roman Britain*, Second edition. Oxford: Clarenden Press.

Hodgkinson, J. 2008. *The Wealden Iron Industry*. Stroud: The History Press.

Holleyman, G.A. 1936. An Early British Agricultural Village Site on Highdole Hill, near Telscombe, *Sussex Archaeological Collections* 77, 202-221.

Lyne, M. 1994. The Hassocks Cemetery, *Sussex Archaeological Collections* 132, 53-85.

Margary, I.D. 1965. *Roman Ways in the Weald*. Third Edition. London: Phoenix House.

Margary, I.D. 1967. *Roman Roads in Britain*. Second Edition. London: John Baker.

Masefield, R. and Machling, T. 1993. The results of a surface artefact collection survey and soil resistivity survey at Mark Cross, Laughton, East Sussex, Unpubl. report, Project no. 1993/59. South Eastern Archaeological Services.

Meaton, C. 2004. An Archaeological Evaluation (Stage 1) at St. Mary the Virgin, Barcombe, East Sussex. Unpubl. report project no. P31. Archaeology South-East.

Millett, M. 1990. *The Romanization of Britain*. Cambridge: Cambridge University Press.

Millum, D. 2013. New evidence of a Romano-British settlement at Upper Wellingham, East Sussex, *Sussex Archaeological Collections* 151, 53-9.

Millum, D. 2014a. Tracing the Roman Road, *Sussex Past & Present* 133, 4-5.

Millum D. 2014b. Bridge Farm 2014, *Sussex Past & Present* 134, 8-9.

Millum, D. 2015. Bridge Farm 2015, *Sussex Past & Present* 137, 6-7.

Millum, D., Rudling, D. and Butler, C. 2013. Reflections on a cold plunge – reporting on the final year's dig in Church Field at Barcombe, *Sussex Past & Present* 129, 4-5.

Millum, D. and Wallace, R. 2013. Bridge Farm Excavation, *Sussex Past & Present* 131, 4-5.

Price, J.E. 1882. On excavations in the camp, the tumulus, and Romano-British cemetery, Seaford, Sussex, *Sussex Archaeological Collections* 32, 167-200.

Robinson, D. 1999. The Coast and Coastal Changes, pages 8-9 in K. Leslie and B. Short (eds), *An Historical Atlas of Sussex*. Chichester: Phillimore.

Rudling, D. 1982. The Romano-British Farm on Bullock Down, 97-142, in P. Drewett, *The Archaeology of Bullock Down, Eastbourne, East Sussex: The development of a landscape*. Lewes: Sussex Archaeological Society Monograph 1.

Rudling, D. 1983. The archaeology of Lewes: some recent research, *Sussex Archaeological Collections* 121, 45-77.

Rudling, D. 1997. Round 'house' to villa: the Beddingham and Watergate villas, pages 1-8 in R.M. and D.E. Friendship-Taylor (eds.), *From Round House to Villa. Fascicule 3 of the Upper Nene Archaeological Society*.

Rudling, D. 1998. The development of Roman villas in Sussex, *Sussex Archaeological Collections* 136, 41-65.

Rudling, D. 2003a. Roman rural settlement in Sussex: continuity and change, 111-126, in D. Rudling (ed.), *The Archaeology of Sussex to AD 2000*, Kings Lynn: Heritage Marketing and Publications.

Rudling, D. 2003b. A Tale of Two Villas: Beddingham and Barcombe, *Bulletin of the Association for Roman Archaeology* 15, 10-15.

Rudling, D. 2008. Roman-period Temples, Shrines and Religion in Sussex, in D. Rudling (ed.), *Ritual Landscapes of Roman South-East Britain*, Oxford: Oxbow, 95-137.

Rudling, D. 2014a. Excavations at Plumpton Roman villa, East Sussex, *Association for Roman Archaeology News* 32, 44.

Rudling, D. 2014b. Bullock Down revisited: The Romano-British Farm, in M.J. Allen (ed.), *Eastbourne, aspects of archaeology, history and heritage*, Eastbourne: Eastbourne Natural History & Archaeological Society, 64-75.

Rudling, D. 2015. The impact of Roman culture on the countryside of Sussex. Unpbl. PhD thesis, University of Roehampton.

Rudling, D. 2016. Plumpton Roman Villa Update, *Sussex Past & Present* 138, 11.

Rudling, D. and Butler, C. 2002. Barcombe Roman Villa, *Current Archaeology* 179, 486-89.

Rudling, D. and Butler, C. 2004. From Iron Age roundhouse to Roman villa: excavations at Barcombe, Sussex, 2001-2003, *Archaeology International* 2003/2004, 17-21.

Rudling, D., Butler, C. and Wallace, R. 2010. Barcombe Roman Villa, *British Archaeology* 111, 22-7.

Rudling, D. and Leigh, G.J. 2013. Southwick Roman villa, Its discovery, excavation, public display and eventual loss – a cautionary tale, *Sussex Archaeological Collections* 151, 27-52.

Rudling, D. and Russell, M. 2015. *Bignor Roman Villa*. Stroud: The History Press.

Russell, M. 1990. Excavations in Friars Walk, Lewes, 1989, *Sussex Archaeological Collections* 128, 141-156.

Russell, M. 2006. *Roman Sussex*. Stroud: Tempus.

Sawyer, J. 1999. The excavation of a Romano-British site at Burgess Hill, West Sussex, *Sussex Archaeological Collections* 137, 49-58.

Smith, A.H. 1956. *English Place-name elements; Part II*. Cambridge University Press.

Smith, V.G. 1939. The Iron Age and Romano-British site at Seaford, *Sussex Archaeological Collections* 80, 293-305.

Spurrell, F. 1852. Roman remains discovered at Newhaven in 1852, *Sussex Archaeological Collections* 5, 263-266.

Staveley, D. Forthcoming. Roman Roads and Roadside Settlements in the South-East, in M.J. Allen and D. Rudling (eds), *Archaeology and Land-use of South-East England to 1066*, Oxford: Oxbow.

Swanton, M.J. 1974. *A Corpus of Pagan Anglo-Saxon Spear-Types*. Oxford: British Archaeological Reports, British Series 7.

Thomas, G. 2010. *The Later Anglo-Saxon Settlement at Bishopstone: a downland manor in the making*. York: Council for British Archaeology Research Reports 163.

Wallace, R. 2014. Culver Archaeological Project: Bridge Farm: East Sussex. Roads, rivers and Romans: A Roman Town on the Upper Ouse? A HLF Funded Community Archaeological Assessment. Unpubl. report, AOC Archaeology Group Report for Project 32227.

Welch, M. 1971. Late Romans and Saxons in Sussex, *Britannia* 2, 232-237.

Welch, M.G. 1983. *Early Anglo-Saxon Sussex*. Oxford: British Archaeological Reports British Series 112.

Winbolt, S.E. 1935. Romano-British Sussex, pages 1-70 in L.F. Salzman (ed.), *The Victoria History of the Counties of England, A History of Sussex,* Volume III. Oxford: Oxford University Press.

Wolseley, G.R. and Smith, R.A. 1927. Prehistoric and Roman settlement on Park Brow, *Archaeologia* 76, 1-40.

9. Anglo-Saxons

Simon Stevens

Writing in the seventh century AD in Northumberland, a monk, known to history as the Venerable Bede, described the coming of the Anglo-Saxons in the fifth century (*Adventus Saxonum*) in the following terms (Colgrave and Mynors 1969, 51):

> The newcomers came from three very powerful nations of the Germans, namely the Saxons, the Angles and the Jutes. From the stock of the Jutes are the people of Kent and the people of Wight, and that which in the province of the West Saxons is to this day called the nation of the Jutes, situated opposite that same Isle of Wight. From the Saxons, that is, from the region that now is called that of the Old Saxons, came the East Saxons, the South Saxons, and the West Saxons ... In a short time, as bands of the aforesaid nations eagerly flocked into the Island, the people of the newcomers began to increase so much that they became a source of terror to the very natives who had invited them.

Bede's account, which is partially based on the work of another monk called Gildas written in the early sixth century (Yorke 1997, 3), masks the complexity of the situation which led to the emergence of so-called *Anglo-Saxon England* in the years *c.* AD 400 to 700 (cf. Welch 1992). Equally the shift to the purported *Viking Age England* of AD 800 to the Norman Conquest (cf. Richards 2000, 10) was not just the result of the appearance of Scandinavian raiders and settlers in the intervening century. The period between *c.* AD 400 and 1066 was a period of manifest social and political upheaval which has left its mark on the landscape of the Ouse corridor, and even in the name of the county. In a period in which archaeological data can often be noticeably thin, even in an area as rich in archaeological remains as Sussex (Gardiner 1990a, 47), this part of the county has a comparative embarrassment-of-riches in this department, including a number of lavishly published sites. Data from cemeteries and settlements provides abundant evidence of the way of life (and death) in this part of the land of the South Saxons from the end of Roman Britain to the Norman Conquest.

The *Adventus Saxonum*

The nature of the transition from *Britannia* to *England* remains obscure. Scholars are divided on the exact mechanisms of change, as well as on an accurate timetable, hamstrung by the paucity of contemporary written sources for the events relating to the arrival of Bede's Angles, Saxons and Jutes. The *Anglo-Saxon Chronicle* (begun in the ninth century) makes only three references to events in early Anglo-Saxon Sussex: the arrival of Aelle and his sons in AD 477, a battle near an unidentified river in 485 and his successful attack on Pevensey in 490/1 (Welch 1983, 255).

Academic theories range from the presence of Germanic mercenaries in Late Roman Britain who took over at the breakdown of centralised rule, much in the style described by Bede (Hawkes and Dunning 1961; Wilson 1976), to a gradual acculturation from the continent preceded by more than a century of proto-Roman continuity (Dark 2000), to a more rapid collapse aided by an evidence-free (and arguably utterly anachronistic) rebellion of the rural proletariat (Faulkner 2000). The fate of Bede's *'natives'* remains open to debate (Lucy 2000, 170-3), however recent studies have suggested the imposition of a form of 'apartheid' by the dominant newcomers, followed by acculturation and eventual assimilation (Härke 2011).

However, what is undeniable is that at the time that Bede's *'newcomers'* are thought to be settling here (by whatever mechanism and originally in whatever numbers or circumstances), new ways of treating the dead start to appear in the archaeological record in the eastern half of the country; cremations (with or without grave goods) and inhumations sometimes accompanied by grave goods, in stark contrast to the prevalent Romano-British method of unaccompanied inhumation (Lucy 2000, 1). The close juxtaposition of settlement and cemetery is also a common early Anglo-Saxon trait (Arnold 1997, 54), reversing the Late Romano-British trend (enforced by law) of 'extra-mural' cemeteries placed away from the living (Lucy 2000, 1).

Similarly, a distinct style of handmade (as opposed to Roman wheelthrown) pottery (Hurst 1976), and a type of building with its origins in continental Europe also begin to appear at this time, the sunken-featured buildings (SFBs), known by the German term *Grubenhäuser* (singular *Grubenhaus*). Although arguably the evidence from the Ouse corridor cannot be used to answer the 'big questions' concerning the apparatus of the changeover from Roman to Saxon Sussex, the available data is relevant to a number of the prevalent themes in early Anglo-Saxon archaeology.

The Excavated Evidence

Despite attempts to highlight the Scandinavian influence in the latter part of the period (e.g. Richards 1991), the Anglo-Saxon period is conventionally divided into three separate phases: *'Early'* (c. 450-650), *'Middle'* (c. 650-800), and *'Late'* (c. 800-1066) (Hills 1999, 177). Published evidence for activity in each of three periods is available for the Ouse corridor, although 'Middle' Anglo-Saxon material has proved the most elusive. The author has deliberately avoided reliance on evidence from placenames, following the wise advice that 'their interpretation is a specialist task best left to the toponymic philologist and there are many potential pitfalls for the inexpert' (Welch 1983, 229)

The Beginning - The Earliest Material

'Squatters'

Arguably the earliest physical evidence of Anglo-Saxon activity in the Ouse corridor comes from so-called 'squatter' occupation at the Roman villa and associated shrine at Beddingham (White, 1999, 28). The term *'squatter'* is perhaps somewhat misleading, suggesting wholesale change of population, rather than a change of circumstances and supply of goods. Pottery dated to the late fourth or fifth centuries was located at the site, including bowls with pedestal feet thought to have fallen out of use by the mid-fifth century (Rudling 1998, 55-9).

There is also potential evidence of immediately post-Roman settlement nearby at Firle, where a scatter of Anglo-Saxon pottery dated by the excavator from the fifth to seventh centuries was recovered in association with a possible Roman villa identified by geophysical survey and trial trenching (Chuter 2005). A sixth century brooch was also recovered, perhaps hinting at the presence of an associated cemetery given the usual juxtaposition of the living and the dead during this period.

Cemeteries

David Rudling (this volume, chapter 8) suggests a link between the post-Roman activity at the villa at Beddingham and the local Anglo-Saxon inhumation cemeteries at Drayton Field, and at Balcombe Pit, Glynde (Welch 1983, 395-401) both partially excavated in the 1800s. Perhaps the presence of a female inhumation at the former site is indicative of the presence of more than a mere handful of warriors using the ruinous villa as a temporary base? Another partially excavated cemetery centred on a group of barrows on Beddingham Hill is also evidence of occupation in the area at an early date, given the presence of a disc brooch dated to *c.* AD 500 among the grave goods (*ibid.*).

Metal detectorists were responsible for the discovery of a previously unknown cemetery at Comps Farm, Beddingham in more recent years. Three accompanied graves dated to the early part of the sixth century were found in October 2008. Burnt material recovered from one of the grave fills suggests that the as-yet-unexplored part of the cemetery may contain cremated remains (Beesley 2009).

Few other early Anglo-Saxon burials in the Ouse corridor have been scientifically excavated in recent years, however a group were examined in a field near the junction of the A26 and the B2192 ('Earwig Corner') in 2002 after metal detectorists had removed material from a known cemetery. The site had been discovered in the 1830s when workmen unearthed a group of graves while road digging, but the 2002 excavation allowed the detailed examination of five inhumations and associated grave goods, some of which were reunited with their 'owners' after removal by the detectorists. The graves were dated to the late fifth or sixth century on the evidence of a range of grave goods (Thomas 2002, 5).

Anglo-Saxon material of fifth to sixth centuries has also been recovered from the site of the Roman villa at Barcombe, where ironworking slag suggested the location of an industrial area (Butler and Rudling 2005, 6). Accompanied Anglo-Saxon burials have been recorded at South Malling (Norris 1956, 11-12), as well as lower down the corridor at South Heighton (Welch 1983, 395) although reporting was minimal and dating uncertain in both cases.

The exact location of these and other known Anglo-Saxon burial sites in the Ouse valley has not been supplied in the text or figures given their vulnerability to illegal metal-detecting. The location of larger sites is given in the map included in the introduction.

Rookery Hill

The most widely known early Anglo-Saxon site in the area is the fifth/sixth century settlement and associated cemetery on Rookery Hill at Bishopstone (Bell 1977). Encountered during construction work, and an excellent example of an early 'rescue' dig, the excavations uncovered evidence of 22 buildings, mostly posthole built, and rectangular in plan (Figure 9.1). These included a larger 'hall' with a trench foundation (although there have been suggestions that this was later in date: Welch 1992, 34) and three *Grubenhäuser*. The remains of these buildings consist of a sub-rectangular pit presumed to have been covered by a roof supported on two posts (Rahtz 1976, 70-81). The subject of an exhaustive recent study (Tipper 2004), these structures are thought to be workshops, and often contain debris associated with weaving, such as loomweights, found

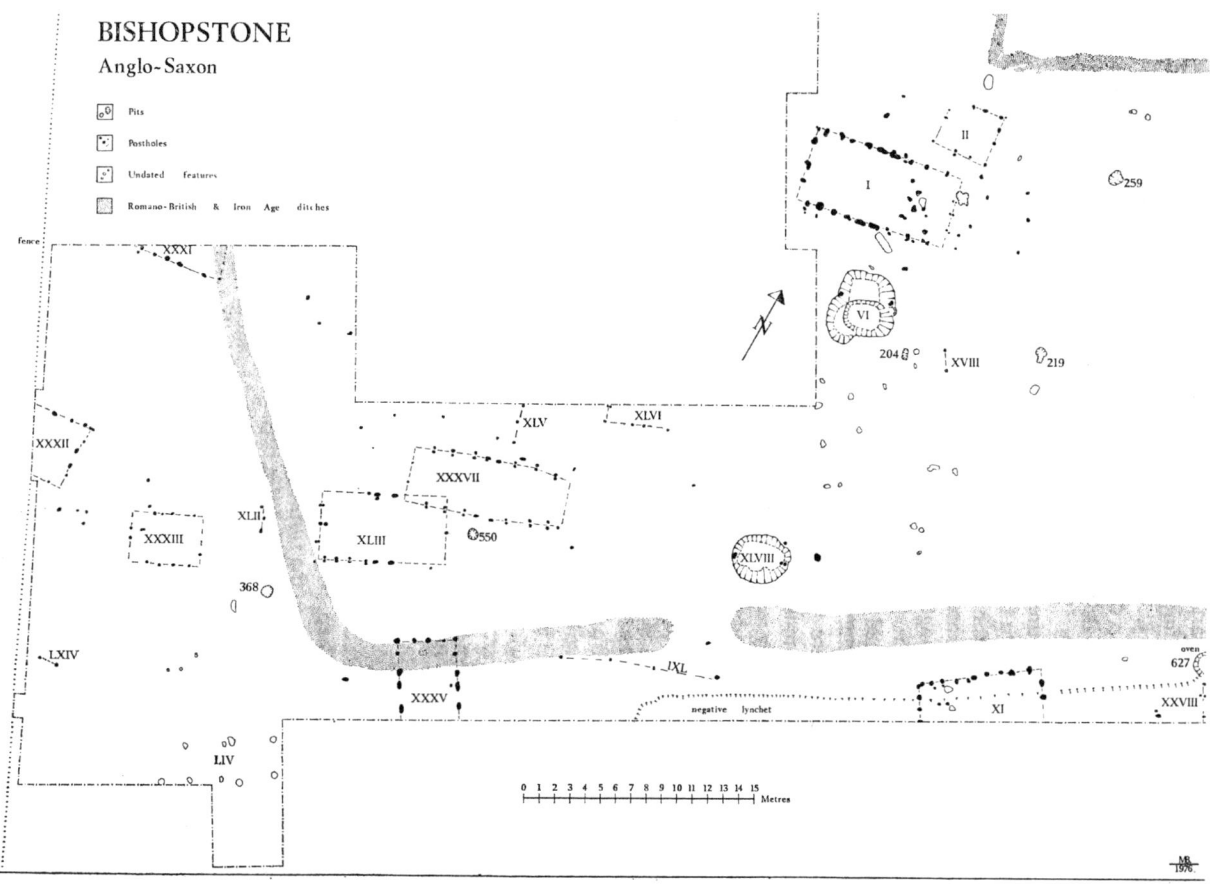

FIGURE 9.1: ANGLO-SAXON BUILDINGS AT ROOKERY HILL, BISHOPSTONE (REPRODUCED BY KIND PERMISSION OF MARTIN BELL)

at Bishopstone, and elsewhere in Sussex (e.g. at Erringham in the Adur valley; Holden 1976).

Arnold (1997, 34) paints a detailed (and rather poetic) picture of life at Rookery Hill from the excavated evidence:

> In the pastures stood sheep, cattle and a few horse and roaming more freely were geese, fowl and cats. Growing in the arable fields during the summer months would have been a crop of barley … food produced in this way was supplemented by marine resources: mussels, limpets and periwinkles gathered on the foreshore, conger eel from the lower shore and whiting taken from the sea ... animals not only provided dairy products, meat, leather and wool for clothing; bone was used to make such things as combs, weaving tools and netting needles. In nearby woodland pigs were reared and red and roe deer were hunted. Also taken from the woodland were oak, hawthorn and hornbeam used for building, for fuel and for wooden implements. Clay and ironstone were brought from the Weald to manufacture pottery, spindle-whorls, loomweights and a variety of implements including nails, knives, spears and shield fittings.

The associated cemetery at Rookery Hill contained 118 inhumation burials and six cremations centred on a prehistoric round barrow, a widespread phenomenon, thought to symbolise legitimisation of land ownership or even associations with the distant past (discussed in Lucy 2000, 124-30). Evidence from Rookery Hill cemetery suggests the presence of at least one post-built structure in the immediate vicinity of the cemetery (Bell 1977, 195). Similar structures have been recorded within Anglo-Saxon cemeteries (so-called *'cremation houses' or 'houses of the dead'*) perhaps reinforcing the link between the living and the dead as suggested at the cemetery at Apple Down to the north of Chichester (Down and Welch 1990).

Itford Farm

The discovery of another fifth/sixth century *Grubenhäus* at Itford Farm near Beddingham demonstrates that people were living in the Ouse valley as well as on the better drained chalk hillsides of the area (Figure 9.2). The structure was uncovered during the laying of a pipeline and hence the area available for excavation was limited and no evidence for associated structures or cemetery was encountered in the narrow easement for the scheme (James 2002).

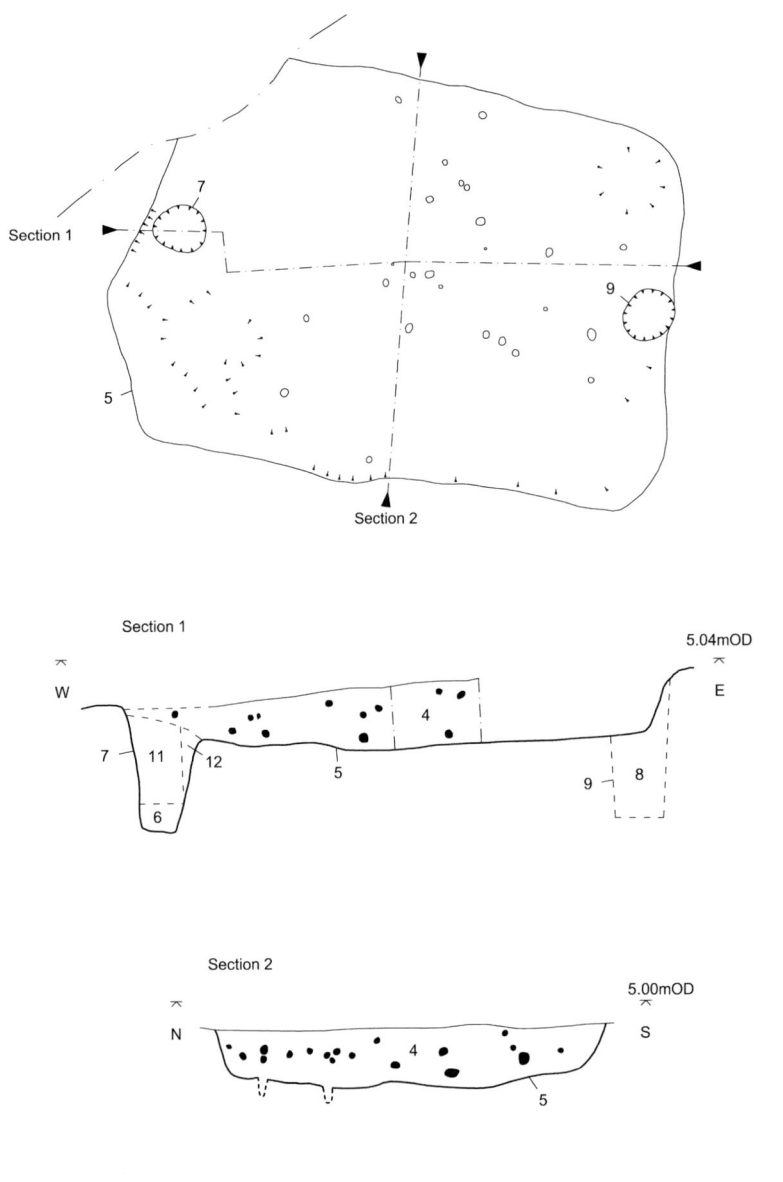

FIGURE 9.2: ANGLO-SAXON GRUBENHAUS AT ITFORD FARM, BEDDINGHAM
(REPRODUCED BY KIND PERMISSION OF RICHARD JAMES)

The Middle - Limited Evidence of Continuity

Saxonbury

The location of a sixth to seventh century cemetery at Saxonbury near Lewes is clearly indicative of later Anglo-Saxon settlement further up the Ouse valley given the usual proximity of the living and the dead (see above). The cemetery was disturbed by workmen in 1891, and the graves were 'excavated' by them, leading to the production of a basic report (Sawyer 1892). The site, which contained 32 or 33 inhumations with some associated grave goods, was eventually more fully published (Craddock 1979).

Itford Farm

Further work at Itford Farm close to the Grubenhaus, suggests some level of occupation into the seventh or even the ninth century, extending the occupation into the otherwise somewhat elusive Middle Anglo-Saxon period (Butler 2009).

Bishopstone

Anglo-Saxon settlements in the Ouse corridor and elsewhere were liable to periodic 'shifts' influence by a variety of factors (for the theory behind the 'Middle Saxon Shift' see Arnold and Wardle 1981, and counter arguments in Thomas 2010), eventually resulting in what has been described as the 'crucial change from fluid to essentially stable communities' (Hamerow 1991, 16). One such *'stable community'* at Bishopstone, in the valley below Rookery Hill has recently been lavishly published (Thomas 2010).

A group of later seventh/eighth/ninth century burials, presumably associated with the Church of St. Andrew (see below) were the earliest evidence of Anglo-Saxon activity encountered in the excavations (Figure 9.3). A total of 37 unaccompanied inhumations were recorded, including the remains of a young woman who had died in pregnancy, the bones of a 23-week-old foetus still in her abdomen (Schoss and Lewis 2010, 80). There was also a relatively high incidence of traumatic injury to bones, explained as the result of an agricultural lifestyle (Schoss and Lewis 2010, 86).

Religious Communities

The evidence from Bishopstone highlights a poorly understood facet of the Anglo-Saxon occupation of the Ouse corridor; the significance of the religious communities. Thomas's putative model suggests that the church of St. Andrew at Bishopstone was founded in the seventh century as a *minster* and became a shrine to St. Lewinna, a local Christian martyr (*op cit.* 215). Taylor notes that Christianity was reintroduced to Sussex in the

9. ANGLO-SAXONS

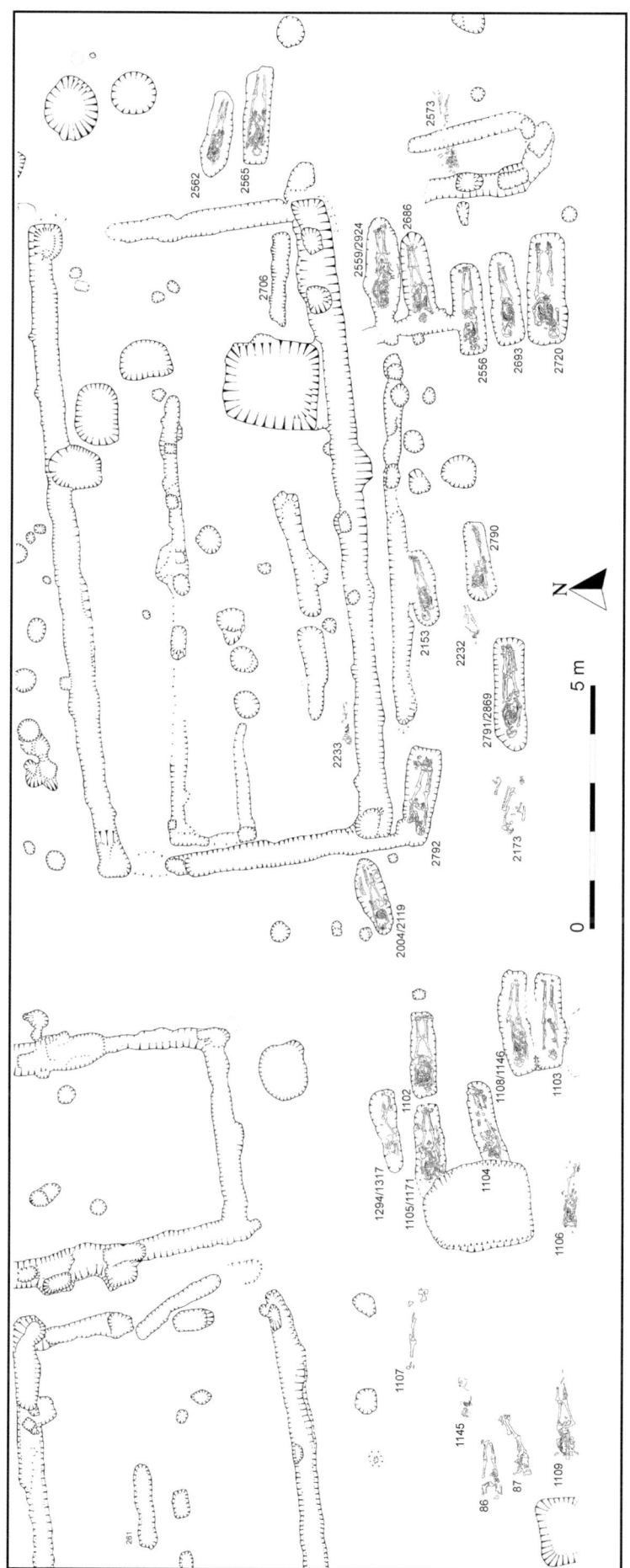

FIGURE 9.3: LATER SEVENTH/EIGHTH/NINTH CENTURY BURIALS AT BISHOPSTONE (REPRODUCED BY KIND PERMISSION OF GABOR THOMAS)

late seventh century by Bishop Wilfred both as a faith and a political force at that time, although there was already an established community of monks at Bosham at the time (Taylor 2003, 161). The missionary work of these new communities led to the foundation of a network of churches including major centres known as *minsters* such as Bishopstone (Combes 2010), where clerics, 'led a common life resembling that of monks' (Taylor 1999, 46). Details of the development and administration of the *minster* system are sketchy (*ibid.*), but the Ouse corridor was the location of other known pre-Conquest religious centres at South Malling and possibly at Beddingham (Taylor 2003, fig. 13.1). Although the survival of recognisable Anglo-Saxon parish church fabric is generally poor in the area (Fisher 1970), the Ouse corridor boasts a unique first. William Camden's *Britannia* published in 1586 includes the earliest surviving illustration from an archaeological volume, a drawing of the chancel arch of St. John-sub-Castro in Lewes (Rodwell 2005, 18), another possible *minster* church (Brent 2004, 27).

The End - 'Stable' and Defended Communities

Bishopstone

The cemetery at Bishopstone was abandoned in favour of the use of the area for buildings and rubbish pits by AD 900 (Figures 9.4 and 9.5). A complex of timber 'halls', some showing clear evidence of rebuilding and/or repair was constructed as well as a building with a cellar, interpreted by the excavator as a tower, a unique discovery on a rural Anglo-Saxon site. Given the complexity of the site, the number of recorded buildings 'can only be expressed as a range of between 22 and 25' (Thomas 2010, 36). Rubbish pits at the site revealed a mass of evidence relating to diet and economy, with exploitation of domestic animals and a range of other species ranging from whales to locally available wild birds. Charred cereals show the cultivation of barley, wheat, oats and rye. There was also a wide range of pottery and domestic artefacts highlighting the more 'stable' lifestyle of the community (Thomas *op cit.*). There was also a hoard of metal objects, interpreted as a 'special deposit', a phenomena borrowed from the lexicon of prehistory (cf. Hill 1995). Mirroring interpretations put forward by Hamerow (2006), the hoard was seen as a 'closure deposit' to mark the cessation of use of the cellared building. Articulated and semi-articulated animal burials were also interpreted in this way (Thomas 2010, 105-6). Morris and Jervis (2011) have further developed Hamerow's theory, stressing the variety of motivations for the creation and deposition of such deposits, and in the process have in fact questioned their very definition as 'special'.

The Burh at Lewes

The Ouse corridor was also the location for one of a chain of planned centres of defense against the threat of Viking incursions initiated by Alfred the Great in the late ninth century and listed in a tenth century document called the *Burghal Hidage* (Hill 1969). A recent study has highlighted the distinctly 'planned' layout of the town of Lewes (Holmes 2010), and archaeological work at the Baxter's site on St. Nicholas Lane has uncovered a 5m wide, 2m deep ditch, which appears to be the first published evidence for the location of the burh defences (Stevens 2008, 5).

Other late Anglo-Saxon features were encountered at the site, and provide clear insight into life in the town in the years immediately preceding the Conquest. Initial assessment of the material suggests a varied diet including the 'usual' domestic animals as well as fresh and saltwater fish and cereals. A range of domestic items was unearthed including a collection of loom weights found in the remains of a building dated to the ninth and tenth centuries (Stevens 2009). A hoard of seventeen silver pennies minted during the reign of Edward the Elder, dated to AD 899-924 was also recovered from the site (Figure 9.6).

Clearly there was a need for communal defence even into the early eleventh century, highlighted by documentary references to a pitched battle in Sussex as late as 1001

FIGURE 9.4: ANGLO-SAXON FEATURES AT BISHOPSTONE (REPRODUCED BY KIND PERMISSION OF GABOR THOMAS)

FIGURE 9.5: RECONSTRUCTION OF ANGLO-SAXON BUILDINGS AT BISHOPSTONE (REPRODUCED BY KIND PERMISSION OF GABOR THOMAS)

FIGURE 9.6: SILVER PENNY OF EDWARD THE ELDER, DATED TO AD 899-924 FROM LEWES (© ARCHAEOLOGY SOUTH-EAST)

(Gardiner and Coates 1987). However, Lewes developed into a major late Anglo-Saxon urban centre of undoubted status, with numerous functions in addition to defence (as defined by Biddle 1976; Reynolds 1999, 160), with a mint and extensive commercial interests (Brent 2004, 21-5).

It has been suggested that Mount Caburn was also refortified in a response to Viking raids but the evidence is thin at best (Drewett and Hamilton 1999, 33).

The Late Saxon Countryside

Metalwork of the ninth to eleventh century date, considered indicative of wealth and status, has been found further upstream at Hamsey (Thomas 2001), highlighting the apparent prosperity of Lewes's late Anglo-Saxon hinterland, although the evidence is arguably somewhat anecdotal. The Late Anglo-Saxon countryside was divided into estates which could be large and potentially prosperous, based on the evidence of a limited number of surviving charters. For instance, the estate of South Malling stretched from near Lewes to the county border at Lamberhurst (Gardiner 1999, 30), but the system of land holding is poorly understood (*ibid.*). Equally, the *Domesday Book* does not offer a particularly clear picture of the pre-Conquest situation in the Ouse corridor, or elsewhere in Sussex (Gardiner and Warne 1999, 34).

However, there is limited, but macabre evidence of the Late Anglo-Saxon judicial system, in the form of a so-called '*execution cemetery*' (Reynolds 1999, 105-10). The site at Malling Down above Lewes was found by a metal detectorist in July 1973 and the subsequent excavation of a mass grave of male skeletons, all with their hands tied behind their backs was never fully published, the exact location was not fully recorded, and the site was to all-intents-and-purposes, lost. It was rediscovered during scrub clearance in November 2004 and further excavation was undertaken in April 2005 by local volunteers under the direction of Greg Chuter, the Assistant County Archaeologist for East Sussex. A further seven burials, all of young males were recorded and again, where evidence was available, it was clear that their hands had been tied, although there was no evidence of trauma on any of the studied bones. A programme of C14 dating of bones from both excavation campaigns suggests a date of burial sometime in the late tenth or early eleventh century (Chuter *et al.* undated). At the time of writing, one of the authors is hoping to gain funding for isotope analysis to ascertain if the individuals were actually of Scandinavian origin in the light of the recent discovery of a mass grave of apparently executed Viking warriors in Dorset (Greg Chuter pers. comm.).

Discussion and future work

Despite the wealth of Anglo-Saxon remains in the Ouse corridor, there are clearly some gaps in the evidence. Arguably the biggest of these is the absence of seventh and early eighth century 'high status' burial sites (Geake 1992, 85-6); for example, barrow cemeteries with lavish grave goods, such as the cemetery of the East Anglian royal family unearthed at Sutton Hoo in Suffolk in the 1930s (Carver 1998). The recent discovery of an opulently accompanied, so-called '*princely burial*' during rescue excavations at Prittlewell in Essex (Hirst *et al.* 2004), has highlighted the possibility that previously unrecorded rich seventh century graves can be unearthed even on 'routine' archaeological investigations. The discovery of the Staffordshire Hoard by legal metal detection in 2009 stimulated huge interest in Anglo-Saxon archaeology (and presumably a rise in metal detector sales). The hoard, which contained more than 1600 items including more than 5kg of gold, appears to date from the late seventh century, and has been valued at over £3 million (Leahy and Bland 2009).

In ideal circumstances a lavishly-funded open area excavation of an early Anglo-Saxon settlement and associated cemetery somewhere in the Ouse corridor might place the river firmly on the Anglo-Saxon map in the way that recent work in the Adur valley has done for one of the Ouse's westerly neighbour (cf. Holden 1976, Gardiner 1990b; 1993, Gardiner and Greatorex 1997). A suitably sumptuous publication to dovetail with those for the other known Ouse sites (and perhaps including some re-evaluation of other smaller sites) might even give the Ouse top billing.

Postscript

The name of the county of Sussex certainly derives from name of the South Saxons, as noted by Bede, and by the late seventh century it had become a geographic entity which essentially matched the extent of Wilfred's diocese (Taylor 1999, 46). It survived as an administrative unit until 1974. It has also been suggested that the name of the river which forms the subject of this study also dates from this period. Ekwall (1928, 291) notes that its Anglo-Saxon name was *Midwin* 'middle winding [river]', from *midde* 'mid' + *winde* 'winding', which survives in *Midwyn Bridge* in Lindfield. But Mawer and Stenton (1929, 6) note that the expression *pontem de wos* is found in an assize roll of 1288, containing a word deriving from Old English *wāse,* the ancestor of *ooze*, which is also its literal meaning, and this has been suspected of contributing to the river-name. However, there remains real doubt as to the antiquity of the current name. It is probable that the river was not actually known as *Ouse* until the seventeenth century, when the name appears for the first time in Michael Drayton's topographical poem of 1620 *Poly-Olbion* (Richard Coates pers. comm.). It may be abstracted from a once-current single-syllable pronunciation of *Lewes*, or it may be his invention.

Acknowledgements

The author would like to thank Dudley Moore for inviting him to contribute to this publication. Thanks are also due to those who have kindly taken time to read various drafts and make valuable additions/comments, sent unpublished material, and/or have kindly agreed for illustrations from their work to be used, namely Martin Bell, Chris Butler, Greg Chuter, Julie Gardiner, Mark Gardiner, Richard James and Gabor Thomas. I am particularly indebted to Richard Coates for his scholarly reworking of the postscript.

References

Arnold, C. J. 1997. *An Archaeology of the Early Anglo-Saxon Kingdom*. London: Routledge.

Arnold, C. J. and Wardle, P. 1981. Early medieval settlement patterns in England. *Medieval Archaeology* 25, 145-9.

Beesley, E. 2009. *Beddingham, East Sussex. Investigative Conservation of Materials from Three Anglo-Saxon Graves,* English Heritage Archaeological Conservation Report no. 56-2009.

Bell, M. G. 1977. Excavations at Bishopstone, Sussex. *Sussex Archaeological Collections* 115, 1-299.

Biddle, M. 1976. Towns. In D. Wilson, (ed.), *The Archaeology of Anglo-Saxon England*, 99-150. Cambridge: Cambridge University Press.

Brent, C. 2004. *Pre-Georgian Lewes c. 980-1714, the emergence of a county town.* Lewes: Colin Brent Books.

Butler, C. 2009. An Archaeological Excavation at Itford Farm, Beddingham, East Sussex. Unpubl. Report no. CBAS 0057, Chris Butler Archaeological Services.

Butler, C. and Rudling, D. 2005. Recent discoveries at Barcombe. Saxon and other activity at Barcombe Roman villa. *Sussex Past and Present* 105, 6-7.

Carver, M. O. H. 1998. *Sutton Hoo. Burial Ground of Kings?* London: British Museum Press.

Chuter, G. 2005. *An Interim Report on a Romano-British site near Compton Wood, Firle, East Sussex.* Unpub. East Sussex County Council Report - Project no. 2005/07.

Chuter, G., Meadows, M. and Allen, M., undated. A late Anglo-Saxon (10th century AD) execution cemetery on Malling Down, Lewes, East Sussex. Unpubl. report.

Colgrave, B. and Mynors, R. (eds), 1969. *Bede's Ecclesiastical History of the English People,* Oxford: Clarendon Press.

Combes, P. 2010. Bishopstone, A Pre-Conquest Minster Church. *Sussex Archaeological Collections* 140, 49-56.

Craddock, J. 1979. The Anglo-Saxon cemetery at Saxonbury, Lewes, East Sussex. *Sussex Archaeological Collections* 117, 85-102.

Dark, K. 2000. *Britain and the End of the Roman Empire.* Stroud: Tempus.

Down, A. and Welch, M. 1990. *Chichester Excavations VII: Apple Down and the Mardens,* Chichester District Council.

Drewett, P. and Hamilton, S. 1999. Marking time and making space: excavations and landscape studies at the Caburn hillfort, East Sussex 1996-98. *Sussex Archaeological Collections* 137, 7-37.

Ekwall, E. 1928. *English river-names.* Oxford: Clarendon Press.

Faulkner, N. 2000. *The Decline and Fall of Roman Britain.* Stroud: Tempus.

Fisher, E. A. 1970. *The Saxon Churches of Sussex.* Newton Abbot, David and Charles.

Gardiner, M. 1990a. The Archaeology of the Weald – a survey and a review. *Sussex Archaeological Collections* 128, 33-53.

Gardiner, M. 1990b. An Anglo-Saxon and Medieval Settlement at Botolphs, Bramber, West Sussex. *Archaeological Journal* 147, 216-75.

Gardiner, M. 1993. The excavation of a late Anglo-Saxon settlement at Market Field, Steyning 1988-89. *Sussex Archaeological Collections* 131, 21-67.

Gardiner, M. 1999. Late Saxon Sussex c. 650–1066. In K. Leslie and B. Short (eds), *An Historical Atlas of Sussex.* Chichester: Phillimore, 30-31.

Gardiner, M. and Coates, R. 1987. Ellingsdean, A Viking Battlefield Identified. *Sussex Archaeological Collections* 125, 251-2.

Gardiner, M. and Greatorex, C. 1997. Archaeological excavations in Steyning 1992-5; further evidence for the evolution of a Late Saxon small town. *Sussex Archaeological Collections* 135, 143-71.

Gardiner, M. and Warne, H. 1999. Domesday Settlement. In K. Leslie and B. Short (eds), *An Historical Atlas of Sussex.* Chichester: Phillimore, 34-5.

Geake, H. 1992. Burial Practice in seventh and eighth-century England. In Carver (ed.), *The Age of Sutton Hoo.* Woodbridge: Boydell Press.

Hamerow, H. 1991. Settlement mobility and the 'Mid Saxon Shift'; rural settlements and settlement patterns in Anglo-Saxon England. *Anglo-Saxon England* 20, 1-17.

Hamerow, H. 2006. Special deposits in Anglo-Saxon settlements. *Medieval Archaeology,* 50, 1-30

Härke, H. 2011. Anglo-Saxon Immigration and Ethnogenesis. *Medieval Archaeology* 55, 1-28.

Hawkes, C. and Dunning, G. 1961. Soldiers and Settlers in Britain, fourth to fifth century. *Medieval Archaeology* 5, 1-70.

Hill, D. 1969. The Burghal Hidage - the establishment of a text. *Medieval Archaeology* 13, 84-92.

Hill, J. D. 1995. *Ritual and Rubbish in the Iron Age of Wessex.* Oxford: British Archaeological Reports British Series 242.

Hills, C. 1999. Early Historic Britain. In J. Hunter and I. Ralston, *The Archaeology of Britain. An Introduction from the Upper Palaeolithic to the Industrial Revolution,* 176-193. London: Routledge.

Holden, E. 1976. Excavations at Old Erringham, Shoreham, West Sussex, part 1: a Saxon weaving hut. *Sussex Archaeological Collections* 114, 306-21.

Holmes, M. 2010. The Street Plan of Lewes and the Burghal Hidage. *Sussex Archaeological Collections* 148, 71-8.

Hirst, S., Nixon, T., Rowsome, P. and Wright, S. 2004. *The Prittlewell Prince: The Discovery of a Rich Anglo-Saxon Burial in Essex.* London, Museum of London Archaeology Service.

Hurst, J. 1976. The pottery. In D. Wilson (ed.), *The Archaeology of Anglo-Saxon England*, 283-348. Cambridge: Cambridge University Press.

James, R. 2002. The excavation of a Saxon *Grubenhaus* at Itford Farm, Beddingham, East Sussex. *Sussex Archaeological Collections* 140, 41–7.

Leahy, K. and Bland, R. 2009. *The Staffordshire Hoard.* London: British Museum Press.

Lucy, S. 2000. *The Anglo-Saxon Way of Death.* Stroud: Sutton.

Mawer, A. and Stenton, F. M. with Gover, J. E. B. 1929-30. The place-names of Sussex. *The Survey of English*

Place-Names 6-7. Reprinted 2001, Nottingham: English Place-Name Society.

Morris, J. and Jervis, B. 2011. What's So Special? A Reinterpretation of Anglo-Saxon 'Special Deposits'. *Medieval Archaeology* 55, 66-81.

Norris, N. E. S. 1956. Miscellaneous Researches, 1949-56. *Sussex Archaeological Collections* 94, 1-12.

Rahtz, P. 1976. Buildings and rural settlement. In D. Wilson (ed.), *The Archaeology of Anglo-Saxon England*, 49-98, Cambridge: Cambridge University Press.

Reynolds, A. 1999. *Later Anglo-Saxon England, History and Landscape.* Stroud: Tempus.

Richards, J. 2000. *Viking Age England,* London: English Heritage/Batsford.

Rodwell, W. 2005. *The Archaeology of Churches.* Stroud: Tempus.

Rudling, D. 1998. The development of Roman villas in Sussex. *Sussex Archaeological Collections* 136, 41-65.

Sawyer, J. 1892). Important Discovery of Anglo-Saxon Remains at Kingston, Lewes. *Sussex Archaeological Collections* 38, 177-82.

Schoss, L. and Lewis, M. 2010. The human remains. In G. Thomas (ed.), *The later Anglo-Saxon settlement at Bishopstone: a downland manor in the making*, 78-86. CBA Research Report no. 163, 78-86.

Stevens, S. 2008. Baxter's Printworks, Lewes. *Sussex Past and Present* 116, 5.

Stevens, S. 2009. Post-Excavation Assessment and Updated Project Design on Archaeological Excavations at the Baxter's Printworks Site, St. Nicholas Lane, Lewes, East Sussex. Unpubl. Report no, 2008082, Archaeology South-East.

Taylor, M. 1999. Religious Foundations. In K. Leslie and B. Short (eds), *An Historical Atlas of Sussex.* Chichester: Phillimore, 46-47.

Taylor, M. 2003. Ecclesiastical Sites in Sussex. In D. Rudling (ed.), *The Archaeology of Sussex to AD 2000*. King's Lynn, Heritage Marketing and Publications, 161-170.

Thomas, G. 2001. Hamsey near Lewes: The Implications of Recent Finds of Late Anglo-Saxon metalwork and its Importance in the Pre-Conquest Period. *Sussex Archaeological Collections* 139, 123-32.

Thomas, G. 2002. Teeth worn down like Iguanodons. New evidence for Early Anglo-Saxon Lewes. *Sussex Past and Present* 96, 4-5.

Thomas, G. 2010. *The later Anglo-Saxon settlement at Bishopstone: a downland manor in the making.* York: CBA Research Report 163.

Tipper, J. 2004. *The Grubenhaus in Anglo-Saxon England*. Landscape Research Centre, Yedingham.

Welch, M. 1983. *Early Anglo-Saxon Sussex.* Oxford: British Archaeological Reports, British Series112, parts I and II.

Welch, M. R. 1992. *Anglo-Saxon England*. London: English Heritage/Batsford.

White, S. 1999. Early Saxon Sussex *c*. 410 – *c*. 650. In K. Leslie and B. Short (eds), *An Historical Atlas of Sussex.* Chichester: Phillimore, 28-29.

Wilson, D. (ed.) 1976. *The Archaeology of Anglo-Saxon England*. Cambridge University Press.

Yorke, B. 1997. *Kings and Kingdoms of Early Anglo-Saxon England*. London: Routledge.

10. The Upper Ouse in the Medieval period (AD 1066 to 1499)

David H. Millum

This chapter aims to provide a balanced review of the main archaeological investigations carried out within the Upper Ouse area where significant data has been gained from the medieval period. The sites and information have been used selectively and it is not intended as a total synthesis of every medieval find from the area.

For much of its length the River Ouse forms the boundary between two of the five medieval administrative divisions of Sussex with the Rape of Lewes to the west bank and that of Pevensey to the east. In the Upper Ouse area the west bank falls within the Hundred of Berecompe (Barcombe), which was mainly held by lay tenants, whilst to the east Lokesfield, formerly Mellinges (Malling), was retained by the Archbishop of Canterbury and included the suburban settlement of Cliffe. To the north the Hundred of Riston, also known as Rushmonden (Morris 1976), was held in multiple lordship (Adams 1999; Gardiner and Warne 1999).

Lewes – the urban centre of the Upper Ouse

Lewes was established as the burh of the Ouse valley during the late Saxon period and William de Warrenne confirmed its local dominance after the conquest by building his double motte castle within the town and subsequently founding the great Cluniac Priory of St. Pancras at Southover by 1082. The town was the trading and judicial centre for the area as well as being the main port for sea-going ships before the coastal port of Seaford took over and subsequently grew into a significant trading centre in its own right by the start of the thirteenth century (Gardiner 1995, 190; Brent 2004, 122). The defended town was enlarged during the medieval period with a new East Gate being built at the bottom of the current School Hill having a Franciscan friary and waterfront beyond and many of the current 'twittens' evidence the layout of this expansion (Stevens 2009).

The medieval town wall survives in only fragmentary form with sections east of Westgate Street, Keere Street, and Southover Road but with little medieval evidence remaining exposed. The lower section of the West Gate's northern bastion and adjacent wall which survive within the Freemason's Hall at 148 High Street are probably of thirteenth century date (Harris 2005, 37).

As Lewes dominated the Upper Ouse, so it does the medieval archaeology listed for the area in the East Sussex Historic Environment Record (ESHER) and *Sussex Archaeological Collections* (SAC) with Grey Friars, St. Nicholas Hospital and the town walls, as well as many domestic sites, in addition to the Priory and Castle (Figure 10.1).

Harris (2005, 38) suggests that the absence of a systematic survey of the townhouses of Lewes has led to a considerable underestimating of medieval building survival. However the ten pre-1500 survivals recorded are significant with four in the High Street area (nos. 66, 70-72, 73 and the Town Hall) including examples of thirteenth to fourteenth century undercrofts. 74-5 High Street is probably the earliest example of a more intact townhouse, dating from probably the fourteenth century, with jettying to two adjacent elevations with *in situ* dragon beam. Fifteenth century structure is found within 67, 92 (Bull House) and 99/100, High Street as well as the cellar beneath the later hall of Anne of Cleves House in Southover (Harris 2005, 38-39).

Lewes has six extant churches that have evidence of medieval origin (Table 10.1) and a further seven that are no longer standing but for which there is historical evidence (see Brent 2004, 30). One of these, St. John-sub-Castro, was probably of minster status suggesting the existence to the east of a much greater precinct than the present churchyard (Harris 2005, 32).

The Battle of Lewes in 1264 also provides a major focus for this period with mass grave sites having been discovered in three pits to the west of the prison crossroads in 1810 and a 'mass of bones crammed' into a 6m by 3m pit adjacent to the cemetery at St. Pancras Priory that was unearthed by railway workers in 1845. The bones from the pit were reputedly removed in 13 wagons to underpin the railway embankment at Southerham Corner (Brent 2004, 66).

Archaeological investigations of major sites in Lewes

Until quite recently most archaeological investigations in the town were undertaken by volunteers or academics as either rescue or training projects with varying degrees of success. Most had strong connections with the Sussex Archaeological Society, whose publications and archive are an invaluable resource, with the Institute of Archaeology also making substantial contributions. The ancient centre of Lewes is now an area where virtually all development requires a mandatory archaeological investigation and report. This has resulted in recent investigations, including several in the heart of the town, being developer funded and conducted by commercial units to a very high standard.

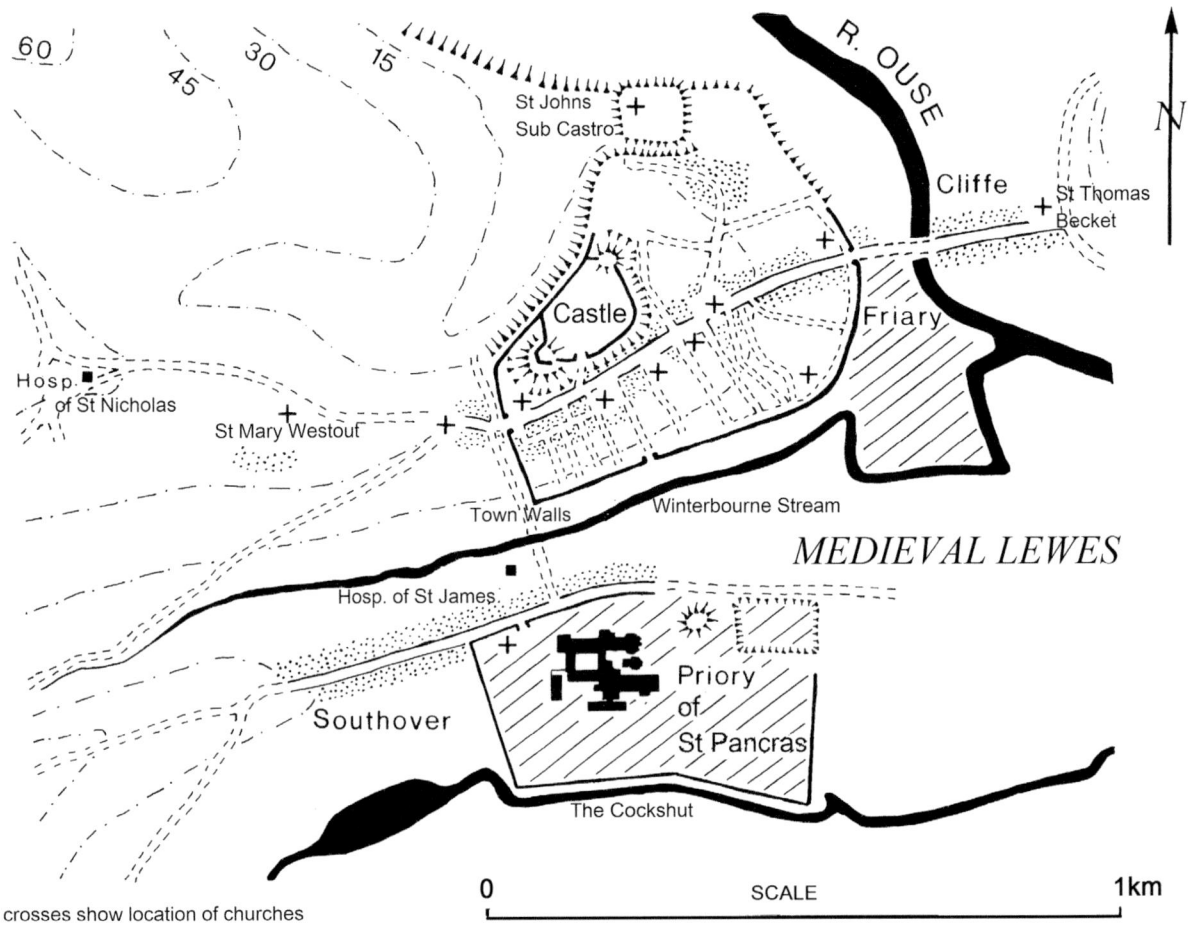

FIGURE 10.1: MAP SHOWING THE MAIN FEATURES OF MEDIEVAL LEWES (FROM RUDLING 1991, FIG. 3), (PLAN BY KIND PERMISSION OF SUSSEX ARCHAEOLOGICAL SOCIETY)

Name	Location	Comments on origin
All Saints	Friars Walk	C15th tower
St Anne formerly St Mary Westout	St Anne's Hill	C12th tower, nave, part chancel and south chapel
St John Sub Castro	St John's Hill	Demolished in 1839 but late Saxon doorway survives
St John the Baptist	Southover High Street	Former hospitium of St Pancras Priory until 1264. C12th arcade, C14th walls
St Michael	High Street	C13th round tower and west wall
St Thomas Becket	Cliffe High Street	Norman chancel, C13th-15th nave & tower

TABLE 10.1: LIST OF EXTANT CHURCHES IN LEWES WITH EVIDENCE OF MEDIEVAL ORIGIN (NAIRN AND PEVSNER 1965; BRENT 2004)

The Castle

The Norman double motte and bailey castle dominates the town with its remaining shell keep on the south western motte above areas of surviving curtain wall and the main gate with protruding fourteenth century barbican (Figure 10.2). It is possible, though unproven, that the eastern motte, Brack Mount, represents the earliest Norman military defences. The castle was falling into disrepair by 1382 beginning its decline into a picturesque ruin.

Walter Godfrey had excavated a series of slit trenches on the north western edge of the motte in 1930 and in 1962 a limited excavation had taken place on Brack Mount. The excavations on the top of the south-western motte of the castle (TQ 413 101) directed by Peter Drewett, for the Institute of Archaeology, University College London (UCL), in 1985-88 are the most extensive to date (Figure 10.3). They revealed two major phases of domestic building including the footings of the Norman kitchen and thirteenth century hall, both possibly tied

10. The Upper Ouse in the Medieval period (AD 1066 to 1499)

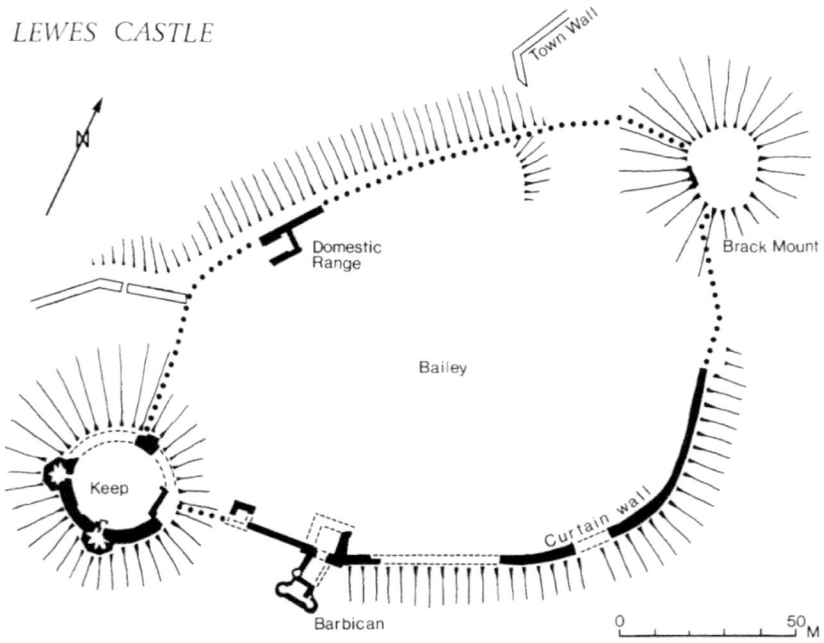

FIGURE 10.2: PLAN OF LEWES CASTLE SHOWING THE SURVIVING DEFENCES (FROM DREWETT 1992, FIG 2) (PLAN BY KIND PERMISSION OF SUSSEX ARCHAEOLOGICAL SOCIETY)

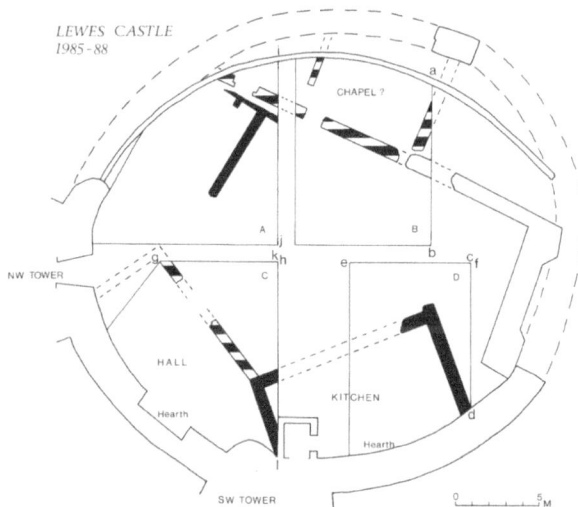

FIGURE 10.3: PLAN OF AREAS EXCAVATED BY DREWETT BETWEEN 1985 AND 1988 (FROM DREWETT 1992, FIG. 4) (PLAN BY KIND PERMISSION OF SUSSEX ARCHAEOLOGICAL SOCIETY)

to major phases of additional fortification in the twelfth and thirteenth centuries. Analysis of the wide range of artefacts and economic data recovered provided an insight into the life of a great baronial family during the early medieval period (Drewett 1992).

St. Pancras Priory

The excavations at the priory (TQ 412 094) directed by Richard Lewis between 1969 and 1982 did a great deal to establish its extent as well as indicating its once fine quality (Figure 10.4). It revealed evidence for Saxon occupation of the site including a small church or shrine beneath the remains of the Cluniac infirmary chapel, possibly built as the first monastic church. Considerable evidence was gained about the internal layout of the eleventh and twelfth century reredorters with much environmental and artefactual evidence collected from the successive sewers. The Priory assemblage goes through to the post–medieval but has some key eleventh to twelfth century ceramic groups (Lyne 1997). In 2007 a ground penetrating radar (GPR) survey was undertaken by Arrow Geophysics enabling an extended interpretation of the ground plan of the priory and the set of superb reconstructive visualisations by Andy Gammon (Mayhew 2008).

The great monastic church and cloister are no longer available for investigation being dissected by the Lewes to Brighton railway line. The visible remains, comprising part of the dormitory and latrine blocks, are managed by the Lewes Priory Trust for Lewes Town Council. In 2009 grants from the Heritage Lottery Fund and English Heritage were obtained to consolidate the remains, allow public access, and provide explanatory signs, paths and seating. Archaeological research by the Trust is ongoing.

Grey Friars

The Franciscan friary (TQ 419 102) was excavated in 1985-6 and 1988-9 by the Field Archaeology Unit of the Institute of Archaeology, UCL and Lewes Archaeological Group prior to redevelopment of the area (Figure 10.5). Eight periods of activity were revealed from a hard for beaching ships covered by twelfth century rubbish to several phases of the friary, founded in 1241 and constructed on the built-up floodplain. The function of many of the friary buildings was determined from the foundations uncovered, the buildings having been demolished following its dissolution in 1538. Notable amongst the wide range of artefacts was the bone assemblage from 55 medieval burials, the majority of which were the complete skeletons of adult males. The pathological analysis, while not representative of the medieval population of Lewes as a whole, adds to the data accumulating for the monastic houses of Britain (Gardiner *et al.* 1996).

St. Nicholas Hospital

Part of the St. Nicholas hospital site was investigated in 1994 by Archaeology South East (ASE). Little structural evidence was found but three quarries were excavated,

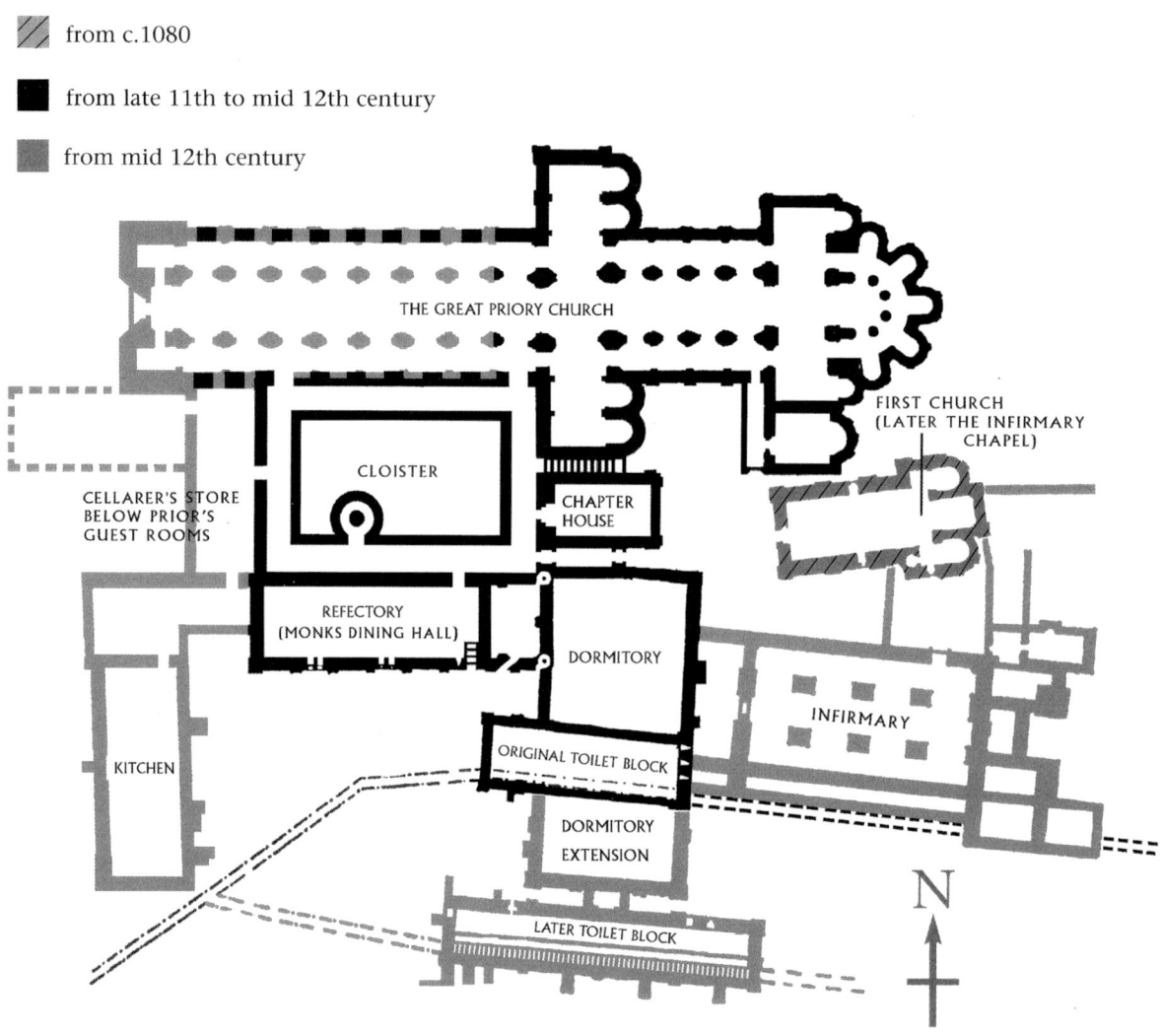

FIGURE 10.4 PLAN OF ST. PANCRAS PRIORY SHOWING THE PHASES OF DEVELOPMENT (GAMMON 2011, 11)
(PLAN BY KIND PERMISSION OF ANDY GAMMON ART & DESIGN AND THE LEWES PRIORY TRUST)

all containing medieval refuse, plus part of the cemetery comprising 103 graves dating from twelfth to early sixteenth centuries revealing valuable data on the use of the hospital (Barber and Sibun 2010). The remains suggest that St. Nicholas' was a non-leper hospital for most of its existence and, although the site is close to the accepted location of the de Montfort/Henry III battlefield, only four bodies showed wounds consistent with violent death suggesting that, despite recent speculation, the cemetery was not used to bury the dead from the battle (Browne 2010, 106).

Baxter's Printworks, Lewes House Library and Residential sites

Possibly of greatest significance to the medieval domestic life of the town is the awaited combined monograph (Swift forthcoming) on the recent, large-scale excavations by Archaeology South East (ASE) of the Baxter's Printworks site in St. Nicholas Lane (TQ 4162 1006) (MES19819) and those at Lewes House, between Broomans Lane and Church Twitten (TQ 4171 1005) (MES19818) for the new Lewes Library and a residential development. Importantly these recent projects offer a greater emphasis on the environmental evidence than was possible in some earlier excavations and examine a substantial area of the town not previously accessible.

Lewes Library

An excavation carried out in advance of the construction in 2004 revealed extensive evidence of medieval activity, predominantly in the form of numerous intercutting rubbish pits, cesspits and wells, largely dating from the twelfth to fourteenth centuries. There is a dramatic decline in evidence after the fourteenth century suggesting that the site was largely abandoned at that time probably marking the impact of the Black Death on Lewes (Griffin 2012).

Baxter's Printworks

At the Baxter's site in 2006 most of the features found consisted of groups of Saxo-Norman and later medieval pits containing a variety of domestic material as well as

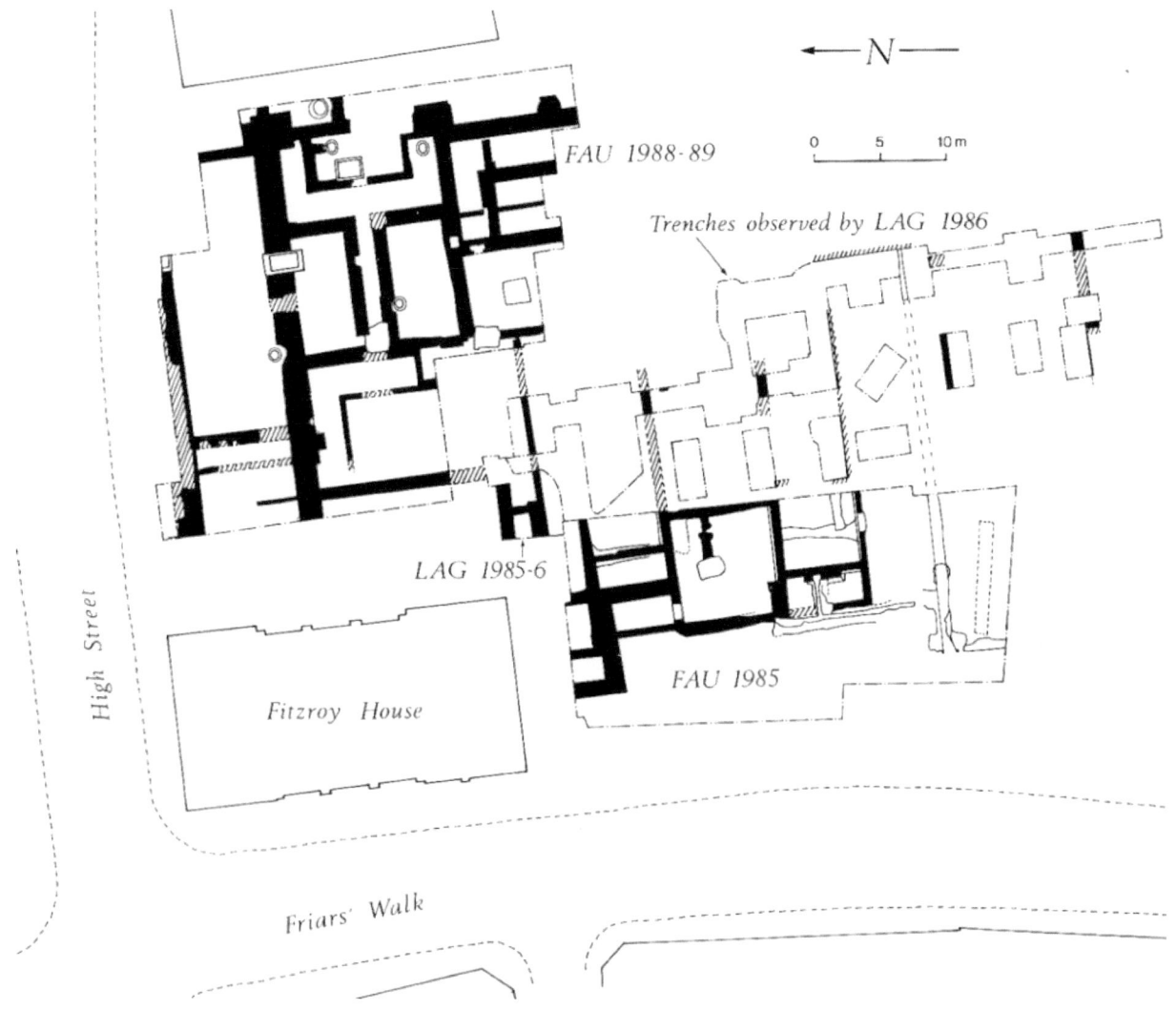

FIGURE 10.5: PLAN SHOWING THE LOCATION OF 1985-9 FRIARY EXCAVATIONS (GARDINER ET AL. 1996)
(PLAN BY KIND PERMISSION OF SUSSEX ARCHAEOLOGICAL SOCIETY)

significant, closely-dated, pottery assemblages. Most notably, a massive north-south aligned ditch was recorded adjacent to the western side of St. Nicholas Lane which was interpreted as marking the eastern limits of the Alfredian burh. There were clear indications of buildings, fronting onto St. Nicholas Lane by the twelfth century, with a variety of pits and cess-pits to the rear and some less obvious signs of building plots along Walwers Lane. It appears that the burh ditch was deliberately backfilled in the early post-conquest period, supporting the view that the medieval town expanded beyond the confines of the Saxon burh at the beginning of the Norman period. In the later medieval period the site clearly continued to be occupied and used for the disposal of domestic refuse in pits, and for some industrial processes, with ovens, kilns and hearths located on both sides of St. Nicholas Lane. There continued to be occupation into the fourteenth and fifteenth centuries represented by at least one household on the western side of the land, stone-lined cesspits on the western side of the lane and a thin scatter of pits in the eastern part of the site (Stevens 2009; Dan Swift pers. comm.).

Lewes House Residential site

The excavation for the Lewes House Residential and Walwers Lane sites in 2008 revealed late Saxon activity and possibly occupation as well as evidence of a significant increase in activity at the site during the eleventh century; predominantly coming from quarrying and refuse disposal. There was also some evidence of structures, and a huge quantity of finds and environmental evidence including animal bone, pottery and ceramic building material, offering insights into the socio-economic status of the area. This activity continues throughout the twelfth and thirteenth centuries with the lost twitten of Pinwell Street visible in the archaeological record for the later thirteenth and fourteenth centuries when there is evidence for at least two buildings on the site and a continuation of the extensive quarrying is also seen (Swift 2010).

Other Archaeological investigations in Lewes

The majority of smaller excavations within the town have been investigations of domestic occupation or the search for the town's defences and/or boundaries. This has mostly resulted in the excavation of a great number of pits together with evidence of a rich material culture reflecting the trade and industry of the period but regrettably with very few, if any, structures. David Freke, who undertook excavations to the north east of the town centre during 1974-5, concluded that the medieval town did not extend as far north as Lancaster Street and that in the twelfth century the area around St. Johns-sub-Castro was a separate fortification outside of the main town's defences. He speculates whether this could be taken as an indication of opposing factions occurring during the 'Anarchy of Stephen' (Freke 1975; 1976). David Rudling provides information on the research undertaken by the Sussex Archaeological Field Unit (SAFU) during the 1970s and early 1980s (Rudling 1983) including reports on 'trial' excavations in Brooman's Lane and Barbican House in 1979, and Grey Friars in 1981, as well as a discussion of the possible medieval origin of Lewes Priory Mount by Fiona Marsden. Another 1970s investigation was of the Clothkits Warehouse site in Brooman's Lane (TQ 417 101) in 1978 by C. E. (Jock) Knight-Farr (Locke 2001) which shows consistency with the later nearby ASE findings. Rudling's excavations to the north of St. Thomas à Becket Church in Cliffe (Rudling 1991) indicates the built-up nature of this area with compacted chalk deposits from the thirteenth to fourteenth centuries. The suburb of Cliffe was largely built on a chalk causeway laid across the Ouse floodplain involving vast amounts of chalk being quarried from the nearby Downs escarpment and compacted into a firm base on which to raise buildings above the alluvium (Mark Gardiner pers. comm.).

The general Upper Ouse area

The rest of the study area has a more dispersed pattern of medieval activity in a mainly rural environment, excepting the market town of Uckfield to the northeast which lying on the River Uck falls outside the area of this report. The survey area ends at the Sheffield Bridge (TQ 406 237) although the Ouse carries on for some distance northwest passing to the north of the village of Lindfield with its High Street rich in medieval vernacular houses.

Following the river northwards out of Lewes the site of the Archbishop's Palace and Dean's College, the hub of the South Malling manor (Brent 2004, 105-7), is located to the east of the river at Old Malling Farm (Table 10.2). Evidence of settlement and a possible deserted village lies on the west bank adjacent to the Church at Hamsey. To the north of Old Malling, Wellingham (TQ 430 134) is an area of great potential as one of the four Saxon settlements that predated the village of Ringmer. The area directly around Barcombe's twelfth century church may also be a shrunken medieval settlement.

Village	Grid Reference	Comments on origin
Fletching	TQ 429234	Norman tower, C13th arcade
Newick	TQ 422208	Norman nave plus C13th
Isfield	TQ 444182	Norman tower plus C13th
Barcombe	TQ 419143	C13th much now C19th
Ringmer	TQ 447128	C13th poss Norman fragments
Hamsey	TQ 415121	Norman nave & chancel
South Malling (palace/college)	TQ 409114	Poss C12th-13th fragments in garden

TABLE 10.2: LIST OF RURAL CHURCHES WITH EVIDENCE FOR MEDIEVAL ORIGIN IN THE UPPER OUSE AREA (NAIRN AND PEVSNER 1965)

Name	Grid Square	Reference/parkland features
Sheffield Park	TQ 4123	Park
Park Wood	TQ 4522	Park plus woodland with curvilinear boundary
Newick Park	TQ 4219	Park adjacent woodland
Lodge Wood	TQ 4419	Lodge, woodland
Old Park Wood	TQ 4118	Park, woodland with curvilinear boundary
Moat Park	TQ 4616	Park
Cooper's Hatch	TQ 4715	Hatch i.e. park gate
Plashetts Park Farm	TQ 4514	Park
Upper Lodge, Broyle	TQ 4814	Lodge
Park Mead, Ringmer	TQ 4312	Park
Lower Lodge, Broyle	TQ 4612	Lodge

TABLE 10.3: LIST OF POSSIBLE REFERENCES TO MEDIEVAL DEER PARKS FROM THE MODERN 1:25000 OS MAP.

10. THE UPPER OUSE IN THE MEDIEVAL PERIOD (AD 1066 TO 1499)

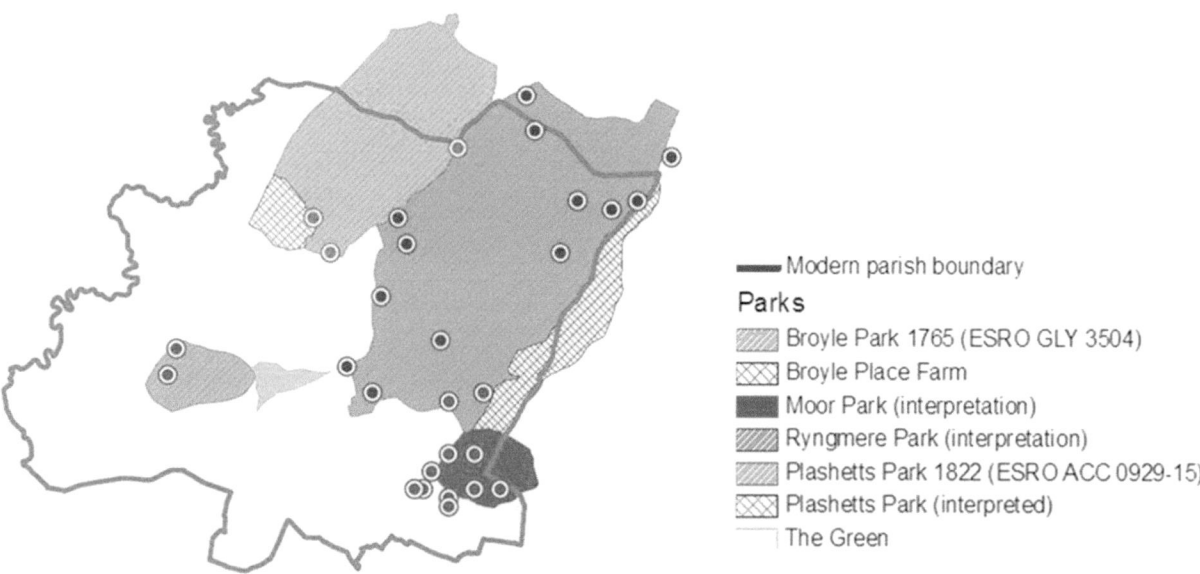

FIGURE 10.6: A PLAN SHOWING AN INTERPRETATION OF THE LOCATION AND APPROXIMATE SIZE OF THE PARKS OF RINGMER FROM MAP RESEARCH TOGETHER WITH THE LOCATION OF PLACE-NAME EVIDENCE (MILLUM 2011).

The northern reaches of the Upper Ouse offer an area of dispersed medieval farmsteads set amidst the remnants of the once vast hunting parks evident in place names and distinctive curvilinear boundaries, such as Old Park Wood at Town Littleworth and Park Wood at Piltdown. Many can be identified even in a cursory inspection of a modern OS map (Table 10.3) but they merit a deeper desk-based assessment subsequently verified by fieldwork. This important aspect of the medieval landscape can be demonstrated by Ringmer where four parks, Broyle, Plashett, Ryngmer, and More, dominated the parish (Figure 10.6). An interesting field study into the evidence available from boundaries undertaken at Ryngmer Park revealed distinct differences between the generally curvilinear park boundaries coinciding with roads, copse edges, and banks with mature trees, to the straight, hawthorn-rich, south-western boundary, interpreted as an eighteenth century realignment (Maloney and Howard 1982).

Further possible deserted and shrunken settlements are listed at Buckham Hill (TQ 451 206), Sharpsbridge (TQ 440 208), Barkham Manor (TQ 439217), around the early church and motte and bailey at Isfield (TQ 442 180) and the eleventh century church at Newick (TQ 421 208). Dredging beside the earthworks at Isfield produced pottery, tile and leatherwork. Spoil sampling suggested it had accumulated in the ditch around the medieval manor house with finds of a twelfth to thirteenth century date range (Gardiner 1992). The motte at Clay Hill (TQ 449 143) is now thought to be associated to the hunting practices of Plashett Park rather than defence (Richard Jones *pers. comm.*) and a late twelfth to early thirteenth century pottery site was excavated just to the west.

There is a surprising scarcity within the study area of recorded medieval iron making sites that might be expected towards the north of the area even though the height of this Wealden industry followed the introduction of the blast furnace at the very end of the fifteenth century with its epicentre located further to the north and east (Cleere and Crossley 1995). Despite the potential of extant building remains it is pottery that figures largely in the archaeological record together with an increasing amount of metal objects including coins and equestrian fittings. The rural area has seen very little archaeological excavation with the parish of Ringmer revealing by far the greatest number of monument records and archaeological investigations outside Lewes, mainly based on its extensive pottery industry (Table 10.4).

During the thirteenth and fourteenth centuries the increasing number of rural pottery kiln sites show no significant technological or functional differences to their urban counterparts. Their location seems largely dictated by convenient access to the bulky raw materials combined with short and easy routes to convey their fragile and cheap product to a sustainable market (Streeten 1981, 327-342). Ringmer epitomises these requirements with ready supplies of clay and sand for pot production plus the timber and furze for firing the kilns, all within a short cart or pack-horse journey from the established market centre of Lewes.

Whilst the data collected to date regarding the trade of medieval Ringmer-ware is scarce and often reliant on a 'spot' visual recognition of the fabric (Figure 10.7, Table 10.5), this is not the case at Battle Abbey, where a sample was identified by thin-section analysis. As the Ringmer-ware pottery has been reported in excavations at several religious houses a factor in the development and longevity

Site location	Grid Reference	Excavator / source	Date of exc.	Period of feature	Type	Description
Potter's Field	TQ44921288 TQ44991278	Martin 1902	1894	Late/Post Medieval	Kiln	2 brick-built parallel flue, up-draught kilns
Kiln Field (Barnetts Mead)	TQ45081287	Hadfield 1981	1970	Medieval	Kiln	Mutsy type 2a kiln C^{14}-dated to c. 1193 with adjacent waster heap
Delves Field	TQ44601280	O'Shea 1973	1973	Medieval	Kiln	Huge waster heap probably close to kiln site
Norlington Lane	TQ44721320	Gregory 1995	1993-4	Medieval	Kiln	2 Mutsy type 2a kilns in series with archaeomagnetic date of 1200-1270 plus 3 waster heaps
Clay Hill	TQ44901435	Jones 1999	1999-2000	Medieval	Kiln	Small semi-temporary kiln with 12th to early 13th C pottery
Lewes Road	TQ45331267	Gregory 2008	2002	Medieval	Waster Heap	Waster heap of early 13th C pottery suggesting adjacent kiln

TABLE 10.4: LIST OF EXCAVATED MEDIEVAL KILN SITES IN RINGMER (MILLUM 2011)

of this industry may have been its location within the manor of the Archbishop. Manorial encouragement may be implied as, amid a general tendency elsewhere for rising clay rents, the nine penny per head payment in Ringmer remained static for over 200 years (Le Patourel 1968, 115). It should however be born in mind that there was a tendency in the area for rents to stay 'fixed by custom' with payments such as some quit rents in the Weald being identical in the nineteenth century to sums paid in the thirteenth (Mark Gardiner pers. comm.).

Many thousands of sherds of medieval pottery have been recovered from the various sites in Ringmer with each project developing their own method of describing the fabrics and forms. It is therefore perhaps understandable, if regrettable, that no one has yet undertaken the task of comparing the descriptions from the various assemblages to compile a comprehensive dated series for Ringmer-made wares, such as that for London (Pearce *et al.* 1985), however the recent paper on the Norlington site (Gregory 2014) does illustrate many of the main forms.

The product range included roof tiles, decorated floor tiles, chimney pots, jars, jugs, skillets, bowls, lids, including possible curfew lid fragments, aquamanile (Figure 10.8) and green-glazed anthropomorphic jug fragments. The pottery from the later phase of the Norlington Lane kiln appeared to fall into a late thirteenth century typology (Gregory 1994) although the 95% confidence archaeomagnetic date for the last kiln firing at AD 1200-1270 (D. Gregory pers. comm.) could imply a slightly earlier date. Much more glazed ware was encountered at Norlington than on other Ringmer sites and the later wares were made of a finer fabric, from

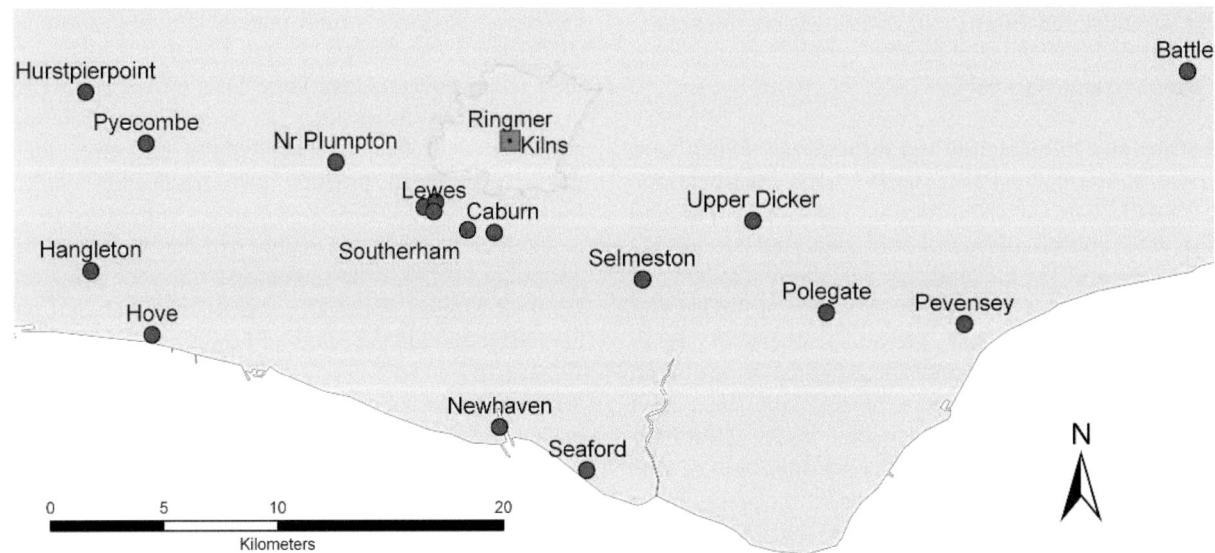

FIGURE 10.7: A MAP OF CENTRAL SUSSEX SHOWING THE LOCATIONS OF RINGMER-TYPE POTTERY AS DESCRIBED IN TABLE 10.5 (MILLUM 2011)

10. The Upper Ouse in the Medieval period (AD 1066 to 1499)

Location	Place	Description	Reference
Lewes	St Pancras' Priory	Ringmer-type pottery from late 11th to 14th century contexts	Lyne 1997, 81-96
Ringmer	Lewes Road	Locally produced wares from 10th to 14th centuries	Barber 2006
Battle	Battle Abbey	Ringmer-type pottery from 12th century context	Streeten 1984, 230
Glynde	Caburn	Ringmer-type 12th century rim sherd	Streeten 1984, 230
Selmeston		Ringmer-type ware	Bleach 1982, 47
Hangleton	Deserted village	Ringmer-type pottery and tiles	Holden 1963, 132 & 147
Upper Dicker	Michelham Priory	Ringmer-type ware	Bleach 1982, 48
Polegate	A27 bypass	Ringmer-type ware	Barber 2007, 126-130
Lewes	Brooman's Lane	Ringmer-type ware	Locke 2001, 229
Pevensey	Old Farmhouse	Ringmer-type ware	Barber 1999, 107
Lewes	Lewes Friary	Ringmer-type ware	Gardiner *et al.* 1996, 102
Pyecombe	Pyecombe Church	Ringmer-type tiles	Butler 1996, 216
Southerham	Grey Pit	Ringmer-type medieval pottery	Allen 1995, 24
Hurstpierpoint	Muddleswood	Ringmer-type fabric	Butler 1994, 111
Lewes	Friars Walk	Late 13th/14th century Ringmer type pottery in pits	Russell 1990, 144-151
Nr Lewes	Ashcombe Bottom	Medieval pottery from Ringmer	Allen 2005, 21-2
Seaford		Pottery from Ringmer	Kay 2000, 5
Newhaven		Pottery from Ringmer	Kay 2000, 5

TABLE 10.5: LIST OF PLACES WHERE RINGMER-TYPE POTTERY OR TILE HAS BEEN DISCOVERED (MILLUM 2011)

both orange and creamy clays. These local wares had previously only been linked to Binstead or Rye which makes future petrological analysis of both production and consumer site wares a high priority (Millum 2011).

Discussion and future work

The outlines of the medieval landscape of the Upper Ouse were shaped by the demands of very conflicting lifestyles; the peasants laboriously creating farmland from former woodland whilst the leisured hunting pursuits of the nobility necessitated the maintenance of vast parkland areas. The latter was however increasingly challenged through the period by need for agricultural land due to changes in population. The river, while still of obvious importance, slowly gives way to terrestrial means of communication and the increased use of pack animals facilitating access to the High Weald hinterland; as demonstrated by the transport of 600 bushels of wheat to the port of Shoreham from Stoneham on the Ouse in 1319 by packhorse rather than by boat (Brent 2004, 126).

Whilst the predominance of monument records in Lewes reflects the town's importance to medieval trade and administration, in the rest of the area the record may be more an indication of where archaeological investigation has taken place rather than a true picture of medieval activity. This is made apparent when looking at the finds

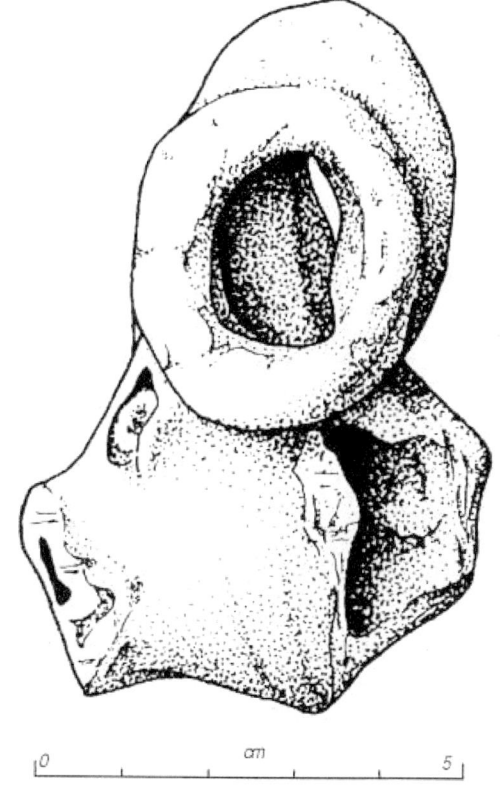

FIGURE 10.8: A DRAWING OF THE AQUAMANILE SPOUT BY JANE RUSSELL (GREGORY 2014, FIG. 19, NO. 80) (REPRODUCED WITH PERMSSION OF THE SUSSEX ARCHAEOLOGICAL SOCIETY)

records which reflect either isolated chance discoveries or patches of systematic field walking and intensive metal detecting. This anomaly can be seen in Ashcombe and Houndean, just west of Lewes (TQ 3809-3909), where clearly a very thorough metal detecting campaign was undertaken. Out of the 205 finds extracted from the ESHER using a broad medieval filter, only 67 could be confidently dated to the post-conquest to pre-Tudor period. Of these 30 were coins (Figure 10.9) and showed a gradual increase in number from the beginning of the twelfth century, peaking in the late thirteenth to early fourteenth centuries, and decreasing again over the next 150 years. This snapshot of the local economy, based on archaeological fieldwork, reflects the rapid increase in coinage minted during the thirteenth century, estimated as increasing from nine million pennies in circulation in 1086 to 216 million in 1300, a 24 times increase funded substantially by the export of wool (Carpenter 2003, 40).

Ashcombe was the Lewes base for the fiefdom of Poynings and the site of a twelfth century chapel, whilst Houndean Bottom was the meeting point of several drove roads. Both are possible shrunken medieval settlements reduced by either the catastrophic effects of the Black Death in 1348-49 and/or the change to larger scale sheep and corn husbandry (Brent 2004, 42).

It is in the medieval period that historical evidence begins to become an increasingly important factor in research, starting with Domesday Book and continuing with manorial custumal and rental documents such as those for the manors of the Archbishop of Canterbury (Redwood and Wilson 1958) and the subsidy rolls for 1296, 1327 and 1332 (Hudson 1910). However if all we had was the written record our knowledge would be sparse; whilst great events may be documented, everyday life would remain a mystery.

What is known about daily life is due largely to archaeology, which far from merely excavation involves exhaustive collation and interpretation of the findings to provide credible explanations of past activity. There is no merit in uncovering past features and artefacts if the knowledge contained therein is not made readily available for subsequent analysis. Fortunately the Upper Ouse valley has not only seen some enthusiastic gathering of data but also some responsible processing of the results to provide valuable insights into this period. In particular the information available for the medieval pottery industry from both archaeological and historical research lays the foundation for a deeper level of analysis to be undertaken in the production of a fabric and form series, to include petrological analysis of both production and consumer site wares; a high priority future project of potentially regional importance.

The archaeological record however imparts another important lesson in that the extent of the data available can often say more about the range of investigation undertaken than of the distribution of finds and past activity particularly in rural areas. The location of many future investigations will depend on the siting of development-led commercial projects, as has occurred recently in Lewes. However, as seen at Baxter's Printworks and Lewes House, this can result in invaluable data being gained in previously under-investigated areas. The proposed, large-scale, redevelopment of the Phoenix Quarter to the northeast of central Lewes could also

FIGURE 10.9: A PENNY, POSSIBLY OF EDWARD II, AD 1307 TO AD 1327 FOUND AT ASHCOMBE
(© PORTABLE ANTIQUITIES SCHEME; RECORD SUR-90EE31)

provide much valuable data for many periods, although the work of Freke (1976) and others suggests that this area is outside the established medieval core of the town. Putting aside the ecclesiastical and baronial sites very few, if any, more domestic structures have been discovered; the later forming a notable gap in the current archaeological record (Luke Barber pers. comm.).

Possible future works for volunteer projects

In Lewes it is difficult to see what actual fieldwork might be undertaken specifically for a volunteer project. Work of a synthetic nature might have to rely on the close monitoring of commercial projects and the resulting 'grey' literature; especially the results of the increasing emphasis on environmental sampling and water-logged deposits which offer insights into the more transient aspects of the archaeological record. Hopefully further environmental evidence will be sourced by The Priory Trust as they continue to investigate the site with a forthcoming project by ASE to excavate the Priory's drains. It is also apparent that the results of some historic excavations within the area have not been published even though their archives have been deposited with local museums and an investigation into which sites still need a written report and what their archive could reveal would be of significance for not only this but all other periods.

In the rural areas there would appear to be greater scope for volunteer-based projects in preparing detailed desktop syntheses of the archaeological record of specific areas or parishes, as undertaken for Ringmer (Millum 2011). This would facilitate greater understanding of the study area and assist in defining appropriate areas and methods of research. However there is no doubt that the use of general landscape archaeology techniques, such as used in the Barcombe and Hamsey project (see www.bandhpast.co.uk), could greatly increase our general knowledge of an area and bring the currently dispersed medieval sites into greater context. A methodical approach should include systematic field-walking and metal detecting followed by geophysical surveys and trial trenching or test pitting in selected locations, including any possible shrunken or deserted settlements. Another area for volunteer activity is to advance the research started by the late Peter Brandon (Brandon and Short 1990, 73) in identifying the medieval deer parks of the area, many of which can be deduced by inspection of the first series OS and local tithe maps before subsequent verification by boundary and earthwork surveys in the field.

The established cooperation between the commercial sector and the local volunteer groups is a great asset which with a greater emphasis on bringing together current and future data could facilitate the production of a more comprehensive picture of this vibrant period.

Acknowledgements

My thanks to Mark Gardiner, Luke Barber, Dan Swift and Simon Stevens, for their invaluable advice and suggested amendments; any errors remaining are entirely mine.

References

Adams, C. 1999. Medieval Administration. In K. Leslie, and B. Short (eds), *An Historical Atlas of Sussex*, 40-1. Chichester: Phillimore & Co Ltd.

Allen, M. J. 1995. The prehistoric land-use and human ecology of the Malling-Caburn Downs. *Sussex Archaeological Collections* 133, 19-43.

Allen, M. J. 2005. Beaker occupation and development of the downland landscape at Ascombe Bottom, near Lewes, East Sussex. *Sussex Archaeological Collections* 143, 7-33.

Barber, L. 1999. The excavation of land adjacent to the Old Farmhouse, Pevensey, East Sussex, 1994. *Sussex Archaeological Collections*, 137, 91-120.

Barber, L. 2006. Pottery. In S. Wallis, Medieval occupation and clay extraction at Lewes Road, Ringmer, East Sussex, 12-18. Unpubl. report 03/61, Thames Valley Archaeological Services Ltd.

Barber, L. 2007. The Pottery. In Stevens, S., Archaeological investigations on the A27, Polegate bypass, East Sussex, *Sussex Archaeological Collections* 145, 125-130.

Barber, L., and Sibun, L. 2010. The medieval hospital of St. Nicholas, Lewes, East Sussex. *Sussex Archaeological Collections* 148, 79-109.

Bleach, J. 1982. The Medieval Potters of Ringmer. In J. Kay, and J. Bleach (eds), *Ringmer History,* Vol. 1, 43-53. Ringmer History Study Group.

Brandon, P. and Short, B. 1990. *The South East from AD 1000.* London: Longman Group.

Brent, C. 2004. *Pre-Georgian Lewes.* Lewes: Colin Brent Books.

Browne, S. 2010. Human Remains, in L. Barber and L. Sibun, The medieval hospital of St. Nicholas, Lewes, Sussex. *Sussex Archaeological Collections* 148, 101-107.

Butler, C. 1994. The Excavation of a Medieval site at Muddleswood, near Hurstpierpoint, West Sussex. *Sussex Archaeological Collections* 132, 101-114.

Butler, C. 1996. Recent archaeological work at Pycombe church, West Sussex. *Sussex Archaeological Collections* 134, 213-39.

Carpenter, D. 2003. *The Struggle for Mastery: Britain 1066-1284.* London: Allen Lane.

Cleere, H. and Crossley, D. 1995. *The Iron Industry of the Weald.* Cardiff: Merton Priory Press Ltd.

Drewett, P. 1992. Excavations at Lewes Castle, East Sussex 1985-1988. *Sussex Archaeological Collections* 130, 69-106.

Freke, D. J. 1975. Excavations in Lewes 1974. *Sussex Archaeological Collections* 113, 66-84.

Freke, D. J. 1976. Further excavations in Lewes 1975. *Sussex Archaeological Collections* 114, 176-194.

Gammon, A. 2011. The development of the site in Franklin, A. *The Priory of St. Pancras Lewes.* Lewes Priory Trust.

Gardiner, M. 1992. Recent work on the earthworks at Isfield, East Sussex. *Sussex Archaeological Collections* 130, 140-146.

Gardiner, M. 1995. Aspects of the history and archaeology of medieval Seaford. *Sussex Archaeological Collections* 133, 189-212.

Gardiner, M., Russell, M., and Gregory, D. 1996. Excavations at Lewes Friary 1985-6 and 1988-9. *Sussex Archaeological Collections* 134, 71-123.

Gardiner, M. and Warne, H. 1999. Domesday Settlement. In K. Leslie, and B. Short (eds), *An Historical Atlas of Sussex* 34-35. Chichester: Phillimore & Co Ltd.

Gregory, D. 1994. Norlington Lane medieval pottery workshop centre. *LAG Newsletter* 106, 3.

Gregory, D. 1995. Norlington earns top award. *Sussex Past and Present* 75, 5.

Gregory, D. 2008. An assemblage of medieval pottery found at the former Police House, Lewes Road, Ringmer, East Sussex (TQ 453 127). *Sussex Archaeological Collections* 146, 206-10.

Gregory, D. 2014. A medieval pottery production centre at Norlington Lane, Ringmer, East Sussex. *Sussex Archaeological Collections* 152, 9-37.

Griffin, N. 2012. *Lewes House Library, Lewes.* [Online] available at: http://www.archaeologyse.co.uk [Accessed 2014].

Hadfield, J. I. 1981. The excavation of a medieval kiln at Barnett's Mead, Ringmer, East Sussex. *Sussex Archaeological Collections* 119, 89-106.

Harris, R. B. 2005. *Lewes: Historical Character Assessment report.* Sussex Extensive Urban Survey.

Holden, E. W. 1963. Excavations at the deserted medieval village of Hangleton, Part 1. *Sussex Archaeological Collections* 110, 54-182.

Hudson, W. 1910. *The three earliest Subsidies for the County of Sussex in the years of 1296, 1327, 1332, (SRS Vol. 10).* Lewes: Sussex Record Society.

Jones, R. 1999. *Clay Hill 1999: an interim report or Anarchy Ordered.* Lewes: Sussex Archaeological Society.

Kay, J. 2000. *Medieval Potteries at Ringmer.* Unpubl. report in ESHER SMR linked documents database.

Le Patourel, H. E. 1968. Documentary Evidence and the Medieval Pottery Industry. *Medieval Archaeology* 12, 101-126.

Locke, A. 2001. Excavations at Clothkits Warehouse Extension, Brooman's Lane, Lewes, by C. E. Knight-Farr, 1978. *Sussex Archaeological Collections* 139, 227-234.

Lyne, M. 1997. *The Priory of St. Pancaras: Excavations by Richard Lewis 1969-82.* Lewes, Lewes Priory Trust.

Maloney, M. and Howard, E. 1982. Report from the Botanical Group on Ringmer Park. *Ringmer History Group Newsletter* 3, 2.

Martin, W. 1902. A forgotten industry: pottery at Ringmer. *Sussex Archaeological Collections* 45, 132-8.

Mayhew, G. (ed.), 2008. *Priory of St. Pancras, Lewes.* Lewes: Lewes Millennium Gallery Trust.

Millum, D. H. 2011. *Mapping the Archaeology of Ringmer Parish to AD 1349.* Unpubl. University of Sussex dissertation held at Lewes, the Barbican House library, Archaeology Room, ref 930.1028.

Morris, J. 1976. *Domesday Book: Sussex.* Chichester: Phillimore.

Nairn, I. and Pevsner, N. 1965. *The Buildings of England: Sussex* (2001 reprint ed.). London: Penguin.

O'Shea, E. W. (ed.), 1973. Ringmer Kiln Site. *Lewes Archaeological Group Newletter* 17, 1-2.

Pearce, J. E., Vince, A. G., and Jenner, M. A. 1985. *A dated type-series of London Medieval pottery, Part 2, London-type ware.* London: London and Middlesex Archaeological Society.

Redwood, B. C., and Wilson, A. E. (eds), 1958. *Custumals of the Sussex Manors of the Archbishop of Canterbury.* Lewes: Sussex Record Society.

Rudling, D. 1983. The archaeology of Lewes: some recent research. *Sussex Archaeological Collections* 121, 45-78.

Rudling, D. 1991. Excavations at Cliffe, Lewes, 1987. *Sussex Archaeological Collections* 129, 165-182.

Russell, M. 1990. Excavations in Friars Walk, Lewes 1989. *Sussex Archaeological Collections* 128, 117-140.

Stevens, S. 2009. Post-excavation assessment and updated project design on archaeological excavations at The Baxters Printworks Site, St. Nicholas Lane, Lewes, East Sussex: ASE Report No. 2008082. [Online] available at: www.archaeologyse.co.uk [Accessed 2014].

Streeten, A. D. 1981. Craft and industry: medieval and later potters in South-East England. In E. L. Morris, *Production and Distribution: a ceramic viewpoint*, 323-346. Oxford: British Archaeological Reports, International Series 120.

Streeten, A. D. 1984. *Medieval and later ceramic production in South-east England* (Vol. II). Southampton. Unpubl. university thesis accessed at the Sussex Archaeological Society library, ref. 738.

Swift, D. 2010. A post-excavation assessment and updated Project Design, report on the Lewes Residential and Walwers Lane Sites, Lewes, East Sussex: ASE Report No. 2009080. [Online] available at: www.archaeologyse.co.uk [Accessed 2014].

Swift, D. forthcoming. Recent Excavations in Lewes, East Sussex: Prehistoric, Roman, medieval and post-medieval findings. Portslade: ASE Monograph Series.

11. Lower Ouse in the Medieval period (AD 1066 to 1499)

David J. Worsell

This chapter presents an archaeological overview of the Lower Ouse valley from Southerham to Seaford. It is primarily based on data contained in the East Sussex Historic Environment Record (ESHER), the *Sussex Archaeological Collections* (SAC), Portable Antiquities Scheme (PAS) and reports produced by archaeological contracting companies and local societies. Other sources include pan-Sussex research reports of the Extensive Urban Survey (EUS) and the Sussex Historic Landscape Characterisation (HLC) project. Given the extensive nature of the evidence only a summary of the medieval period is presented.

The Lower Ouse valley is *c.* 10km in length presenting a bulbous outline, widest to its north (*c.* 2.5km) and tapering as it progresses south. The river valley geology is mainly marine alluvium with occasional gravel deposits at its margins. Elsewhere on rising land, chalk formations underlie well drained silty soils (see Allen, Chapter 2).

Government initiatives on the planning process resulted in Planning Policy Guidance Note 16: Archaeology and Planning (PPG16) being replaced by The National Planning Policy Framework (NPPF). Like its predecessor the NPPF includes heritage as a component of the planning process with developers continuing to fund 'developer-led' archaeology. Hence it should be no surprise that most of the archaeological investigations, related here, were delivered by professional contracting companies funded by developers.

The chapter commences with an overview of the Lower Ouse valley, followed by a section on Seaford, an archaeological view of the valley and finally a discussion.

Lower Ouse valley Overview

In the Norman period Rapes divided Sussex into five administrative areas, becoming feudal baronies under French overlords. The Lower Ouse formed a boundary between the Rapes of Lewes to the west and Pevensey to the east.

Settlements developed along the valley with ready access to the river. Those described here lie in the contour range 6-17m on the edge of the chalk zone and near to fertile soils. They take various forms, probably as unplanned development, with the main ones being linear (Rodmell) and nucleated (Piddinghoe). Churches often provide the only visible medieval evidence of Norman and later medieval architecture. Archaeological investigations demonstrate a pattern of dispersed settlements and isolated farmsteads in the thirteenth and fourteenth centuries.

The Ouse must have been a tidal inlet since numerous salt-works were recorded in the Domesday Book (Robinson and Williams 1983) with the river deep enough for navigation by sea-going vessels. Flooding during the winter sometimes extended into the summer months. Land reclamation (inning) of marshland at the margins of the river had a major but unrecognised consequence. Narrowing of the river reduced the volume of flood-tide water causing shingle to be deposited at the river's mouth (Farrant 1972, 45). Combined with longshore drift the river's mouth moved eastwards to Seaford from Newhaven (Brandon 1971, 94). In 1422 a Commission of Sewers was appointed, suggesting devastation of the valley by the great flood the previous year (Brandon 1971, 97).

Following the Conquest Lewes became the administrative centre with pre-Conquest Saxon estates restructured and sub-divided during the twelfth and thirteenth centuries. Change is also reflected in church buildings with many remodelled or completely rebuilt. Churches dominate the study area with those at Iford, Rodmell and Southease mentioned in the Domesday Survey. The valley's economy relied on agriculture, in particular sheep rearing for wool production and as a food source. Other industries were milling, salt production, fishing and possibly craft working. An exception to this is Seaford which developed as a port and town exporting goods to other parts of Britain and the continent.

Settlements of the Lower Ouse valley

A survey (Figure 11.1) of medieval settlements listed Deserted Medieval Villages (DMV) and Shrunken Medieval Villages (SMV) (Burleigh 1973; 1976). Burleigh had indicated a number of sites under threat or destroyed by the plough, later reported in a survey of Sussex by McAvoy (2002). Fourteen DMV, SMV and Domesday sites (Figure 11.1) are identified mainly in the Lower Ouse valley by Burleigh, ESHER and the Domesday Book (DB) (Table 11.1).

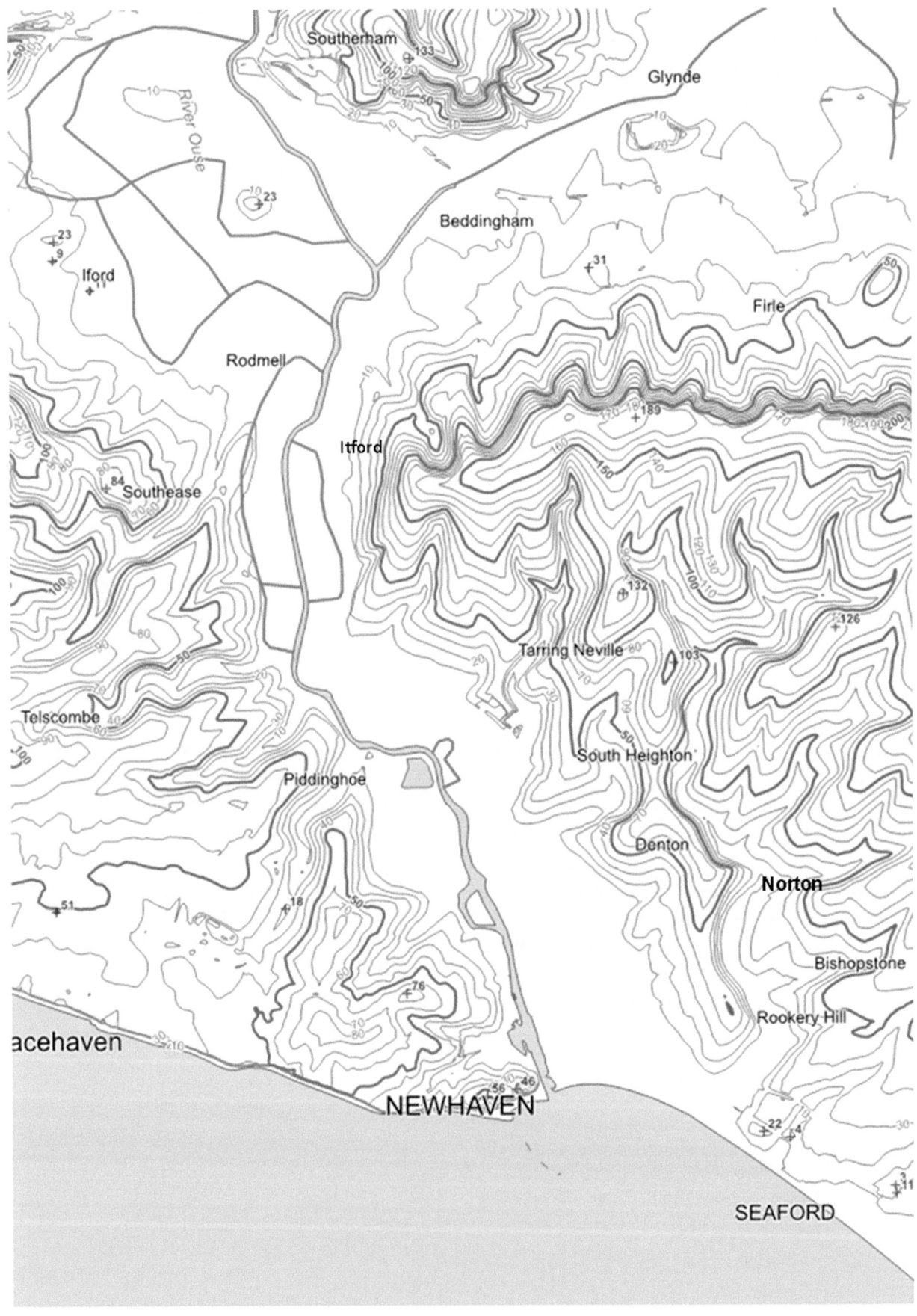

Figure 11.1. Medieval villages (DMV, SMV and Domesday) Crown copyright/database right 2014. Ordnance Survey/EDINA supplied service.

11. Lower Ouse in the Medieval period (AD 1066 to 1499)

Settlement	Grid Ref	Type	Church	Source	Evidence
Beddingham	TQ 445078 & TQ 446075	SMV	Yes	Burleigh (73) DB	None Listed
Bishopstone	TQ 472010	SMV	Yes	Burleigh (73) Burleigh (76) DB	None Listed Documentary only
Denton	TQ 455026 & TQ454026	SMV	Yes	Bell (1979) Westley (1979)	Findspot Excavation
Harpingden	Lost	Village		DB	
Iford	TQ 408073	SMV	Yes	Burleigh (73) DB	None Listed
Itford	TQ 434055	DMV		Burleigh (76) DB	Documentary only
Norton	TQ 455024	SMV		ESHER (1978)	Field survey
Piddinghoe	TQ 436031 & TQ431033	SMV DMV	Yes	Burleigh (73) Burleigh (76) DB	None Listed The Lydds earthworks
Preston	Lost	Village		DB	
Rodmell	TQ 420063	SMV	Yes	Burleigh (73) DB	None Listed
Seaford (Sutton)		DMV	Yes	Burleigh (73) Burleigh (76)	Maps/docs/excavation Documentary only
Southease	TQ 423053	SMV	Yes	Burleigh (73) DB	None Listed
South Heighton	TQ 451028	SMV		Burleigh (73) Burleigh (76) DB	None Listed Documentary only
Tarring Neville	TQ 443039	SMV	Yes	Burleigh (73) DB	None Listed

TABLE 11.1: SETTLEMENTS (DMV, SMV AND DOMESDAY)

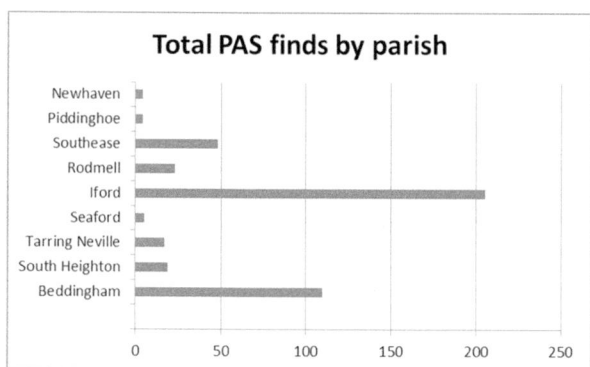

FIGURE 11.2: TOTAL PORTABLE ANTIQUITIES SCHEME (PAS) FINDS BY PARISH

Portable Antiquities Scheme (PAS)

Lewes district, which includes the lower Ouse, recorded 864 medieval finds (Figure 11.2).

Most of the 429 medieval findspots occur in two parishes: Beddingham and Iford. The distribution pattern may be indicative of medieval activity or possibly skewed where concentrated searches have taken place, for example metal detecting or fieldwalking. Metallic items accounted for 98.4% of the finds, with coins the largest category (Figure 11.3) followed by buckles and mounts (Figure 11.4).

Finds under the Household items are: Lamps (1), Thimbles (1), Bells (1), Keys (9) and Candle Holder (1). Sword/Dagger finds are mainly chapes (Figure 11.5).

The contrast between Iford and Beddingham is intriguing with finds of personal adornment double the number for Iford than Beddingham whilst the opposite is true for 'Other' items. Perhaps this shows more journeys through Iford parish or that Beddingham finds indicate a higher level of domestic activity with Lewes. A third possibility is that increased activity in Iford parish is due to Lewes being the administrative centre of Lewes Rape, whereas Beddingham lies on the margins of Pevensey Rape. The overall chronological spread for finds between Beddingham (AD 1066–1499) and Iford (AD 1100-1483) is similar, with small variances between finds groups.

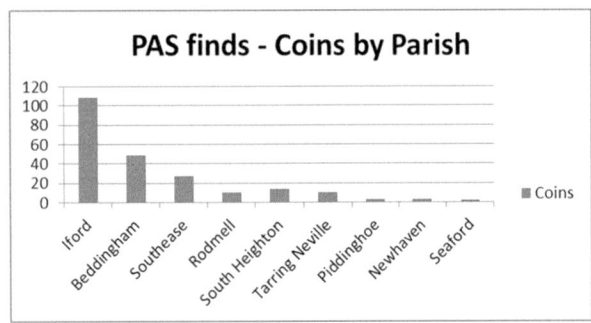

FIGURE 11.3: TOTAL PAS FINDS – COINS BY PARISH

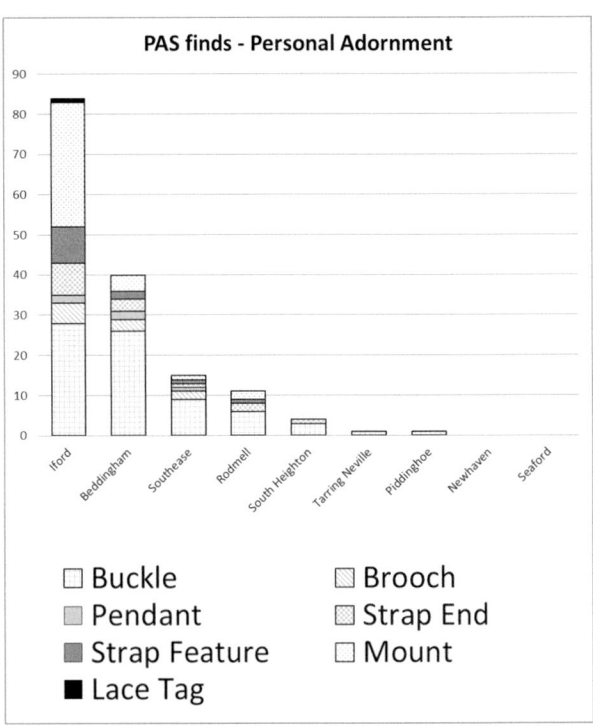

FIGURE 11.4: PAS FINDS – PERSONAL ADORNMENT

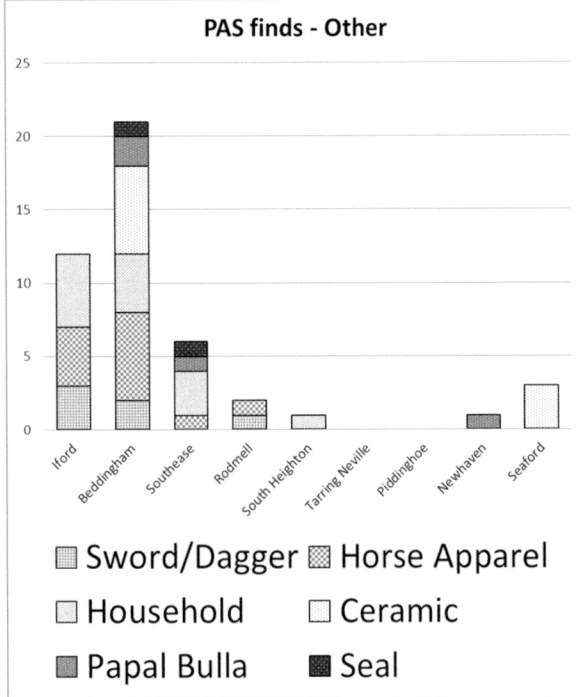

FIGURE 11.5: PAS FINDS – OTHER

Seaford

From an archaeological viewpoint Seaford dominates the archaeology record. It has had numerous archaeological investigations contributing to our understanding of the medieval period. As such it stands alone archaeologically and requires to be treated separately.

Historical context

Seaford is not mentioned in the Domesday Book, coming to prominence after the mouth of the Ouse deflected eastwards from Newhaven to beneath Seaford Head (Brandon 1971, 94) (Figure 11.6).

Documentary sources suggest the town existed in the eleventh century. A grant of land in c. 1140 confirmed the same gift probably made between 1088 and 1138 (Harris 2005, 13). By c. 1200 sea-going trade along the Ouse to Lewes appears to have stopped, although smaller vessels continued to operate (Brent 2004). Seaford rose to prominence in the thirteenth and fourteenth centuries after replacing Lewes for sea-going trade, possibly being used as an out-port for Lewes. Wool and other locally produced goods were traded with the Continent or other British ports. Increased trade in turn enabled the town to flourish, becoming a Cinque Port as a limb of Hastings by 1229-30 (Wynter 1922, 7). During this period two hospitals were founded: St. Leonard's in 1147 for treating lepers, sited outside of the town (ESHER 1690) and St. James of Sutton by 1260. A watermill, probably tidal, is recorded operating next to the marsh (Harris 2005, 15). The vibrancy of Seaford towards the end of the late thirteenth century can be judged by the changing occupation patterns of the original burgage plots, with tenements being sub-divided suggestive of increased economic activity. Unlike Lewes, Seaford did not benefit from a town wall and in the fourteenth century French raids, an inundation of the sea and the plague all contributed to Seaford's demise. Today Seaford has absorbed smaller settlements such as Sutton and East Blatchington which documentary sources show as medieval hamlets (ESHER 19364).

11. Lower Ouse in the Medieval period (AD 1066 to 1499)

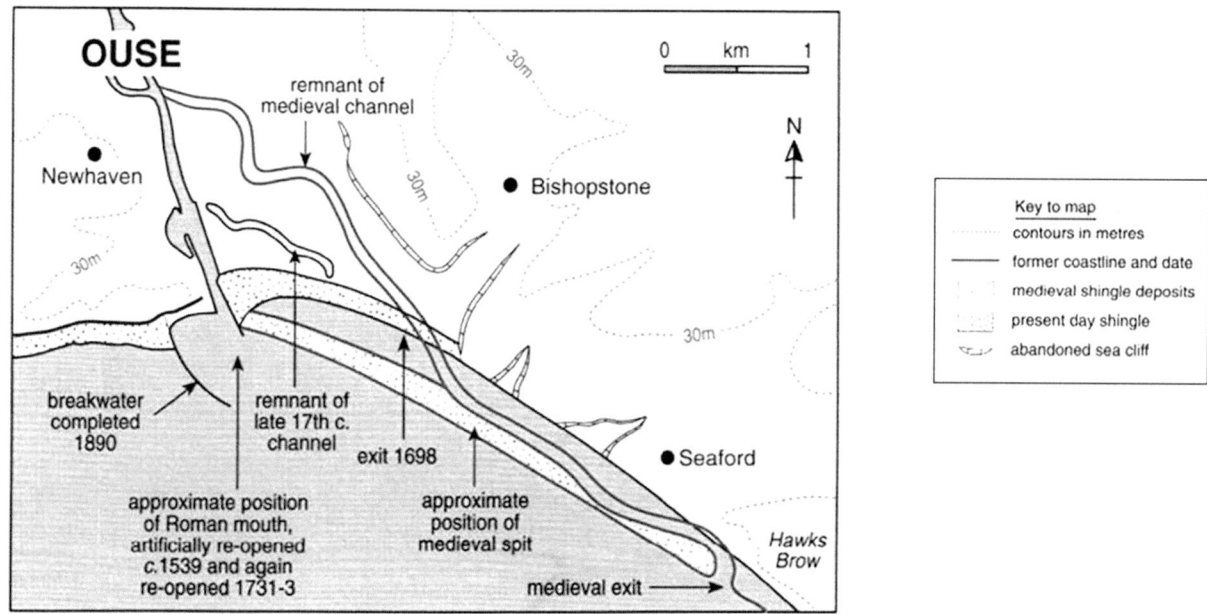

FIGURE 11.6: RIVER OUSE RELOCATION (ROBINSON 1999) (REPRODUCED WITH PERMISSION OF PHILLIMORE AND CO. LTD.)

Archaeological investigations in Seaford

In the following section excavation locations are shown in Figure 11.7 unless specifically mentioned as otherwise.

A small number of buildings exhibit aspects of medieval architecture including the church of St. Leonard, a Norman font at St. Peters, and the Crypt, a thirteenth century undercroft. Excavation of land between St. Leonards and the Crypt, on Church Street, found 'intense late medieval occupation' in the form of 'thirty-two pits, a well and corner of a timber framed building' (Freke 1978). The Church Street investigations concluded 'that the early town was further to the south and east

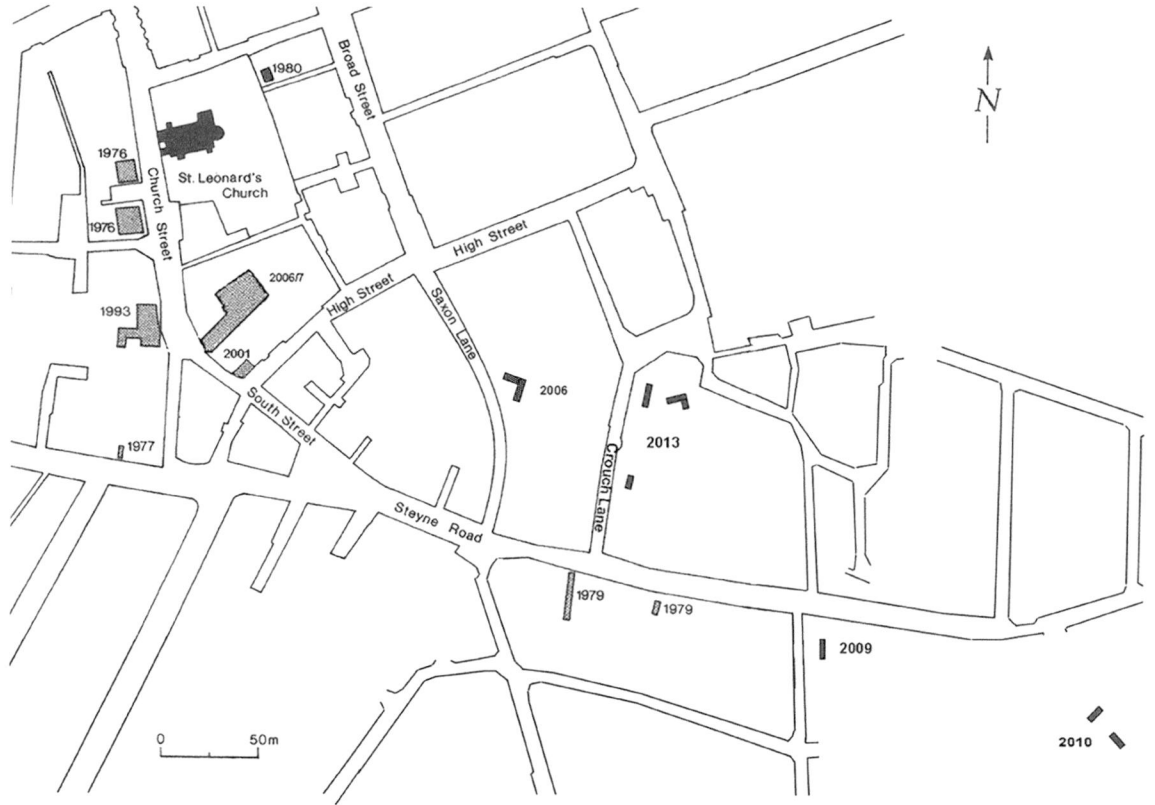

FIGURE 11.7: ARCHAEOLOGICAL INVESTIGATIONS IN SEAFORD (1976–2013), BASED ON GARDINER (1995, FIG. 1) ADDITIONS BY THE AUTHOR (FOR POST 2000 EXCAVATIONS) (REPRODUCED WITH PERMISSION OF THE SUSSEX ARCHAEOLOGICAL SOCIETY)

perhaps nearer the quay' (Freke 1978). Lack of twelfth century finds in a trench between the church and Broad Street may confirm the hypothesis and if correct place the church at the town's western edge, sited on rising ground (Freke and Rudling 1983). Trenching at Seaford Constitutional Club on Crouch Lane has potentially extended the town's medieval eastern footprint beyond Saxon Lane (Russell 2013). A west-east aligned ditch, dated by pottery *c.* 1275-1350, with some sherds of early/mid-thirteenth century, together with building material as fill suggest 'a substantial medieval building stood within close proximity'.

Freke (1979) had assumed the quay to be along the line of Steyne Road but excavation on the north side revealed a medieval floor, well and fence line. Beneath a wall various medieval features dated no earlier than the twelfth century, with a fourteenth century beam slot and pottery of possibly twelfth century to late medieval date (Freke 1979). Freke reported 'The site is probably not on the medieval quay' requiring a 're-appraisal of Seaford's medieval layout.' Trenching along the south side of Steyne Road, *c.* 250 metres east of the previous excavation, revealed thirteenth/fourteenth century pottery suggesting its position to be 'near the medieval river bank but is not the site of the medieval quay' (Freke and Rudling 1983). The marine environment was examined on the south side of Steyne Road, *c.* 140 metres east of the 1979 investigation (Butler 2009). It found 'evidence for flooding events' possibly linked to breaches of sea defences. A geoarchaeological evaluation at Seaford Head School, further to the east on the south side of Steyne Road, shown as trenches 2010 (Figure 11.7) confirmed it lies within a former marine inlet which has 'undergone a process of progressive intertidal silting and eventual isolation from the sea' and is the most likely location for Seaford Port (Porteus *et al.*, 2010).

The Crypt

Although called The Crypt this medieval structure is an undercroft, forming part of a merchant's house and unusual in having an internal stair to upper levels. Archaeological investigations presented the possibility to examine aspects of medieval trade and economy. A survey of the street frontage to the Crypt followed by excavation 'between the present street frontage and the undercroft, and around the undercroft' (Gardiner 1995; Figure 11.8) revealed three or possibly four tenements (1, 2A, 2B, 3) with 'most of the excavated remains belonging to the thirteenth or fourteenth centuries'. Pottery finds were generally of the thirteenth/fourteenth centuries with one cesspit yielding sherds of the late twelfth/early thirteenth century. A small number of overseas manufactured sherds were also recovered with the majority from northern France and a single sherd originating from southern Brittany. The absence of twelfth century features however could be attributed to removal by subsequent rebuilding hence Freke's assertion for the town centre to be located elsewhere cannot be substantiated.

Excavations on the corner of High Street and South Street revealed postholes, pits and a possible beam slot. Pottery finds were of the twelfth to early-fifteenth century similar in composition to those found at the Crypt, most of thirteenth/fourteenth century date (Stevens 2004; ESHER 7246). German lava quernstone fragments demonstrate trading connections with the Continent. The earliest phase (AD 1125–1250) included a truncated pit containing building rubble suggesting a stone building of some status, possibly sited on the street frontage. Other examples of stone-built buildings are normally found in larger settlements, e.g. Canterbury. The majority of structural evidence is of fourteenth century date possibly suggesting one or two buildings aligned at right angles to the street.

Prior to building redevelopment on Saxon Lane, two phases of insubstantial timber framed buildings were recorded and suggested to be sheds dating to the thirteenth/fourteenth century (Hunter and Pine 2006; ESHER 7341). Analysis of rubbish pits, with a similar date, showed they continued in use after the buildings were abandoned. On South Street Mews, medieval buildings of the thirteenth or fourteenth century and later, were discovered with rubbish pits containing thirteenth to fourteenth century pottery and tile (Meaton 2009; ESHER 8736). One structure appeared to be a vault or cellar but later was interpreted as a corridor and chalk floors, dated by tile to the thirteenth/fourteenth centuries. Possibly this thirteenth/fourteenth century structure represents a tenement fronting South Street.

The Church Street excavations provided an insight into everyday life. Caprovids (generally sheep or goat) and cattle remains in fourteenth century pits/wells were likely food animals (Brothwell 1979, 231). Also found were pig, horse, a few cats, limited deer, possibly dogs, two whale fragments and rodents. The latter may be important since two skulls were of the black rat possibly suggesting infestation in Seaford. Butchery marks were noted on caprovid and cattle bones, with a significant lack on pig remains. Bones with burning and chewing marks were also noted.

Archaeology of the Lower Ouse

Beyond the bounds of Seaford archaeological investigations of the valley are few, with most villages, DMV's and SMV's invisible archaeologically. Exceptions are the many churches with medieval features. Often these are of the simplest kind with a nave and chancel occasionally separated by a tower (Nairn and Pevsner 1965, 43). The close association of Sussex with France may explain the use of apses, which are

11. Lower Ouse in the Medieval period (AD 1066 to 1499)

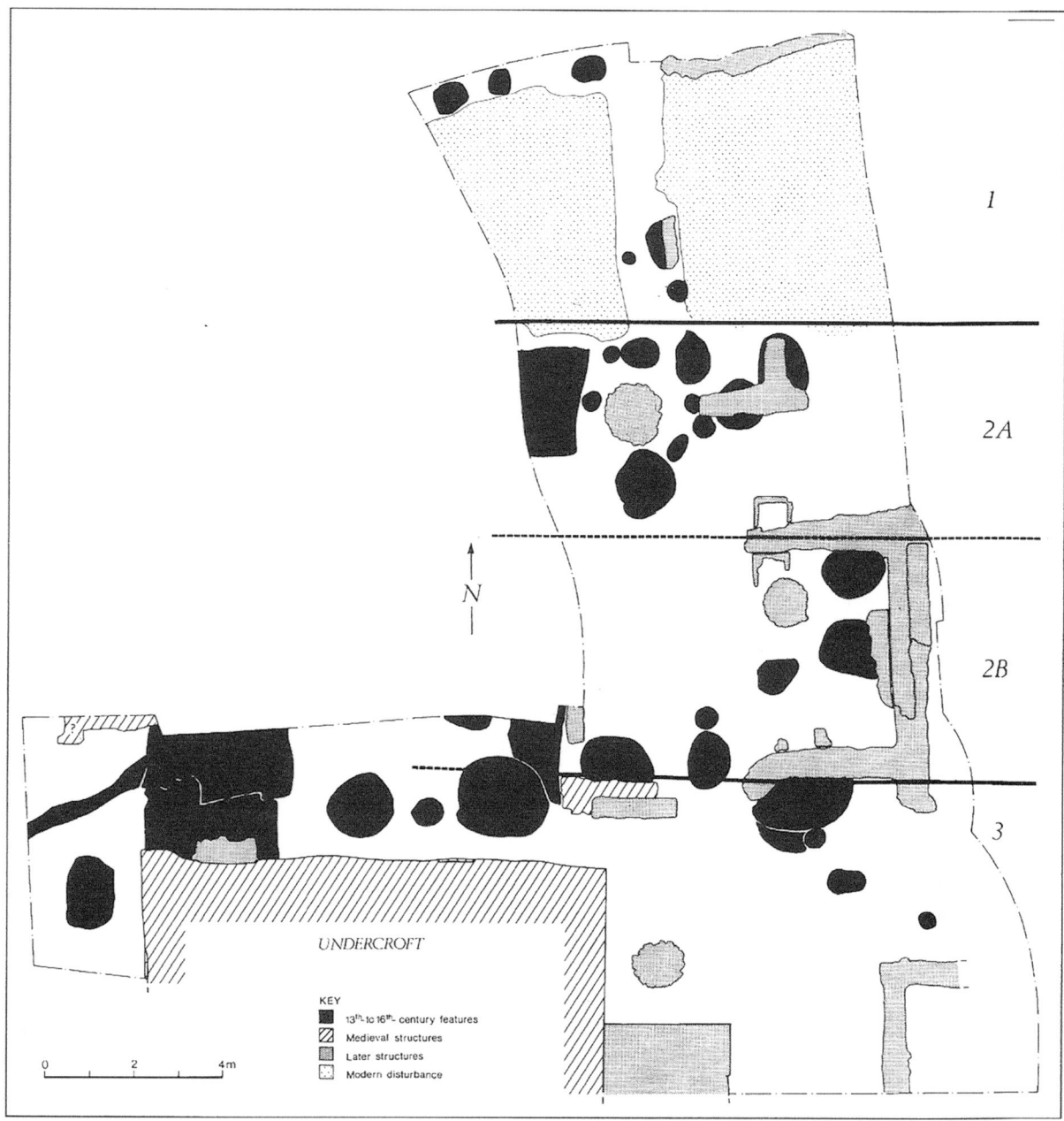

Figure 11.8: The Crypt, Seaford – plan of excavated features (from Gardiner 1995, fig. 3, reproduced with permission of the Sussex Archaeological Society)

more common in France than England. The locations of places mentioned in text are shown in Figure 11.1.

Newhaven

Newhaven, originally called Meeching or Mechinges c. 1090, is absent from the Domesday Book, and may be of Anglo-Saxon origin (Mawer and Stenton 1930, 323). Documentary sources trace its development from the eleventh century through land grants and taxation records. William de Warenne, in c. 1090, granted the church to the Cluniac priory of St. Pancras at Lewes along with a mill and four acres of land. In c. 1253-62 a ferry is first recorded (Field 1935) and appears to have continued at the same location for the following centuries.

The paucity of archaeological data is demonstrated by Newhaven, which has only one surviving medieval building (Harris 2005, 20) - St. Michael's church (Figure 11.9). This was built in the twelfth century of which the eastern tower with twin-arch bell openings, apse and corbel table which includes heads and monsters remain (Nairn and Pevsner 1965, 570). Built of Caen stone, ashlar for quoins and rubble that includes ferruginous sandstone (Harris 2005, 20) the church shows the close contact between Sussex and Normandy. Prior to the ring road development, excavations took place at South Way within close proximity of the High Street. Medieval finds consisted of two shallow pits cut into the Ouse flood-plain alluvium and thirteenth/fourteenth century pottery, mainly coarse ware cooking pots, found 10m west of the subway (Bell 1976, 299). If Meeching developed as a nucleated settlement then St. Michael's and the manor house, suggested to be Court House Farm, should be in close association (Harris 2005, 20). This appears not to be the case, a distance of 350m separating them and each 300m from the eighteenth century mapped town centre. To explain this Harris (2005) suggested either a town centre shift or development as a polyfocal settlement. Industrial activity is shown by three medieval salterns (TQ 4559 0111) located *c.* 1km SE of the swing bridge (ESHER 7253).

Piddinghoe

Piddinghoe, to the north of Newhaven, is a typical nucleated medieval village with the Norman church of St. John (TQ 4351 0308) having a round tower (ESHER 1838). Only two other round towers exist in Sussex: Southease (St. Peter) and Lewes (St. Michael). Round towers, which are found mainly in East Anglia (164), possibly indicate Saxon origins. Although remodelled in 1882, medieval features still exist, such as the north and south (*c.* 1200) arcades and chancel (thirteenth century) (Whiteman and Whiteman 1994, 122). Close-by is an area known as The Lydds (TQ 431 033), thought to be a DMV (Burleigh 1976, 67) below which are broad lynchets. The word Lydd though is possibly an alternative for lynchet hence the designation as a DMV is uncertain. Piddinghoe has a number of mill sites: the first *c.* 1km SSW where a possible bowl barrow has been converted to a windmill stead (ESHER 1843) and two medieval windmills on its' northern fringe (TQ 4318 0327) (ESHER 1860). Farming practices are frozen in the landscape with strip lynchets (TQ 4300 0262) well preserved in woodland (ESHER 1850) and to the NW (*c.* 0.75km) where medieval strip lynchets and terraces are visible on aerial photographs (ESHER 1845).

Southease

Southease village is similar in aspect to Piddinghoe, having a nucleated form. The church of St. Peter (TQ 423 053) dates from AD 966 with Norman features: a small round-headed window, the nave and jambs of the former north doorway. There is some debate as to an eleventh century date for the earliest part of the building and the existence of a separate Chancel is disputed. However an eleventh century date is suggested by excavations revealing possible foundations of porticus, found more often pre-Conquest. Several thirteenth century paintings are displayed on the north wall (Nairn and Pevsner 1965, 608: ESHER 1996) and the pair of bells are dated 1296 (treble) and *c.* 1260 (tenor). The round tower is of probable twelfth century date and its construction phasing with the nave is controversial. Allen (1985, 262) summarised the debate (Figure 11.10), concluding that the tower and nave were roughly contemporaneous, with the tower built after the nave.

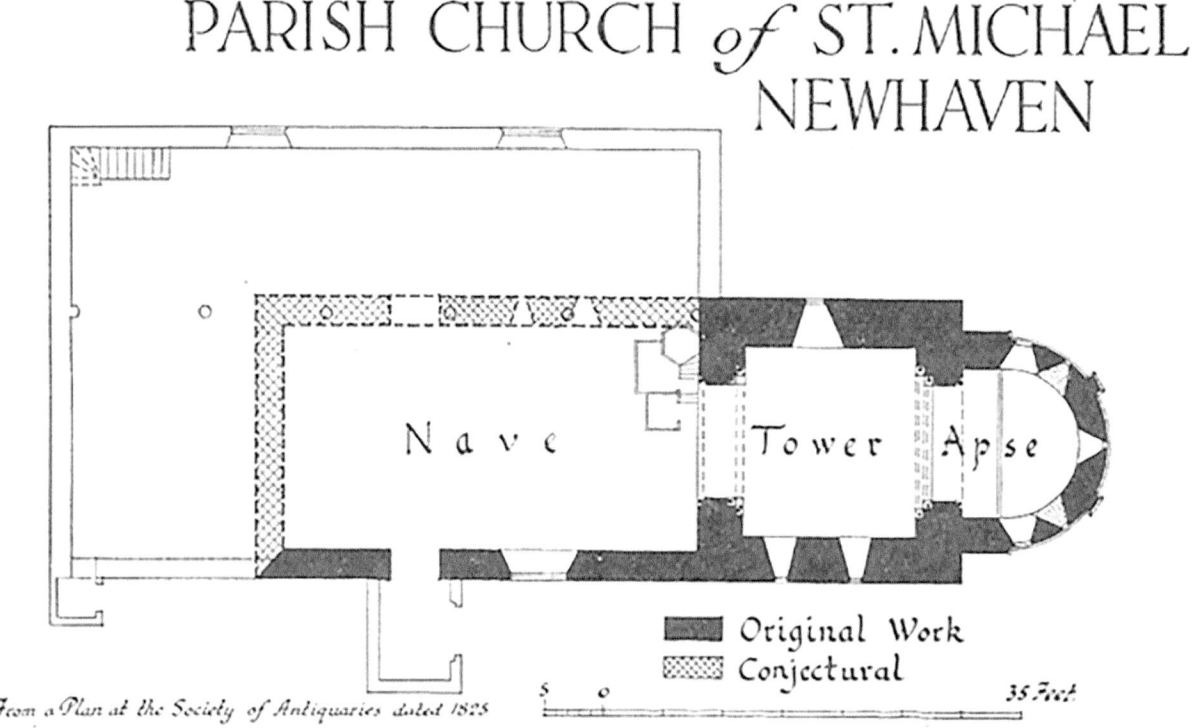

FIGURE 11.9: PLAN OF ST. MICHAEL'S CHURCH, NEWHAVEN (FROM GODFREY 1940, FIG 2, REPRODUCED WITH PERMISSION OF THE SUSSEX ARCHAEOLOGICAL SOCIETY)

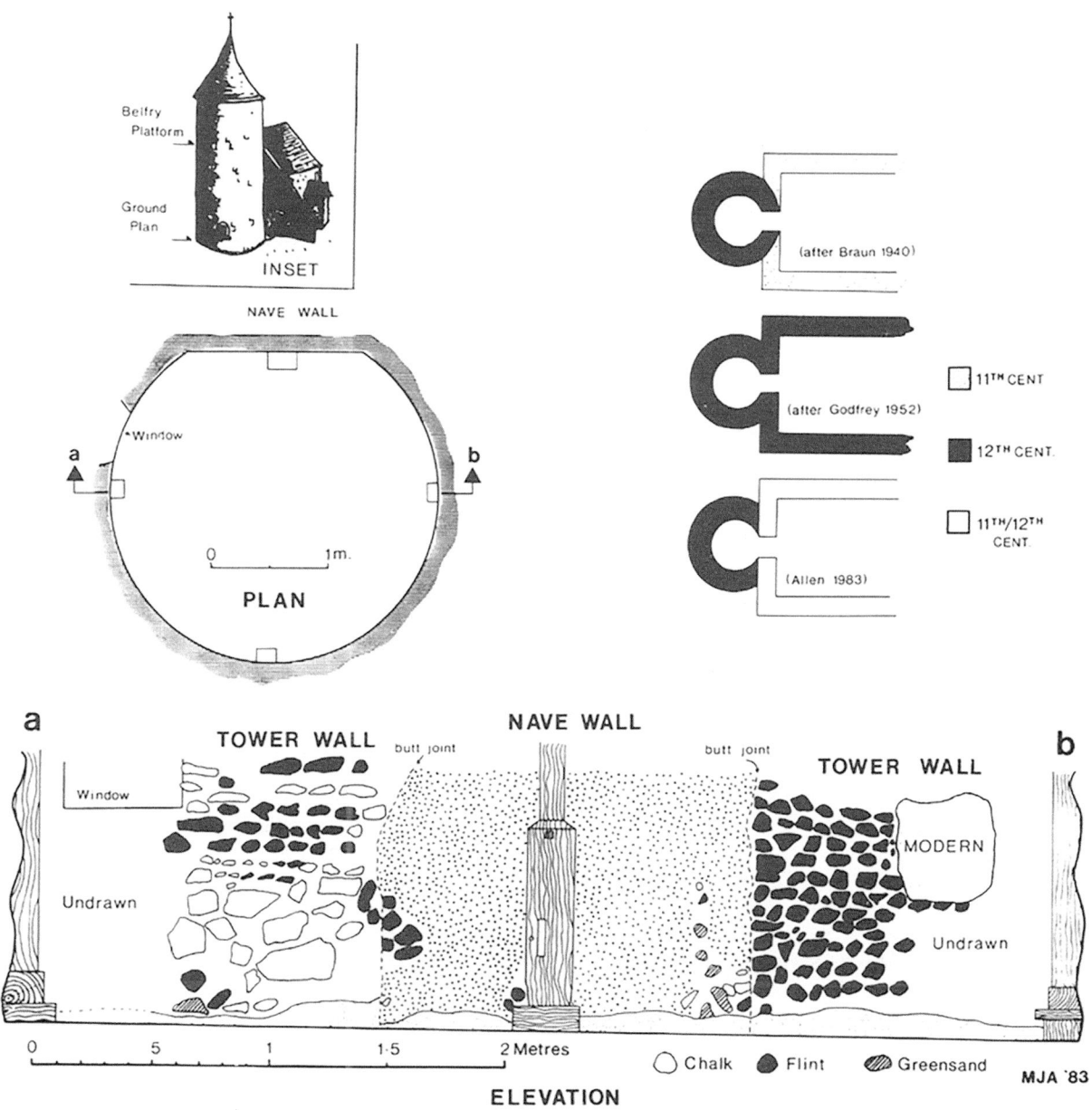

FIGURE 11.10: ST. PETER'S SOUTHEASE TOWER AND NAVE VIEWS (FROM ALLEN 1985, FIG. 23, REPRODUCED WITH PERMISSION OF THE SUSSEX ARCHAEOLOGICAL SOCIETY)

Rodmell

Rodmell is mentioned in the Domesday Survey as Redmelle or Ramelle. It existed before the Conquest, with St. Peter's church possibly built on the site of a Saxon church and granted to St. Pancras priory in Lewes c. 1090 by William de Warenne. Northease Manor, operated by monks, on the road to Lewes probably became the principal farm in the area.

St. Peter's church is of early Norman date retaining much of its twelfth century fabric, notable for its flint elevations and is reputed to have a Saxon font. The building is small with thirteenth century features and a tower of late-twelfth or early-thirteenth century with an attached room (the Baptistry) of the same date. The south aisle was thrown out not later than the twelfth century in a manner similar to St. Anne's at Lewes and at Beddingham (Nairn and Pevsner 1965, 590). Unlike Southease and Piddinghoe, Rodmell is a linear settlement lying in a roughly parallel orientation to the River Ouse. To the immediate south of the church, within the village, is Rodmell Place the home of the de la Chambre family. All that remains are cellars, largely filled in, above which are walls of late medieval date. To the church's west, about one kilometre distant, is Northease manor house which was once a chapelry. An early medieval wall may represent the west wall of the chapel of Northease which possibly had a nave and chancel. Almost due west of the church is Monk's House where investigations found evidence for medieval occupation (TQ 42115 06414). This excavation included a small part of extensive earthworks which suggest they are man-made and possibly dated to the Norman period. Minor flooding events may be represented by localised layers of a possible ditch and bank enclosure possibly showing attempts to consolidate the ground. A litharge fragment is suggestive of silver working maybe in a specialised craft centre at Rodmell. Interpretation of finds and environmental data support a 'wide range of activities happening in the vicinity, including domestic settlement, crop-processing, grain storage and lead working' during the mid-twelfth to fourteenth centuries. Little material was recovered dated to the mid-fourteenth to mid-fifteenth centuries implying close links with Lewes which had declined in this period (Doherty 2014).

Iford

St. Nicholas church at Iford, represents in Pevsner's view one of the simpler Norman styles of a church with a nave and chancel separated by a tower (Figure 11.11).

Between Iford and Kingston near Lewes is Swanborough Grange (TQ 40102 07802) an L shaped building, the earliest part being a Grange of St. Pancras, Lewes (Figure 11.12). Dated to *c.* 1200 the hall and part of the chapel to the east have an east-west orientation (Godfrey 1936, 3). The grange was extensively remodelled and extended at the turn of the fourteenth and fifteenth centuries (ESHER 1525).

About 1km south-southwest of the Grange is an enclosure (TQ 3917 0738) identified by a bank and outside ditch, considered to be a possible medieval stock enclosure (ESHER 1540).

Beddingham

Beddingham was a Saxon royal minster, with the manor of Preston in Beddingham held by the Abbey of Bec. A farm is recorded at Beddingham (ESHER 16223) in 1327.

Excavations (1987–1992) uncovered a Roman villa with one building later hollowed out, possibly in Saxon times, as a grubenhaus. With the arrival of the Normans the church of St. Andrew's, owned by Wilmington Priory, was rebuilt in local flint. The church underwent remodelling in the mid-fourteenth century with little of the Norman aspects remaining. To the east of St. Andrews, *c.* 100m, a concentration of 64 unabraded sherds of medieval pottery were found, of the twelfth to fourteenth centuries (ESHER 7173). These may indicate a nearby settlement, possibly situated to the east of the A26, opposite the church, where earthworks are visible.

To the south south west of Beddingham is Itford Farm (TQ 433 059), a thirteenth century farmhouse. Excavations revealed a grubenhaus and later medieval ditch just north of the farm (James 2002). The ditch's fill probably dated to the Saxo-Norman period is in keeping with similar sherds, found south of the farm, from topsoil and the grubenhaus fill. Burleigh (1976) identified a DMV (TQ 4330 0553) at Itford, recorded in the Domesday Book, and considered to be a farm in the sixteenth century (Brandon 1963, 356).

Tarring Neville

Tarring Neville Parish church of St. Mary (TQ 4441 0378) has a thirteenth century chancel and tower, with

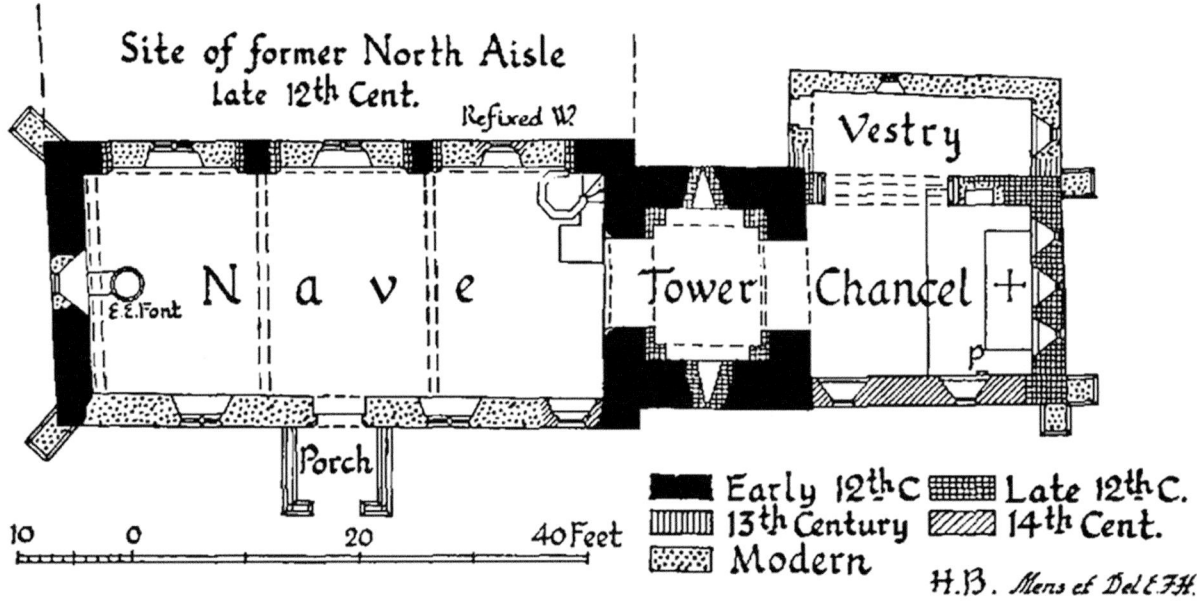

FIGURE 11.11: PLAN OF ST. NICHOLAS CHURCH, IFORD (FROM GODFREY 1940, FIG. 5, REPRODUCED WITH PERMISSION OF THE SUSSEX ARCHAEOLOGICAL SOCIETY)

11. Lower Ouse in the Medieval period (AD 1066 to 1499)

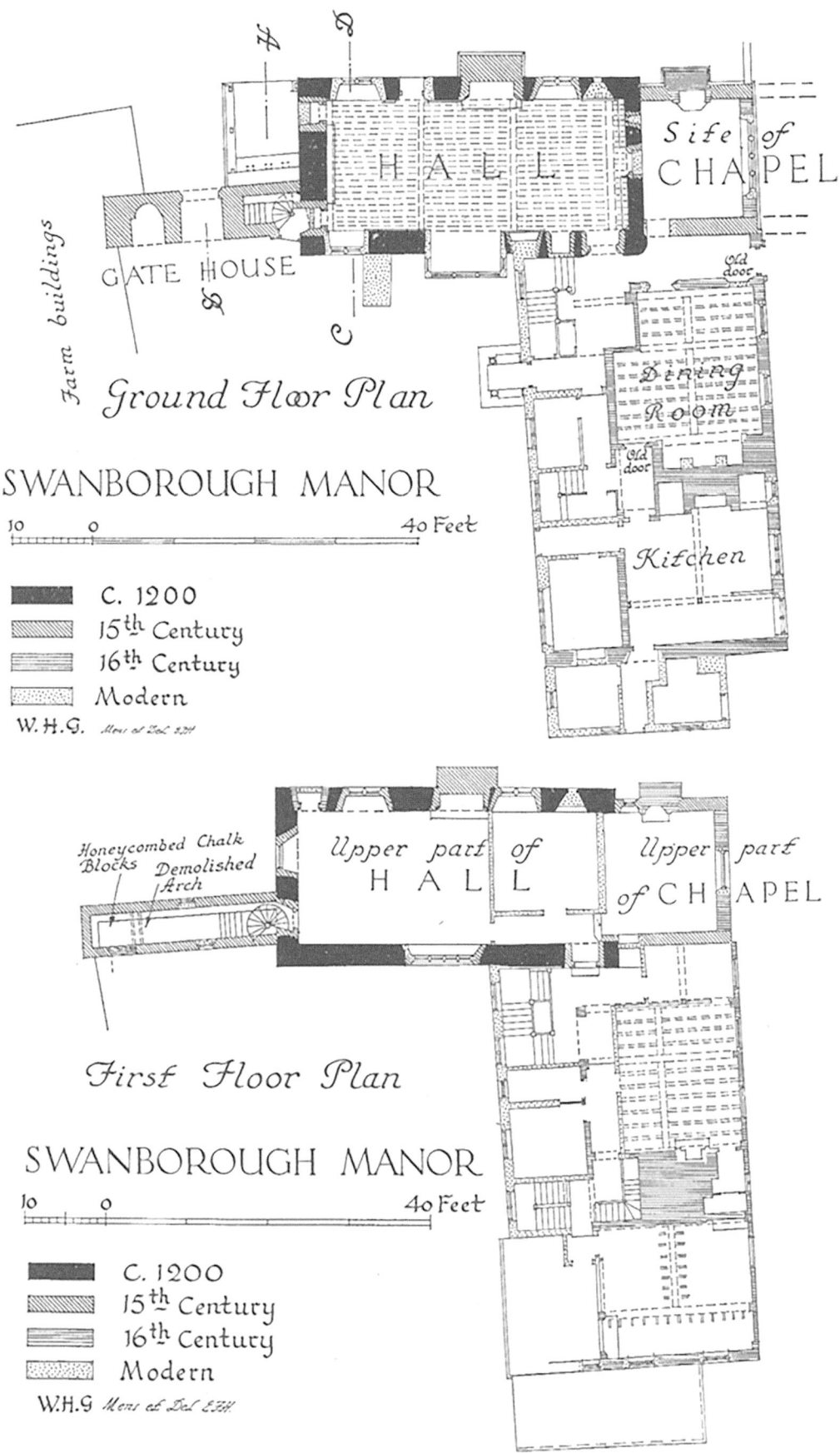

Figure 11.12: Plan of Swanborough Grange c. 1936 (from Godfrey 1936, fig 2, reproduced with permission of the Sussex Archaeological Society)

transitional Norman nave and aisle (ESHER 2037). A fourteenth century font is built into the south wall of the aisle. The name Tarring may allude to the process of waterproofing ships with tar and the Neville added after the Conquest when the village was owned by a family of that name. Opposite Tarring Court Farm a linear feature, interpreted as a ditch or dyke yielded a small amount of medieval pottery dated to the thirteenth to fourteenth century (Thorpe 2010, 78: ESHER 15550). Possibly the feature is associated with drainage works in the fourteenth century. Three former quarries (TQ 4431703587), south of the village, were found to contain a small quantity of twelfth and thirteenth century pottery, however these may be residual. Further medieval finds are: pottery recovered from a furrow (TQ 4445603461) and a buckle from the topsoil nearby (Thorpe 2010, 81).

South Heighton

An evaluation at The Hall, South Heighton (TQ 4500 0280) found substantial flint and mortar wall foundations, interpreted as the west end of St. Martin's church (Score 2000; ESHER 1954). The north wall return was constructed on a chalk platform cut into the hill slope. A buttress foundation pit, robber trenches and postholes were also uncovered together with a stone baptismal font. The most northerly barrow (TQ 4656 0116) in a linear form of barrows, extending from Rookery Hill, has been converted to a Windmill mound probably in medieval times (ESHER 1956).

Denton

The parish church of St. Leonard contains a Norman font of tub-shape and there is a ruined priest's house adjacent: both are of thirteenth century date. Opposite the church (TQ 455 026), parts of a quern showing considerable wear and two large sherds of eleventh to twelfth century pottery were recovered (ESHER 1813). During building of the Church Hall (TQ 454 026) a medieval pit was found roughly midway between the church and surviving walls of the priest's house. This yielded thirteenth to mid-fourteenth century pottery along with animal, bird and fish bones (Bell 1979; Westley 1979). The latter comprised both freshwater and marine species, including Conger and Ling common in northern waters, indicating likely trading links.

Norton

To the south east of Denton and north of Bishopstone is Norton Farm (TQ 472 018). From documentary sources a large medieval farmstead existed here (ESHER 19368). Medieval agricultural practices are recorded in ploughed fields by 'a few very abraded flint-tempered pot sherds' possibly of later medieval date, probably used for manuring (Nielsen and Rapson 2010). Excavations of a chapel-of-rest exposed collapsed flint walls and foundations of an extensive building having two levels. The lower level produced pottery dated to the thirteenth to fourteenth century. Interestingly fragments of glazed floor tile suggest a building of some status (O'Shea 1978; ESHER 1977). Norton (TQ 472 019) has possible platforms with associated trackways, as extensions of present streets, with banked enclosures possibly of medieval date (Webster and Cherry 1978; ESHER 1978). Documentary evidence shows a fourteenth century beacon on Beacon Hill (TQ 4759 0179), *c.* 0.5km east of the farm (ESHER 19391).

Bishopstone

Bishopstone likely succeeded the early Anglo-Saxon settlement at Rookery Hill by the second half of the eighth century. Excavations in the core of the village, just to the north of St. Andrew's church (2002–2005), suggest abandonment within the excavated area, no later than the turn of the tenth century (Marshall *et al.* 2010, 202; Thomas 2010, 220). Listed in the Domesday Survey, as being held by the Bishop of Chichester (ESHER 19367), the hideage remained the same prior to 1066 and in 1086. It is likely by this time, that Bishopstone's core had shifted to south of the church as suggested by test pitting about 15m to the south-west of the churchyard. This revealed a rubbish pit containing 'rich concentrations of domestic refuse including an unabraded assemblage of Ringmer-ware pottery dating to the twelfth century' (Thomas 2010, 223). The lack of stratified twelfth century material north of the churchyard and the assemblages' unabraded nature, suggesting little or no movement after deposition, both support the shift theory. To the west of the village two large ovens and ditches were discovered with Saxo-Norman to fifteenth century pottery (TQ 472 011) (Webster and Cherry 1978). More ephemeral finds are of medieval pottery sherds found as scatters in fields on the north-east of the village at Manor Farm. Although of limited archaeological importance these demonstrate medieval activity, probably from manuring (Nielsen and Rapson 2010). On the north-west margins are Field Cottages. 153m to the south of their gateway a trial hole found 'a few abraded fragments of fine flint tempered medieval pottery along with occasional charcoal flecks, oyster and winkle shell' (Nielsen and Rapson 2010). The later medieval period may be shown by the remains of a flint wall found in the village along the roadside (Nielsen and Rapson 2010). Medieval habitation is also suggested by the identification of a possible house platform *c.* 48m north of St. Andrew's (ESHER 54).

Industry

Salt was a vital commodity for preserving meat and fish especially for winter use and shipping. The Ouse, as a tidal estuary, enabled the development of salterns, along its lower reaches in similar fashion to that along the Adur (Holden and Hudson 1981 117-148). They were considered sufficiently important to be specifically mentioned in the Domesday Book. Four salt-houses are listed within Totnore hundred near Beddingham (Morris 1976) and eleven at Rodmell. Three medieval salterns (TQ 4559 0111) lie opposite Newhaven in the Ouse Estuary Nature Reserve (Meaton 2006, 18; ESHER 7253) and a further excavated saltern between Newhaven and Bishopstone (Griffin 2006).

Beyond the floodplain, on the upper levels of rising ground, mills were built (Mill Mounds), often on pre-existing raised areas, such as Bronze Age barrows as at Beddingham (ESHER 1219), Piddinghoe (Grinsell 1934, 268) and South Heighton (Grinsell 1934, 272). Even Rookery Hill, with its linear form of barrows, has had its most northerly barrow (TQ 4656 0116) converted to a windmill mound (Grinsell 1934, 272; ESHER 1956). Mills were important in the eleventh or twelfth century as shown by the gift of a mill and four acres of land at Meeching (Newhaven) given by the Earl Warenne Sheriff to the Priory of St. Pancras at Lewes (Online British History – rape and honour of Lewes). Other mill sites are: Mill Hill, Southwest of Rodmell; Piddinghoe (*c.* 1km SSW) where a possible bowl barrow has been converted to a windmill stead (ESHER 1843) and on Piddinghoe's northern fringe (TQ 4318 0327) two mill-steads were aligned east-west (ESHER 1860). Water also provided power for mills with water-mills mentioned in the Domesday Book at Beddingham and Iford (Brent 2004, 24).

The economy of the Lower Ouse valley relied heavily on agriculture. Topographically the valley was ideally suited for both land and sea exploitation, with distinct zones available: riverside pastures, arable at the foot of the Downs and sheep rearing on higher land. Transportation of produce could be effected by both river and land routes on the well-drained chalk Downs. In 1225 monastic houses imported building materials by boat along the Ouse (Brent 2004) and Brandon (1974) has suggested sea-going boats were capable of navigating the river to Lewes.

Today the landscape displays visible signs of this medieval activity in the form of strip lynchets and field systems. Examples of lynchets may be found in the Piddinghoe area (TQ 4300 0262) well preserved in woodland (ESHER 1850) and to the NW of Piddinghoe (*c.* 0.75km) where lynchets and terraces show on aerial photographs (ESHER 1845). Enclosures, possibly for stock, are found in the valley to the north of Heighton Hill, now visible as weak banks about 0.5m high together with ditches (ESHER 1968) and about 1km SSW of Swanborough Manor (TQ 3917 0738) identified by a bank and outside ditch (ESHER 1540). Medieval pottery sherds found as scatters in fields on the north-east of Bishopstone at Manor Farm and Norton Farm (TQ 472 018) may represent manuring practices.

Chalk production, used for marling and building purposes, took place south of Tarring Neville at three quarries (TQ 44317 03587). The quarries were found to contain a small quantity of twelfth and thirteenth century pottery, possibly of a residual nature. A further proposed medieval chalk pit has been recorded at Denton (ESHER 1811).

Land based activities were also supplemented by fishing. The Domesday Survey indicated the strength of the Lower Ouse fishing trade in recording tax levied on tenants at Southease of 38,500 herring, Iford 16,000 and Rodmell 3,000. The latter with Piddinghoe were engaged in the North Sea herring fishery (Brandon 1974, 116).

Discussion and future work

Much of the detailed evidence for this period comes from historical sources. The archaeology contributes to this view, but is sparsely and randomly represented within the Lower Ouse valley. Excavations have generally been undertaken in isolation, as pre-development investigations or watching briefs with limited intrusiveness.

The archaeological timeline for Seaford commences in the twelfth century at the junction of the High Street and South Street with a potential stone building, possibly of some status and occupation of the area in front of the Crypt. The thirteenth century saw buildings along Saxon Lane, the street frontage of the Crypt, Crouch Lane and at South Street Mews. Occupation is shown by pottery of the thirteenth to fourteenth centuries along the south side of Steyne Road and at South Street Mews. The buildings discovered vary considerably from stone construction to insubstantial timber framed structures. A beam slot from north of Steyne Road and possible buildings aligned at right angles to the street on the corner of the High Street and South Street date to the fourteenth century. Late medieval occupation, along Church Street, is shown in thirty-two pits and the corner of a timber framed building. All of this activity probably relates to the town of Seaford with the location of the port area undetermined. The most likely location, to date, is provided by work at Seaford Head School along the south side of Steyne Road showing this area as a marine inlet.

Seaford has received most attention archaeologically however questions remain unanswered for the medieval period. In terms of the following discussion the word 'settlement' is used to include both the town and port areas. Of key consideration is whether the original medieval settlement form, including extent and location, can be described and how this developed over time. In particular can evidence be found to explain the settlement's fourteenth century decline and its consequent effect? Elucidation of the settlement's form would assist in answering questions about the economy and whether organised development took place. The relationship between the port and town areas is crucial to an understanding of the urban morphology. Industrial and trade aspects are currently the domain of historical sources, through archaeological investigations these could be confirmed and industrial centres defined. In turn these may help to refine the relationship between Seaford and Lewes. Nowadays Seaford has assimilated smaller villages of Chinting, Sutton and Blatchington originally existing as distinct entities. Again the question of relationships, morphology and trade links are important both between these villages and Seaford.

The discussion above could well apply to Newhaven where the settlement's medieval morphology is little understood. For both Seaford and Newhaven the wider context needs exploration in order to correctly place these within the Lower Ouse medieval community. This exploration has to include the smaller settlements along the Ouse and their physical relationship both between each other and the larger urban centre of Seaford.

Based on the archaeological evidence a picture emerges of the valley, excluding Seaford, from the eleventh to fifteenth centuries. In the eleventh century is seen a relatively limited view of activity on both sides of the river. On the western side, activity is centred about half way between Seaford and Lewes with remodelling of the church at Southease and the possible construction of extensive earthworks at Rodmell. Both of these indicate organisation, effort and funding probably by the Norman overlords. It may be that these works were connected with the Ouse crossing to Itford on the eastern bank (Brandon 1974, 120). The eastern side demonstrates quite a different profile, mainly of domestic activity. Near the church at Denton, quern and pottery is suggestive of domestic use whilst Bishopstone demonstrates continuity of habitation from the Anglo-Saxon period. The twelfth century sees construction of churches at Newhaven and Rodmell representing a consolidation of Norman power which may have attracted silver working artisans to the Rodmell area. Elsewhere at Beddingham and Bishopstone, quantities of unabraded pottery probably show local settlement activity. The thirteenth century is a period of growth in terms of settlements and religion. Religious houses continued to build and develop their organisation. New churches were built on both sides of the river at Piddinghoe, Tarring Neville and Denton. Other construction works were the priest's house at Denton and at nearby Norton a two level chapel-of-rest, with further works at Southease and Rodmell churches. This religious activity also saw the building of a grange, Swanborough Manor, between Iford and Kingston near Lewes. The fourteenth century sees domestic and industrial activities at Rodmell including crop processing, grain storage and lead working. Activity at rural settlements is matched by the building of isolated farmhouses, as at Itford Farm. Religious activity is on a more modest scale: a new font in the church at Tarring Neville and at Beddingham the church is rebuilt in local flint by Wilmington Priory for use by the local community. Perhaps to consolidate religious influence and power Swanborough Manor underwent extensive remodelling and enlargement. Although activity appears diminished this does not seem to have affected the Denton priest, who possibly continued to enjoy a varied diet of animal, bird and occasional North Sea fish. Land management at Tarring Neville is suggested by a ditch possibly used for drainage purposes and at Monks House with defences against flooding. It is possible the chapel-of-rest at Norton may well have continued into the fourteenth century. The fifteenth century is a time of virtual archaeological invisibility with three settlements at Bishopstone, Rodmell and Swanborough Manor all providing evidence for little activity.

Overall the archaeological record shows a period of growth peaking in the thirteenth century, followed by a gentle but accelerating decline. Coin data from PAS (Figure 11.13) with a lifetime within a specific century supports this timeline. The two parishes with the largest coin concentrations, Iford and Beddingham, show a remarkably similar profile.

The difficulty in interpretation of archaeological data from the valley is compounded by the sparse and random nature of the investigations. A way forward for the smaller rural settlements may be to use a structured approach similar to that established by Dr Carenza Lewis at Cambridge University. This is called the Currently Occupied Rural Settlement (CORS) project and has operated from Derbyshire to Hampshire and Hertfordshire to Kent. It seeks to 'advance knowledge and understanding of the ways in which rural settlements that are still inhabited today developed in the past' by conducting systematic small scale excavations, typically sondage based. Applying this methodology could well provide new information in a community based environment and structured fashion.

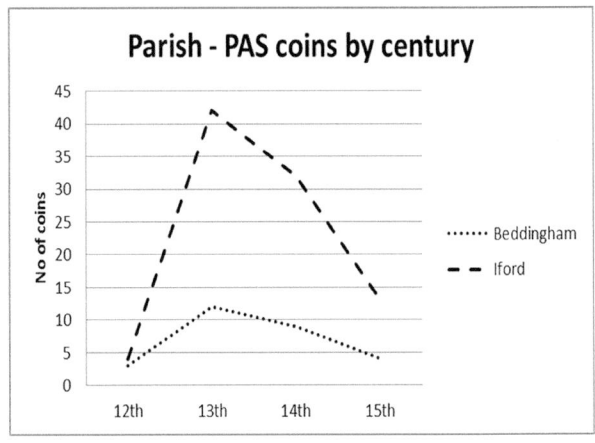

FIGURE 11.13: BEDDINGHAM AND IFORD: MEDIEVAL COIN FINDS BY CENTURY, RECORDED BY PAS.

Acknowledgements

My thanks to Greg Chuter (Assistant County Archaeologist for East Sussex County Council) for providing ESHER maps and data. Also to Luke Barber for his thoughtful review comments and Archaeology South East for allowing access to the Monk's House draft report. For permission to reproduce illustration (Figure 11.6) I am grateful to Phillimore and Co Ltd. Any omissions or errors are entirely the responsibility of the author.

References

Allen, M. J. 1985. Southease Church (TQ 423053). *Sussex Archaeological Collections* 123, 261.

Bell, M. 1976. The excavation of an early Romano-British site and Pleistocene landforms at Newhaven, Sussex. *Sussex Archaeological Collections* 114, 299-301.

Bell, M. 1979. Medieval Finds from Denton (1). *Sussex Archaeological Collections* 117, 238.

Brandon, P. F. 1963. The Common Lands and Wastes of Sussex. Unpublished PhD Thesis, accessed at Ethos, Ref 337324, available at: www. Ethos.bl.uk [accessed 2015].

Brandon, P. 1971. The Origin of Newhaven and the drainage of the Lewes and Laughton Levels. *Sussex Archaeological Collections* 109, 97.

Brandon, P. 1974. *The Sussex Landscape*. London: Hodder and Stoughton Limited.

Brent, C. 2004. *Pre-Georgian Lewes c. 890-1714 the emergence of a county town*. Lewes: Colin Brent Books.

British History Online. http://www.british-history.ac.uk/ [accessed 6 May 2010].

Brothwell, D. 1979. Notes on the Mammal remains in Medieval pits and well at Seaford Church St. 1976. *Sussex Archaeological Collections* 117, 231.

Burleigh, G. R. 1973. An introduction to deserted Medieval Villages in East Sussex. *Sussex Archaeological Collections* 111, 56-73.

Burleigh, G. R. 1976. Further notes on Deserted and Shrunken Medieval Villages in Sussex. *Sussex Archaeological Collections* 114, 65.

Butler, C. 2009. A Standing Building Survey and Evaluation Excavation at 1 Cricketfield Road, Seaford, East Sussex. Unpubl. report no. CBAS 0089, CBAS Ltd.

Doherty, A. 2014. Archaeological Excavations at Monk's House, Rodmell. Unpubl. report no. 2013326, Archaeology South East.

ESHER, 2012. *East Sussex Historic Environment Record*. Lewes: East Sussex County Council.

Farrant, J. H. 1972. The evolution of Newhaven Harbour and the Lower Ouse before 1800. *Sussex Archaeological Collections* 110, 45.

Field, L. F. 1935. 'Meeching Ferry and Stockferry', *Sussex Notes and Queries*, 5, 171-4.

Freke, D. J. 1978. Excavations in Church Street, Seaford, 1976. *Sussex Archaeological Collections* 116, 199-224.

Freke, D. J. 1979. Excavations in Steyne Road, Seaford, 1977. *Sussex Archaeological Collections* 117, 233-234.

Freke, D. and Rudling, D. 1983. Recent Archaeological Trial Trenching in Seaford. *Sussex Archaeological Collections* 121, 209-210.

Gardiner, M. 1995. Aspects of the history and archaeology of medieval Seaford. *Sussex Archaeological Collections* 133, 189-212.

Godfrey, W. H. 1936. Swanborough Manor House. *Sussex Archaeological Collections* 77.

Godfrey, W. H. 1940. Axial towers in Sussex churches, *Sussex Archaeological Collections* 81, 97-120.

Griffin, N. 2006. The Archaeological Excavation of a Medieval Saltern on the Ouse Estuary Near Newhaven, East Sussex, 2002. Unpubl. report, project no. 1556, Archaeology South East.

Grinsell, L. V. 1934. Sussex Barrows. *Sussex Archaeological Collections* 75.

Harris, R. B. 2005. *Seaford: Historic Character Assessment Report*. Lewes: Sussex Extensive Urban Survey.

Holden, E. W. and Hudson, T. P. 1981. Salt making in the Adur Valley, Sussex. *Sussex Archaeological Collections* 119, 117-148.

Hunter, P. and Pine, C. 2006. Summary Report of the Archaeological Evaluation at Land at Saxon Lane Seaford East Sussex (HER 7341). Unpubl. assessment report, Development Archaeology Services.

James, R. 2002. The excavation of a Saxon grubenhaus at Itford Farm, Beddingham, East Sussex. *Sussex Archaeological Collections* 140, 41-7.

Marshall, P., van der Plicht, J., Cook, G. T., Grootes, P. M., Athfield, N. B., and Buzinny, M. 2010. *The later Anglo-Saxon settlement at Bishopstone: a downland manor in the making*. York: Council for British Archaeology.

Mawer, A. and Stenton, F. M. 1930. *The Placenames of Sussex*. London: Cambridge University Press.

McAvoy, F. 2002. *The Management of Archaeological Sites in Arable Landscapes - Appendix B Details of Regional Plough Damage Surveys*. Oxford: Oxford Archaeology.

Meaton, C. 2006. An Archaeological Desk-Based Assessment on the Proposed Site of the Newhaven Desalination Plant. Unpubl. report, project no. 2536, Archaeology South East.

Meaton, C. 2009. An Archaeological Watching Brief at South Street Mews, Seaford, East Sussex. Unpubl. report no 2008160, Archaeology South-East.

Morris, J. 1976. *Domesday Book*. Chichester: Phillimore and Co. Ltd.

Nairn, I., and Pevsner, N. 1965. *The Buildings of England: Sussex* (2003 reprint ed.). London: Yale University Press.

Nielsen, R. and Rapson, G. 2010. EDF Bishopstone to Norton AONB Undergrounding. Unpubl. report ref ES-BNU09: MoL Archaeology, London.

O'Shea, E.W. 1978. Excavation at Norton Farm, Bishopstone (TQ 472018). *Sussex Archaeological Society Newsletter* 26 Dec 1978, p. 161.

Porteus, S., Pope, M. and Whittaker, J. 2010. An Archaeological and Geoarchaeological Evaluation at Seaford Head Community College, Seaford, East Sussex. Unpubl. report no. 2010001, Archaeology South-East.

Robinson, D. and Williams, R. B. G. 1983. The Sussex coast past and present. In A. Sutton ed. *Sussex: Environment, Landscape and Society*. Falmer: University of Sussex

Robinson, D. 1999. The Coast and Coastal Changes. In K. Leslie, and B. Short (eds), *An Historical Atlas of Sussex*. Chichester: Phillimore and Co. Ltd.

Russell, C. 2013. An Archaeological Evaluation at Seaford Constitutional Club, Crouch Lane, Seaford East Sussex. Unpubl. report CBAS 0354, CBAS Ltd.

Score, D. 2000. Land at The Hall, Heighton Road, South Heighton, East Sussex Archaeological Evaluation Report. Unpubl. report ref. LEWSA: 2000.4, Oxford Archaeological Unit.

Stevens, S. 2004. Excavations at 1-3 High Street, Seaford, East Sussex. *Sussex Archaeological Collections* 142, 79-92.

Thorpe, S. 2010. Ouse Valley Transfer Scheme archaeological assessment and Updated Project Design. Unpubl. report 414, Network Archaeology Ltd.

Thomas, G. 2010. *The later Anglo-Saxon settlement at Bishopstone: a downland manor in the making.* York: CBA Research Report 163.

Webster, L. E. and Cherry, J. 1978. Medieval Britain in 1973. *Medieval Archaeology,* 18, 218.

Westley, B. 1979. Medieval Finds from Denton (2), *Sussex Archaeological Collections* 117, 238 - 239.

Whiteman, K. and Whiteman, J. 1994. *Ancient Churches of Sussex.* Seaford: S. B. Publications.

Wynter, W.R. 1922. *Old Seaford*. Lewes: Farncombe and Co Ltd.

12. Research priorities for the Ouse valley

Michael J. Allen and David Rudling

Following from the original aims of this book to engage both students and staff involved in Sussex University CCE archaeology courses to discuss and investigate aspects of the archaeology of the Ouse valley, the writing of the chronological chapters has driven an area-specific research agenda for further archaeological engagement in this fascinating, topographically well-defined landscape. The research priorities below highlight both clear gaps in our knowledge and identifies some key themes and issues to be addressed; some of which are derived at a local scale, and others in part reflect some of the South East Regional Research Framework (SERF) priorities. It seems logical, therefore, to conclude this collection of period reviews with a new research agenda; one that can be followed by individual scholars, active research groups, and fed into developer-funded commercial archaeology. We hope that together, they might improve our understanding and lead, ultimately perhaps, to a revised volume with a greater understanding and comprehension of the archaeology of the Ouse valley.

It is surprising that the Ouse valley has rarely been considered as a topographic entity in itself worthy of archaeological review, though it has more commonly been approached as a region via several more historical or ecological themes (Holmes 2011; Holmes and Pilkington 2011). The research and archaeological work in the Ouse valley to date is both disparate and varied as the chapters clearly demonstrate. Almost none of that archaeological work has been directed at looking at this landscape *per se*. An exception was an archaeological project instigated by the Lewes Archaeological Group in the 1970s which set out to survey a number of 'deserted' medieval villages in the Ouse valley, with the ambitious hope of making some regional overview. After surveys at Hamsey and Beddingham (Allen 1981; 1985), the project became moribund. Further attempts to bring together some of the archaeological fieldwork which had been undertaken in and around the town of Lewes and in the Lewes area respectively, included an article on Lewes in the *Sussex Archaeological Collections* (Rudling 1983) and a collection of papers published by the Lewes Archaeological Group (Allen *et al.* 1987). A similar review of archaeological fieldwork and historical sources was produced for Seaford (Gardiner 1995). Between 2004 and 2008 three towns within the valley, Lewes, Newhaven and Seaford, were studied by Roland Harris as part of a much larger, Sussex-wide, Extensive Urban Survey. Additionally, a 'Millennium Project' featuring both archaeological fieldwork and the study of historical sources was undertaken for the parishes of Hamsey and Barcombe on behalf of the Sussex Archaeological Society by Pam Combes (https://sussexpast.co.uk/research/excavations/barcombe-hamsey-project).

Any river valley provides a clear, convenient and coherent landscape for archaeological study and review; it not only provides a clear communication route, but traverses and samples the landscape through which it flows, and presumably attracted human activities in the past. A successful research project undertaken in the much less densely occupied and developed Cuckmere valley (i.e. the next river valley to the east of the Ouse), for instance, surveyed the whole of the valley, but was centred solely on the analysis of a large scale fieldwalking programme undertaken in just one winter (Garwood 1984; 1985). Another multi-period archaeological landscape study in East Sussex was undertaken on a block of chalk downland centred on Bullock Down Farm, Beachy Head (to the east of the Cuckmere near Eastbourne). Whilst this intensive research provides a very thorough understanding of one block of downland (Drewett 1982), the area reviewed is tiny compared with the whole of the Ouse valley. All three of these landscape projects, together with two others in West Sussex (Chilgrove and Up Marden, Down 1979; and Chichester / Fishbourne, Manley 2008) and major developer funded rescue projects which provide large transects across the landscape, such as the A27 Brighton by-pass (Rudling 2002), and Westhampnett by-pass (Fitzpatrick *et al.* 2008), demonstrate, however, the desirability for more such micro-studies so that we can begin to compare both similar and different parts of the wider landscape.

As the previous chapters have shown there is far more information to be gleaned from the archaeological resources being exposed, excavated, eroded and buried within the Ouse valley. The Ouse valley is therefore an obvious and important landscape unit to study; its corridor and interfluves providing the transport route from the sea via Lewes to the Weald, it bisects the chalk which overlooks the valley in its southern reaches, and in the upper valley it fans out encompassing a large mass of the Weald.

A Research Framework

Over and above the chronologically-defined research themes outlined below, the collection of papers clearly highlights a series of broad research themes that can be applied to the Ouse valley.

Research Themes

- Archaeological visibility and bias
- The archaeology of, and beneath, the floodplain floor
- Settlement and settlement location shifts
- Continuity and change
- Transport, communication and trade
- The valley may provide a political and social barrier, boundary or corridor
- Variation in settlement patterns between the Upper (Weald) and Lower (Downs) valley
- Problems of locating the remains of the dead (in various periods)
- The potential for Portable Antiquities Scheme (PAS) data
- The need to examine dry and river valleys for colluvium and alluvium, both sealing archaeological sites but also containing long stratified sequences of land-use history (geoarchaeology, snails and pollen)

Various research methods could be adopted, for instance transects of survey including fieldwalking across both Lower and Upper valley, and comparing overall finds and period distributions by topography within the valley in a similar fashion to Shennan's East Hampshire Survey (1985). Stronger and more uniform comparison between both Weald (upper) and Downland (lower) portions of the valley would clearly be beneficial, A fieldwalking programme is desperately needed in the Wealden part of this valley in order to locate and examine prehistoric material. It is especially important to examine any contrasts between the claylands and greensand ridges; together providing a database to compare with the better studied chalklands to the south.

The presence of the Ouse valley alluvium many metres deep has not been taken into account by many archaeologists; there is a large amount of landscape concealed and buried that may have been utilised in the past. It may contain another waterlogged and well-preserved Shinewater (Eastbourne) or Must Farm (Cambridgeshire).

The edges of the Lower Ouse valley provided the main communication routes and the locations of occupation in the medieval period; but this situation may also have earlier historic or prehistoric antecedents. Fieldwork including fieldwalking, survey and test-pitting could examine this on a village by village and/or site by site basis.

Period by Period Research Context

The chapters above, and authors of those chapters, have highlighted a series of clear research topics which are presented below. These are defined as a series of main topics that we perceived as the most significant or important. They are presented by period divisions more commonly used in research frameworks, rather than those simple chronologies discussed in the previous chapters.

Lower and Middle Palaeolithic

- The Ouse valley has an established but poorly understood record. A lack of firm dating frameworks for the valley, and of associated palaeo-environmental remains, hampers any meaningful synthesis.
- There is enough demonstrable potential in the Ouse valley to form the basis for a complete re-evaluation of Palaeolithic archaeology in the county.
- A dating program focused on the terrace deposits could both unlock understanding of the existing record, and bring into focus new sites and new areas of potential.

Upper Palaeolithic and Mesolithic

- Broad landscape studies are needed to examine palaeo-environmental evidence synchronous with Mesolithic artefacts, as well as excavations that secured high quality information from securely stratified and dated contexts.
- Testing local assumptions about the Mesolithic, such as preference for the Greensand, the use of tranchet axes for forest clearance and the identification of and examination of Mesolithic pits (some formerly defined as 'dwellings'), are also to be encouraged.
- Geoarchaeological analysis of sediments at small sites is thought to be particularly important for building up the overall mosaic of environmental information over time.
- Specific attention needs to be paid to rare peat sites with waterlogged preservation and palaeo-environmental remains (e.g. The Wilderness, Barcombe and as recently studied outside the valley in the Pett Levels), and possibly peats below the Ouse valley floodplain.

Earlier Neolithic

- Extensive field walking programmes are needed to characterise and compare the Upper (Weald) with the Lower (Downs) valley.
- Examine the distribution of flint axes in the valley as significantly more work has been done in the Weald since the last surveys were undertaken (e.g. Gardiner 1988).
- Examine buried soils beneath Neolithic monuments to reconstruct the pre-monument landscape (cf. French *et al.* 2003; 2007).

- Examine the long palaeo-environmental sequences surviving in long barrow and causewayed enclosure ditches.
- Strongly consider sites that may be buried under the 8m of alluvium in the valley (Note that Neolithic pollen was 8m down at Wellingham, Wing 1980).

Later Neolithic and Early Bronze Age

- Look at the mosaic of land-use, via flint scatters, monument distributions and palaeo-environmental land-use reconstruction.
- Re-evaluate the later Neolithic flint assemblages, especially components of both the Houndean-Ashcombe artefact scatters (Biggar 1978), and those from the Ashcombe Bottom dry valley (Allen 2005b).
- Compare burial monuments and settlement evidence archaeology in both the north (upper) and south (lower) Ouse valley.
- Systematic field walking in the Weald is a high priority, especially in order to attempt to identify Late Neolithic-Early Bronze Age flint assemblages comparable with those identified on the chalk (e.g. Gardiner 2014).
- Transect surveys (fieldwalking, field survey, walkover survey, augering) – recognising that there are apparent 'blanks' where subsequent deposits have buried part of the landscape, such as dry valleys (some of which are known to contain Beaker sites: Allen 2005a; 2005b; 2005c), and the largely unexplored Ouse valley alluvium itself.
- Search for henges (currently there is an absence of these in East Sussex and perhaps only one, at Lavent, in West Sussex) and other monuments, especially on the chalkland valley footslope overlooking the floodplain of the Ouse.
- Examination of aerial photographs in both public and private collections for ploughed out barrows, barrow cemeteries and possible settlement evidence.
- Examination of buried soils beneath Bronze Age barrows to reconstruct the pre-monument landscape (cf. French *et al.* 2003; 2007).

Later Bronze Age and Early Iron Age

- Address the imbalance of the north-south divide in terms of the numbers of sites and finds.
- Further excavations need to occur at Barcombe (e.g. the villa and in its environs) to further understand Bronze Age activity in this area which has revealed Middle Bronze Age burials, a waterlogged post and a later axe hoard.
- Whilst there are numerous barrows and burials in the Ouse valley, there is only one known Middle Bronze Age settlement; the discovery of additional domestic activity and associated settlements is thus a priority.
- South Heighton with finds of a copper alloy axe, later socketed axes, Early Bronze Age/Middle Bronze Age burial sites, and a multi-ditched feature, is an area worthy of further investigation.
- The Ouse valley contains Bronze Age peat (Thorley 1971; 1981), and has the potential for excellent waterlogged preservation, possibly of the quality discovered at Shinewater, near Eastbourne (Greatorex 2003) or Must Farm, Cambridgeshire.
- Examining social and economic changes between the later Bronze Age and the development of the earlier Iron Age hilltop enclosures.
- An improved understanding of the first hill-top ditched enclosures / 'hill-forts'; as at Seaford, Newhaven and Caburn.
- Finding and defining non-enclosed settlements of the Early Iron Age (as at Heathy Brow, Bullock Down, Beachy Head: Bedwin 1982, 73-88).

The Later Iron Age

- Investigate the settlement pattern and land-use of the valley immediately prior to the Roman Conquest in AD 43. Some of the Portable Antiquities Scheme (PAS) finds may help in the location of new sites. Various Roman-period villas and farmsteads have revealed evidence of continuity from the Late Iron Age.
- Undertake a detailed analysis of all Late Iron Age coin finds within the valley to see if these reveal any significant changes in their supply over time. Type 1 potin coins, which feature so prominently at the Caburn, warrant special attention.
- Further study of Structured Deposition as strongly represented at Mount Caburn.
- Further survey and much closer dating of iron-working sites to the north of Barcombe. Do any sites precede the Roman Conquest?

Roman

- Further refining of the routes of the major Roman-period roads in the Ouse valley.
- Continued investigation of the nature and dating of the recently discovered nucleated settlement at Bridge Farm. What was the function of, and precise dating for, the double ditched enclosure?
- Full post-excavation reporting on the excavations at Beddingham, Firle and Barcombe. Such research should enable the study of local variability of cultural practices and of social identities at nearby villa settlements.

- A detailed study of the PAS data for the valley (both coins and other artefacts).
- A high priority should be given to any Roman-period burials or shrine/temple sites if they are discovered in the valley.
- A detailed survey and excavation (i.e. not just of the furnace shaft) of at least one iron-working site in the north of the valley.
- Continued study of the discovery at consumer sites of the products of the Wickham Barn (Chiltington) pottery kilns. Can any marketing patterns be discerned?
- High priority should be given to any possibility of excavating further traces of the early villa at Newhaven, or the settlement associated with the cremation cemetery at Seaford.
- A detailed survey and excavation at the Furlongs site at Beddingham in order to establish the nature and dating of a farmstead settlement off the downs and in very close proximity to a villa.

Saxon

- Publication of the cemetery associated with the early settlement site at Rookery Hill, Bishopstone.
- Further investigations at the Romano-British villa site at Beddingham, especially to the west of the main house where quantities of very early Saxon pottery have been discovered. Do such finds represent limited continuity of occupation or new 'squatter' settlement?
- There are large gaps in the evidence and arguably the biggest of these is the absence of 7th and early 8th century 'high status' burial sites, sometimes barrow cemeteries with lavish grave goods.
- Detailed studies of the PAS finds from the valley.
- Continued investigations regarding the nature of the Saxon burgh at Lewes.

Medieval

- In urban areas an increasing emphasis on environmental sampling and waterlogged deposits which offer insights into the more transient aspects of the archaeological record.
- In the rural areas there would appear to be greater scope for volunteer-based projects in preparing detailed desktop syntheses of the archaeological record of specific farms, areas or parishes.
- Systematic field-walking and metal detecting followed by geophysical surveys and trial trenching or test-pitting in selected locations, including any possible shrunken or deserted settlements.
- Identifying the medieval deer parks of the area, many of which can be deduced by inspection of the first series OS and local tithe maps and the use of LIDAR surveys of woodland, before subsequent verification by boundary and earthwork surveys in the field.
- Investigation of round towered churches and why they seem specific to the Ouse valley: Southease, Lewes, etc.
- Characterising the original settlement form, location and distributions, and defining a site's development over time.
- Examination of the port/s and town areas [Lewes, Newhaven, Seaford etc.] and their relationship to trade to, through and within the valley.

Geoarchaeology and Palaeo-environment

- The prehistory of the valley floor is completely lacking as it is buried under metres of alluvium, but there are for instance, thick and extensive peat beds of Bronze Age date across much of the Vale of The Brooks. These could bury whole riverside well-preserved Bronze Age settlements (e.g. as at Must Farm, Cambridgeshire).
- The environment and land-use of the valley floor is largely undefined and unknown.
- The environment and land-use of the Wealden catchment is poorly understood in comparison with the smaller, more clearly defined chalkland catchment.
- When were the major phases of human activity in the Wealden catchment, and when did sediment inputs occur in the valley as a result of those human activities?
- Apart from the coast (and Lewes), is there any evidence of landing points dating from prehistoric to historic times along the course of the river?

Summary

The above clearly shows gaps in our knowledge, some quite major, highlighted by the summaries provided by the authors of the chronological chapters. Obviously any or all of these can be tackled in an *ad hoc* or piecemeal fashion. There is, however, the possibility of designing targeted research projects encompassing a specifically selected range of the fieldwork techniques (fieldwalking, survey, augering and test-pitting), and desk-based research (HER, NMR, PAS, aerial photographs, LIDAR images), or ones specifically attempting to concentrate on specific chronological timeframes. Moreover, the above provides a framework of archaeological, landscape and historical questions to be addressed by all types of fieldwork, research, and developer-led interventions in the region. We hope that this will help direct archaeological enquiry, and rapidly increase our knowledge. If this is done, and this volume becomes out-of-date, then we will have collectively succeeded.

References

Allen, M. J. 1981. Hamsey, Sussex, *Medieval Village Research Group 28th Annual Report for 1980.*

Allen, M. J. 1985. Hamsey, East Sussex, *Medieval Archaeology* 9, 242.

Allen, M. J. 2005a. Beaker settlement and environment on the chalk downs of southern England, *Proceedings of the Prehistoric Society* 71, 219-45.

Allen, M. J. 2005b. Beaker occupation and development of the downland landscape at Ashcombe Bottom, near Lewes, East Sussex, *Sussex Archaeological Collections* 143, 7-33.

Allen, M. J. 2005c. Beaker and Early Bronze Age activity, and a possible Beaker valley entrenchment, in Cuckoo Bottom, near Lewes, East Sussex, *Sussex Archaeological Collections* 143, 35-45.

Allen, M. J., Seager-Smith, R. H., Somerville, E. M., Stevens, P. and Norman, P. 1987. *Aspects of Archaeology in the Lewes Area*. Lewes: Lewes Archaeological Group.

Down, A. 1979. *Chichester Excavations 4, The Roman Villas at Chilgrove and Up Marden*. Chichester: Phillimore.

Bedwin, O. 1982. The Pre-Roman Iron Age on Bullock Down. In P. Drewett 1982, 73-96.

Biggar, J. T. M. 1978. A field survey of Houndean-Ashcombe and other Downland fields west of Lewes, 1972–1975, *Sussex Archaeological Collections* 116, 143-153.

Drewett, P. 1982. *The Archaeology of Bullock Down, Eastbourne, East Sussex: The Development of a Landscape.* Sussex Archaeological Society Monograph 1. Lewes: The Sussex Archaeological Society.

Fitzpatrick, A. P., Powell, A. B. & Allen, M. J. 2008. *Archaeological Excavation on the Route of the A27 Westhampnett Bypass, West Sussex, 1992; vol. 1: Late Upper Palaeolithic-Anglo-Saxon*. Salisbury: Wessex Archaeology Report 21

French, C., Lewis, H., Allen, M. J., Scaife, R .G. and Green, M. 2003. Archaeological and palaeo-environmental investigations of the upper Allen valley, Cranborne Chase, Dorset (1998-2000): a new model of earlier Holocene landscape development, *Proceedings of the Prehistoric Society* 69, 201-234

French, C., Lewis, H., Allen, M. J., Green, M. Scaife, R. G. & Gardiner, J. 2007. *Prehistoric landscape development and human impact in the upper Allen valley, Cranborne Chase, Dorset.* Cambridge: McDonald Institute Monograph.

Gardiner, J. P. 1988. *The Composition and Distribution of Neolithic Surface Flint Assemblages in Central Southern England.* Unpublished Ph.D. thesis, University of Reading.

Gardiner, J. 2014. Evidence for Neolithic activity at the Eastbourne Edge of the South Downs. In Allen, M.J. (ed.), *Eastbourne, aspects of archaeology history and heritage*, 44-52. Eastbourne: Eastbourne Natural History and Archaeological Society.

Gardiner, M. 1995. Aspects of the history and archaeology of medieval Seaford, *Sussex Archaeological Collections* 133, 189-212.

Garwood, P. 1984. The Cuckmere Valley Project fieldwalking programme 1982–83, *Bulletin of the Institute of Archaeology* 21, 49–68.

Garwood, P. 1985. Unpublished. The Cuckmere Valley Project Fieldwalking Programme Archive. Unpubl ms, Barbican House Library, Lewes.

Greatorex, C. 2003. Living on the margins? The late Bronze Age landscape of the Willingdon Levels. In D. Rudling (ed.), *Archaeology of Sussex to AD 2000*, pp 89-100. King's Lynn: Heritage Marketing.

Holmes, A. 2011. The Ouse Project: A Case Study of Applied Oral History. In S. Trower. *Place, Writing and Voice: Studies in Oral History*, New York: Palgrave Macmillan, 127-148.

Holmes, A. and Pilkington, M. 2011.Storytelling, floods, wildflowers and washlands: oral history in the River Ouse project, *Oral History* 39, no. 2 (Autumn), 83-94.

Manley, J. (ed.), 2008. *The Archaeology of Fishbourne and Chichester, a framework for its future*. Lewes: Sussex Archaeological Society.

Rudling, D. 1983. The Archaeology of Lewes: some recent research, *Sussex Archaeological Collections* 121, 45-77.

Rudling, D. (ed.), 2002. *Downland Settlement and Land-use, The Archaeology of the Brighton Bypass*, UCL Field Archaeology Unit Monograph 1. London: Archetype Publications.

Rudling, D. 2015. The impact of Roman culture on the countryside of Sussex. Unpubl. PhD thesis, University of Roehampton.

Shennan, S. 1985. *Experiments in the Collection and Analysis of Archaeological Survey Data: the East Hampshire Survey.* Sheffield: University of Sheffield.